BASEBALL GENERATIONS

Career Value Index–

A New Look at the Hall of Fame and
Ranking the Greatest Players of All Time

BY DAVID J. GORDON

SUMMER
GAME
BOOKS

ISBN: 978-1-955398-06-0 (print)
ISBN: 978-1-955398-07-7 (ebook)

For information about permission, bulk purchases, or additional distribution, write to Summer Game Books

P. O. Box 818
South Orange, NJ 07079
or contact the publisher at www.summergamebooks.com

Front cover photograph courtesy of the National Baseball Hall of Fame and Museum. Shown: Mel Ott, whose CVI of 131.0 puts him at 22nd on the list of greatest players of all time.

Photo credits for the interior of the book appear at the back on page 399.

DEDICATION

I dedicate this book to my son Sam, a millennial baseball fan who (like his dad) has grown up rooting for a hapless team (the Orioles), but never gives up hope. He encouraged me to write this book for young fans like himself, who love the game and are hungry to know more about its legends and lore. Sam did the artwork, entitled "First Game," below.

ACKNOWLEDGMENTS

I am grateful to Walt Friedman of Summer Game Books for his invaluable contributions and advice in helping to organize and bring focus to what was once a sprawling 800-page manuscript. I also want to give special thanks to Carole Sargent, Director of Scholarly Publications at Georgetown University, for her generous advice and assistance in navigating the nearly impenetrable maze of the publishing world.

I am also grateful to the support staff at Baseball-Reference.com for their generous assistance with using their Stathead tool to extract arcane statistics like Inside-the-Park HR and Reached-Base-on-Error and to the Society of American Baseball Research (SABR) editor Cecil Tan and her editorial staff for inviting me to publish my work on the Deadball Era and Racial Parity in the Hall of Fame in the Autumn 2018 issue of Baseball Research Journal.

Indeed my approach owes much to the pioneering work of Bill James and to those in SABR and elsewhere who built on his work. I also want to than various friends and relatives who have read parts of the book at various stages of development and offered feedback and encouragement – my brother Jeff, my longtime friends Dan Opitz and Jack Roney, and my wife's cousin Cris Arguedas.

I also want to thank my wife, Susan, who helped me proofread my work and endured long silent periods and late nights when I was glued to my computer, as well as my daughter Emily for her encouragement and support.

TABLE OF CONTENTS

BASEBALL GENERATIONS

Henry Aaron, with permission from the National Baseball Hall of Fame and Museum

INTRODUCTION

Ghosts and Numbers

Several news outlets carried a story about a 68-year-old Cubs fan, who drove 650 miles from his home in Fuquay-Varina, North Carolina to Greenwood, Indiana in early November 2016 with a portable radio and a lawn chair to listen to Game 7 of the 2016 World Series at his father's graveside.[1] He was honoring a promise he made to his dying 53-year old father in 1980 more than 35 years earlier. It was a chilly and rainy night, and the game didn't end until after 1:00 AM, but still he stayed to the very end and was rewarded when the Cubs won and finally ended their 108-year "curse." Such devotion to a sports team transferred from one generation to the next and extending even beyond the grave is most easily imagined in baseball.

To fully appreciate how big a deal this was, you must understand that to be a Cub fan over the course of the preceding 108 years was to be trapped in endless futili-ty.[2] In most years, it has been clear by June that the Cubs had no chance. But even those rare good Cubs teams had a knack for inventing new ways to snatch defeat from the jaws of victory. It was like being trapped as Charlie Brown in an endless Peanuts cartoon, each year believing that this time Lucy will finally let you kick the football, only to have her snatch the ball away at the last moment yet again, leaving you on your back with stars circling around your head. For example:

— In Game 6 of the 2003 NLCS, with the Cubs leading 3-0 and five outs away from the NL pennant, the infamous Steve Bartman play followed by a blown double play grounder kicked off a decisive eight-run inning.

— The 1984 Cubs, who jumped out a 2-0 NLCS lead over the Padres in Wrigley Field, but could not win even one game in San Diego to clinch the series. A key error by Cubs 1B Leon Durham helped decide the clincher.

— The 1969 Cubs, fielding five future Hall-of-Famers, built a nine-game lead over the Mets through August 16, then collapsed while the Mets blew right by them, denying Ernie Banks his best chance to reach the World Series.

— The seven-game loss to the Tigers in the 1945 World Series, where they in-curred the "Curse of the Billy Goat."

— Babe Ruth's famous called home run in the 1932 World Series at Wrigley Field – a four-game wipeout by the Yankees.

— With the Cubs leading 8-0 in the seventh inning and on the verge of tying the 1929 World Series 2-2, a routine Mule Haas fly ball that Cub CF Hack Wilson lost in the sun triggered a decisive 10-run inning,

Indeed, one had to go back to the ragtime days of Three-Finger Mordecai Brown and Tinker to Evers to Chance and then even further back to the Cap Anson-led White Stockings teams of the 19th century to find a happy ending. The backstory of the Cubs' World Series opponent in 2016, the Cleveland Indians, was barely less bleak, with the second longest streak of 68 years since their last World Series victory in 1948, led by 30-year-old MVP SS-Manager Lou Boudreau. Three Indians teams had reached the World Series since then, but all had lost.

In truth, all 30 major league teams have a narrative in which ghosts and shadows of past events mingle with the present and color the imaginations and attitudes of baseball fans. The haughty and coldly dominant Yankees and their foil, the perennial underdog Red Sox, the Dodgers, who went from Bums to heroes when they paved the way for integration, but then became the Yankees West in Los Angeles, are three examples. Individual players also come with backstories. A baseball fan cannot watch Maris or Aaron or McGwire or Sosa or Bonds pursue home run records without conjuring the image of Babe Ruth. Similarly, the quests of Carew, Brett, Boggs, and Gwynn to hit .400 are inseparable from the legacy of Ted Williams. Every player who compiles a 30-game hitting streak is chasing DiMaggio. Stolen base kings Maury Wills, Lou Brock, and Rickey Henderson were chasing the ghost of Ty Cobb, as was Pete Rose when he broke Cobb's all-time hit record. Cal Ripken was chasing Lou Gehrig when he complied his iron man streak. When a new superstar like Mike Trout comes along, he is hailed as the next Mickey Mantle, who in turn was once the next Joe DiMaggio. Every year players pursue awards named after Cy Young, Mariano Rivera, Edgar Martinez, and other hallowed icons of the game.

I could go on, but you get the point. Every baseball franchise has its collection of stars and memorable players and teams, and its stories of victories against all odds and bitter heartbreaking defeats. Every new star competes not only with his peers but with the shadows of past stars. In baseball, more than any other sport, these personalities, these stories bring emotional texture and resonance to a fan's experience of the game, beyond the context of how compelling the game one is watching on a given day or its impact on the pennant race that season might be. A baseball fan who is ignorant of or impervious to these stories of shadows and ghosts is like someone who listens to "Over the Rainbow" pecked out note by note on a toy piano but has never heard Judy Garland sing it. It may be the same tune, but without the loneliness and longing and memories of when you first saw *The Wizard of Oz*, there is no emotional resonance, nothing that would make you drive 650 miles to listen to a game in a cold and rainy cemetery rather than stay home and watch it on TV.

The other aspect of baseball that is unique in American sports is its intense preoccupation with and reverence for numbers. While fans of other sports seem to care mainly about the game at hand, we baseball fans are obsessed with which players are the best and argue passionately about who belongs on the All-Star team, who deserves the postseason awards, and who belongs in the Hall of Fame. And we back up our opinions with all sorts of statistics. Indeed, ghosts and numbers are the yin and yang of baseball. Stories populated with ghosts and shadows of the past are what fire our imagination and take it beyond a contest between two teams of contemporary players, and the numbers and statistics give shape and substance to these shadows and make them as real and palpable as the players on the field.

Statistics are the scaffolding on which we hang our stories, and no sport has more statistics than baseball. We have simple counts like home runs, wins, strikeouts, and errors, averages like batting average, ERA and WHIP, complex derived statistics like WAR and Win Probability Added (WPA), that can only be generated by computers from complex databases, and new technical stats like exit velocity, launch angle, and spin rate that break the game down to its elements, and require high-tech equipment even to measure.

Perhaps our obsession with numbers comes from the fact that baseball is a game of serial one-on-one encounters of pitcher versus batter. The batter is alone when he hits a home run and alone when he strikes out. When a batted ball comes toward a fielder, he either catches it or he doesn't, and if he does catch it, he either throws accurately or he doesn't. These events happen consecutively rather than simultaneously, and each is clearly visible to even the neophyte fan. More importantly, they can be counted and manipulated into meaningful statistics. At the opposite extreme, football is a series of 11-on-11 match-ups in which it is hard to dissect the contributions of individual players. If a pass is completed, does the credit go to the quarterback, the receiver, to another potential receiver who decoyed the defense, someone who threw a key block, poor coverage by the defense, or brilliant play calling by the coach? Individual statistics can't fully capture what is going on.

Baseball fans' reverence for statistics is nowhere more evident than in our debates about who belongs in the Hall of Fame (HOF). Back in the 1950s, kids on the New York sandlots would endlessly debate the greatness of the three iconic players who brilliantly patrolled center field for the Giants, Yankees, and Dodger and are immortalized in song: Willie, Mickey, and the Duke.[3] Seasonal metrics like a .300 batting average, 60 home runs, 20 wins, and career milestones like 714 home runs, 300 wins, and 3000 hits need no further elaboration to baseball fans. So, of course, fans were outraged when the onset of performance-enhancing steroid usage in the late 1990s trivialized the longtime home run milestones.

To a lesser extent, fans were also discomfited by the more gradual change in pitcher usage, which really began in organized baseball's earliest days in the 1870s, when a team's ace pitcher typically pitched and earned decisions in most of his team's games, so that a pitching win was really an individual accomplishment, not just crediting the guy who happened to be in the game when the winning run scored.

Although baseball was popular before the Civil War and its origins can be traced back to colonial times, our story begins when the first organized professional league, the National Association (NA), was established in 1871.[4,5] The NA (1871-75) which debuted on May 4, 1871 in Fort Wayne, IN with a 2-0 victory for the home team Kekiongas over the visiting Cleveland Forest Cities. was actually a loose alliance of player-run clubs playing short and variable schedules, a far cry from the enduring configuration of teams we have today.[6,7] A total of 25 teams played in the NA over its five-year duration but never more than 13 (or fewer than eight) in any year.

In the chapters that follow, I will tell the story of how MLB has evolved from these humble beginnings as a small-time provincial enterprise, played by white men in a collection of northeastern cities and towns, to a multi-billion dollar international game played by diverse races and nationalities, and I will rank and describe its top players at each stage of this evolution.

CHAPTER 1

BASEBALL ACROSS THE AGES

My objective in **Baseball Generations** is to identify, compare, and contrast the greatest stars of major league baseball (MLB) across its 150 years (1871-2020) of existence. To do so, I introduce a metric called Career Value Index (CVI), which is derived from Wins Above Replacement (WAR). I will define and explain CVI in chapter 2.

To appreciate and measure the all-time greats across the generations, one must appreciate that the modern game of baseball did not spring into the world fully formed and eternal like Botticelli's Venus emerging from the sea foam. Many modern fans may be aware of recent phenomena like the increasing dominance of home runs and strikeouts, the specialization of pitchers, and the steroid years but are unaware of the profound differences between the modern game and the game of our great-great-grandparents and even more the recent game of the first half of the 20th century.

Each of chapters 3 to 9 each begins with an overview of the state of the game in each of seven distinct historical eras – generations, if you will – and describes the greatest players of that generation as determined by CVI. Then, in Chapters 10, I integrate the player evaluations from chapters 3 through 9, to rank the all-time greats, and relate these rankings to the Hall of Fame. A critical historical review of the Hall of Fame follows in Chapter 11. I have also included two appendices – one containing tables and graphs of historical time trends over 150 years of baseball history and another providing illustrations of the calculation of CVI.

The statistical data in **Baseball Generations** are taken from Baseball-Reference. com and are complete and accurate through the 2020 season, including the 2020 postseason results.[1] (Note that almost all the analyses performed in this book predated the incorporation of Negro Leagues statistics into the Baseball-Reference database in spring 2021. Thus, the term "MLB" in this book and the statistics I have cited refer to the white or integrated major leagues, not the Negro Leagues. I have also used Baseball-Reference's Stathead tool liberally to count players with WAR above a specific threshold and to identify players with similar career WAR.[2] Note that Baseball-Reference.com occasionally tweaks their historical data and WAR calculations; thus, readers wishing to cite the most up-to-date statistics should go directly to the source. I have drawn heavily (but not exclusively) from the Society of American Baseball Research (SABR) BioProject for my biographical "Beyond the Numbers."[3] Readers looking for detailed biographies are encouraged to turn to these excellent online resources.

Finally, let me stipulate that statistics are and always will be imperfect. Fielding is notoriously difficult to quantify, since the key aspect is what balls fielders can get to and make a play on, rather than how many errors they make on balls they reach. With advancing technology, baseball researchers are increasingly able to measure this aspect of fielding, but retroactive data are unavailable for much of MLB's history. Even today, we have no good metric to capture the full defensive contribution of catchers, whose hitting stats are diminished because they typically play fewer games than other position players and the physical demands of the position are so heavy.

We also lack a definitive metric for closers, who pitch too few innings to show well in advanced metrics, while the saves statistic rewards usage patterns as much as skill level. The leveraged WAR metric I have devised for calculating CVI is the latest take on an eternal question until something better comes along. We also have no good method to incorporate postseason performance into an overall performance metric. I will come back to some of these questions in subsequent chapters. I don't pretend to have all the answers, but I hope I can at least advance the conversation.

CHAPTER 2

BEYOND WAR: CAREER VALUE INDEX (CVI)

Some "old school" fans would echo Edwin Starr and say WAR, or "wins above replacement," are good for "absolutely nothing!"[1] Wins above replacement means the number of games a team would win with the player being measured compared with a hypothetical "replacement-level" player.[2,3] Although WAR has now become the standard metric used by major league front offices to evaluate players and determine how best to deploy their player acquisition budgets, old school fans prefer the familiar counting stats and simple averages they can find in a box score. But these traditional stats are simply not up to the task of evaluating players meaningfully across eras or rating candidates for the Hall of Fame (HOF). But as Marvin Gaye sang, "WAR is not the answer" – or at least not the full answer.[4] I will propose something better in this chapter.

Although baseball statistics have become more sophisticated over time and are used more than ever in evaluation of player performance and greatness, the process for electing players to the HOF remains somewhat subjective and haphazard. Although most voters are conscientious and try to apply rigorous standards, they often rely on a hodgepodge of context-dependent statistics, many of which apply to one kind of player more than another or which mean different things in different ballparks or different eras. In addition, they are asked to consider intangible qualities like leadership and character. This is all well and good when all the indicators all point in the same direction, as for Derek Jeter in 2020. But when these indicators point in differing directions, we are left in a situation resembling the Indian parable of the six blind men examining the different parts of an elephant.[5] Each comes to a different conclusion of what elephant looks like, depending on whether he is examining the trunk, an ear, a tusk, or a leg. No one can quite wrap his mind around the whole animal.

Consider the case of Jack Morris, a fine pitcher who played from 1977-1994, lingered on the BBWAA ballot for 15 years (2000-2014), never attaining the required 75% of votes, and was ultimately elected to the HOF by the Modern Era Veterans Committee in December 2017.[6] His supporters pointed to his 254 career wins, his contributions as the ace of three different World Series (WS) Champions, in 1984, 1991, and 1992, including his unforgettable 10-inning Series-clinching 1-0 win in Game 7 of the 1991 WS. They also spoke of him being a "warrior" on the mound. His detractors pointed to his 186 career losses, his unimpressive 3.90 ERA and 1.296 WHIP, and his 3.80 overall postseason ERA. Everyone agreed that Morris was a good and durable pitcher, but was he a Hall of Famer?

While some subjectivity is unavoidable, a comprehensive context-independent yardstick to evaluate a player's career is needed to advance the discussion. In this chapter I will describe and define a metric that does this — the Career Value Index (CVI). CVI is based on WAR, which is an offshoot of the linear weights construct advanced by Pete Palmer and John Thorn in their seminal 1984 book, *Hidden Baseball*, in which standard linear regression analysis was used to assign weights to every measurable outcome of a plate appearance based on its contribution to runs scored, the currency of how games are won or lost.[7] The weights vary from park to park and from season to season; a HR does not receive the same weight in Coors Field in 2019 as it did in the Polo Grounds in 1951. The method is a little more complicated for pitchers; at one extreme, one may use earned runs allowed, or at the other, one may use the expected runs allowed based on more fundamental components like walks, hits, extra-base hits, etc.

WAR then compares a player's runs produced or saved with a conceptual entity called the replacement player – a hypothetical freely available journeyman minor leaguer or bench player who could fill in at that position if the player of interest were removed from the team for whatever reason. The value of a replacement player varies by position and is greatest for DH, LF, and 1B (which have few defensive demands) and smallest for C and SS (where players with the required defensive skills are relatively scarce). WAR incorporates this factor by adding or subtracting a positional adjustment ranging from -15 runs per 1350 innings. for DH to + 9 runs for catchers.[8] In addition, WAR for positional players incorporates defensive as well as offensive metrics. The interpretation of WAR is relatively straightforward, with 0 WAR signifying no value above a freely available minor league replacement, 2 WAR signifying a solid everyday player or rotation pitcher, 5 WAR signifying an All-Star candidate, and 8 WAR signifying someone on the short list of the best players in baseball that season. Unlike traditional statistics like AVG, HR, and RBI or even newer statistics like OBP or SLG, the WAR of a position player who played in the time of Ty Cobb may be fairly compared to one who played in the time of Babe Ruth, Willie Mays, Mike Schmidt, or Barry Bonds. The situation for pitchers and for position players before the adoption of the 154-game schedule in the 1890s is more complicated, as we shall see later.

Although you can't find WAR in a box score, seasonal and career WAR totals are readily available online for every player who ever played in the major leagues and are updated daily for active players during the season. Unfortunately for those who value transparency, many teams and baseball websites (like Baseball-Reference and Fan Graphs) use their own proprietary versions of WAR, deciding which variables to use in the regression model that assigns the weights.[9] For example, Baseball-Reference bases pitcher WAR on earned runs, while Fan-Graphs bases it on the more fundamental outcomes of individual batters faced. FanGraphs WAR treats the sequence Out-Out-BB-BB-HR-Out (3 ER) the same as HR-Out-Out-BB-BB-Out (1 ER), while Baseball-Reference WAR views the former sequence as more damaging.

What's more, the regression models are tweaked periodically and retroactively, so one may suddenly find that the WAR of a player who played 100 years ago has changed slightly, even on the same website. However, the beauty of WAR, whatever the version, is that it translates hitting, pitching, and fielding stats to a common and highly relevant scale – their incremental contribution to team wins by either producing or preventing runs. In this book, I have used Baseball-Reference WAR values through the end of the 2020 season.

WAR is not the only statistic that is useful for comparing players of different generations. In this book, I have also relied on two adjusted rate statistics, OPS+ and ERA+, to compare hitters and pitchers, respectively, across ballparks and eras.[10,11] For each of these statistics, 100 is average, and higher is better. But like all rate statistics, OPS+ and ERA+, are not useful for small sample sizes. For example, if I tell you that Pedro Martinez (291 ERA+ in 2000) was nearly three times as stingy in allowing runs as the average MLB pitcher that year, and that his ERA+ was the best of any pitcher except for Tim Keefe in 1880 under very different rules and conditions, that says something important about his peak value. But Dennis Eckersley's 603 ERA+ in 1990, when he faced only 262 batters, cannot be compared to Pedro, who faced 817 batters.

The Problem With Comparing Pitchers Across Generations

WAR works well for comparing position players across generations because there have always been nine men in the lineup and on the field at any time, and the distribution of PA has not changed significantly since MLB began in 1871, although changes in the length of the schedule have affected the absolute numbers of PA available, especially before 1892 (Figure 2.1). However, the distribution of IP and BF among pitchers has changed dramatically and continuously over 150 years of baseball history (Figure 2.2).

The top five SP in the mid-1880s averaged 600 IP per season — about three times the workload of modern pitchers circa 2018-19. The impact on pitching stats

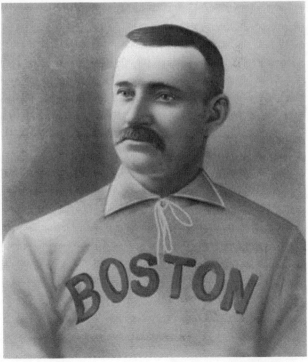

Hoss Radbourn

was profound. It is as if one compared modern batting statistics to those compiled in an era that featured three-man instead of nine-man batting orders, and where each starting position player was given 2000 PA. For example, when Charles "Old Hoss" Radbourn won a record 60 games (and lost 12) for the Providence Grays (NL) in 1884, he started – and completed – 73 games and pitched 678.2 innings, almost two-thirds of the 1036.1 innings pitched by his team.[12] Providence finished 84-28 overall; thus, non-Radbourn pitchers went 24-16.

Radbourn's 1884 season was no anomaly. The top 23 places on the leaderboard for pitcher wins in a season are occupied exclusively by 19th century pitchers, many of whom are quite obscure. The highest 20th century pitcher on the lead-

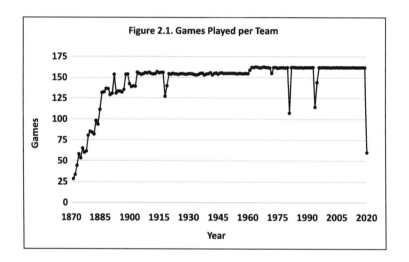

Figure 2.1. Games Played per Team

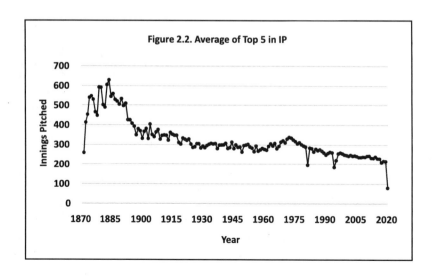

Figure 2.2. Average of Top 5 in IP

erboard is spitballer Jack Chesbro of the 1904 New York Highlanders (AL), who was in a group of six pitchers tied for 24th place at 41 wins. You must scroll down to Walter Johnson's 36 wins in 1913 (tied for 50th) to find someone who pitched after 1910, and all the way down to Jim Bagby (1920), Lefty Grove (1931), and Denny McLain (1968), who tied for 107th with 31 wins, to find a pitcher from after 1920.

Obviously, pitcher wins are nearly useless for comparing pitchers across generations, since a pitcher win today does not mean what it did in 1884 – or even 1968 – when pitchers routinely pitched complete games and really owned their wins and losses. Pitching WAR (WAR_p) is a better metric than wins, but since it also measures quantity as well as quality, it does not completely fix the problem of changing pitcher usage patterns. Other than Walter Johnson's 15.1 in 1913 (7th) and 13.2 in 1912 (tied for 17th) and Cy Young's 12.6 in 1901 (tied for 23rd) the top 25 pitching seasons by WAR_p all occurred in the 19th century. Dwight Gooden's 12.2 WAR_p in 1985 (26th) is the best of the past 100 years. So, should the Hall of Fame be populated predominantly with 19th century pitchers?

The Win is not the only "classical" statistic that does not mean what it used to mean. The evolution of the "small ball" game of 1871-1919 to the modern "three true outcomes" game has made it impossible to compare HR or SO totals across the decades. Babe Ruth's 54 HR in 1920 and Rube Waddell's 349 SO in 1904 are far more remarkable than Alex Rodriguez's 54 HR in 2007 and Randy Johnson's 347 SO in 2000. Conversely, George Brett's .390 AVG in 1980 and Pedro Martinez's 1.74 ERA in 2000 are far more remarkable than Al Simmons's .390 AVG in 1931 and Vic Willis's 1.73 ERA in 1906. While we may not like being forced out of our comfort zone of familiar stats you can find in a box score, relying on these old friends to evaluate players of different generations for the HOF is no longer defensible (if it ever was). Clearly, we need to go beyond our familiar box score statistics and beyond WAR to compare players across generations.

Career Value Index (CVI)

So, if WAR is a comprehensive metric for evaluating players on a common scale across the decades, why go beyond WAR to CVI? While WAR is very good for comparing individual seasons (at least over the past 100 years or so), just summing seasonal WAR values over the course of a player's career leaves something to be desired as a metric for evaluating players for the HOF. WAR has two major limitations:

- It undervalues players with high but short peaks and overvalues "compilers" with long careers who were never superstars. For example, Don Sutton's career WAR was 66.7 – far higher than Sandy Koufax's 48.9. There is nothing wrong with a player like Sutton, who performed at a 2- to 5-WAR level for 23 years, won 324 games, and played in four All-Star games. However, as Bill James has espoused, the Hall of Fame is meant for players who were recognized as among the very best of their time, as evidenced by MVP and Cy Young awards, All-Star selections, league-leading performances in important statistical categories ("black type"), and championships.[13] In general, players are elected to the Hall of Fame because their achievements were memorable, not just because they were serviceable for a long time. So we need a metric that gives extra emphasis to the years is which a player was among the best in MLB.

- As explained above, the fact that WAR is a function of usage is very problematic for comparing pitchers across generations. In 1884, three pitchers racked up >600 IP and ten more threw 500-600 IP. The number of IP required to lead MLB fell below 500 after 1892, below 400 after 1908, below 350 from 1946-1970, below 300 after 1980, below 250 after 2011, and below 225 after 2016. Relief pitchers also do poorly in WAR because they pitch so few innings.

To address the first issue, Jay Jaffe devised the Jaffe WAR Score (JAWS), which is the simple average of a player's career WAR and the total WAR for a player's seven best seasons.[14] Thus, when you compare two Hall of Famers with identical career WAR (67.8), Fred Clarke and Ernie Banks, JAWS gives greater value to the player with the higher seven-year peak – Banks (52.1) versus Clarke (36.1). So, Banks winds up with a 60.0 JAWS versus 52.0 for Clarke. But while JAWS does a better job than plain WAR of differentiating players who were true stars in their prime from "compilers" who were merely pretty good for a long time, what is the rationale for seven years? Babe Ruth had 18 seasons with WAR $\geq$5, 14 seasons with WAR $\geq$8, and 11 years with WAR $\geq$10. Why should seven of Ruth's fourteen 8-WAR seasons get no extra weight, while three of Don Sutton's seasons with 4.6, 4.5, 3.5, and 3.5 WAR_p receive double weight for being among his top seven? In my view, JAWS doesn't go far enough. JAWS also doesn't even begin to address the usage issue described above.

For the analysis of baseball's greatest across the generations that follows, I have developed a new metric called Career Value Index (CVI), which starts with seasonal WAR but introduces several enhancements and adjustments to create a more comprehensive indicator of a player's career value as it pertains to their qualifications for the HOF. Rather than defining player excellence to an arbitrary number of peak seasons CVI identifies and rewards <u>all</u> seasons above a defined threshold of excellence — typically WAR $\geq$5.0 — be it three seasons for Sutton or 18 for Ruth. Unlike JAWS, which gives double weight to seasons well below All-Star level if they are among that player's seven best, CVI gives extra credit only for seasons in which a player is among the best in MLB. Specifically, in seasons for which the "threshold of excellence" is 5 WAR, the player gets a "bonus" of 2*(WAR-5).

Table 2.1: CVI Calculations for Fred Clarke and Ernie Banks

Fred Clarke (67.8 WAR)					Ernie Banks (67.8 WAR)				
Year	WAR$_H$	Bonus	CVI Season	CVI Cumulative	Year	WAR$_H$	Bonus	CVI Season	CVI Cumulative
1894	0.3	0.0	0.24	0.24	1953	0.5	0.0	0.40	0.40
1895	3.0	0.0	2.40	2.64	1954	2.5	0.0	2.00	2.40
1896	3.1	0.0	2.48	5.12	1955	8.2	6.4	11.68	14.08
1897	6.6	3.2	7.84	12.96	1956	5.3	0.6	4.72	18.80
1898	3.8	0.0	3.04	16.00	1957	6.7	3.4	8.08	26.88
1899	4.4	0.0	3.52	19.52	1958	9.3	8.6	14.32	41.20
1900	2.4	0.0	1.92	21.44	1959	10.2	10.4	16.48	57.68
1901	5.0	0.0	4.00	25.44	1960	7.9	5.8	10.96	68.64
1902	5.0	0.0	4.00	29.44	1961	4.6	0.0	3.68	72.32
1903	4.3	0.0	3.44	32.88	1962	2.8	0.0	2.24	74.56
1904	2.1	0.0	1.68	34.56	1963	0.3	0.0	0.24	74.80
1905	3.7	0.0	2.96	37.52	1964	3.1	0.0	2.48	77.28
1906	3.6	0.0	2.88	40.40	1965	1.9	0.0	1.52	78.80
1907	5.1	0.2	4.24	44.64	1966	0.4	0.0	0.32	79.12
1908	4.8	0.0	3.84	48.48	1967	2.4	0.0	1.92	81.04
1909	5.3	0.6	4.72	53.20	1968	3.5	0.0	2.80	83.84
1910	1.9	0.0	1.52	54.72	1969	-0.7	0.0	0.00	83.84
1911	3.8	0.0	3.04	57.76	1970	-0.2	0.0	0.00	83.84
1912			0.00	57.76	1971	-0.7	0.0	0.00	83.84
1913	-0.2	0.0	0.00	57.76					
1914	0.0	0.0	0.00	57.76					
1915	0.0	0.0	0.00	57.76					

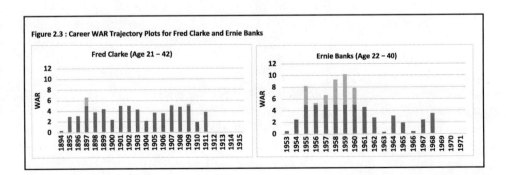

Figure 2.3 : Career WAR Trajectory Plots for Fred Clarke and Ernie Banks

The calculation of CVI is illustrated for Fred Clarke and Ernie Banks — two players with identical 67.8 career WAR totals — in Table 2.1 and Figure 2.3. In these simple examples, each player receives a "bonus" of 2*(WAR$_H$ – 5.0) for each sea-

Ernie Banks

son in which WAR_H >5. In effect, this gives triple weight to the portion of WAR_H over the 5.0 threshold. Seasons with negative WAR are rounded up to zero and do not count against CVI; this avoids penalizing players (like Banks) who were kept on past their prime for their leadership value or fan appeal. The total for each season is multiplied by a 0.8 scaling factor to put CVI on the same scale as career WAR (something that JAWS does not do), while preserving its rank order. Thus a CVI ≥60, like a career WAR ≥60, is a rough indicator of a player in the HOF conversation. The right columns of the tables show the cumulative CVI after each season of the player's career. This partition of each player's WAR_H into a portion <5.0 (black) and a triple-weighted portion >5.0 (gray) is illustrated graphically in Figure 2.3.

By giving triple weight to WAR in excess of 5.0 in all seasons with WAR >5.0—i.e., six seasons for Banks and three for Clarke – CVI highlights the difference (83.0 versus 58.0) between Banks, the 6-year superstar and two-time MVP of the 1950s, and Clarke, the steady compiler of 1894-1911, far more than JAWS (60.0 versus 52.0). CVI's elevation of players who achieved elite peak performance levels, albeit over a shorter period, comes closer than JAWS (in my opinion) to distinguishing the great players from the very good. I will use "career WAR trajectory plots" like those in Figure 2.3 throughout this book.

In general, a CVI that far exceeds career WAR signifies a player who dominated for much of his career. For example, Babe Ruth had a CVI of 270.0 and a career WAR of 182.4. Some other players with WAR in the 40-80 range whose CVI exceeded their WAR by at least 10 because their value was concentrated in

Fred Clarke

relatively few seasons are Wilbur Wood (74.7 vs 50.0), Roy Halladay (88.4 vs 64.2), Sandy Koufax (70.2 vs 48.9), Shoeless Joe Jackson (82.5 vs 62.1), Dazzy Vance (77.8 vs 60.1), and Arky Vaughan (93.8 vs 78.0). At the other extreme, Hall of Famer George Kell, who had no 5-WAR seasons, had a 30.2 CVI, exactly 80% of his 37.6 career WAR. Other "compilers" whose CVI fell significantly of their WAR because their value was spread out over a long period with no prominent peaks are Jake Beckley (50.1 vs 61.3), Jack Quinn (48.7 vs 58.6), Tommy John (51.8 vs 61.6), Luis Aparicio (46.4 vs 55.9), Lou Whitaker (66.9 vs 75.1), and Don Sutton (58.7 vs 66.7). In the middle, we find Derek Jeter, whose 71.3 CVI was identical to his career WAR.

Unfortunately, just applying a simple threshold or 5.0 to define the "bonus level" for primary WAR is inadequate to account for fluctuations in the length of the season (Figure 2.1) and the profound changes in pitcher usage (Figure 2.2) over 150 years of MLB history. CVI addresses this by varying this threshold to reflect the length of the season (for position players) or the average of the top 5 IP totals (for pitchers) during a particular era (Table 2.2).

Table 2.2: Thresholds for WAR "Bonus" – 1871-2020

Years	H	P	Years	H	P
1871	2.0	5.0	1918	4.0	6.0
1872-1873	2.0	7.5	1919-1923	5.0	6.0
1874-1878	2.0	10.0	1924-1967	5.0	5.0
1879-1882	3.0	10.0	1968-1978	5.0	5.5
1883-1884	3.0	11.0	1979-1980	5.0	5.0
1885-1886	4.2	10.0	1981	3.5	3.5
1887-1891	4.2	9.0	1982-1993	5.0	5.0
1892	5.0	9.0	1994	3.7	3.5
1893-1895	5.0	7.5	1995	5.0	4.0
1896-1898	5.0	7.0	1996-2011	5.0	4.5
1899-1908	5.0	6.5	2012-2019	5.0	4.0
1909-1917	5.0	6.0	2020	2.0	2.0

The threshold of 5.0 is used for hitters in most seasons after 1891, except for those truncated by labor stoppages (1981, 1994) and pandemics (1918, 2020). However, while the threshold for pitchers was 5.0 in 48 seasons, it was as high as 11.0 in 1883-1884 and as low as 4.0 in 2012-2019 (not counting truncated seasons). In effect, changing the threshold in this fashion puts all pitching seasons on a more or less equal footing without taking WAR away from any pitcher. For example, when Tim Keefe accrued 19.9 WAR_p in 619 IP (9.9 over the threshold of 10.0) in 1883, he earned 0.8*(10+3*9.9) = 37.6 in CVI. This is identical to the CVI accrued by Lefty Grove in 1931-32 when he accrued a combined 19.9 WAR_p (10.4+9.5) in a combined 590.3 IP and the bonus threshhold was 5.0. Thus, in effect, CVI counts one 20-WAR-600-IP Tim Keefe season as equivalent to two 10-WAR-300-IP Lefty Grove seasons, which seems fair.

CVI also incorporates the following additional tweaks for catchers, designated hitters and relief pitchers.

- For players who played at least 75% of their games at catcher (who make fewer plate appearances) or designated hitter (whom WAR penalizes by deducting 15 runs per 1350 innings from their offensive value <u>and</u> by assigning them a negative dWAR even if they make no appearances in the field), I have lowered the threshold to 3.2. Thus, these players receive triple credit for WAR_H in excess of 3.2. For players, who split times between these and other positions, the theshold becomes 3.8 for players who appear in 50-74% of their games at C or DH and 4.4 for players who appear in 25-49% of their games at C or DH. The default CVI formula (threshold = 5.0) was used for players with <25% of their games at C or DH. As a result, the CVI values for Johnny Bench, Gary Carter, Mike Piazza, Edgar Martinez, Ivan Rodriguez, and Mickey Cochrane all exceed their career WAR by at least 15.

- Relief pitchers, who have become important specialists in today's game but do not pitch enough to generate high WAR totals, are a special case, since no simple threshold adjustment can level the playing field. For example, even Mariano Rivera has only 56.3 career WAR, which places him only 79th on the all-time list. Over the past 40 years, baseball has relied on a deeply flawed metric – the save – to evaluate relief pitchers.[15] The save recognizes only the pitcher who gets the final out of a winning game (even if he gives up a couple of runs along the way) and not the pitcher who gets his team out of a game-deciding late-inning jam to preserve a lead or keep a game within reach. Saves are also unfair to earlier generations of RP, who were often deployed in high leverage situations in the seventh and eighth innings and had fewer save opportunities than recent RP. CVI uses a statistic that I call "leveraged WAR" – the "product of WAR as a relief pitcher and a statistic that Baseball-Reference.com calls game entering Leverage Index (gmLI) – to evaluate pitchers who accrued a significant proportion of their career value in relief. Seasonal values of gmLI may range from 0.4 for RP deployed

Mariano Rivera

mainly in "mop-up" situations to as high as 2.5 for RP who are deployed mainly in the late innings of close games. For pitchers who saw significant activity as both SP and RP within a single season, I have partitioned their WAR_p into starting WAR and relief WAR by multiplying the proportion of games started or relieved times the seasonal WAR. The starting WAR is treated the same as the WAR for SP. The relief WAR for each season is multiplied by the pitcher's gmLI. No extra credit is given for values of leveraged WAR over 5.0 in a relief role, and no 0.8 scaling factor is used. This is illustrated for Dennis Eckersley in Appendix 2 (Table A2.8).

CVI also incorporates a few special adjustments for the following situations:

- Time Missed for Wartime Military Service: Many great players missed several prime years for wartime military service, particularly in World War II. I have adjusted CVI for affected players by interpolating the WAR for their "missing" years, Ted Williams, Bob Feller, Joe DiMaggio, Hank Greenberg, and Johnny Mize all gained at least 15 CVI from this adjustment. Details and a complete listing are provided in Appendix 2 (Table A2.1).

- I have back-extrapolated the WAR trajectory curves for four players whose careers were delayed by segregation and for Ichiro Suzuki (who played nine years in Japan before starting his MLB career at age 27). Records from the Negro Leagues and Japan suggest that these players were MLB-ready long before they were permitted to play in the major leagues. A table of adjusted CVI for these five players is in Appendix 2 (Table A2.2).

- Steroid Usage: I have discounted WAR by 20% for hitters and 10% for pitchers for all seasons when that player was known or strongly suspected to have been using illegal performance enhancing drugs (PED). The basis of this adjustment is explained in Chapter 8. A table of PED users affected by this adjustment is provided in Appendix 2 (Table A2.3)

Some illustrative examples of the calculation of CVI in various scenarios are provided in Appendix 2 (Tables A2.4-10). Appendix 2 also includes a table (A2.12) of CVI rankings without these three special adjustments.

CVI and the Hall of Fame[16]

In considering what might be the appropriate selection criteria for entry to the Hall of Fame, it is useful to think of CVI in terms of percentile rankings. For this purpose, I have used the 16,008 players who made their MLB debuts before opening day of the 2004 season as a denominator (see Appendix 2).[17] Thus, a player whose CVI ranks 160th among such players has a percentile ranking of 160/16,008 or 1.00%. The relationship of CVI to percentile is plotted in Figure 2.4; some examples are tabulated in Table 2.3.

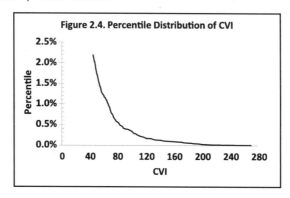

Table 2.3: CVI Percentiles

CVI	Percentile
108.6	0.25
83.5	0.50
72.6	0.75
66.7	1.00
58.6	1.25
53.9	1.50
50.2	1.75
47.6	2.00

The shape of this distribution is very crowded in the lower range of CVI, but thins out as CVI increases. The 25.1 CVI gap between players at the 0.25 and 0.50 percentile is greater than the 24.9 CVI gap between the 0.75 and 2.00 percentile. Moreover the CVI gap between the 0.25 percentile and Babe Ruth's 270 CVI far exceeds the gap between the 0.25 percentile and 0 CVI.

What are the practical implications of these percentiles for the entry criteria for the Hall of Fame? Think about the 16,008 players who debuted before 2004 as being distributed randomly into 80 "leagues," each with eight teams of 25-man rosters. If we set our HOF entry criterion at the 2.0 percentile (47.7 CVI), we should ultimately expect to find four Hall of Famers in the average "league." I think most would agree that this is too lenient. If we set our entry criterion at the 0.5 percentile (83.5 CVI), we would accept only the best player in each league. Most would agree that this is too strict. If we set the criterion at the 1.0 percentile (66.7 CVI), we would admit the two best players in each league, which seems about right if we are open to making exceptions for players near this threshold whose historical significance is not fully captured by CVI.

As of December 2020, the HOF includes 235 men who were elected based on their accomplishments as MLB players. The 235th player (Bobo Newsom), whose CVI is 53.04, sits at the 1.55 percentile, a level that would admit approximately three players in each of our 80 hypothetical leagues. (Of course, the HOF election committees have not chosen the best 235 players by CVI or any other metric, as we shall see.) Throughout this book, I will use the term "CVI-Plus" to refer to the top 235 HOF-eligible players and ineligible players with CVI ≥53.04. I have classified them into four subcategories: Elite (CVI ≥100), Great (CVI ≥70 but <100), Near Great (CVI ≥62 but <70), and Very Good (CVI ≥53.04 but <62). Here are a few examples from each group:

- Elite: Mays (232.3), Mantle (143.0), Seaver (120.5), Ripken (113.3), Carter (103.1)

- Great: Beltre (98.8), Keefe (88.5), Rose (83.6), Ryan (79.9), Berra (74.1), Lofton (70.6)

- Near Great: Mauer (69.7), Palmer (69.3), Gwynn (68.3), Tiant (65.0), Sabathia (63.4)

- Very Good: Edmonds (61.0), Terry (57.8), Killebrew (56.3), Fingers (55.0), Kaat (53.3)

The "Very Good" category for players who are CVI-Plus but fall a bit short of what I would consider a reasonable threshold for "greatness" is adopted from the "Hall of the Very Good" (HOVG) descriptor that "Small Hall" proponents often apply somewhat dismissively to players whose HOF candidacies they do not support. While I placed this threshold at CVI ≥62, this is just a rule of thumb. I do not view every player with CVI ≥62 as belonging in the HOF, nor do I view every player with CVI <62 as a pretender. Players with CVI <53.04 are deemed "CVI-Minus." This group includes 72 Hall of Famers. Conversely, 72 HOF-eligible CVI-Plus players – more than 30% - have not been elected to the HOF. We will be exploring many of these inequities in the coming chapters.

In Chapters 3-9, I have parsed the history of baseball into seven eras or generations:

- CH3: The Founding Generation of the wild and woolly 19th century (1871-1900)

- CH4: The Deadball Generation (1901-19) who played when runs were hard to come by

- CH5: The Classical Generation (1920-46) who pioneered the transition from "small ball" to "long ball"

- CH6: The Boom Generation (1947-72) when MLB spread across the continent and opened its doors to diverse races and nationalities

- CH7: The Free Agent Generation (1973-1993), a period of open warfare broke out between management and labor over the distribution of expanding TV revenues, which brought down the venerable reserve clause

- CH8: The Steroid Generation (1994-2011), when home runs became cheap and records fell

- CH9: The Analytics Generation (2012-2020), when new technologies and approaches to statistics have taken the game in new and unexpected directions.

Each chapter reviews the top players of its generation — as defined by the midpoint of their career (the season during which a player reaches 50% of his eventual career WAR) — in the context of the state of MLB in that historical period. The players are grouped thematically within each generation, and their CVI percentile rankings, and other HOF credentials are discussed and compared. CVI-Minus players who have been elected to the HOF despite weak credentials are also reviewed in Chapters 3-7. Integrated ranked lists of CVI across generations are provided in Chapter 10.

CHAPTER 3

THE FOUNDING GENERATION (1871-1900)

The Game

When we think of MLB's stability and rich traditions, we are thinking of the past 120 years since the start of the 20th century. MLB's first 30 years were anything but stable and traditional, with turmoil and radical change on every front. While it is convenient to cover the 30 years of 19th century professional baseball in a single chapter, the game changed more radically in those 30 years than in the 120 years that followed. The rules and the configuration of leagues and teams changed nearly every year.[1,2] The number of MLB teams, which started at nine in 1871 when there was only the NA, mushroomed to as high as 25 in 1890 (when there were three competing leagues) and fell back to eight by 1900, when the NL enjoyed a brief monopoly.[3]

Restrictions on pitchers, who were originally required to throw underhand from 45 feet away and put the ball where the batter requested, were removed by 1884

Bid McPhee

(see Table A1.2 in Appendix 1). However, the pitching distance was gradually lengthened, reaching its current 60.5' in 1893, and the number of balls required to give the batter a free base decreased from nine in 1879 to its current four in 1889. The final 5' increase in pitching distance in 1893 (which allowed 9% more time for hitters to react to pitches) had a cataclysmic effect on the smallish pitchers of that era, driving many of them from the game and precipitating a two-run rise in the leaguewide ERA from 3.28 in 1892 to an all-time high 5.33 in 1894 (Fig. 3.1).[4] Hard-throwing power pitchers like 6'2" 210-pound Cy Young and 6-1" 200-pound Amos Rusie made the transition successfully; many smaller pitchers, like 31-year-old 5'10" 155-pound future Hall of Famer John Clarkson and 33-year-old 5'9"

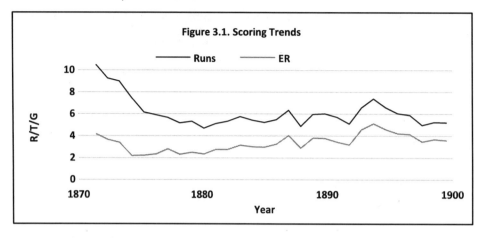

Figure 3.1. Scoring Trends

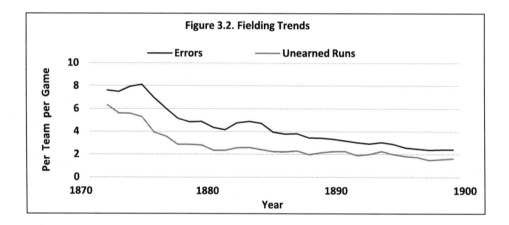

Figure 3.2. Fielding Trends

175-pound Bill Hutchison, who averaged 40 wins and a 2.76 ERA from 1890-92, struggled to adjust and quickly vanished from MLB.[5]

Defense was terrible, especially early on, mainly because fielders played barehanded.[6,7] NA teams averaged 7-8 unearned runs per team per game and more than half the runs scored were unearned (Fig 3.2). In the late 1870s and 1880s players (especially 1B and C) began to wear gloves to protect their non-throwing hand as the frequency of games increased and pitchers were permitted to throw overhand. However, their gloves were primitive by modern standards, and even in 1900, the 2.4 errors per team per game were quadruple the 0.60 errors per team per game in 2019.

The most striking stylistic contrast between 19th century baseball and the modern game was the emphasis on "smallball," which prioritized contact over power. Batters ranging from the hulking Cap Anson and to the diminutive Willie (hit 'em where they ain't) Keeler shortened their swings to maximize contact and almost never struck out. The ball was put in play on 81% (1891) to 97% (1874) of PA, compared to 64% in 2019 (the most recent "normal" season). Due to the high error rate, batters reached base safely on 33% (1898) to 42% (1873) of balls in play, compared to 31% in 2019. Home runs and strikeouts were far scarcer than they are today. Except for the offensive explosion of 1894, HR rates never exceeded 0.31 per game (compared to 1.39 in 2019). Except for the low-offense years of 1888-92, SO rates never exceeded 3 per game (compared to 8.8 in 2019, when there were actually more SO than H).

Because of the dominance of smallball and scarcity of HR, modern fans often conflate this era with the Deadball Era of 1901-19. However, contrary to the popular image of hitters scraping and scratching for runs, this was actually a high-scoring era, with teams averaging no fewer than five and as many as 10 runs per game (Figure 3.1). Although shoddy defense contributed significantly to these high scoring rates (Figure 3.2), especially in the 1870s, the 5.12 earned runs per team per game in 1894 is the highest in MLB history, easily exceeding the 4.73 ER/team/game in 1930 and the 4.72 ER/team/game in 2000 at the peak of the Steroid Era.

Equally striking is the profound difference in how pitchers were used in this era. From 1871-1886, the lion's share of IP belonged to no more than two pitchers per team. Teams also carried a handful of position players who could fill in as relief pitchers when the starters were ineffective or hurt.[8-10] However, by the mid-1880s, the rapid growth of the schedule from 30 to 120 games per season led to inning totals of 500-700. It was therefore common for ace pitchers to win 40 games and compile >12 WAR_p in a season, far exceeding anything seen today, when teams typically carry 13 pitchers, complete games are a rarity, and pitchers rarely compile as many as 220 IP or 20 W. As the schedule grew further to 140 games by 1900, teams increasingly relied on four-man pitching rotations and carried 8-10 pitchers on their rosters, but 350-400 IP workloads and 30+ W remained the norm for pitching aces.

KEELER, N. Y. AMER.

Willie Keeler, 1909

Baseball does not exist in a vacuum but is a microcosm of our society at large. Thus, a history of 19th century baseball would be incomplete without describing the origins of two grossly unjust and long-lasting policies – the establishment of the Reserve Clause in 1879 and the "gentleman's agreement" to exclude players of color in 1889. MLB was born in the aftermath of the Civil War and Reconstruction and in the age of the capitalist "robber baron." These themes played out in our National Pastime.

When the NA was founded in 1871, professional baseball was only a part-time job, in which men of sufficient skill could earn extra money by playing on weekends with their local baseball club for a share of the modest gate receipts.[11] There were no wealthy owners or financiers. Players were free to play with a club of their choosing. However, the founders of the NL in 1876 were businessmen with their eyes on the bottom line. Their first order of business was to bring stability and continuity by controlling costs.

They standardized rules, schedules, ticket prices, and player contracts. Their most far-reaching policy, implemented in 1879, was to establish the Reserve Clause, binding players to their teams in perpetuity at salaries set at the owner's discretion.[12] Some rationalized this system as essential to preventing the wealthiest teams from hoarding the best players and thereby destroying competitive balance. But empirically, this system did not prevent big-market teams like the New York Yankees of 1921-64 from doing exactly that and dominating their competition for decades. Nor did it prevent teams like the Philadelphia Phillies from winning more games than they lost only once (78-76 in 1932) in a 31-year stretch from 1918-1948.

The Reserve Clause's nearly 100-year reign (1879-1975) drove much of the ferment in the configuration of MLB. The establishment of the American Association (AA) in 1882, the Union Association (UA) in 1884, and the Players League (PL) in 1890 (as well as the American League and Federal League in the 20th century) were all driven in large part by the desire to break the NL's dominance, but each of these leagues quickly either joined with the NL in honoring the reserve clause (the AA) or were run out of business (the UA and PL).[13-17]

Although the AA, which lasted 10 years, was the longest lived of these rival leagues, the eight-team PL, which operated for only one year (1890), came closest to toppling the reserve system. This league was established by John Montgomery Ward's Players' Brotherhood under the aegis of the newly passed Sherman Anti-Trust Act.[18-26] The PL successfully solicited substantial financial backing and attracted many of the top stars of the game (with the notable exception of Cap Anson), including future Hall of Famers Ward (as player-manager of the Brooklyn "Ward's Wonders"), Roger Connor, Dan Brouthers, Tim Keefe, Buck Ewing, Hoss Radbourn, and Deacon White. Worse still for the establishment, the PL competed directly with the NL and AA in their biggest markets, undercutting ticket prices. The competition among the 25 major league teams, all in the northeast quadrant of the US, was so fierce that everyone lost money, but the PL had the best product and could have prevailed.

Unfortunately, the PL's financial backers in New York, Brooklyn, and Chicago, were unwilling to continue to lose money for another year to solidify their league and joined forces with NL ownership in those cities. Without these flagship franchises, the PL had no choice but to fold after only one season. The 10 year-old AA folded a year later, leaving the NL, which absorbed the four strongest AA franchises, with an uncontested 12-team monopoly (fewer than half the number of teams that existed in 1890) and its reserve clause intact. Player salaries immediately plummeted. Only eight MLB teams remained by 1900.

Given that organized professional baseball was established in the Reconstruction era and against a backdrop of the Klu Klux Klan and lynchings, it is not surprising that players of color were unwelcome. In 1883, Chicago White Stockings team captain, Cap Anson, refused to let his team take

Cap Anson

the field for an exhibition game against the Toledo Blue Stockings, who employed an African American catcher named Moses Fleetwood Walker.[27] Although Anson relented when faced with the loss of his share of gate receipts, that was not the end of it. In 1884, when Toledo joined the AA, Anson's continuing call to ban African-American players was taken up by other players and managers, who won the shameful acquiescence of ownership. Walker's release in 1889 following a reprise of the 1883 Anson-Walker incident in 1888 led to a *de facto* ban of players of color from MLB, which endured almost 60 years until Branch Rickey finally brought Jackie Robinson to the Dodgers in 1947. We will take up this story again in Chapter 6.

The premier teams of this era were the Boston Beaneaters and Chicago White Stockings, whose origins go back to the NA and who survive today as the Braves and Cubs. The Providence Grays (1883-84), St. Louis Browns (1885-88), New York Giants (1887-88), also enjoyed success in the 1880s.The Brooklyn Bridegrooms (who survive today as the Dodgers) and Baltimore Orioles (no relation to today's Orioles) were the top teams of the 1890s.

The Players

This is the most difficult generation of players to evaluate because the game was so different from other eras and changed so much from year to year. Still, I believe CVI provides a useful general ranking of the top players of this generation, even if it is not perfect.

This generation produced 19 players (eight hitters and eleven pitchers) with CVI ≥62, of whom 13 are in the Hall of Fame. Only Cy Young was elected to the HOF by the BBWAA; the rest were elected by the VC (see Chapter 11). It also produced

Table 3.1: CVI-Plus Players

A) Players (Position)	Midcareer	HOF	AVG/OBP/SLG	OPS+	WAR$_{\mathrm{H}}$	CVI
Anson, Cap (1B)	1886	VC	.334/.394/.447	142	94.4	108.8
Connor, Roger (1B)	1888	VC	.316/.397/.486	153	84.3	102.7
Brouthers, Dan (1B)	1888	VC	.342/.423/.520	171	79.8	102.3
Davis, George (SS)	1899	VC	.295/.362/.405	121	84.7	83.3
Delahanty, Ed (LF)	1897	VC	.346/.411/.505	152	69.6	80.5
Glasscock, Jack (SS)	1887	No	.290/.337/.374	112	62.0	74.8
Dahlen, Bill (SS)	1899	No	.272/.358/.382	110	75.3	68.8
Hamilton, Billy (CF)	1894	VC	.344/.455/.432	141	63.3	64.7
Burkett, Jesse (LF)	1899	VC	.338/.415/.446	140	62.8	56.3
Ward, Monte (SS)	1883	VC	.275/.314/.341	92	34.3	54.0

B) Pitchers	Midcareer	HOF	ERA/WHIP	ERA+	WAR$_{\mathrm{P}}$	CVI
Young, Cy (SP)	1899	BBWAA	2.63/1.130	138	165.7	194.0
Nichols, Kid (SP)	1895	VC	2.96/1.224	140	116.7	119.9
Clarkson, John (SP)	1889	VC	2.81/1.209	133	84.9	96.0
Keefe, Tim (SP)	1885	VC	2.63/1.123	126	89.1	88.5
Galvin, Pud (SP)	1884	VC	2.85/1.191	107	83.3	82.5
Radbourn, Old Hoss (SP)	1884	VC	2.68/1.149	119	73.2	76.6
Rusie, Amos (SP)	1893	VC	3.07/1.349	129	65.2	70.7
McCormick, Jim (SP)	1882	No	2.43/1.132	118	76.0	69.4
Bond, Tommy (SP)	1877	No	2.14/1.091	115	61.0	68.2
Buffinton, Charlie (SP)	1888	No	2.96/1.234	115	60.7	65.8
Mathews, Bobby (SP)	1874	No	2.86/1.237	104	62.3	62.7
Spalding, Al (SP)	1874	MGE	2.13/1.193	132	53.6	59.8
Griffith, Clark (SP)	1898	MGE	3.31/1.313	121	59.3	56.4
King, Silver (SP)	1889	No	3.18/1.122	121	50.1	56.2
Welch, Mickey (SP)	1885	VC	2.71/1.226	113	63.1	55.9
Mullane, Tony (SP)	1887	No	3.05/1.237	117	61.1	55.3
Breitenstein, Theodore (SP)	1895	No	4.03/1.449	110	51.8	54.3
Ward, Monte (SP)	1883	VC	2.10/1.043	119	28.1	54.0

eight additional CV-Plus players (one hitter, six pitchers, and one two-way player) of whom three were elected to the Hall of Fame as players (all by the VC) and two as managers/executives (MGE). The careers and HOF credentials of these players, partitioned into thematic groupings, are presented in this chapter. For each player, I have provided his full name, CVI, the main teams he played for (and his

WAR accrued with each team in parentheses), and a summary of the high points of his career. Later in this chapter, a similar table will be provided for CVI-Minus players of this era who have been elected to the HOF. Chapters 4-9 will follow a similar format.

What Greatness Looked Like

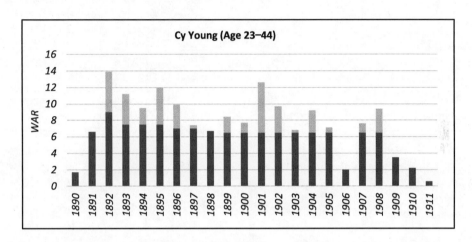

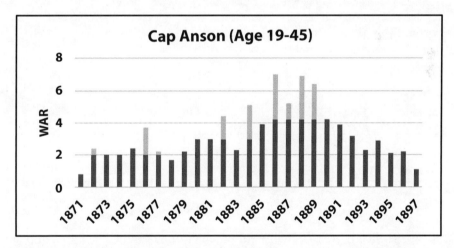

Cy Young and Cap Anson were the top players of the Founding Generation. Cy Young never pitched 500+ innings or achieved a 15-WAR season like many of his predecessors of the 1880s, but he far outlasted them and was still producing great seasons in his 40s in 1907-08. Cap Anson superficially looks like a compiler but his WAR values are limited by the fact that the baseball season lasted <100 games until 1886, when he was already 34 years old.

The Four Hoss-Men

John Clarkson (SP):
96.0 CVI – Boston NL (42.3),
Chicago NL (36.5)

Tim Keefe (SP):
88.5 CVI – New York NL (34.9),
New York AA (28.5), Troy NL (13.1)

Pud Galvin (SP):
82.5 CVI – Buffalo NL (52.7),
Pittsburgh NL (20.0)

Old Hoss Radbourn (SP):
76.6 CVI – Providence NL (54.0),
Boston NL (13.0)

These four pitchers exemplify the pitching style before the substitution of a pitcher's mound for the pitcher's box and the establishment of the current 60.5' pitching distance in 1893, when pitchers were almost everyday players, and walks and strikeouts were infrequent. Their productivity was generally confined to a relatively small number of spectacular seasons whose production levels far exceeded anything since. Table 3.2 summarizes their seasons with 10 or more WAR.

Table 3.2: The Four Hoss-Men –Seasons with ≥10.0 WAR

Year	Pitcher	IP (% of Team)	CG/GS	W-L	SHO	ERA+	WAR$_p$	WAR
1883	Keefe	619.0 (70.8%)	68/68	41-27	5	145	19.8	20.2
1884	Radbourn	678.7 (65.5%)	73/75	60-12	11	205	19.1	19.4
1884	Galvin	656.3 (63.6%)	71/72	46-22	12	155	20.5	18.4
1889	Clarkson	620.0 (53.2%)	68/72	49-19	8	150	16.7	16.2
1887	Clarkson	523.0 (46.5%)	56/59	38-21	2	145	14.9	15.0
1883	Radbourn	632.3 (72.6%)	68/76	48-25	4	150	13.1	13.4
1885	Clarkson	623.0 (61.3%)	68/70	53-16	10	163	12.9	12.8

Each man pitched more than half of his team's innings and racked up 2-to-3 modern seasons' worth of IP, wins and WAR. Indeed, no post-1892 pitcher has more than 482 IP (Amos Rusie), 41 wins (Jack Chesbro), or 15.1 WAR$_p$ (Walter Johnson) in a season. It is therefore hard to compare them with modern pitchers. CVI places them as no-doubt Hall of Famers, in the 0.38-0.63 percentile range. All relied on inducing groundballs; none had a 3TO rate higher than 0.19, and only Keefe racked up as many as 0.5 SO/H. All were washed up by their mid-30s. Still, they each pitched long enough to have won 300 games and to rank in the top 30 in IP and ranking 21st, 24th, 29th, and 37th among SP, respectively, in CVI.

Beyond the Numbers

- Clarkson and Keefe came from well-to-do families.[28,29] Radbourn's parents were immigrant farmers.[30] Galvin grew up in abject poverty in the slums of St. Louis.[31]

- Keefe was reportedly the inspiration for the pitcher who struck out the mighty Casey with men on 2B and 3B and two outs to seal a 4-2 victory over Mudville in the iconic 1888 Ernest Thayer poem "Casey at the Bat."[32] In real life, the game was played in August 1887 between the Giants and Phillies, the bases were loaded, the score was 5-3, and Dan Casey hit a game-tying single.[33] But Thayer's vignette makes for a more dramatic story.

- Keefe and Radbourn were active in the Players Brotherhood and jumped to the Players League in 1890. Keefe's sporting goods company supplied equipment to the new league.

- Radbourn's 60 wins in 1884 is an all-time record that will never be equaled. Clarkson's 53 wins in 1885 ranks second — and it wasn't even his best season.

- Galvin was baseball's first known steroid user, taking part in an 1889 experiment with the Brown-Sequard elixir, which contained extracts from guinea pig and dog testicles.[34] The rotund Galvin, who was well past his prime, pitched a two-hit shutout. But we all know now that the impact of steroids is not instantaneous and requires a rigorous training regimen, so the experiment really proved nothing.

The First Great Modern Pitchers

Cy Young (SP)	Kid Nichols[6] (SP):
194.0 CVI – Cleveland NL (75.6), Boston AL (67.1), St. Louis NL (15.7)	119.9 CVI – Boston NL (107.2)

There is no "Kid Nichols Award," but in the high-scoring 1890s, Nichols was on a par with Cy Young, as they thrived under the rules changes of 1892-93 that wrecked so many other pitching careers. Young and Nichols entered the NL together in 1890 and pitched most of their careers from 60.5' under mostly modern rules. Although

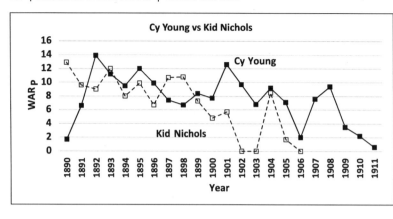

both were work-horses by today's standards, neither ever had more than 453 IP, 49 CG, 36 W, or 14.0 WAR_p, in a season and neither ever pitched more than 34% of his team's innings.

When one compares their career WAR trajectories, Nichols was actually the slightly superior pitcher in the 1890s, accruing 96.9 WAR_p (31.5 in 1890-92, and 65.4 afterwards) versus 87.4 WAR_p (22.2 in 1890-92, and 65.2 afterward) for Young. Nichols also had 30 more wins (297-267), eight more shutouts (36-28), 32 more CG (418-386), and 369 more SO (1484-1125) than Young in the 1890s, with a lower ERA (2.97-3.05) and WHIP (1.234-1.242) and a better ERA+ (146-139).

Kid Nichols

However, Nichols left MLB in 1901 after a 19-win season to co-own and manage a minor league franchise, while Young went on pitching exceptionally for 10 more years and finally retired at age 44. Nichols came back successfully in 1904 (21 wins) but was out of baseball by age 36. So it is Young who stands high atop the career leaderboards with 7356 IP, 749 CG, 511 W, and 165.6 WAR_p, who was among the original HOF inductees in 1939, and who was honored by the establishment of the eponymous award for pitching excellence. Nichols's 5067.1 IP (11th), 532 CG (4th), 361 W (7th), and 116.7 WAR_p (4th) also rank high on the career leaderboards, but he was a HOF afterthought, winning recognition from the VC in 1949. Young and Nichols are both elite Hall of Famers, whose CVI rank second and tenth, respectively, among SP, and seventh and 28th, among all HOF-eligible players.

Beyond the Numbers

- Young's decision to sign with the Boston Americans in 1901 (along with the defection of Nap Lajoie) brought the new AL instant credibility. He threw the first pitch of the first modern World Series for Boston in 1903 and was the only pitcher to win a game in both the Temple Cup and the World Series.

- In 1907, Young became the only pitcher to throw three consecutive 1-0 CG shutouts. He was also one of only six men to throw three or more no-hitters, including the first modern perfect game in 1904 at age 37. Only Ryan and Koufax have thrown more.

- According to Bill James, Kid Nichols had a decisive impact on five close pennant races in 1891, 1892, 1893, 1897, and 1898; only Babe Ruth and Mickey Mantle outdid him in that regard.[35]

The Giants

Cap Anson (1B):
108.8 CVI – Chicago NL (84.8),
Philadelphia NA (8.7)

Roger Connor (1B):
102.7 CVI – New York NL (53.0),
St. Louis NL (9.5), Troy NL (9.4)

Dan Brouthers (1B):
102.3 CVI – Buffalo NL (24.5),
Detroit NL (20.1), Brooklyn NL (12.6)

MLB's big men of the 19th century were 1B, not pitchers. Anson (6'2" and over 200 pounds), Connor (6'3" and 220 pounds), and Brouthers (6'2" and 207 pounds) were imposing figures in their day; indeed it was Connor's bulk that gave rise to changing the name of the New York NL team from "Gothams" to "Giants" in 1885. These three 1B were the outstanding hitters of the 1880s.

None of these men was a slugger in the modern sense. Although Connor held the MLB career HR record until Babe Ruth came along, his 138 HR are hardly reminiscent of Babe Ruth (or even Babe Herman). Brouthers held the career home run record (107) before Connor. Brouthers (.520 SLG and .178 ISO), Connor (.486 SLG and .170 ISO) had substantial extra base power; his 233 triples rank fifth on the all-time leaderboard. On the other hand, Anson (.447 SLG and .113 ISO) swung strictly for contact. All three players struck out infrequently. Anson (31.15) and Brouthers (28.26) rank 21st and 30th on the career leaderboard for AB/SO. Connor's 17.14 AB/SO, though less impressive, is still three times better than Bonds and Ruth, twice as high as Henry Aaron, and comparable to Joe DiMaggio, who combined elite contact skills with power. Connor had the highest 3TO rate (0.185) and SO/H (0.184), while Anson's 3TO and SO/H are among the lowest in history.

In an era when defensive play was primitive, none of these players was a strong fielder. Indeed, Anson holds the all-time record with 658 errors at 1B (.970 fielding average) and was even worse at 3B (.784 fielding average in 220 games). By contrast, Dick Stuart, a Red Sox 1B of the 1960s whose fielding misadventures earned him the nickname "Dr. Strangeglove," racked up only 169 errors in his 10-year career (.982 fielding average), and David Ortiz (whose defensive deficiencies limited him to only 265 games at 1B in his 20-year career) committed only 22 errors (a fielding average of .990). To be fair, Anson played the first half of his career without a fielding glove. Connor was also a terrible fielder when he broke in as a bare-handed 3B, with 60 errors and an .821 fielding percentage, and was only slightly better at 1B the following year. After a shoulder injury limited him to 1B, he worked hard to improve and later led all 1B in fielding percentage four times.

One cannot write about Anson without mentioning that he is one of the least admirable players in the Hall of Fame. Anson was an intimidating presence on the field and was known for his belligerence toward opponents and umpires. He earned the nickname "king of kickers" for the dirt he kicked while arguing with umpires. More importantly, Anson was on the wrong side of history regarding the two major issues of his era – the reserve clause and the color line – which stained MLB for decades to come. It was his refusal to play in an 1883 exhibition game with a Black player that instigated the chain of events that led to segregation of MLB. Unlike Connor and Brouthers, he failed to support the Players Brotherhood in 1890, yet later had the temerity to complain about the NL's monopolistic tendencies in his 1900 autobiography when Al Spalding blocked him from establishing Western League franchise in Chicago in the late 1890s.[36]

CVI ranks Anson, Connor, and Brouthers fourth, fifth, and sixth, respectively, among 1B and 39th, 47th, and 48th among all HOF-eligible players. They are all elite Hall of Famers.

Beyond the Numbers:

- Anson debuted at age 19 on May 6, 1871, in the Rockford Forest City's first game of the first national Association season. He played for 27 years.

- Anson bought a semipro club in Chicago in 1907 and even donned a uniform in 1908, although at age 56, he could no longer play. Ironically, Anson allowed his team to play several exhibition games against the Chicago Leland Giants, a prominent Negro League team, without comment or complaint.

Beyond the Numbers (cont'd)

- Anson ended his days in vaudeville, performing with his daughters in a routine written by Ring Lardner.

- Unlike Anson, Connor was a soft-spoken, dignified man, who sought no attention – sort of a 19th century version of Henry Aaron. In an odd twist of fate, it was Aaron himself who inadvertently rescued Connor from obscurity with Aaron's record-breaking 715th HR in 1974, making Connor the answer to the trivia question, "Whose career home run record did Babe Ruth break?" His newfound fame led to his belated election to the Hall of Fame two years later.[37]

- Strangely, Connor never led the major leagues in HR but finished second four times. He led the Players League with 14 HR in 1890.

- Connor's game-winning grand slam against the last-place Worcester Ruby Legs in 1881 was the first in NL history.

- Brouthers was forced to find a new team four times in his career when his current team folded – in 1885 (Buffalo NL), 1888 (Detroit NL), 1890 (Boston PL), and 1891 (Boston AA). Indeed, he played for Boston teams in three different leagues in 1890-92.

Three Slick Shortstops

George Davis (SS):
83.3 CVI – New York NL (44.6),
Chicago AL (33.1)

Jack Glasscock (SS):
74.8 CVI – Cleveland NL (15.3),
Indianapolis NL (14.6), Salem NL (1)

Bill Dahlen (SS):
68.8 CVI – Chicago NL (34.0),
Brooklyn NL (20.7), New York NL (14.5)

Dahlen, Davis, and Glasscock did not compare with Anson et al as hitters, but they set the defensive standard at the most important position on the field, ranking 8th, 15th, and 25th in dWAR among all SS. Glasscock, who began his career a

Jack Glasscock, 1888

decade before Dahlen and Davis and was dubbed the "King of Shortstops," did it mostly without wearing a glove. Yet, only Davis is in the Hall of Fame, and even he was not recognized until 1998, after a 30-year campaign led by baseball historian Lee Allen, almost 30 years after his death from tertiary syphilis in a mental hospital in 1940.[38] Dahlen and Davis were better hitters than one may glean from their raw stats, since they played much of their careers in the offensive doldrums of the early Deadball Era; they hit .298 and .314, respectively in the 1890s. CVI ranks Davis, Glasscock, and Dahlen 8th, 10th and 17th, respectively, among SS and at the 0.51, 0.67, and 0.92 percentile overall. Glasscock and Dahlen deserve to join Davis in the HOF.

Beyond the Numbers:

- Dahlen and Davis played for World Series champions in successive years – Dahlen for the Giants in 1905 and Davis for the White Sox "hitless wonders" in 1906. Glasscock never played in a postseason, and the three main teams he played for vanished without a trace – which helps explain his present obscurity.

- Davis began his career with the Cleveland Spiders and came to the Giants in an 1892 trade for over-the-hill Hall of Famer Buck Ewing. He jumped to the AL White Sox a decade later.

- Dahlen was a notorious rule-breaker and umpire baiter, especially in the first half of his career in Chicago.[39] He came full circle when he managed the Brooklyn Superbas/Dodgers in 1910-14 and had no more success managing his players than he had managing himself.

- Dahlen was largely forgotten after he retired and never received much support for the Hall of Fame. In 2012, SABR's Nineteenth Century Committee singled him out as its "overlooked legend of 19th century baseball."[40]

Phillies Stars of the 1890s

Ed Delahanty (LF):
80.5 CVI - Philadelphia NL (60.9),
Washington AL (8.0).

Billy Hamilton (CF):
64.7 CVI – Philadelphia NL (36.4),
Boston NL (23.8)

The Phillies of the high-scoring 1890s were an offensive juggernaut that never had enough pitching or defense to win a pennant. "Big Ed" Delahanty and "Slidin' Billy" Hamilton, who comprised two-thirds of their HOF outfield (Sam Thompson was the third), epitomized this offensive powerhouse. Delahanty was the big slugger whose .346 career AVG ranks fifth on the all-time leaderboard, but who unfortunately is better remembered for jumping or falling to his death from a bridge spanning the Niagara river in 1903 after leaving his team in midseason and embarking on a prolonged drinking binge.[41] The diminutive 5'6" Hamilton, by contrast, was the Ricky Henderson of his day – a base-stealing, run-scoring machine, who was the quintessential lead-off man of his generation. Hamilton stole >100 bases four times in his 14-year career (and 97 once) and his .344 lifetime AVG ranks only two spots behind Delahanty. He was also one of the first hitters to make drawing walks a big part of his game, leading the NL in OBP and BB five times each. His .521 OBP in 1894 was the major league single-season record until Ruth came along, and it is still the ninth best of all time. He also batted .403 that year and set the all-time record with 198 runs scored (one of four times he led the league in that category). His .455 career OBP ranks behind only Ted Williams, Babe Ruth, and John McGraw.

Delahanty's and Hamilton's gaudy stats were no mere artifacts of the high-scoring environment in which they played, as their 154 and 141 OPS+ attest. Unlike Delahanty, who compiled a more than respectable .505 SLG, Hamilton totally lacked power, with only 522 more TB than hits. Thus, his .083 ISO falls well below that of other speedy contact-hitting smallball superstars like Cobb, Wagner, Speaker, and Lajoie.

Surprisingly, Delahanty was the better defensive OF, since Hamilton's bad hands and weak throwing arm offset his superior speed. Delahanty's and Hamilton's stats are all the more impressive because each played a shorter schedule than modern players (130-140 games) during their peak years. Neither was able to compensate with longevity, playing 16 and 14 years, respectively. Still, CVI ranks Delahanty 7th among LF (0.56 percentile overall) and Hamilton 13th among CF (1.09 percentile overall). Both deserve their plaques in Cooperstown.

Beyond the Numbers

- Hamilton's lofty SB totals must be taken with a large grain of salt because extra bases taken on batted balls (like scoring from 1B on a single or going from 1B to 3B on a bunt) were counted as SB until 1898.[42]

- Hamilton played for two NL champions in Boston in 1898-99 after he was traded to the Beaneaters in November 1895. Delahanty remained with the Phillies until he jumped to the AL Senators in 1902 and never played for a pennant winner.

The Hoosier Thunderbolt

Amos Rusie (SP):
70.7 CVI – New York NL (67.5)

At first blush, there seems to be a disconnect between Amos Rusie's unimpressive conventional stats and the subject of John McGraw's comment, "You can't hit 'em if you can't see 'em."[43] Indeed, sportswriters of the time attributed the 1893 rule change moving the pitching rubber back five feet to 60.5' to the hitters' fear of Rusie's thunderous but erratic fastball. Was he really the Nolan Ryan of the 19th century? Statistically, the only obvious commonalty with Ryan (who walked 0.52 per IP versus 0.45 for Rusie) is subpar control. But unlike Ryan, who also struck out a spectacular 1.06 per IP over a 27-year career and gave up only 0.73 H/IP, Rusie struck out only a tepid 0.52 per IP. His 0.575 SO/H was not even the best of his era and pales next to Ryan's 1.46. And how to reconcile Rusie's 13.7 WAR$_p$ in 1894 with his merely respectable 2.78 ERA and pedestrian 1.41 WHIP and with the fact that his walks exceeded his strikeouts that year?

The answer is context. Rusie pitched in the highest scoring era in baseball history — if you don't count the error-inflated run totals in the NA in the early 1870s. The NL ERA from 1893-97 (Rusie's peak years) soared to levels never seen before or since, exceeding 4.30 in all five years and peaking at 5.33 in 1894. So, Rusie's 3.07 career ERA was 29% better than the league average (129 ERA+), far more impressive than it looks, and his 2.78 ERA in 1894 was a whopping 88% better than the league average (188 ERA+). Similarly, the league WHIP rose to unheard of levels above 1.50 during this period, peaking at 1.71 in 1894. Again, Rusie's 1.35 career WHIP and 1.41 WHIP in 1894 were quite decent in that context, despite his suboptimal 0.45 BB per IP. So, when viewed through an 1890s lens, Rusie really was one of the NL's best pitchers during his brief 10-year career, and one of few who successfully navigated the transition to the 60.5-foot pitching distance in 1893. Rusie's 70.7 CVI ranks at the 0.81 percentile, making him a solid Hall of Famer.

Beyond the Numbers

- Rusie's career was short but paid one last dividend for the Giants in 1901, fetching future Hall of Famer Christy Mathewson (who would dominate the next decade) in a lopsided trade with the Cincinnati Reds. This was the second time in less than a decade – the 1893 Buck Ewing-George Davis trade with Cleveland was the first — that the Giants had virtually stolen a young player embarking on a HOF career in exchange for the spent remains of a Hall of Famer whose best years were behind him. Rusie went 0-1, with an 8.59 ERA in three starts for the Reds before his release; Mathewson went on to win 372 games over 17 years with the Giants.

A Man for All Seasons

John Montgomery Ward (SS/SP):
54.0 CVI – Providence NL (27.5), New York NL (20.7), Brooklyn NL (6.7)

Born into a well-to-do family but orphaned at age 14, Ward was a brilliant self-made man who is difficult to pigeonhole. He was a very good pitcher, but his pitching career was cut short by injury and did not merit HOF recognition. He re-invented himself as a speedy versatile slap-hitting SS when his arm became too sore to pitch, but he was not among the best offensive players of his time. He was a winning player-manager for seven seasons, but his teams never won a pennant – although his second-place New York Giants swept the first-place Baltimore Orioles to win the 1894 Temple Cup. He never ran a team. Yet he was one of the most influential players in MLB history because of his fierce advocacy for players' rights as the founder of the Players Brotherhood, as the father of the Players League, which nearly succeeded in toppling MLB's power structure in 1890, and later as a lawyer for players wishing to jump from the NL to the new AL (or back to the NL) in the early 1900s. Think of him as a 19th century hybrid of Marvin Miller and Scott Boras.

Ward's biography (which I can only touch on here) is more remarkable than his accomplishments on the playing field.[44] As a teenager attending Penn State University, he pitched for their first baseball team and won acclaim at age 15 by conducting a public lecture/demonstration of how a thrown ball could be made to curve. He got a law degree and a Bachelor of Philosophy in political science from Columbia University while playing with the Giants in 1985-86,. An eloquent and persuasive writer, he penned a prescient article entitled "Is the Baseball Player a Chattel?" in 1887, deconstructing the reserve clause.[45] When the NL owners rebuffed Ward's attempt to negotiate modifications in the reserve clause that would permit a more equitable distribution of MLB's growing revenues, Ward persuaded his furious

John Montgomery Ward, 1887

members to call off plans for a strike and to focus instead on securing financing for a new league with player control.

Thus was born the Players League (PL) in 1890. Citing the newly passed Sherman Anti-Trust Act, Ward argued successfully in the courts to defeat attempts by NL owners to enjoin other players from defecting to the PL.[46] The PL attracted many of the top stars of the game, who were members of the Brotherhood. But the competition among the three leagues was so fierce that they all lost money. Unfortunately, the PL's financial backers were the first to blink, and the league folded. So, Ward and the others had no choice but to return to the NL in 1891.

After his playing career ended, Ward became a successful corporate lawyer, gradually moving away from baseball after a few high-profile reserve clause cases – two involving his friend and former teammate George Davis in 1901 and 1903. He almost returned to baseball in 1909 as NL president, but he had alienated too many members of MLB's establishment – notably Ban Johnson – to get the job.

The Lesser Hoss-Men

Jim McCormick (SP):
69.4 CVI – Cleveland NL (53.8),
Chicago NL (9.9), Cincinnati UA (7.8)

Tommy Bond (SP):
68.2 CVI – Boston NL (40.2),
Harrisburg NA-NL (21.9)

Charlie Buffinton (SP):
65.8 CVI – Philadelphia NL (26.6),
Boston NL (24.2)

Bobby Mathews (SP):
62.7 CVI – New York NA-NL (34.6),
Philadelphia AA (12.7)

Like Clarkson, Keefe, Galvin, and Radbourn, these four pitchers compiled HOF-caliber careers by posting a small number of seasons with WAR_p >10, in which they started and finished most of their team's games. But they weren't quite as good for quite as long; all four fell short of 300 career wins and election to the Hall of Fame. The Glasgow-born McCormick was perhaps the best of the bunch with 265 W, a 118 ERA+, and 76.0 WAR_p. Bond had an extraordinary five-year run in the late 1870s in which he averaged 36 wins and 7.9 WAR_p per season, baffling hitters with a low sidearm delivery of questionable legality at a time when the rules required pitchers to throw underhand. However, he faded fast and performed below replacement level (-0.2 WAR_p) for the remainder of his 11-year career. Buffinton was more consistent, winning 234 games in 11 years. Mathews, who hurled the Fort Wayne Kekiongas to a 2-0 victory in MLB's first-

Bobby Mathews

ever game, pitched for 17 years and fell only three wins shy of 300 but had a five-year midcareer dry spell in 1877-81 that reduced his career ERA+ to 104. His four best years came in the NA in 1872-75. CVI ranks McCormick, Bond, Buffinton, and Mathews at the 0.89, 0.94, 1.03, and 1.15 percentiles. One could argue for their inclusion in the HOF, but their omission is understandable.

Hall of the Very Good

Al Spalding (SP):
59.8 CVI – Boston NA (59.2)

Clark Griffith (SP):
56.4 CVI – Chicago NL (46.3),
Chicago AL (7.8), New York AL (7.4)

Jesse Burkett (LF):
56.3 CVI – Cleveland NL (29.2),
St. Louis NL (18.1), St. Louis AL (10.4)

Silver King (SP):
56.2 CVI – St. Louis NL (29.9),
Chicago PL (12.4)

Mickey Welch (SP):
55.9 CVI – New York NL (51.0),
Troy NL (10.8)

Tony Mullane (SP):
55.3 CVI – Cincinnati AA-NL (38.4),
Toledo AA (13.3)

Ted Breitenstein (SP):
54.3 CVI – St. Louis NL (32.6), Cincinnati NL (18.0)

Four of the seven players in this group – Spalding Griffith, Burkett, and Welch – are in the HOF. Spalding and Griffith were selected for their careers as executives. Spalding was a truly great pitcher, winning 204 games in five years in the NA, but ended his playing career in 1877 at age 27 to become manager and co-owner of the Chicago White Stockings – the NL's flagship franchise of the time – and went on to become president of the NL in 1882.[48] Griffith, who was merely a very good SP who pitched for 24 years, was among the chief founders of AL as player-manager of the White Sox, led the movement to abolish the spitball and other "freak" pitches in 1917, and owned the Senators from 1919 until his death in 1955.[49]

Burkett was a terrific hitter, who hit over .400 twice and over .350 four more times and had a .415 career OBP. Although he played much of his career in the high-scoring 1890s, his 140 OPS+ shows that he was more than just a product of his times. He was a consummate singles hitter, with a .108 ISO, but he also knew how to draw a walk. Weak defense (-12.3 dWAR) held down his CVI, which is at the 1.35 percentile – a little light for the HOF.

Welch and Mullane (who is not in the HOF) were in the same mold as their contemporaries McCormick, Bond, Buffinton, and Mathews – workhorse pitchers who posted a small number of 10-WAR seasons in which they pitched 500+ IP. Welch is the only one of the six who made it to the HOF, probably because he was the only one to attain the magical 300 win milestone (Mathews won 297 and Mullane won 284). He would not be in my Hall of Fame.

The two remaining players on this list are Silver King and Ted Breitenstein, two relatively obscure pitchers with short careers (10 and 11 years, respectively) who racked up some high IP and WAR totals in the late 1880s and 1890s. Neither is really a legitimate HOF candidate – especially Breitenstein whose 4.03 career ERA and 1.45 WHIP cannot be totally explained away by the high-scoring environment of the 1890s.

Other Hall of Famers

All 12 players on the CVI-Minus list for this era were hitters. I do not generally support the HOF candidacy of CVI-Minus players (especially those who fall outside the top 2% by CVI), but I cannot be dogmatic about this era. The game was just too different! Many of these hitters were handicapped by not playing what would now be considered a full schedule. The CVI threshold adjustment (Table 2.2) helps but does restore the extra WAR they might have earned in a full 154 or 162 game schedule. Capsule comments on these players are provided below.

One can make a strong argument that **Buck Ewing** deserves his plaque in the HOF. He was considered by many of his peers, including Connie Mack, as the best player of his time and was the first catcher to be elected to the HOF.[50] Not only did he spend his prime years in an era when teams played only 80-120 games per season,

Table 3.3: CVI-Minus Hall of Famers

Players (Position)	Midcareer	HOF	AVG/OBP/SLG	OPS+	WAR$_{11}$	CVI
Ewing, Buck (C)	1888	VC	.303/.351/.456	129	48.0	51.8
Jennings, Hughie (SS)	1897	VC	.312/.391/.406	118	42.3	51.8
White, Deacon (3B)	1879	VC	.312/.346/.393	127	45.7	51.3
Beckley, Jake (1B)	1896	VC	.308/.361/.436	125	61.7	50.1
Kelly, King (RF)	1894	VC	.307/.368/.438	138	47.0	49.8
Keeler, Willie (RF)	1899	BBWAA	.341/.388/.415	127	54.3	49.1
Kelley, Joe (LF)	1897	VC	.317/.402/.451	134	50.5	48.2
O'Rourke, Jim (LF)	1884	VC	.310/.352/.422	134	52.1	48.0
McPhee, Bid (2B)	1891	VC	.272/.355/.373	107	52.5	44.5
Thompson, Sam (RF)	1892	VC	.331/.384/.505	147	44.4	39.6
Duffy, Hugh (CF)	1894	VC	.326/.386/.451	123	43.1	38.1
McCarthy, Tommy (RF)	1891	VC	.292/.364/.375	102	16.2	16.3

Ewing himself never played more than 105 games nor made more than 444 PA until 1893 (when he was 33 years old). **Ewing's** 48.0 WAR ranks 13th among all catchers. All of the 11 HOF-eligible catchers ahead of him are in the HOF. Ewing also ranks first among all C (and 18th among all players) in triples and first among catchers in SB, fourth in R, tied for fourth in OPS+, and eighth in AVG. In that context, his 1939 election to in the Hall of Fame is understandable, if not compelling.

The next seven players on this list — **Jennings**, **White**, **Beckley**, **Kelly**, **Keeler**, **Kelley**, and **O'Rourke** — all had CVI in the top 2%, but their case for the HOF is more of a stretch. **White**, who played in MLB's first game on May 5, 1871 and was active through 1890, is probably the most deserving, since his CVI was most affected by playing shorter schedules. He was regarded as the game's best catcher until Ewing came along.[51] **One** might also give a nod **to Willie Keeler** as the only player on this list elected by the BBWAA, which historically has had stricter standards than the VC (see Chapter 11). His .341 AVG, 127 OPS+, and incredible 63.17 AB/SO for his career (the best of all time) indicate that he was more than just a product of his high-octane offensive era. On the other hand, Keeler had no power (.074 ISO) and was a mediocre fielder (-9.9 dWAR) despite his speed. **Jennings** was a good offensive SS (118 OPS+), a solid defender (9.0 dWAR), and a sparkplug for the 1890s Orioles. He also managed the Tigers successfully for 14 years (1907-1920). **King Kelly** was a strong hitter (139 OPS+) and had extra value as a catcher. **Beckley** played for 20 years and was a solid hitter (125 OPS+), but never had more than 4.6 WAR in a season despite spending the last half of his career playing 154-game seasons. **Kelley** and **O'Rourke** (who played for 23 seasons) were also strong hitters but poor fielders (-7.4 and -9.6 dWAR, respectively).

There are also things to like about **McPhee** and **Thompson**. McPhee's 16.2 dWAR ranks 15th among all 2B. **Thompson** was a prolific hitter (147 OPS+) and run-producer (1308 RBI), including 166 RBI in 127 G for Detroit in 1887 and 165 RBI in 119 G for Philadelphia in 1895. Although he had a strong arm, his defense was subpar (-7.2 dWAR), and his prime was relatively short.

Finally, we have Boston's "heavenly twins" of the 1890s, **Hugh Duffy** and **Tommy McCarthy**, who were known for their innovative OF defense and for inventing the hit-and-run play. **Duffy** was also an excellent contact hitter, whose .4397 AVG in 1894 was the highest ever recorded in MLB. Although he had no power and his AVG was inflated by playing in MLB's highest scoring era, his 123 OPS+ was respectable.

Bottom of the Pile

Tommy McCarthy (16.3 CVI) earns this dubious distinction, not only for his own generation, but for the HOF as a whole. As his WAR trajectory plot shows, he was no better than replacement level for five of his 13 years in MLB and a league-average player for seven of his remaining eight years. His 16.2 WAR_H, .292 AVG, 102 OPS+, and -3.0 dWAR were no better than ordinary. While a 13-year career with 16.2 WAR is nothing to sneer at, 11.1% (997) of the 8955 non-pitchers who made their MLB debut before 2004 have exceeded McCarthy's 16.2 primary WAR total.[52] (I have used WAR, rather than CVI, to make this comparison, since I have not calculated CVI for the top 1000 players. Since 5-WAR seasons are rare for most players with WAR_H <30, the rank orders for WAR_H and CVI should be similar in this range.) I have no idea what the VC was thinking in 1946 when they chose McCarthy. It is as if the VC got together today and elected Orlando Merced (who also had 16.2 WAR_H) to the HOF.

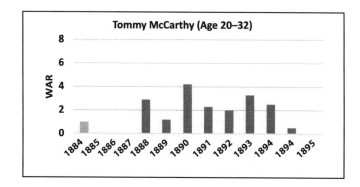

CHAPTER 4

THE DEADBALL GENERATION (1901-1919)

The Game

The NL started the new century with franchises in Boston, Brooklyn, Chicago, Cincinnati, New York, Philadelphia, Pittsburgh, and St. Louis. It was joined in 1901 by a new major league with staying power, the American League (AL), which evolved from the minor league Western Association of the 1890s, with new franchises in Baltimore, Boston, Chicago, Cleveland, Detroit, Milwaukee, Philadelphia, and Washington.[1] Although the AL began in open competition with the NL and poached two of its biggest stars – Cy Young and Nap Lajoie – the two leagues were soon honoring each other's reserve clauses and (after a one-off in 1903) made a permanent agreement to play an annual World Series matching their two champions starting in 1905. After the AL's Milwaukee franchise moved to St. Louis in 1902 and its Baltimore franchise moved to New York in 1903, the two leagues remained remarkably stable for the next 50 years.

The turn of the century also brought us the Deadball Era, MLB's two-decade offensive famine, when scoring averaged 3.93 runs/team/game – 3.4 runs below the high point of 7.38 in 1894.[2,3] After reaching an all-time high in 1894, scoring began to decline to 6.58 runs per team per game in 1895 to 6.04 in 1896 to 5.88 in 1897 to 4.96 in 1898 (Fig. 4.1). This decline may have reflected the gradual replacement of the smaller finesse pitchers of the 1880s by bigger stronger men who were better able to acclimate to the new 60.5' pitching distance and to leverage the advantage of throwing downhill from an elevated pitchers' mound.[4]

After a small uptick in 1899-1900, the scoring decline picked up steam, falling below 4.5 in 1902-03, below 4.0 in 1904-07 and reaching an all-time low of 3.36 in 1908. The introduction of the Foul Strike Rule in the NL in 1901 and in the AL in 1903 was a significant factor.[5] Under this new rule, foul balls which had previously been scored as "no pitch" were now scored as strikes (except on strike 3). This attempt to curb batters who wore down pitchers by fouling off their best pitches had the unintended (but predictable) consequence of causing strikeout rates to spike and accelerating the tailspin in scoring (Table 4.1).[6,7]

Correspondingly, scoring in the NL fell from 5.21 to 4.63 runs/team/game in 1901 and scoring in the AL fell from 4.89 to 4.10 runs/team/game in 1903.

The introduction and popularization of the spitball and similar "adulterated" pitches is sometimes cited as a significant contributor to the Deadball era.[8] The

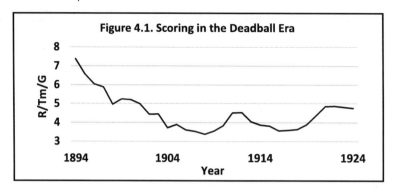

Figure 4.1. Scoring in the Deadball Era

Table 4.1: Impact of Foul Strike Rule on Strikeouts as a Percentage of PA

Year	NL	AL	Foul Strike Rule
1900	6.3%	–	
1901	10.1%	6.6%	Implemented by NL
1902	9.5%	6.7%	
1903	9.1%	10.5%	Implemented by AL
1904	9.5%	11.3%	

spitball was introduced into MLB in 1902 and became popular following the success of future Hall of Famers Jack Chesbro and Ed Walsh, who relied heavily on the pitch, in 1904.[9] Thus, the Deadball Era was well underway before the spitball became prevalent. Moreover, the time line of the gradual phaseout of the spitball in 1919-34 does not match the rapid transition to longball in the early 1920s.[10]

Specifically, each team was allowed to designate no more than two legal spitballers in 1919. In 1920, a general ban of the spitball was imposed, but 17 pitchers who had relied on the spitball were grandfathered and allowed to use the pitch for the rest of their careers. Three of these 17 grandfathered spitballers were Hall of Famers (Stan Coveleski, Red Faber, and Burleigh Grimes) and four others (Dutch Leonard, Jack Quinn, Dick Rudolph, and Urban Shocker) had substantial careers; the other 10 were relatively obscure. All but four of the 17 grandfathered pitchers were still pitching in 1925; Faber (1933), Quinn (1933) and Grimes (1934) lasted into the 1930s. Table 4.2 tracks these 17 grandfathered spitballers during the home run-fueled scoring revival of 1918-22. These 17 pitchers accounted for 12% of all MLB batters faced (BF) in 1918, 17% in 1919, and 16% in 1920, 14% in 1921, and 10% in 1922. Spitballers were nearly as HR-prone as other pitchers; they gave up slightly fewer HR in 1919

Table 4.2: Home Run Trends for Grandfathered Spitballers vs Other Pitchers, 1918-22

Year	Grandfathered Spitballers			All Other Pitchers		
	BF	HR	% HR	BF	HR	% HR
1918	9,443	28	0.30%	66,289	207	0.31%
1919	13,990	62	0.44%	68,731	385	0.56%
1920	15,115	101	0.67%	78,004	529	0.68%
1921	13,095	115	0.88%	82,505	822	1.00%
1922	9,158	105	1.15%	87,014	950	1.09%

and 1921, slightly more in 1922 and the same in 1918 and 1920. HR rates rose similarly – more than 3.5-fold in four years — in both groups of pitchers. Thus, the hypothesis that spitballers were uniquely invulnerable to the HR and that their phaseout led to the rise in HR and in scoring in the 1920s cannot withstand scrutiny.

So how then can we explain the Deadball Era? It was clearly not about the characteristics of the baseball; the same ball was used in 1894 (when scoring was at its all-time high of 7.38 runs/team/game) as was used in 1901-1910.[11] When MLB finally replaced the baseball's hard rubber core with cork in 1910, the scoring famine continued unabated. By the time that MLB implemented a new policy to remove dirty and scuffed balls from play in the wake of Ray Chapman's fatal beaning in September 1920, Babe Ruth was already putting the finishing touches on his first 50+ HR season and the famine was over.[12]

I view the Deadball Era as the product of a 20-year lag between the failure of the "smallball" paradigm and the adoption of and popularization of a new "longball" approach that sacrificed some contact for power. As described in Chapter 3, MLB in the 1870s was a free-wheeling game with very few walks and strikeouts and lots of baserunners, aided and abetted by porous defenses. The rules were set up to give the batter a chance to hit the pitch he wanted and restricted the pitcher's options for "missing bats" by forcing them to throw underhand and attempting (ineffectively) to limit their ability to spin the ball to make it break. In this environment, a contact-oriented "scientific" approach to hitting flourished.

Even big strong players like Chicago White Stockings star Cap Anson, who stood 6'2" and weighed well over 200 pounds, choked up on his bat and just half-swung, using his wrists to generate line drives rather than risk hitting lazy flyballs or (worse yet) striking out.[13] This made perfect sense. If you could just hit the ball into fair

Honus Wagner, 1910

territory, there was a better than 40% chance that something good would happen and that you would reach 1B safely. This "smallball" paradigm was both logical and effective and produced an inelegant but entertaining high-scoring game. But as the game evolved to feature better defense and bigger stronger pitchers, an increasing proportion of balls in play were converted into outs and the smallball paradigm became increasingly inefficient.

Still, managers kept doubling down on the old smallball strategies, treating every run as precious. If their teams couldn't score a lot of runs, they would capitalize on every scoring opportunity and deny runs to their opponents. Pitching, defense, and speed took on new prominence. Bunts, hit-and-run plays, and stolen bases moved to the fore, and power took a backseat. In 1906, a Chicago White Sox team nicknamed the "hitless wonders" upset the 116-win Chicago Cubs in the World Series after hitting only .230/.301/.286 during the season.[14] The Cubs only hit .262/.328/.329 that year – better than the Sox, to be sure, yet not exactly "murderers' row."

In 1920, the light bulb finally went on. Through 1918, the record for most HR in a season was 27, set by Ned Williamson in 1884 (who played in Chicago's short-lived Lake Front Stadium whose fences were <200' from home plate in the corners and 300' in CF).[15] The career HR record was 138, held by Roger Connor. When a 24-year old Red Sox pitcher/OF, Babe Ruth, hit 29 HR in 1919, outhomering runner-up Gavvy Cravath by 17, it caused only a minor ripple. After all, 29 was only two more than 27, and there had been other 20-HR-seasons in the interim. But then, after Ruth was sold to the Yankees and became a full-time OF, his 54 HR—35 more than runner-up George Sisler and almost double his record total from the previous season — put MLB on notice that their world had changed.

Suddenly, this new phenomenon, the home run, had made the time-honored scientific smallball approach seem old-fashioned and quaint. Smallball may have been the most efficient run scoring strategy under the conditions that prevailed in the 19th century — but not in an environment where fielders converted 70% of balls in play into outs. In four short years between 1918 and 1922, scoring increased by 34% from 3.63 to 4.87 runs per team per game, despite continuing declines in errors and unearned runs. Viewed through a historical lens, the surprise is not that this paradigm shift took place, but that it took so long. Teams that adopted the new paradigm simply scored more runs and won more games. We will see the results in Chapter 5.

The most successful teams of the Deadball era were the Giants, Cubs, and Pirates in the NL and the Red Sox, Athletics, White Sox, and Tigers in the AL. The baseball world was rocked at the end of the Deadball era by the Black Sox scandal, in which professional gamblers paid off eight members of the star-laden but seriously underpaid AL champion Chicago White Sox to deliberately lose the World Series to the underdog Cincinnati Reds.[16] The scandal cost those eight players their careers and also led to the hiring of a new autocratic commissioner, Kenesaw Mountain Landis, who ruled baseball with an iron fist until his death in 1944. The good news is that the upright and moralistic Landis rid the game of the influence of gamblers. The bad news is that he did more than any other man to keep the game segregated during his long tenure and that he steadfastly defended the Reserve Clause and the resulting economic exploitation of players by wealthy owners that fostered the conditions in which the Black Sox scandal happened.

In 1914-15, MLB endured its final significant challenge by a rival league, the Federal League (FL), which competed for players and revenues with the established leagues. Unlike the AA (1882), the PL (1890), and the nascent AL (1901), which attracted many of the best players in baseball and shook the established order, the FL, which began as a minor league in 1913, was more of a nuisance than a threat. It attracted a few big names (Bender, Brown, Plank, and Tinker) who were looking for one last payday at the end of their HOF careers, but Edd Roush was the only ascending Hall of Famer who played in the FL. When the FL folded, it left two enduring legacies. First, it gave us Wrigley Field, the home field of the 1915 league champion Chicago Whales. Second, it gave us the infamous 1922 US Supreme Court decision (Federal Baseball Club v. National League) holding that baseball was an entertainment, not commerce, and was therefore exempt from the Sherman Anti-Trust Act, which applied only to interstate commerce.[17] Baseball's new commissioner Kenesaw Mountain Landis enthusiastically welcomed this specious ruling and used it to justify ever-increasing encroachments on player autonomy and compensation, including incorporating the minor leagues into organized baseball, capping prices for the purchase of minor league players by major league teams, and in the 1930s, establishing extensive minor league farm systems that effectively restricted player movement from the day they signed a professional contract.[18] Landis and his successors jealously guarded this right and moved quickly to squelch all challenges.

The Players[19,20]

Baseball talent in the Deadball era was more concentrated at the top than in any period before or since. Although this era produced approximately 10% of the 19,902 players who have ever played MLB, it placed four players in the Top 12 in CVI (Cobb, Johnson, Speaker, and Wagner) and four more in the Top 25 (Collins, Alexander, Lajoie, and Mathewson). Three other players in the Top 12 (Ruth, Young, and Hornsby) played at least five years in the Deadball Era, although they compiled most of their career WAR in other eras. The talent thinned out rapidly after Mathewson; there are only 13 additional CVI-Plus Deadball era players, and two of them (Jackson and Cicotte) were banished in the Black Sox scandal of 1919.

Another illustration of the great gap between the best and the masses in this era is that in a period when MLB batting averages were stuck below .260 and dipped as low as .239 in 1908, Cobb (twice), Lajoie, and Jackson all hit over .400, and there were nine other .380+ batting averages (four by Cobb). Many of the top players had extra base power, but home runs were at an all-time low. Speed was emphasized, and stolen bases were plentiful. On the pitching side, pitching workloads no longer exceeded 500 innings and declined rapidly as teams carried more pitchers on their rosters. Although most games started still resulted in complete games, win totals of the leading pitchers declined. However, IP totals above 350, win totals near and above 30, and complete games were still common.

This generation included ten CVI-Plus hitters and ten CVI-Plus pitchers; all but Jackson and Cicotte are in the HOF (Table 4.3). As in Chapter 3, the careers and HOF credentials of these players, grouped thematically, are presented below.

Table 4.3: CVI-Plus Players

A) Players (Position)	MidCareer	HOF	AVG/OBP/SLG	OPS+	WAR$_H$	CVI
Cobb, Ty (CF)	1915	BBWAA	.366/.433/.512	168	151.0	198.0
Speaker, Tris (CF)	1917	BBWAA	.345/.428/.500	157	134.3	174.6
Wagner, Honus (SS)	1906	BBWAA	.328/.391/.467	151	130.8	172.4
Collins, Eddie (2B)	1915	BBWAA	.333/.424/.429	141	123.9	154.8
Lajoie, Nap (2B)	1906	BBWAA	.338/.380/.466	150	107.3	130.6
Jackson, Shoeless Joe (RF)	1914	Banned	.356/.423/.517	170	62.1	82.5
Wallace, Bobby (SS)	1904	VC	.268/.332/.358	105	70.3	73.8
Baker, Home Run (3B)	1913	VC	.307/.363/.442	135	62.7	70.6
Crawford, Sam (RF)	1908	VC	.309/.362/.452	144	75.3	68.2
Clarke, Fred (LF)	1903	VC	.312/.386/.429	133	67.8	57.8

B) Pitchers	MidCareer	HOF	ERA/WHIP	ERA+	WAR$_P$	CVI
Johnson, Walter (SP)	1915	BBWAA	2.17/1.061	147	151.9	211.8
Alexander, Grover (SP)	1917	BBWAA	2.56/1.121	135	116.0	146.6
Mathewson, Christy (SP)	1908	BBWAA	2.13/1.058	136	99.8	129.2
Walsh, Ed (SP)	1910	VC	1.82/1.000	146	63.7	83.5
Plank, Eddie (SP)	1908	VC	2.35/1.119	122	87.7	80.4
McGinnity, Joe (SP)	1902	VC	2.66/1.188	120	61.3	72.6
Willis, Vic (SP)	1903	VC	2.63/1.209	118	67.5	69.4
Waddell, Rube (SP)	1904	VC	2.16/1.102	135	60.8	69.0
Cicotte, Eddie (SP)	1917	Banned	2.38/1.154	123	57.5	63.6
Brown, Mordecai (SP)	1908	VC	2.06/1.066	139	57.2	57.1

What Greatness Looked Like

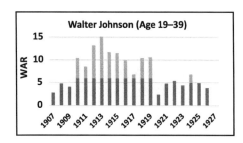

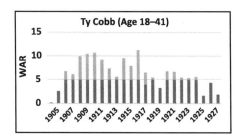

Walter Johnson and Ty Cobb were the top players of the Deadball Generation. Johnson attained the highest seasonal WAR_p totals of any pitcher since John Clarkson in 1889 without ever pitching more than 375 IP in a season. And unlike the top pitchers of the 1880s, he maintained his elite productivity for a solid decade and remained productive through age 38. Cobb, with the advantage of the 154-game season, far outstripped his 19th century predecessors and like Johnson, was an elite player for nearly two decades.

Deadball Batting Masters

Ty Cobb (CF):
198.0 CVI – Detroit AL (144.8)

Tris Speaker (CF):
174.6 CVI – Cleveland AL (74.3),
Boston AL (55.7)

Honus Wagner (SS):
172.4 CVI – Pittsburgh NL (120.1),
Louisville NL (10.7)

Nap Lajoie (2B):
130.6 CVI – Cleveland AL (79.8),
Philadelphia NL (17.6), Philadelphia AL (9.8)

Cobb, Speaker, Wagner, and Lajoie were men of differing temperaments, who were all supremely gifted players and elite Hall of Famers. They dominated an era when contact hitting and aggressive base running reigned supreme, strikeouts were shunned, and home runs were an afterthought. Each could drive the ball, but that ability showed up in doubles and triples. They posted 24 8-WAR seasons – seven by Wagner, six each by Cobb and Speaker, and five by Lajoie. Their career AVG ranged from .328 for Wagner (35th on the career leaderboard) to .366 for Cobb (best of all time), and their OBP ranged from .380 for the free-swinging Lajoie to .433 for Cobb (ninth on the career leaderboard). But their SLG percentages were unremarkable and their ISO (SLG minus AVG) ranged from .128 for Lajoie to .155 for Speaker.

Ty Cobb, 1924

These four players provided the MLB batting champion in 17 of the 20 seasons between 1900 and 1919 – a string interrupted only by Cy Seymour (1905), George Stone (1906), and Benny Kauff (1914). They also won 25 of the 40 league batting titles among them during this period (eleven for Cobb, eight for Wagner, five for Lajoie, and one for Speaker). There were 15 instances of players hitting over .380 between 1900 and 1919; 12 of those instances were produced by these four players – seven by Cobb alone. Cobb also hit over .380 twice after 1920 and three times hit over .400 (1911-12 and 1922). Joe Jackson (.387 in 1910, .408 in 1911, and .395 in 1912) was the only player beside these four "masters" to hit over .380 during this period. The annual MVP awards did not exist until 1922, but Cobb and Speaker were honored as the top players in MLB with the first two Chalmers awards in 1911 and 1912. CVI ranks Cobb, Speaker, Wagner, and Lajoie 6th, 11th, 12th, and 23rd, respectively, among HOF eligible players.

Cobb was perhaps one of the most driven man ever to play any professional sport. To say that he was competitive is like saying that hell is hot. He played in a barely controlled rage that could turn murderous when he was provoked. Once, in 1912, he went into the stands and beat a disabled heckler so severely that his teammates had to intervene to prevent Cobb from killing him.[21] He hated defeat in any form. In 1921, when he was the Tigers' player-manager, and protege and teammate Harry Heilmann completed his breakout season by edging him for the AL batting championship, Cobb became so enraged that he refused to speak to him. Evidently, Cobb's unquenchable thirst for victory pertained more to personal than team achievements.

Cobb's hostile worldview was profoundly amplified by a sordid and tragic 1905 incident in which his mother shot and killed his father (whom he idolized) after mistaking him for a prowler. The senior Cobb, suspecting his wife of infidelity, had been spying on her through her bedroom window.[22] Yet Cobb was not an unmitigated villain. Thirty years later, Cobb lobbied for Heilmann's election into the HOF and kindly told him as he lay dying of cancer that he had been elected, although the vote had not yet been taken.

Cobb ranks among the all-time top 10 in H, R, RBI, 2B, 3B, TB, SB, OBP and OPS+ as well as leading the pack in career AVG. He also held the career records for hits and runs and the modern record for SB for many years until Rose, Henderson, and Brock surpassed him. Although Cobb was widely disliked, his on-field accomplishments were held in such high esteem that he was easily elected to the inaugural class of the Hall of Fame in 1936, receiving 222/226 votes, more than any of his more congenial peers.

Although he was also an elite hitter, Speaker was known especially for his brilliant defense. Nicknamed the Gray Eagle, he reinvented the CF position, playing shallow, but sprinting back effortlessly to reach most deep fly balls, and keeping baserunners honest with his powerful arm. Even if he fell slightly short of Cobb at bat, he was among the best, with a string of 15 consecutive 5-WAR seasons – and 17 of 18 from 1909-26. He is the all-time career leader in doubles and ranks in the top 10 in H, AVG, and 3B. Unlike the high-strung Cobb, Speaker performed well in his three World Series opportunities with Boston in 1912 and 1915 and as a player-manager in Cleveland in 1920; his teams won all three Series. The BBWAA elected him as part of the second HOF class in 1937.

The "Flying Dutchman," Honus Wagner, was baseball's greatest SS and its first superstar of the 20th century, but he didn't look the part. Awkward, barrel-chested, and bow-legged with oversized hands and feet and his arms whirling as he ran the bases, the 5'11" 200-pound Wagner earned no style points. Still, he was a rangy fielder (21.3 dWAR) and stole 723 bases. And, of course, the man could really hit. In addition to his eight NL batting championships, Wagner led the NL twice in H and R, three times in 3B, four times in OBP, RBI, and SB, six times in TB, SLG, and OPS+, and seven times in 2B. In 1908, his best season, he led the NL in 10 of the 11 categories listed above – all except runs. He was in the inaugural HOF class of 1936 and ranks in the top 10 in career H, 2B, 3B, and SB.

Lajoie's career (like Wagner's) began in the waning years of the 19th century. He was one of the first players to jump to the new AL in 1901 and immediately became one of its showcase stars; his team (the Cleveland Naps) was even named after him. At 6'1" and 200 pounds, Lajoie was a big man for his time and hit the ball hard. His power was evident in his 657 doubles (eighth on the career leaderboard) and 163 triples. Lajoie was a free-swinger and notorious bad ball hitter, who rarely walked. Lajoie was also known for his hot temper and frequent run-ins with umpires. His .426 AVG in 1901 is the highest of the 20th century and ranks fourth on the all-time leaderboard. Lajoie was sure-handed and elegant at 2B, far more graceful than Wagner, with "soft hands" and a powerful arm. The BBWAA elected Lajoie to the second HOF class in 1937, and he attended the first induction ceremony in 1939.

Beyond the Numbers

- While in his early 20s, Cobb led the Tigers to three consecutive pennants in 1907-1909. Unfortunately, he did not play well in 17 World Series games and the Tigers lost all three Series with a combined 5-12 record. He never appeared in another World Series.

- Some of Cobb's most publicized off-field rages were directed against black people whom he believed had insulted him. Although these incidents earned him a reputation as a racist, Cobb was in favor of integrating baseball and once wrote that segregation was "a lousy rule."[23]

- In 1926, pitcher Hubert "Dutch" Leonard implicated Cobb and Speaker in a 1919 game-fixing scandal, which forced them to resign from their respective managerial positions in Detroit and Cleveland.[24] However, the investigation was dropped after Leonard declined to testify, and they were permitted to resume their playing careers elsewhere.

- Although Speaker's interpersonal skills were better than Cobb's, he aligned with an anti-Catholic Protestant clique in Boston. He once told sportswriter Fred Lieb that he had joined the Ku Klux Klan.[25] Religious tensions with Catholic players (including young Babe Ruth) led to his trade to Cleveland after the 1915 season.

- In the faceoff between Cobb's Tigers and Wagner's Pirates in the 1909 World Series, the stoical veteran SS thoroughly outplayed his fiery young rival, hitting .333 to Cobb's .237 and adding 6 RBI and 6 SB; the Pirates prevailed 4-3. However, the story of Wagner responding to an ethnic slur by Cobb in Game 1 of that Series by planting a hard tag that bloodied Cobb's mouth is probably apocryphal, given that the two men went hunting together a month later.[26]

- Lajoie's 14 HR in 1901 was briefly an AL record until it was surpassed by Socks Seybold's 16 in 1902 (which held until Babe Ruth's 29 in 1919).

The Four Aces

Walter Johnson (SP):
211.8 CVI – Washington AL (164.5)

Grover Cleveland Alexander (SP):
146.6 CVI – Philadelphia NL (61.1),
Chicago NL (43.0), St. Louis NL (14.8)

Christy Mathewson (SP):
129.2 CVI – New York NL (106.1)

Ed Walsh (SP):
83.5 CVI – Chicago AL (65.9)

In a low-scoring era, it should be no surprise to find three pitchers on the short list of the best ever and another (Walsh) who was similarly brilliant over a shorter period. Johnson (417), Mathewson (373), and Alexander (373) won more games than anyone except Cy Young and lead all pitchers with 110, 90, and 79 career shutouts, respectively. They also top the post-1900 pitching leaderboard in CG. Walsh had a shorter but still brilliant career; his 1.816 ERA and 0.9996 WHIP rank first and second, respectively, on MLB's career leaderboards.

Walter Johnson

Johnson threw harder than anyone of his time, with a whip-like sidearm delivery that earned him the nickname "Big Train." Ty Cobb said his fastball "hissed with danger."[27] His strikeout records have long been surpassed by stars like Feller, Koufax, Ryan, and Randy Johnson (when strikeouts were far more frequent leaguewide). There were no radar guns then, so we will never know who threw hardest, but it is indisputable that no pitcher before or since has ever dominated his era as Walter Johnson did. His WAR_p totals of 15.1 in 1913 (when he went 36-7) and 13.2 in 1912 are the two highest for post-1900 pitchers. He could also handle a bat (12.8 WAR_H), and his WAR totals for those two years, 16.5 and 14.3, respectively, are the top two figures since the 1880s. He won the Chalmers award (forerunner of the modern MVP) in 1913 and the AL MVP award in 1924.

Johnson compiled 12 seasons with 20+ wins, and 11 seasons with ERA <2.00 over the course of his career. Johnson also posted five seasons with ERA+ >200. His career ERA and WHIP rank tied for sixth and tenth, respectively, of all time. His career record 110 SHO are 20 more than his nearest rival (Alexander). His amazing 0.780 WHIP in 1913 is the second best since 1900 and third best ever, and his 1.14 ERA and 259 ERA+ for that season rank fifth. He was among the inaugural class of players elected to the Hall of Fame in 1936. CVI ranks Johnson first by far among SP and third overall.

Named after the incumbent US president in his birth year (1887), Grover Cleveland Alexander, affectionately known as Old Pete, ranks fifth among all pitchers and 17th overall in CVI. His 11.9 WAR_p in 1920 is tied for the fifth best of the 20th century. Alexander had a shambling gait and didn't look the part of a great athlete. Although his strikeout totals were unimpressive by modern standards, they were good enough to lead the NL five times, before he evolved into a finesse pitcher at age 30. Alexander shares the single-season SHO record with 16 in 1916 (tied with George Bradley in 60 starts in 1876), and his 28 SHO in consecutive seasons (1915-16) are unequaled. Alexander won 30 or more games three times. His peak ERA (1.220), ERA+ (225), and WHIP (0.8423) occurred in 1915, a year in which he also went 31-10. He won 30+ games three times (1915-17) and also won 28 in 1911 and 27 in 1920. He was elected to the HOF in 1938 in time to join the first group of inductees in 1939.

Christy Mathewson, the greatest pitcher of the first decade of the 20th century, was a key contributor to the Giants' 1904-5 and 1911-3 NL pennants and to their 1905 World Series Championship. His trademark was the "fadeaway" pitch or screwball, which he is thought to have invented. He had six 8-WAR$_p$ (and a 7.9-WAR$_p$) seasons, topped by 11.7 in 1908, when he went 37-11 with a 1.43 ERA (169 ERA+) and 0.827 WHIP. Moreover, that was only the fourth best ERA of his career, which included a microscopic 1.144 (224 ERA+) in 1909 and 1.276 (230 ERA+) in 1905. Matty is also one of 30 men to throw two or more no-hitters. Mathewson was the hard-luck losing pitcher in the one-game playoff against the Cubs in 1908, necessitated by the infamous "Merkle's Boner," when the 19-year-old Fred Merkle neglected to touch 2B on what would have been a game-winning, pennant-clinching base hit.

Tragically, Mathewson's career and eventually his life were shortened by pulmonary disease, starting with a life-threatening bout of diphtheria in 1905 and what was thought to be influenza but was probably tuberculosis in 1914. He sustained further lung damage when he was exposed to mustard gas during his wartime work at a munitions factory in 1918 and died of tuberculosis in 1925. Mathewson was held in such high regard that he was elected posthumously to the first Hall of Fame class in 1936, with more votes than even Walter Johnson. CVI ranks him seventh among SP and 24th among all HOF-eligible players.

As post-1900 pitchers transitioned from the 19th century workhorse paradigm to a more moderate and sustainable workload, Ed Walsh was a throwback. In 1906-12, "Big Ed," who stood 6'1" and weighed 193 pounds, put up stats that would have been right at home in 1890. Indeed, since Walsh pitched in the nadir of the Deadball era, his 1.816 ERA (the best of all time) and 0.9996 WHIP (second to Addie Joss) were correspondingly lower. However, Walsh's 146 career ERA+ attests that his record was not a mere artifact of his era. Walsh's signature pitch was a devastating spitball, about which contemporary and fellow Hall of Famer Sam Crawford joked: "I think that ball disintegrated on the way to the plate and the catcher put it back together again. I swear when it went past the plate it was just the spit that went by."[28] In 1908, Walsh was the last pitcher with 40 W or 400 IP. Walsh had only seven good years, won only 195 games, and had to wait until 1946 for election to the HOF. CVI ranks Walsh as the 28th best SP and at the 0.50 percentile overall.

Beyond the Numbers

- Although Johnson's 5.3 SO9 and 0.70 SO/H seem pedestrian by modern standards, he led the AL in SO 12 times, including eight consecutive seasons in 1912-19.

- Pitching mostly for losing teams, Johnson won 30+ games only twice (in 1912-13) but won 25+ games for seven consecutive years from 1910-16.

- Despite his brilliance, Johnson had to wait until 1924 (age 36) to reach the World Series. He pitched four innings of scoreless high-pressure relief to win Game 7 on Buddy Ruel's bad-hop grounder over Freddy Lindstrom's head in the 12th inning to upset the favored Giants.

- Johnson was one of baseball's nice guys but had a mischievous sense of humor. He is said to have deliberately eased up on his friend – and Ty Cobb's teammate – Sam Crawford while saving his nastiest fastballs for the hyper-competitive Cobb. Cobb never caught on and was furious that Crawford hit Johnson better than he did.[29]

- Johnson retired to Germantown, MD and dabbled in politics, serving as Montgomery County commissioner, but was defeated for Congress in 1938. Still, he remains a local icon to this day.

- Alexander suffered a fateful injury in July 1909 when a baseball struck him in the head as he was running from 1B to 2B. He would be prone to epileptic seizures for the rest of his life.[30]

- Alexander's seven weeks at the front in World War I nearly destroyed him, leaving him shell-shocked, deaf in his left ear, and with muscle damage in his right arm. He began drinking heavily and his epileptic seizures became more frequent. He recovered enough to post two strong seasons, including his career best 11.9 WAR_p with the Cubs in 1920, but thereafter was no longer the same dominant pitcher, relying heavily on finesse.

- Alexander's final career highlight came in the seventh inning of Game 7 of the 1926 World Series when Old Pete entered with a 3-2 lead with the bases loaded and two out. He struck out Tony Lazzeri (after a long foul into the RF stands), to end the threat. He then retired the next five Yankee batters before walking Babe Ruth, who inexplicably tried to steal 2B but was thrown out to end the Series. This game was immortalized in a 1952 movie starring future president Ronald Reagan as Alexander.[31] Thus, Alexander is karmically connected with two U.S. presidents, who served 100 years apart. Unfortunately, life denied him a Hollywood ending. His marriage fell apart as his alcoholism and epilepsy got the best of him; he died broke and alone at age 63.

- Mathewson first won national acclaim in football at Bucknell as their fullback, punter, and drop-kicker. He is buried near the Lewisburg, PA campus.[32]

Beyond the Numbers (cont'd)

- The clean-cut, well-built, college-educated Mathewson, who joined the Giants in a lopsided 1901 trade which sent the washed up Amos Rusie to Cincinnati, made quite a contrast with the 5'7" 155-pound, profane, rough-hewn, hard-drinking John McGraw, who managed him for most of his career and loved him like a son.

- Mathewson helped uncover the Black Sox scandal as a baseball reporter in 1919-20.

- Walsh was not the ace of the 1906 White Sox "hitless wonders" World Series champions but won Games 3 and 5 over the heavily favored Cubs in the World Series, yielding only 1 ER in 15.0 IP.

Connie Mack's First Dynasty

Eddie Collins (2B):
154.8 CVI – Chicago AL (66.6),
Philadelphia AL (57.3)

Eddie Plank (SP):
80.4 CVI – Philadelphia AL (77.5)

Home Run Baker (3B):
70.6 CVI – Philadelphia AL (42.2),
New York AL (20.5)

Rube Waddell:
69.0 CVI – Philadelphia AL (44.5)

Connie Mack was an ex-player and an astute judge of baseball talent, who twice assembled and dismantled great baseball teams, while operating the A's on a shoestring budget from 1901-50. His first dynasty in 1905-14 featured four CVI-Plus players—Eddie Collins, Eddie Plank Home Run Baker, and (in the early years) Rube Waddell — as well as CVI-Minus HOF pitcher Chief Bender. The dynasty culminated in 1910-14 when they won four AL pennants in five years (finishing second to Boston in 1912). Only a historic upset by the 1914 "Miracle Braves" prevented them from winning four World Series. Yet they were all gone by 1915 when the A's tumbled to the AL cellar with a dismal 44-108 record. One could say that Mack's actions were the forerunner of "tanking."

Collins, whose CVI ranks second only to Rogers Hornsby at 2B and 16th overall, was a "Deadball Batting Master" and an elite Hall of Famer. He was a slick-fielding singles hitter extraordinaire, who made a science of studying pitcher tendencies to become a prolific base-stealer and run scorer. He had almost no power; his .095 ISO was among the lowest in the HOF. His 1499 career bases on balls was unusu-

Eddie Collins, 1911

ally high for this era, amplifying the offensive value of his baserunning. His .424 OBP was comparable to Cobb's and Speaker's and ranks 12th on the career leaderboard. Collins also ranks seventh with 741 SB and 12th with 187 3B (reflecting speed more than power). He won the fourth and final Chalmers award in 1914 as MLB's best player, but that didn't save him from being sold off to the White Sox as part of the financially motivated purge of the team's biggest stars.

Collins spent eleven years with the White Sox, one more than he spent with the A's, and continued to excel. His high point with the White Sox was the 1917 World Series, in which he hit .409/.458/.455 to spark a 4-2 victory. The low point was the infamous 1919 World Series. Collins was the captain of the faction-riven "Black Sox," but was not implicated in the scandal. The BBWAA elected Collins to the HOF in 1939; he attended the inaugural induction ceremony.

Never considered the best pitcher in the AL or even the ace of his own team, underrated southpaw Eddie Plank quietly outlasted and outshone most of his peers while winning 326 games over the course of his 17-year career. He also pitched superbly in four World Series, compiling a 1.32 ERA and 0.878 WHIP in 54.7 IP, although his W-L was only 2-5. His excellent 6.4-WAR_p season in the inferior Federal League at age 39 in 1915 contributed 5.8 to his CVI, it was 74.6 even without counting that season. CVI ranks him at the 0.57 percentile overall, making him a solid Hall of Famer.

"Home Run" Baker seems an incongruous nickname for someone who never hit more than 12 HR in a season and had more than twice as many SB (235) as HR (96) in his career. Baker's nickname derives from two key HR he hit in the 1911 World Series in consecutive games against future Hall of Famers Rube Marquard and Christy Mathewson, rather than high annual home run totals. However, he did pack a lot of muscle into his 5'11' 173-pound frame and swung his 52-ounce bat with great force. In his six-year prime (1909-14), Baker hit .321/.376/.471 (153 OPS+) and averaged 8 HR, 102 RBI, 95 R, 268 TB, 29 SB, and 7.0 WAR per season. His consecutive AL HR titles in 1911-14 further attest that his nickname was not entirely undeserved.

Baker got into a salary dispute with Connie Mack after the great sell-off and sat out the entire 1915 season. Finally, Mack gave in and sold his contract to the Yankees, where he was solid but not a star. Baker sat out the 1920 season after his family was struck with scarlet fever, which killed his wife and afflicted his two infant daughters.[33] Baker finished his career with the Yankees as a complementary player on their 1921-22 AL champions. CVI ranks Baker 10th among 3B and at the 0.82 percentile overall.

Amos Rusie may have been the Hoosier Thunderbolt, Walter Johnson may have been the Big Train, and Bob Feller may have been "Rapid Robert," but Rube Waddell was MLB's premier strikeout pitcher until Sandy Koufax came along in the 1960s. Over the course of his 13 career, Waddell struck out 7.0 batters per 9 IP and 0.94 batter per hit allowed. Before Koufax, only Bob Feller (6.7 SO per 9 IP and 0.79 SO per hit allowed) even came close to Waddell. By contrast, Walter Johnson had only 5.3 SO per 9 IP and 0.71 SO per hit allowed, while Rusie had only 4.6 SO per 9 IP and 0.58 SO per hit allowed. Waddell was no one-trick pony. In 1902-06, he won 112 with 1344 SO, a 1.94 ERA, and 1.060 WHIP and accrued 43.8 WAR_p with the Athletics. But his prime

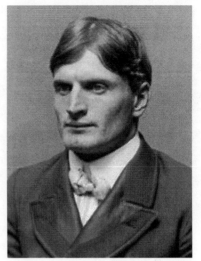

Rube Waddell, 1901

was relatively brief, and he won only 193 games in his career. Although Waddell was the ace of the Athletics' 1905 AL champs, he was long gone by 1910 when they won their first World Series. Still, CVI ranks him at the 0.92 percentile. He clearly deserves his plaque in Cooperstown.

Beyond the Numbers

- The Columbia-educated Collins was an exceptionally smart ballplayer and was resented by some of his rough-hewn teammates, especially when he wrote analytic magazine articles that exposed their vulnerabilities.[34]

- In 1933, Collins finally left the playing field after 25 major league seasons to accept the general manager position for the Boston Red Sox under new owner and fellow Irving Prep School alumnus Tom Yawkey. Although he signed future Hall of Famers Ted Williams and Bobby Doerr during his 14-year tenure and revived a long-dormant Boston franchise, his last major decision for the Red Sox (with Tom Yawkey) was failing to pursue and sign Jackie Robinson. The Red Sox were the last MLB team to integrate.[35]

- Plank was known for his outstanding control (despite an unorthodox across-the-body motion), his painfully slow and fidgety demeanor on the mound, and his lack of a good pickoff move to 1B.[36]

- Plank was born in Gettysburg only 12 years after the great Civil War battle. In retirement, he supplemented his income by conducting battlefield tours.[37]

Beyond the Numbers (cont'd)

- Although Baker was bow-legged and ran clumsily, he showed surprising speed, stealing at least 20 bases every year from 1909-13, topped by 40 in 1912. He was also a fine defensive 3B (9.7 dWAR).

- Born on April Fool's Day, Waddell is best remembered for his eccentricity, often taking time off during spring training to play marbles with street urchins, lead a parade, or wrestle an alligator.[38]

The Damned

Shoeless Joe Jackson (RF):
82.5 CVI – Cleveland AL (34.9), Chicago AL (27.8)

Eddie Cicotte (SP):
63.6 CVI – Chicago AL (50.0), Boston AL (8.3)

Two of the eight players who forfeited their careers by accepting payment from professional gamblers to lose the 1919 World Series were on a HOF track before they fell from grace. Shoeless Joe Jackson, the illiterate South Carolina country boy, was the more sympathetic of the two. He was a speedy line-drive hitting OF with extra-base power, whose lifetime .356 AVG ranks third behind only Cobb and Hornsby. He hit .408 in 1912, when he posted a career-high 9.5 WAR, and more than .380 in three other seasons in his short career. Although he hit only 54 career HR, his 307 doubles and 168 triples gave him a robust .161 ISO – higher than any of the "Deadball Masters." The fact that he hit .375 during the 1919 World Series and never received the money he was promised is sad but makes him no less guilty.

Eddie Cicotte is better remembered as the ringleader of the infamous "Black Sox" than for his fine career as MLB's first master of the knuckleball, which otherwise could have made a nice story. It was Cicotte who instigated the plot and got paid in advance. Unlike the hapless Jackson, his complicity in the fix was obvious from his play. He hit Cincinnati's leadoff hitter in Game 1, gave up six runs in 3.7 innings, and deliberately muffed a throw that could have started a double play. Cicotte pitched well in Game 4 but made two errors to let in two unearned runs in a 2-0 loss. One error involved needlessly deflecting a relay throw that he should never have touched, allowing a runner who had already stopped at 3B to score. So as not to be too obvious or perhaps because he did not receive as much money as he was promised, he pitched well in a 4-1 Game 7 victory to narrow the Reds advantage to 4-3 before the underdog Reds came back to rout co-conspirator Lefty Williams to clinch the Series. Cicotte freely accepted responsibility for what he did and lived a long and productive life after baseball.[39]

One can sympathize with the naïve Jackson and even his not-so-naïve co-conspirators since MLB players had been exploited and underpaid for years. They were not the first or only players to be involved with professional gamblers. But regardless of extenuating circumstances, accepting money to deliberately lose games (let alone the World Series) is a capital sin in any sport.

Beyond the Numbers

- When Cleveland fans voted Jackson into the team's Hall of Fame in 1951, Ed Sullivan booked him to appear on his Sunday night TV show before Christmas. But Jackson died of a heart attack on December 5, just two weeks before his scheduled appearance. He was only 64 years old.[40]

- Cicotte was a late bloomer, who was considered an underachiever for the first eight years of his career, bouncing from Detroit to Boston to Chicago. Cicotte's career years with the White Sox came in 1917, when he went 28-12, 1.53 ERA (174 ERA+), 0.912 WHIP and 11.7 WAR$_P$, and 1919, when he went 29-7 with a 1.82 ERA (176 ERA+), 0.995 WHIP, and 9.6 WAR$_P$.

King of the Deadball Shortstops

Bobby Wallace (SS):
73.8 CVI – St. Louis AL (48.4), St. Louis NL (14.1), Cleveland NL (13.7)

Baseball "lifer" Bobby Wallace, who is among the most underappreciated stars in MLB history, followed Young and Lajoie into the new AL in 1902, jumping from the Cardinals to the crosstown St. Louis Browns and signing a lucrative $32,500 five-year contract.[41] He was a spectacular defensive SS with a wide range, a fluid motion, and a powerful arm, who revolutionized how SS was played. His 28.7 dWAR ranks eighth among all SS, just ahead of Dahlen and well above Davis. The impact of his excellence on defense was amplified by the prevalence of groundballs in the Deadball era. Indeed, Wallace set a still-standing record by handling 17 fielding chances at SS in a nine-inning game; that record is unlikely to be matched in today's era of "three true outcomes."

Wallace's 105 OPS+, while above league average, ranks well below Davis and Dahlen, although he was often among the league leaders in hits, SLG, RBI, and

Bobby Wallace

other offensive categories during his 14-year prime. From 1897-1910, Wallace accrued WAR totals between 4.2 and 7.8 in 12 of 14 seasons. Unfortunately, Wallace
toiled in relative obscurity for second division teams in St. Louis and Cleveland
throughout his career. It took Wallace until 1953 to reach the HOF, but he lived
long enough (87 years) to attend his induction ceremony. CVI ranks him 13th
among SS and at the 0.72 percentile overall.

Beyond the Numbers

- Wallace began his career as a pitcher, compiling a 24-22 record with a 3.89 ERA
  (125 ERA+) with the Cleveland Spiders in 1894-96.

Iron Men

Iron Man Joe McGinnity (SP):	**Vic Willis (SP):**
72.6 CVI – New York NL (31.6),	69.4 CVI – Boston NL (42.6),
Baltimore AL (13.3), Brooklyn NL (8.4)	Pittsburgh NL (21.2)

McGinnity and Willis were both workhorse pitchers who won 246 and 249 games,
respectively, in careers straddling the 19th and 20th centuries. McGinnity won 26+
games with 339+ IP six times but lasted only 10 seasons. Willis was an eight-time
20-game winner, who completed 388 of the 471 games he started in his 13-year

career and exceeded 300 IP eight times, including 410 IP in 1902. Both were key contributors to championship teams – McGinnis with the 1905 Giants and Willis with the 1899 Beaneaters and 1909 Pirates.

McGinnity relied on a rising curveball, which he threw underhand, and a hard sinker which he threw overhand.[42] Sometimes he pitched both games of a double-header throwing overhand in one game and underhand in the other. The 6'2" Willis threw harder and missed more bats (3.7 SO per 9 IP versus 2.8 for McGinnity), but he was no Rube Waddell. Their ERA+ numbers (120 for McGinnity and 118 for Willis) were very good but not great. CVI ranks them at the 0.75 and 0.88 percentile, respectively, making them solid Hall of Famers.

Second Fiddles

Sam Crawford (RF):
68.2 CVI – Detroit AL (63.6),
Cincinnati NL (11.7)

Fred Clarke (LF):
57.8 CVI – Pittsburgh NL (46.7),
Louisville NL (21.2)

These two steady compilers, whose careers straddled the 19th and 20th centuries, shared the common fate of playing second fiddle on their own teams to two of the most transcendent superstars of their time, Ty Cobb and Honus Wagner. Crawford was a legitimate Hall of Famer in his own right and even outshone Cobb in two areas. He hit 309 triples, 14 more than Cobb, to top the career leaderboard, and he outhit Cobb against the great Walter Johnson. Crawford was also one of baseball's strongest men, who unlike most pre-Ruthian sluggers, did not pull his punches at the plate. His simple approach – just hit the ball hard and let the chips fall where they may – produced more 2B and 3B than HR. Although he hit only 97 HR and never led the league in SLG, he finished in the top 10 in SLG for 15 consecutive years (1901-15), and his ISO was a solid .143. Like Cobb, Crawford was unproductive in the Tigers' consecutive World Series defeats in 1907-09. His 68.2 CVI ranks 15th in RF and at the 0.94 percentile overall. He is a deserving Hall of Famer.

Clarke, who played his entire 21-year career as Wagner's teammate in Louisville as well as Pittsburgh, was (as discussed in Chapter 2) a classic compiler with a 133 OPS+ including eight 4-WAR seasons but only one with >5.3 WAR. His 57.8 CVI ranks 13th in LF and at the 1.27% percentile overall, placing him in HOVG territory.

Beyond the Numbers

- Crawford and Cobb had a complicated relationship. Crawford was older than Cobb and led the merciless hazing Cobb received as a rookie in 1905. Cobb always resented the easy going but sharp-witted Crawford for his role in this hazing but still lent his voice to the successful campaign to elect Crawford to the Hall of Fame in 1957.[43]

- In 1917, Crawford retired to a walnut orchard in California and immersed himself in the study of literature and philosophy. His insightful interview in Lawrence Ritter's *The Glory of their Times* is a must read.[44]

- Clarke is the only man with over 2000 H as a player and over 1000 wins as a manager.

The Man With Three Fingers

Mordecai "Three Finger" Brown (SP):
57.1 CVI – Chicago NL (48.3)

Born in the Centennial year of 1876, "Three Finger" Brown, whose pitching hand was mangled in a childhood accident, won 148 with a 1.63 ERA (164 ERA+), 0.972 WHIP, and 40.2 WAR$_p$ as the ace of the outstanding Cubs teams of 1906-11, which won four pennants and two World Series. He dueled Christy Mathewson to a stalemate in many head-to-head matchups during that period and won their most famous faceoff – the 1908 playoff game necessitated by Fred Merkle's notorious "boner" two weeks earlier – shutting down the Giants with one run in 8.3 IP in relief of starter Jack Pfister. Brown was also the Cubs "closer," with 41 saves in 1906-11, However, CVI cannot fully capture this aspect of his career because gmLI

Three Finger Brown hand

data from the deadball era are unavailable (I used 1.6 as a conservative estimate to calculate his CVI). Unfortunately , Brown (who did not reach the major leagues until age 26 declined rapidly after 1911. Still, he finished his career with 239 wins and a sparkling 2.06 ERA (146 ERA+). CVI ranks him at the 1.30 percentile, placing him in the HOVG, but he may have been better than that.

Other Hall of Famers

Table 4.4: CVI-Minus Hall of Famers

A) Players (Position)	MidCareer	HOF	AVG/OBP/SLG	OPS+	WAR$_H$	CVI
Flick, Elmer (RF)	1903	VC	.313/.389/.445	149	53.0	52.4
Wheat, Zack (LF)	1919	VC	.317/.367/.450	129	60.1	52.3
Collins, Jimmy (3B)	1901	VC	.294/.343/.409	113	53.4	50.1
Tinker, Joe (SS)	1908	VC	.262/.308/.353	96	53.2	47.4
Carey, Max (CF)	1919	VC	.285/.361/.386	108	54.5	45.2
Bresnahan, Roger (C)	1907	VC	.279/.386/.377	123	42.5	44.5
Hooper, Harry (RF)	1918	VC	.281/.368/.387	114	53.2	44.2
Chance, Frank (1B)	1905	VC	.297/.394/.395	135	45.8	44.1
Evers, Johnny (2B)	1909	VC	.270/.356/.334	106	47.7	41.2
Maranville, Rabbit (SS)	1919	BBWAA	.258/.318/.340	82	42.9	40.2
Schalk, Ray (C)	1917	VC	.253/.340/.316	83	33.0	32.4

B) Pitchers	MidCareer	HOF	ERA/WHIP	ERA+	WAR$_P$	CVI
Joss, Addie (SP)	1906	VC	1.89/0.968	142	47.7	42.1
Chesbro, Jack (SP)	1904	VC	2.68/1.152	111	42.7	42.6
Bender, Chief (SP)	1909	VC	2.46/1.113	112	42.3	40.9
Marquard, Rube (SP)	1914	VC	3.08/1.237	103	34.8	31.3

The 15 CVI-Minus Hall of Famers from the Deadball Generation – 11 hitters and 4 pitchers – are listed in Table 4.4. Most were elected by the VC in their hyperactive pre-1980 years (see Chapter 11). None quite measures up as a Hall of Famer. As in Chapter 3, I have provided capsule comments on these 15 players below.

On the pitching side, **Joss** has the most credible HOF case. He was a truly brilliant pitcher, whose career and life ended at age 31 due to a bacterial infection. In his nine MLB seasons, he accrued 160 W with 45 SHO and two no-hitters (including a perfect game). He trails only Ed Walsh with a 1.89 ERA (142 ERA+), and his 0.968 WHIP tops the MLB career leaderboard.

Bender and **Chesbro** have weak HOF credentials. **Bender**, an ace SP for Connie Mack's dynasty teams, was a good but not great pitcher. Spitballer **Chesbro** made the HOF based largely on a single spectacular season in 1904, when he won 41 games in 454.2 IP, tops in the 20th century. His 10.6 WAR_p that year was nearly twice as high as in any other season. He won 157 games and accrued 31.9 WAR_p in his other 10 seasons.

Flick and **Wheat** are the strongest hitters in Table 4.4, with 149 and 129 OPS+, respectively, but neither played great defense (-5.5 and -6.9 dWAR). **Flick** had nine 4-WAR seasons, six with >5.3 WAR, but played only 13 seasons. **Wheat**, who along with **Bender** and Early Wynn are the only Native Americans in the HOF, had WAR >4 in only six of his 18 seasons.[45]

Table 4.4 contains several other interesting players. **Tinker** and **Maranville** (the only BBWAA selectee in this group), who stand fourth and sixth among all SS with 34.3 and 30.8 dWAR, represent the leading edge of the good-field-no-hit SS, who are a special favorite of HOF voters, extending to Omar Vizquel today.

Tinker's ticket to the HOF was as the leading man of the **Tinker-to-Evers-to-Chance** double play combination (immortalized in poetry) at the heart of the 1906-08 Chicago Cubs teams that won an all-time record 116 games in 1906 and consecutive World Series in 1907-08.[46] Neither he nor Maranville hit like Hall of Famers, although their defensive prowess was undeniable. **Collins** and **Evers** also rank high defensively at 3B (16.8 dWAR, 10th) and 2B (15.4 dWAR, 16th), respectively.

Chance's CVI is unimpressive, but this is largely because he was injured so often and amassed only 5135 PA in 17 154-game seasons. His 135 OPS+ indicated that he was a very good hitter when he took the field. Both **Chance** (who managed the Cubs to three pennants and two World Series championships in 1906-08) and **Collins** (who managed the Red Sox to consecutive pennants in 1903-04 and to victory in the first modern World Series) get extra points.

Bresnahan was a good-hitting catcher-OF and a solid defender (6.5 dWAR), who played for 17 years and peaked at 5.8 WAR in 1908. He ranks second among catchers with 212 SB, fifth with a .386 OBP, sixth with 71 3B, and tied for seventh with a 126 OPS+.

Carey and Hooper were good but not great players. **Hooper** may have gotten a boost from ex-teammate Waite Hoyt on the VC.

Bottom of the Pile

Two Deadball Generation players earned this dubious accolade.

Ray Schalk was an excellent defensive catcher (18.3 dWAR) and team leader, who was well liked by everyone and untainted by the Black Sox scandal, but he was not good enough to be in the HOF. His .253 AVG (with a meager .063 ISO) is the lowest

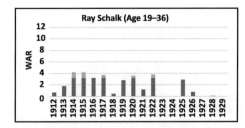

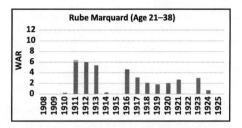

in the HOF, his OPS+ was only 83, and his WAR never exceeded 4.2 in any season. If you like defense-first catchers, Jim Sundberg, who played from 1974-1989, mostly with Texas, was a better player (42.5 CVI) and a better defender (25.3 dWAR).

Except for an outstanding three-year run in 1911-13, in which he compiled a 73-28 W-L with a 2.52 ERA (131 ERA+) and a 1.151 WHIP for three consecutive Giants NL pennant winners, **Rube Marquard** had a relatively undistinguished 18-year career. His ticket to the HOF was his 19-game winning streak in 1912, which still stands as an MLB record today, His career ERA+ was a mediocre 103. There are 219 pitchers with more than Marquard's 34.8 career WAR$_p$. A close contemporary comp is Jared Weaver (34.9 WAR$_p$), who was a fine pitcher but no one's idea of a Hall of Famer.

CHAPTER 5

THE CLASSICAL GENERATION: (1920-1946)

The Game

The Classical Era, which coincided roughly with the interval between the ends of the two World Wars, marked the eclipse of smallball by longball. While the arrival of an extraordinary talent, ex-pitcher Babe Ruth, who became a full-time outfielder in 1919, was the spark that lit the fire, the ground was fertile for change after two decades of low-scoring baseball in which the old smallball strategies were increasingly stifled by great pitching and improving defense.[1] Rather than use the "scientific approach" championed by Deadball stars like Ty Cobb, who thrived by using his contact skills, speed, and intensity to extract every advantage from his prodigious talent, Ruth embraced a new paradigm: "I swing big with everything I've got. I hit big or I miss big. I like to live as big as I can."[2] Now, one man's performance, no matter how sensational, does not make a trend. At first, Ruth stood nearly alone, outhomering his nearest competitor 29-12 in 1919, 54-19 in 1920, and 59-24 in 1921. In 1921, the Yankees, taking Ruth's cue after years of irrelevance, began to win pennants.

In baseball as in life, success breeds imitation. When something works, it is quickly adopted by your rivals. Rogers Hornsby, a contemporary of Ruth, who had been an exemplar of the Cobb/Speaker/Collins approach and had never hit as many as 10 HR in six major league seasons, suddenly hit 21 HR in 1921 and doubled down with an MLB-leading 42 in 1922. The Yankees added more home run sluggers, most notably Lou Gehrig. Mel Ott, Jimmy Foxx, and others came along to challenge Ruth's and the Yankees' supremacy. By 1930, paralleling the rise in HR, scoring was up to 5.55 runs per team per game, the highest it had been since 1897 (Figures 5.1-2). By 1930, the 30-HR club had swelled to 19 members.[3]

But it was not just HR. There was an increase in hard-hit balls, leading to increasing AVG and OBP. Strikeout rates actually fell during the 1920s, then began to creep upward, but did not really take off until after World War II. Proponents of the old smallball decried the change but to no avail. Smashing the ball over or through the defense simply produced more runs and more victories than trying to finesse the defense with smallball. The offensive explosion did not slow down until 1942-45, when many of MLB's best players served in the military.

As the Classical Era drew to a close, the transition from small ball to long ball appeared to have plateaued. However, as we shall see in subsequent chapters, the thinning of MLB talent during World War II produced only a temporary lull in what would become a 100-year trend toward increasing predominance of not just

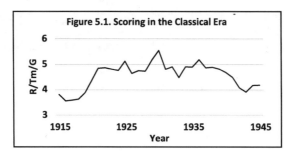

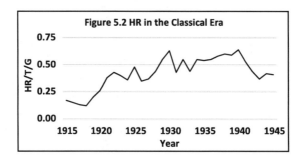

home runs, but the "three true outcomes" (out-of-the-park HR, SO, and BB/HBP) in which the ball is not put in play.[4] Before 1920, Jimmy Sheckard (1897-1913) was the all-time leader among players with at least 7500 PA with 3TO in 23.4% of his PA (see Table A1.4). Babe Ruth's (1914-1935) 39.1% 3TO rate left Sheckard's standard in the dust. But 80 years later, Adam Dunn's (2000-2014) 51.0% 3TO rate would far surpass Ruth. On the pitching side, Rube Waddell (1897-1910), a man decades ahead his time, led all pre-1920 pitchers with at least 7500 BF with 3TO in 27.9% of BF (see Table A1.5). His standard was displaced by Bob Feller (1936-56) with 3TO in 28.6% of BF. Randy Johnson (1988-2009) is the current standard bearer with 3TO in 40.9% of BF. However, leaguewide 3TO percentages generally remained between 16-20% during the Classical era, similar to the Deadball era, with increasing HR offset by decreasing SO.

The slugging Yankees were the dominant team of this high-flying era, winning 14 pennants and 10 World Series in 27 years. Their AL dominance was briefly interrupted by the Senators, Athletics, and Tigers. The other four AL teams were mostly dreadful. Their main NL challengers were the Cardinals, Giants, Pirates, and Cubs. Off the field, Commissioner Kenesaw Mountain Landis reigned supreme after ridding the game of the influence of gamblers, and the Reserve Clause stood unchallenged. If anything, its reach was extended into the minor leagues by Branch Rickey's introduction of the "farm system," which built the Cardinals from an afterthought to a power.[5]

Awards and honors became increasingly prominent in the Classical Era. The Chalmers award honored MLB's best player in 1911-14 but was dropped after four years. Starting in 1922, the BBWAA began selecting an MVP for each league. There was no special award for pitchers until the Cy Young award was introduced in 1956 after Young's death. The annual All-Star game (ASG) was introduced in 1933 to allow fans of each league to see their favorite stars face off against the best of the other league. Starting in this chapter, ASG appearances will be featured for players who were still productive in 1933. Finally, the Hall of Fame (HOF) opened in Cooperstown in 1939.

Professional baseball remained strictly segregated. MLB was all white, except for the occasional American Indian or fair-skinned Latino. Dark-skinned players were confined to the Negro Leagues and Cuban and other Caribbean leagues. However, in 1946, as the Classical era drew to a close, Jackie Robinson, MLB's first player of color in more than 60 years, was playing for the Montreal Royals, a Dodger farm team, preparing for his debut with the 1947 Brooklyn Dodgers, which would herald the dawn of a new era.

The Players

The Classical Generation included 41 CVI-Plus players – 25 hitters, 15 pitchers, and one player who did both (Table 5.1). All but Ferrell, Uhle, Shocker, Walters, and Newsom are in the HOF. As in Chapters 3 and 4, the careers and HOF credentials of these players, partitioned into thematic groupings, are presented below.

Table 5.1: CVI-Plus Players

A) Players (Position)	MidCareer	HOF	AVG/OBP/SLG	OPS+	WAR$_H$	CVI
Ruth, Babe (RF)	1926	BBWAA	.342/.474/.690	206	162.1	270.0
Hornsby, Rogers (2B)	1923	BBWAA	.358/.434/.577	175	127.1	185.0
Gehrig, Lou (1B)	1931	BBWAA	.340/.447/.632	179	114.1	165.4
Ott, Mel (RF)	1936	BBWAA	.304/.414/.533	155	110.7	131.0
Foxx, Jimmie (1B)	1934	BBWAA	.325/.428/.609	163	93.1	117.2
DiMaggio, Joe (CF)	1941	BBWAA	.325/.398/.579	155	79.1	107.4
Mize, Johnny (1B)	1941	VC	.312/.397/.562	158	71.3	97.2
Gehringer, Charlie (2B)	1934	BBWAA	.320/.404/.480	124	83.8	95.3
Vaughan, Arky (SS)	1937	VC	.318/.406/.453	136	78.0	93.8
Appling, Luke (SS)	1940	BBWAA	.310/.399/.398	113	77.0	85.9
Greenberg, Hank (1B)	1938	BBWAA	.313/.412/.605	158	55.7	82.3
Heilmann, Harry (RF)	1924	BBWAA	.342/.410/.520	148	72.1	77.8
Frisch, Frankie (2B)	1926	BBWAA	.316/.369/.432	110	70.8	73.8

(continued)

Table 5.1 (cont'd)

A) Players (Position)	MidCareer	HOF	AVG/OBP/SLG	OPS+	WAR$_H$	CVI
Boudreau, Lou (SS)	1944	BBWAA	.295/.380/.415	120	63.0	73.7
Simmons, Al (LF)	1930	BBWAA	.334/.380/.535	133	68.0	72.7
Waner, Paul (RF)	1932	BBWAA	.333/.404/.473	134	73.9	71.7
Dickey, Bill (C)	1936	BBWAA	.313/.382/.486	127	57.3	71.0
Gordon, Joe (2B)	1942	VC	.268/.357/.466	120	55.7	69.2
Cronin, Joe (SS)	1933	BBWAA	.301/.390/.468	119	64.1	67.2
Goslin, Goose (LF)	1928	VC	.340/.379/.468	128	66.2	66.6
Sisler, George (1B)	1920	BBWAA	.320/.419/.478	125	54.0	65.2
Cochrane, Mickey (C)	1931	BBWAA	.316/.387/.500	129	49.1	64.8
Hartnett, Gabby (C)	1932	BBWAA	.297/.370/.489	126	56.9	60.7
Terry, Bill (1B)	1931	BBWAA	.341/.393/.506	136	55.8	57.8
Herman, Billy (2B)	1937	VC	.304/.367/.407	112	56.0	57.7
Medwick, Joe (LF)	1937	BBWAA	.324/.362/.505	134	54.3	54.2

B) Pitchers	MidCareer	HOF	ERA/WHIP	ERA+	WAR$_P$	CVI
Ruth, Babe (SP)	1926	BBWAA	2.28/1.159	122	20.3	270.0
Grove, Lefty (SP)	1932	BBWAA	3.06/1.278	148	113.3	161.4
Feller, Bob (SP)	1941	BBWAA	3.25/1.316	122	65.2	107.0
Vance, Dazzy (SP)	1927	BBWAA	3.24/1.230	125	62.9	77.8
Newhouser, Hal (SP)	1946	VC	3.06/1.311	130	60.0	77.1
Hubbell, Carl (SP)	1934	BBWAA	2.98/1.166	130	68.9	75.7
Coveleski, Stan (SP)	1920	VC	2.89/1.251	127	66.4	74.2
Faber, Red (SP)	1922	VC	3.15/1.302	119	67.7	70.4
Ferrell, Wes (SP)	1932	No	4.04/1.481	116	48.9	69.6
Lyons, Ted (SP)	1932	BBWAA	3.67/1.348	118	66.8	67.6
Ruffing, Red (SP)	1935	BBWAA	3.80/1.341	109	55.4	62.8
Uhle, George (SP)	1926	No	3.99/1.405	106	45.1	56.0
Shocker, Urban (SP)	1922	No	3.17/1.255	124	54.8	54.4
Grimes, Burleigh (SP)	1924	VC	3.53/1.365	108	46.8	53.4
Walters, Bucky (SP)	1937	No	3.30/1.324	116	46.4	53.2
Newsom, Bobo (SP)	1939	No	3.98/1.463	107	51.3	53.0

What Greatness Looked Like

Babe Ruth and Lefty Grove were the top hitter and pitcher of the Classical Generation. Each posted a long, steady stream of outstanding seasons – 19 for Ruth, with a one-year interruption in 1925, and 14 for Grove, with a one-year interruption in

1934. Since Ruth was primarily a pitcher in his early years, his career trajectory graph depicts his total WAR, not just his WAR_H.

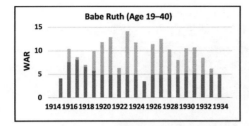

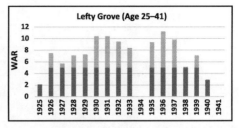

The Babe

Babe Ruth (RF/SP):
270.0 CVI – New York AL (143.0), Boston AL (39.8)

Babe Ruth was the most dominant player ever — perhaps in any sport — and he tops the CVI list by far. He owns six of the top 13 seasonal WAR_H of all time in 1920-21, 1923-24, and 1926-27 and eight of the top 20 seasonal OPS+, in 1919-21, 1923-24, 1926-27, and 1931. In his sixth best season (1926), his 11.4 WAR_H tops the *best* season of such luminaries as Cobb (11.3), Mantle (11.3), Musial (11.3), Mays (11.2), and Morgan (11.0). Indeed, only Yastrzemski (12.5 in 1967), Hornsby (12.2 in 1924), Bonds (11.9 and 11.7 in 2001-02), and Gehrig (11.8 in 1927), and Ripken (11.5 in 1991) ever outperformed Ruth's sixth best season. Ruth is the only hitter whose lifetime OPS+ exceeds 200 (making him more than twice as good as his average contemporary).

As MLB's first three true outcomes hitter, with 39% of his PA ending in a HR, BB, HBP, or SO, Ruth will be remembered as the man who fundamentally changed the way baseball was played. He eschewed the "scientific" smallball approach that his predecessors held dear. Ruth's 54 HR in 1920, his first year with the Yankees, represented nearly 15% of all the HR (369) hit in the AL that season, nearly 9% of all HR (630) hit in both leagues, and more HR than the total output of any of the 15 other major league *teams*. He hit 60 HR in 1927 (a record that stood for 34 years), 59 in 1921, 54 in 1920 and 1928, and 40 or more in seven other seasons.

During his 15 years as a Yankee, his WAR_H exceeded 5.0 in every year except 1925, when he missed two months with what may have been an intestinal abscess. His career home run record of 714 stood until Henry Aaron surpassed it in 1974 and still ranks third best of all time. And in addition to his many hitting records, Ruth posted 20.4 WAR_P and is the only pitcher to have pitched in 10 seasons with a winning record in all of them. His 2.277 career ERA (122 ERA+) is the 17th best of all time (12th among post-1900 pitchers), and his 7.18 H9 is tied for 15th. His record

29.2 consecutive scoreless innings in the 1916 and 1918 World Series endured until Whitey Ford's 33.2 in 1960-61. Ruth was one of five players elected by the BBWAA to the HOF class of 1936 and attended the Hall's inaugural ceremony in 1939.

Babe Ruth, 1916

Beyond the Numbers

- Ruth led the league in strikeouts four times in the 1920s, but even his highest total—93 in 1923—was paltry by modern standards. He ranks 16th in 3TO (39.1%) but only 155th in SO/H (0.463).

- Every fan knows about Babe Ruth's outsized personality. He was a big, flamboyant, irrepressible man-child, who ate too much, drank too much, smoked too much, frequented the hottest night spots in New York wearing his full-length camel hair coat with a woman on each arm, and could down 25 hot dogs and a beer for breakfast without missing a beat. But he was fundamentally good-natured and was known for visiting sick children in the hospital and promising to hit a home run for them – and often delivering. Then, there was his famous and controversial "called-shot" home run in 1932 against Charlie Root and the Cubs in Wrigley Field.[6]

- Ruth won just one MVP award, in 1923. He appeared in the first two ASG in 1933-34.

The New Wave

Lou Gehrig (1B):
165.4 CVI – New York AL (114.1)

Mel Ott (RF):
131.0 CVI – New York NL (110.7)

Johnny Mize (1B):
97.2 CVI – St. Louis NL (39.2), New York NL (27.0)

Hank Greenberg (1B):
82.3 CVI – Detroit AL (53.0)

While Ruth remained the exemplar of the new slugging paradigm throughout his career, he was soon joined by many others. Gehrig, Ott, Foxx (who will be covered later in this chapter), Mize, and Greenberg were all powerful men who successfully swung for the fences, although without Ruth's flair. Ott, who joined the Giants at age 17, hit 511 HR over a 22-year MLB career, while Gehrig, who was struck down by amyotrophic lateral sclerosis (ALS) at age 36, had 493 HR in 16 years. While Mize's and Greenberg's career HR totals were held down by their wartime military service (3 and 4.5 years, respectively), each enjoyed a 50-HR season. Although Ott and Gehrig rank ninth and 17th, respectively, on the career BB leaderboard, they seldom struck out (<0.32 SO/H).

Soft-spoken Lou Gehrig earned the nickname "Iron Horse" by playing in 2130 consecutive games, an iconic record that stood until 1995 when it was finally surpassed by Cal Ripken, Jr. His streak also created a new baseball verb, to be "Wally Pipped," from Gehrig's unlucky predecessor at 1B, who took the day off when Gehrig's streak began and never got his job back.

But Gehrig was about much more than durability. Although he was a quiet man and was overshadowed – first by the flamboyant Ruth, then by the elegant DiMaggio – over much of his career, he was a monster slugger in his own right. In his peak year of 1927, when he won the MVP award, he amassed 447 total bases (more than Ruth) and had a higher SLG than anyone in history not named Ruth or Bonds. But of course, that was the year Ruth hit 60 HR and hogged the spotlight. Gehrig hit .347/.456/.650 (186 OPS+) and averaged 37 HR, 150 RBI, 141 R, 375 TB, and 8.7 WAR per season during his 12-year prime. He scored 167 runs in 1936, and his 185 RBI in 1931 is still an AL record.

Gehrig's career .6324 SLG is topped only by Ruth and Ted Williams. Gehrig was also Ruth's equal in seven World Series, six of which were won by the Yankees (four in sweeps). His best World Series was the four-game sweep of Pittsburgh in 1928, where Gehrig hit .545/.706/1.727 with 4 HR, 9 RBI, and 6 R in 11 AB, but he also had an OPS >1.000 in the 1927, 1932, and 1937 Series wins. A special election was held in 1939 to put Gehrig in the HOF while he was alive to enjoy the honor. Gehrig tops all 1B in CVI and ranks 14th among all players.

Standing only 5'9" and instantly recognizable by the distinctive cocking of his right leg when he started his swing, lifelong Giant Mel Ott was among MLB's most consistent sluggers. From 1929 (when he became the Giants everyday RF) to 1942, Ott terrorized NL pitchers, hitting .309/.420/.549 (159 OPS+) and averaging 30 HR, 111 RBI, 109 R, 166 H, 98 BB, 294 TB, and 6.8 WAR per year, which more or less describes any single Ott season from that period.

He led the Giants in HR for 18 consecutive seasons (1928-45) and is their all-time RBI leader (one ahead of Willie Mays). Ott was more consistent than spectacular, and never had more than 42 HR or 8.9 WAR in a season or won an MVP. However, he led the NL six times in HR and BB and four times in OBP and was selected for 12 consecutive ASG in 1934-45. Ott's 131.0 CVI ranks third, behind only Ruth and Aaron among RF, and 22nd among all HOF-eligible players. He is an elite Hall of Famer.

Although he was never an MVP and not quite on a par with the top sluggers of his time, Mize was a 10-time all-star, who could be counted on by the Cardinals (1936-41) and Giants (1942-48) for 5.4-8.0 WAR per year over a 13-year stretch from 1936-48 (interrupted by three years of military service in World War II) when he hit .324/.409/.588 (168 OPS+) and averaged 35 HR, 127 RBI, 111 R, and 351 TB per 162 games and accrued 65.4 WAR.

Mize's calling card was power, topped by 51 HR in 1947. He was a solid all-around hitter who rarely struck out; indeed, he is still the only man to hit 50 or more HR in a season with <50 SO. For his career, Mize ranks 14th all-time in SLG and tied for 16th in OPS+. Although CVI ranks Mize ranks seventh at 1B and at the 0.37 percentile overall, he had to wait until 1981 for the Veterans Committee to elect him to the HOF. Perhaps, this is because he played mostly for mediocre teams in his prime and because of the time he missed in military service.

The original "Hammerin' Hank," Greenberg lost more than four years to military service in 1941-45 and another prime year to injury in 1936 but was otherwise one of the most prolific sluggers in baseball from 1934-1946. During that interrupted 13-year period, MLB's first Jewish Hall of Famer hit an elite .321/.417/.631 (165 OPS+) and averaged 42 HR, 158 RBI, and 130 R per 162 games. Although he topped out at 7.7 WAR in 1935, he also gained fame in 1938 by falling only two HR short of Ruth's 1927 record of 60 HR, while enduring a barrage of ethnic slurs.

Although his active career was too short to place high on any career leaderboards in counting stats, his career OBP was a robust .412, and his career .605 SLG was topped only by Babe Ruth, Ted Williams, Lou Gehrig, Jimmy Foxx, and Barry Bonds. He was the MVP for two pennant winners in 1935 and 1940 and starred for two others (1934 and 1945). He was outstanding in four World Series — wins in 1935 and 1945 and losses in 1934 and 1940. Greenberg's 82.3 CVI ranks ninth at 1B and at the 0.53 percentile overall.

Beyond the Numbers

- Gehrig played in the first seven ASG and won MVP awards in 1927 and 1936.

- Gehrig stole home 15 times – five more than any other 400+ HR slugger. Babe Ruth is next with 10 steals of home.

- In his emotional farewell speech at Yankee Stadium in June 1939, immortalized by Gary Cooper in "Pride of the Yankees, Gehrig called himself the "luckiest man on the face of the earth."[7,8]

- As one of the best-liked players in the game, Ott became the Giants' player/manager in 1942 and was retained as a manager until 1948 but enjoyed little managerial success. Indeed, Ott was the target of Leo Durocher's famous aphorism "Nice guys finish last."[9] Ott eventually found his niche in broadcasting from 1955 until his death at age 49 in an automobile accident in 1958, which sent the entire baseball world into mourning.

- Mize's played his last five seasons as a part-time 1B and pinch hitter extraordinaire for the Yankees and helped them win five consecutive World Series championships in 1949-53.

- Mize was a subpar defensive 1B. His nickname "The Big Cat" was bestowed ironically by teammates.[10]

- Greenberg played his final season in Pittsburgh in 1947, while mentoring young future Hall of Famer Ralph Kiner. Also, having himself been the target of ethnic slurs, he provided advice and comfort to Dodger rookie Jackie Robinson, who was carrying the burden of being the first black major leaguer in more than 60 years.[11]

- Greenberg enjoyed success as the general manager of the Cleveland Indians and Chicago White Sox in the 1950s and 1960s, including pennants in 1954 and 1959, under the tutelage of his close friend Bill Veeck.

Flawless

Joe DiMaggio (CF):	Charlie Gehringer (2B):
107.4 CVI – New York AL (79.1)	95.3 CVI – Detroit AL (83.8)

There have been other players with gaudier stats, but none that embodied perfection on the diamond like DiMaggio and Gehringer. Both combined power and consistency at the plate and artistry and reliability on defense, as few had before or since.

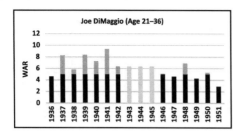

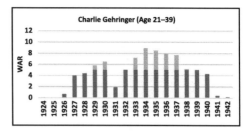

If baseball were judged like figure skating, 13-time All-Star and three-time MVP Joe DiMaggio would have been a perfect 10. Lean and graceful, the "Yankee Clipper" glided through CF seemingly without effort, rarely taking the wrong route on a fly ball or throwing to the wrong base. At bat, his powerful swing was so controlled that he struck out (369) only slightly more often than he homered (361). His iconic 56-game hitting streak in 1941, which has never come close to being equaled, was actually only the second longest of his professional career, falling five games shy of his 61-game streak for the San Francisco Seals (AAA) in 1933. DiMaggio's career bests in counting statistics were attained in his 8.3-WAR sophomore season (1937) when he hit 46 HR, with 167 RBI, 418 TB, and 151 R.

In 13 major league seasons, he played at a high level for 10 AL pennant winners (in 1936-39, 1941-42, 1947, and 1949-51), nine of which won the World Series, and he won AL MVP awards in 1939, 1941, and 1947. Like many high-performance sports cars, DiMaggio was fun to experience but spent a lot of time in the garage. Injuries frequently interrupted his career and eventually forced his retirement at age 36. These injuries and the loss of three prime years to wartime military service at ages 28-30 held down his career stats. But even in his prime, his mystique was about more than stats. His 107.4 CVI ranks sixth in CF and 41st among all HOF-eligible players. He is an elite Hall of Famer.

Six-time All-Star Charlie Gehringer was an exemplary ballplayer who lived an exemplary life. Nicknamed the "mechanical man" for his consistent, understated excellence, Hall of Fame SP Lefty Gomez once said of him, "You wind him up in the spring, and he goes all summer. He hits .330 or .340 or whatever, and then you shut him off in the fall."[12] His career WAR trajectory was almost a perfect bell-shaped curve spanning 19 years and peaking at MVP level (8.9) at age 31, although his only actual MVP award came three years later. In his five-year peak from 1933-37, Gehringer hit .347/.428/.512 (140 OPS+) and averaged 14 HR, 111 RBI, 128 R, 8.0 WAR and 1.5 dWAR. He had a little power (184 HR and 574 2B) and a little speed (181 SB) and was a strong defender at 2B (10.7 dWAR). Gehringer performed well in three World Series (4-3 losses to the Cardinals and Reds in 1934 and 1940 and a 4-2 win over the Cubs in 1935). Gehringer's 95.3 CVI ranks sixth at 2B and 59th among all HOF-eligible players, barely missing the elite category.

Beyond the Numbers

- Off the field, DiMaggio was elegant, but aloof and private. Teammate Jerry Coleman described him as having an "imperial presence." He was revered more than beloved as a teammate and took little interest in mentoring his young heir apparent, Mickey Mantle, while they were teammates in 1951.[13]

- DiMaggio's brief marriage to Marilyn Monroe in 1954, which put him back in the public limelight in the role of "prince consort" to a Hollywood queen, did not end well, but DiMaggio remained devoted to her and continued to send flowers to her grave after her death in 1962.

- After he retired, DiMaggio insisted on being introduced as baseball's greatest living ball player, a title bestowed on him by a public poll in 1969. He was not greater than Willie Mays, Ted Williams, Henry Aaron, Stan Musial, and other still-living ballplayers, but he was perhaps the most famous. How many ballplayers have been featured in four popular songs and an Ernest Hemingway novella? In the 1960s and 70s, he was the TV spokesman for Mr. Coffee, as Simon and Garfunkel plaintively pled, "Where have you gone, Joe DiMaggio?"[14]

- Gehringer missed his 1949 HOF induction ceremony due to preparations for his wedding. After that, however, he was a regular attendee and served on the VC and as a HOF Board member from 1953-1990.[15]

- Gehringer was the Tigers GM in 1951-53; the team was awful, but he did sign Al Kaline.

The Great Challenge Trade

Rogers Hornsby (2B):	Frankie Frisch (2B):
185.0 CVI – St. Louis NL (91.4), Chicago NL (16.0), New York NL (10.2), Boston NL (9.0)	73.8 CVI – New York NL (37.6), St. Louis NL (33.2)

It is almost unheard of for two teams swap Hall of Famers in their prime, but that's what happened on December 20, 1926 when the Cardinals traded 30 year-old 2B Rogers Hornsby for 29 year-old 2B Frankie Frisch. Just looking at the numbers, this trade seemed to heavily favor the Giants. In the six years leading up to the trade (1921-26), Hornsby had averaged .388/.460/.653 with an astounding 191 OPS+, along with 26 HR 118 R, 115 RBI, 8 SB, and 9.0 WAR (0.5 dWAR). Frisch's numbers for this same period – .332/.381/.461 (121 OPS+) with 8 HR, 104 R,

70 RBI, 29 SB, and 5.7 WAR (1.8 dWAR) per year – were excellent, but he was no Hornsby. Clearly, the Giants obtained the far superior hitter, although at the cost of some speed and defense. And the Cardinals were just coming off their first NL pennant and an upset win over the Yankees in the World Series. Yet, Cardinals owner Sam Breadon was more than willing to make the trade because Frisch was many things that Hornsby was not — a superior defender, an unselfish teammate, and a natural leader, who had led the Giants to four consecutive NL pennants in 1921-24 and World Series championships in 1921-22. And sure enough, it was the Cardinals who won

Frankie Frisch

the trade. Frisch spent 11 years with the Cardinals and contributed to four more NL pennants and two more World Series championships, while Hornsby lasted only a year with the Giants. Hornsby was traded to Boston and then to the Cubs 10 months later, where he helped them win the 1929 pennant in his last great year, and was washed up by 1932.

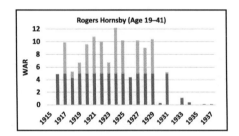

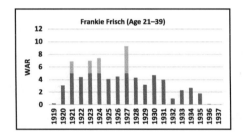

In his early years, Hornsby was a small-ball clone of Cobb and Speaker, never hitting double digits in HR, but he changed with the times when the calendar turned to 1921 and combined the best of both worlds. From 1917-29, Hornsby had nine 8-WAR seasons and hit .367/.442/.596 (182 OPS+) while averaging 21 HR, 104 RBI, 108 R, and 8.9 WAR per season. He hit .424 (the highest for anyone after 1901) in 1924, but he also hit .401 and won the Triple Crown in 1922 (when he tallied career highs with 42 HR, 152 RBI, and a staggering 450 TB) and .403 in 1925 (when he attained a career high .756 SLG).

Rogers Hornsby

He also banged 39 HR in 1925 and 1929, to go along with his 42 in 1922, and was named MVP in both seasons. Hornsby's career .358 AVG ranks second only to Cobb, and he also ranks in the top 10 for OBP, SLG, and OPS+. Although Hornsby's play declined sharply in his 30s, he had done more than enough before then to make him an elite Hall of Famer. CVI ranks Hornsby first among all infielders and eighth overall.

Frisch was a speedy, high-contact, switch-hitting 2B/3B, who seemed to have a knack for winning. In his prime (1920-34), Frisch's teams played in eight World Series and won four. During these same 15 years, the Giants and Cardinals each won only one pennant without him. Frisch won the NL MVP award in 1931, although this was far from his best season, and played in the first three ASG in 1933-35. His .316 career AVG notwithstanding, Frisch was probably most valuable for his defense. His unimpressive 110 OPS+ indicates that his flashy offensive stats were largely an inflated product of his era. Frisch's 73.8 CVI ranks 11th among 2B and at the 0.72 percentile overall.

Beyond the Numbers

- After excelling as the Cardinals player-manager in 1933-37, Frisch went on to manage the Cardinals (1938), Pirates (1940-46) and Cubs (1949-51) but was disengaged and could not repeat his early success. The Cubs fired him in 1951 for reading a book in the dugout.[16] Hornsby, who had a caustic personality that alienated his players, also failed to sustain the managerial success he enjoyed as the Cardinals' player/manager in 1926 and had a 701-812 record in 14 years as a manager with six teams. [17]

- Hornsby's heavy betting on horse races put him on Commissioner Landis's blacklist in the 1940s, although he was never formally banned. He was restored to good standing when Landis died in 1944.

- Although he was a witty, sophisticated, and well-read man with a hearty sense of humor, Frisch became something of a curmudgeon as he aged, romanticizing the past and deriding the modern game. As member of the VC in 1967-72, the opinionated and persuasive Frisch was responsible for what Bill James has called some "simply appalling selections" as he advocated for players in the nether regions of Table 5.3 whom he played with or managed.[18] More on this later.

Connie Mack's Second "Dynasty"

Lefty Grove (SP):
161.4 CVI – Philadelphia AL (64.8),
Boston AL (41.9)

Jimmy Foxx (1B):
117.2 CVI – Philadelphia AL (62.4),
Boston AL (32.7)

Al Simmons (LF):
72.7 CVI – Philadelphia AL (50.9),
Chicago AL (10.8)

Mickey Cochrane (C):
64.8 CVI – Philadelphia AL (37.3),
Detroit AL (11.8)

In his 50 years at the helm of the Philadelphia Athletics, Connie Mack's teams had only a net .484 winning percentage. However, during his long tenure, Mack was also able to build and dismantle two dominant teams, which won nine pennants and seven World Series — second only to the Yankees. The second of these teams, which was more of an interregnum in the long reign of Yankee dominance than a true dynasty, began to take shape in 1925 after 10 consecutive dreary losing seasons — six with between 98 and 117 losses – and culminated in three consecutive 100-win pennants in 1929-31 and World Series wins in 1929-30. Grove, Foxx, Simmons, and Cochrane were the stars. But as the Depression reversed his fortunes, Mack sold them off one by one—Simmons in 1932, Cochrane and Grove in 1933, and Foxx in 1935. By 1934, the Athletics had embarked on another 13-year streak of losing seasons. They would not win another AL pennant until 1972.

Lefty Grove, 1933

Known for his fiery temper as well as his blazing fastball, Lefty Grove had the best career winning percentage (0.680) of all 300-game winners. His lifetime 3.06 ERA and 1.278 WHIP are not particularly impressive at face value but must be considered in the context of pitching in hitter-friendly home parks during 16 seasons (1925-1940) in which the MLB ERA ranged from 3.81 to 4.82 and the MLB WHIP ranged from 1.384 to 1.521. Grove's seemingly pedestrian ERAs were good enough to lead the AL a record nine times, and his lifetime 148 ERA+ trails only Mariano Rivera, Clayton Kershaw, Pedro Martinez, and Jim Devlin, who had far fewer IP.

In his 31-4, 10.4-WAR_p 1931 MVP season, his 2.06 ERA translated to a remarkable 217 ERA+. Similarly, although his SO9, which never exceeded 6.8 and averaged 5.2 for his career, was unimpressive by modern standards, Grove was one of the hardest throwers of his time and led the AL in strikeouts seven times. After a sore arm ruined his first season in Boston in 1934, Grove reinvented himself as a finesse pitcher. He posted his best WAR_p (11.2) in 1936 at age 36, when he went 17-12 with a 2.81 ERA for a weak Red Sox team. He continued to pitch effectively through age 40. Grove's 161.4 CVI ranks fourth among all SP and 15th overall. He is an elite Hall of Famer.

Nine-time All-Star Jimmy Foxx was the closest thing to Ruth in his time. He had two 50-plus HR seasons, including 58 in 1932 when he threatened Ruth's 60 from five years earlier, and his 34.2% 3TO rate was second only to Ruth up to that point in baseball history. He struck out more often than Ruth; his 0.495 SO/H, though modest by current standards, was the highest of any pre-integration player with

≥7500 PA. Foxx's career paralleled that of Mel Ott with higher but less sustained performance peaks. During an amazing four-year stretch from 1932-35, Foxx accrued 36.1 WAR and hit .350/.457/.687 (195 OPS+), averaging 46 HR, 144 RBI, 128 R, 383 TB and 109 BB.

Foxx's lifetime SLG trails only Ruth, Williams, and Gehrig, but his .325 AVG, .428 OBP, and sub-100 annual strikeout rate (lower than his walk rate) attest that Foxx was no one-dimensional slugger. He was also a good defensive 1B with a strong enough arm to fill in at 3B and C. He even tried pitching in 1945 with the Phillies and posted a 1.52 ERA in 23.2 IP. CVI ranks Foxx third at 1B, behind Gehrig and Pujols, and 31st among all HOF-eligible players. He is an elite Hall of Famer.

Three-time All-Star Al Simmons was a right-hand-hitting slugger and a passable OF (at best), who combined a high AVG and power, despite an unorthodox "bucket-footed" batting stance. In his eight-year heyday with the Athletics from 1925-32, Simmons hit a robust .365/.408/.611 (155 OPS+) and averaged 25 HR, 132 RBI, 111 R, and 6.2 WAR per season. After leaving the A's, Simmons had two excellent years with the White Sox in 1933-34 before playing out his career with multiple teams as a journeyman in the late 1930s and early 1940s. Simmons's 72.7 CVI ranks eighth in LF and at the 0.75 percentile overall.

Two-time All-Star Mickey Cochrane became the first catcher elected to the Hall of Fame by the BBWAA in 1947. Until he suffered a nervous breakdown in 1936 and a career-ending (and nearly fatal) beaning in 1937, he was on his way to even better things. Although his shortened career (6208 PA) limited his counting stats, his .320 AVG and .419 OBP still top all catchers.

Cochrane was also known as a winning player, whose teams never finished below third place. His two MVP awards in 1928 in Philadelphia and 1934 in Detroit attest to his leadership qualities and the high regard in which he was held by contemporary writers. He was the emotional leader not only for the A's but for the AL champion Tigers of 1934-35 as their catcher-manager. The 1935 pennant was unfortunately his last hurrah, as the addition of general manager responsibilities to his portfolio tipped the tightly wound Cochrane over the edge in 1936. Cochrane's 64.8 CVI ranks 11th among catchers and at the 1.08 percentile overall.

Beyond the Numbers

- Perhaps more than any other Hall of Famer, Grove's career suffered from the Reserve Clause. He was held back in AAA for five years, winning 111 games, before getting his first chance to pitch in the major leagues at age 25. When the Orioles sold his contract to the Athletics for the then outlandish sum of $100,600, he went only 10-12 with a 4.75 ERA and led the AL with 131 BB in his rookie season and was viewed as a costly flop.[19] It took him another year to get on track.

Beyond the Numbers (cont'd)

- Grove was outstanding in three World Series, going 4-2 with a 1.75 ERA and 1.013 WHIP. He even picked up two saves in 1929, when he was used as a super-reliever, pitching a Bumgarner-like 4.1 three-hit six-strikeout scoreless innings in relief of George Earnshaw in Game 2, and adding a perfect two-inning four-SO save in the A's 10-8 comeback win over the Cubs in Game 4.

- Foxx was also a strong postseason performer and hit the Series-clinching Game 6 HR against the Cardinals in 1930.

- Foxx continued to play at a high level for the Red Sox from 1936-41 and mentored emerging superstar Ted Williams, who became his lifelong friend.[20]

- Foxx's later years were marred by alcoholism and financial problems. The Jimmy Dugan character played by Tom Hanks in the popular 1992 movie, "A League of Their Own" was likely based at least in part on Foxx.[21]

- In the 1929 Series, Simmons was the catalyst in the pivotal Game 4 comeback when the Cubs were cruising to a Series-tying 8-0 win. Simmons opened the 10-run seventh inning with a HR and then singled in his second AB of the inning and scored the winning run. The A's wrapped up the Series in Game 5.

- Cochrane was of Scottish (not Irish) descent and preferred Mike or Black Mike to Mickey.[22] In retrospect, it was for the best, since Mickey Mantle was named after him; Gordon Stanley Mantle and Black Mike Mantle just don't have the same flair.

The Power Pitchers

Bob Feller (SP):
107.0 CVI – Cleveland AL (63.4)

Dazzy Vance (SP):
77.8 CVI – Brooklyn NL (59.0)

Hal Newhouser:
77.1 CVI – Detroit AL (61.4)

"Rapid Robert" Feller, "Prince Hal" Newhouser, and "Dazzy" Vance were the pre-eminent power pitchers in an era dominated by power bats. Although their raw power statistics pale in comparison to their post-1960 counterparts, these three men rank first, seventh, and tenth, respectively, among all pre-integration pitchers in 3TO, and second, seventh, and fourth in SO/H. So, let us appreciate them in the context of their times.

Eight-time All-Star Bob Feller was the original Nolan Ryan. He broke into the major leagues as a 17-year-old high school junior who threw harder than any of his peers and walked almost as many batters as he struck out. In his first start with the Indians, he struck out 15 batters in a 4-1 complete game victory. He struggled mightily with control early in his career; his 208 BB in 1938 tops all post-1900 pitchers. Although Feller's control improved as he matured, walks were always his Achilles heel; his 1764 BB rank fifth on the career leaderboard, despite being held down by his four-year absence in 1942-45 for military service.

Starting in 1939, at age 20, Feller put together a stretch (1939-1946) of four almost equally superb seasons (sandwiched around his military service) in which he went 107-51 with a 2.67 ERA (146 ERA+) and 1.229 WHIP with 7.5 SO9 and 4.1 BB9. He posted his highest pitching WAR_p (10.0) in 1946 and set what was thought to be an MLB record with 348 SO until researchers unearthed six extra SO for Rube Waddell in 1904, raising his total to 349 for that season.

Feller seemed to lose something after his 371.1 IP in 1946 (probably encompassing an enormous pitch count, given his 348 SO and 143 BB). From 1948-56, he was no better than average, and he was ineffective in his only World Series appearance in 1948. Inexplicably, he was not used at all in the 1954 World Series, when the Giants swept the Indians.

Feller's three no-hitters were topped only by Nolan Ryan (7) and Sandy Koufax (4), and his 12 one-hitters are tied with Ryan for the major league record. With the interpolation of his missed wartime seasons, CVI ranks Feller 14th among SP and for 42nd among all HOF-eligible players. He is an elite Hall of Famer.

No baseball player has had a career quite like that of Dazzy Vance, the fun-loving 6'2" 200-pound fireballer and prankster, who got his nickname from his dazzling fastball.[23] He was a sore-armed journeyman who won 133 minor league games in 1915-21 but was ineffective in three major league cameos with the Pirates and Yankees. The turning point came when Vance banged his pitching elbow on a card table during a poker game. The intense pain sent him rushing to a doctor, who diagnosed his problem and operated on his elbow.

The nature of the operation is uncertain, but it left Vance pain-free. He won 21 games in 1921 and was up with the Dodgers for good in 1922 at age 31. From there, Vance went on to a 62.9-WAR_p HOF career. His career year came in 1924, at age 33, when he went 28-6 with a 2.16 ERA (174 ERA+) and 1.022 WHIP and led the NL with 262 SO. He racked up 10.5 WAR_p and beat out Rogers Hornsby (who hit .424) for the NL MVP award. Vance led the NL in strikeouts for seven consecutive years in 1922-28 (despite an injury-shortened season in 1926), averaging 19-11, 191 SO, a 3.00 ERA (131 ERA+), and a 1.198 WHIP. He pitched a no-hitter in 1925. The closest match to Vance in the Hall of Fame is Red Faber, who had 12.9 WAR_p by age 30 (versus -0.6 for Vance) en route to 67.4 career WAR_p. Looking outside the

HOF, one can point to Jamie Moyer, who had 7.0 WAR_p through age 30, en route to 49.9 career WAR_p. Vance's 77.8 CVI ranks 35th among SP and at the 0.61 percentile overall.

Seven-time All-Star Hal Newhouser was baseball's top pitcher of the 1940s (other than Satchel Paige), but his career was often discounted (and he was snubbed by the BBWAA) because he dominated the AL at a time when many of its best players were at war. Newhouser was classified 4-F because of a heart condition (mitral valve prolapse). However, Newhouser continued to be one of the AL's top pitchers through 1949, four years after MLB had returned to full strength.

When he hit the big leagues at age 19, Newhouser's dour demeanor, Coke-bottle-smashing dugout tantrums, and complete disinterest in anything but his own pitching, alienated his teammates.[24] When he finally learned to master his temper, the Tigers' faith in him was rewarded. From 1944-49, Newhouser averaged 23-11 (including 29-9 in 1944) with 190 strikeouts, a 2.52 ERA (152 ERA+), and a 1.212 WHIP. He was named AL MVP in both 1944 and 1945. His 12.1 total WAR in 1945 were exceeded by only seven post-1900 pitching performances (four by the same man, Walter Johnson). He pitched the Tigers to the 1945 AL pennant and added two wins (including the clincher) in the 4-3 World Series victory over the Cubs, after being routed 9-0 in the Series opener. CVI ranks him 36th among SP just behind Vance and at the 0.62 percentile overall,. There is no doubt that he belongs in the HOF, as the VC finally affirmed in 1992.

Beyond the Numbers

• A prodigy who could throw a baseball 267 feet when he was nine years old, Feller's father began grooming him as a ballplayer before he could walk and played catch with him every day at age four.[25] When he was 12, his dad built a baseball field on his Iowa farm (the original "Field of Dreams?") to showcase his son's talent. He charged 25 cents admission to crowds of as many as 1000 fans.

• They didn't have radar guns in Feller's day, but a film exists of Feller trying to measure the speed of his fastball against a speeding (86 mph) motorcycle.[26] Feller's fastball beat the motorcycle to the finish line despite (unintentionally) giving the motorcycle a 10-foot head start; they calculated that Feller's fastball must have traveled 98-103 mph in that test. So, if Walter Johnson was the "Big Train," perhaps Feller was the "Big Chopper." In another test, Feller fired his fastball through a military device called a "Lumiline Chronograph," which gave a reading of 98.6 mph. This would correspond to 101-107 mph using a modern radar gun (which measures the ball's speed as it leaves the pitcher's hand rather than after traveling 60 feet).

Beyond the Numbers (cont'd)

- Feller supplemented his post-War income by organizing off-season barnstorming tours against a team of Negro League All-Stars led by Satchel Paige. He and Paige would generally pitch an inning or two in every game. While Feller's motives were not entirely altruistic, these tours gave Paige and his teammates valuable exposure and income at a time when MLB had only begun to integrate.[27]

- Feller continued to throw a baseball daily into his 80s and once claimed credibly, if not provably, that he had probably thrown a baseball more times than any man in history.[28]

- Vance's only World Series came with the Cardinals in 1934 at age 43; he pitched 1.1 innings of scoreless relief.

- After his playing career, Newhouser remained in baseball as a scout for the Orioles, Indians, Tigers and Astros for 36 years, signing Milt Pappas and Dean Chance, among others. He quit scouting in 1992 after the Astros overrode his recommendation to draft Derek Jeter with their #1 overall pick; they chose Phil Nevin instead.[29]

Heavy Hitters

Harry Heilmann (RF):
77.8 CVI – Detroit AL (67.6)

Paul Waner (RF):
71.7 CVI – Pittsburgh NL (69.4)

Goose Goslin (LF):
66.6 CVI – Washington AL (43.0),
St. Louis AL (13.7), Detroit AL (9.4)

George Sisler (1B):
65.2 CVI, St. Louis AL (52.0)

Bill Terry (1B):
57.8 CVI –New York NL (55.8)

Joe Medwick (LF):
54.2 CVI – St. Louis (37.4),
Brooklyn NL (8.6)

These four OF and two 1B, were not big HR hitters like Ruth, Gehrig, Ott, Foxx, et al. but exemplified the slashing high-AVG hitting style of the Classical Generation. Although Goslin, Terry, and Medwick displayed occasional 25+ HR power, none approached Ruth's 35% or even Ott's 28% 3TO, and their career HR totals were 183, 113, 248, 102, 154, and 205, respectively. All six players hit over .370 at least once (Heilmann did it four times), and Sisler (twice), Heilmann, and Terry each hit over .400. Their slugging percentages ranged from .468 (Goslin) to .520

(Heilmann), but only Medwick (.181) and Heilmann (.178) had an isolated power (SLG minus AVG) above .165.

Harry Heilmann

The Tigers' Harry Heilmann, the last AL player to hit over .400 before Ted Williams in 1941, was one of the best pure hitters of the 1920s, picking up where Ty Cobb left off, but without Cobb's speed and aggressiveness. Heilmann was a poor outfielder and even worse at 1B, and his -14.0 dWAR detracted significantly from his CVI. Starting when he narrowly beat out his manager/teammate Cobb for the 1921 batting title, Heilmann enjoyed a seven-year run of 5.8-8.9 WAR seasons in 1921-27, in which he hit .380/.452/.583 (167 OPS+) and averaged 15 HR, 104 R, 116 RBI, and 6.7 WAR per season. Heilmann's power numbers were dwarfed by the new breed of Ruthian sluggers, but he hit more HR than any of MLB's top pre-1920 sluggers. Heilmann never played for a pennant winner; his career began after the great Cobb-Crawford Tiger teams of 1907-09 and ended before the Tiger pennants of 1934-35, featuring Gehringer, Greenberg, and Cochrane. He also never won an MVP award but finished second to Gehrig in 1927. Heilmann's 77.8 CVI ranks 10th in RF and at the 0.60 percentile overall.

Four-time All-Star Paul Waner was a colorful 5'8" 155-pound hard-drinking .333 hitter, who sprayed doubles and triples all over the field but rarely homered or struck out. Although he didn't start his career until 1926, he never got the memo about the new longball paradigm. Waner's .140 ISO, .150 3TO rate, and .119 SO/H resembled Tris Speaker more than his contemporaries.

Waner believed he was at his best when he was relaxed, so he drank a swig of whisky from a hip flask before every at bat. Casey Stengel once quipped about him, "He had to be a very graceful player because he could slide without breaking the bottle on his hip."[30] When Pie Traynor managed the Pirates, he reportedly asked Waner to cut back on the hard liquor and just stick to beer. Waner complied, but when he started the season hitting .240, Traynor ordered him to go out drinking. He went 4-for-4 the next day.[31]

During his 12-year peak in 1926-37, Waner averaged .348/.417/.507 (142 OPS+) with 206 H, 86 RBI, 110 R, 40 2B, 14 3B, 300 TB and 5.5 WAR. His WAR would have been higher except for his lackluster defensive play (-0.4 dWAR per year). His peak came in 1927, his sophomore season, when he hit .380/.437/.549 (154 OPS+), led the NL with 342 TB, and won the NL batting title and MVP award, while leading the Pirates to the pennant. Although the Pirates were swept by the powerful Yankees, Waner went 5-for-15 with a double and 3 RBI, in what would be his only World Series. His 71.7 CVI ranks 12th in RF and at the 0.78 percentile overall.

Goose Goslin was a free-swinging slugger and fun-loving prankster, who played the horses and was the antithesis of the hypercompetitive "scientific" contact hitters of previous decades.[32] His corkscrew left-handed swing, which he started in an extreme closed stance and turned almost 180 degrees, was entertaining to watch (especially when he missed and spun to the ground) and quickly made him a fan favorite. Although no one swung harder than Goslin, he never struck out more than 54 times in a season. Goslin had a 14-year run (1923-1936) as a solid-to-excellent everyday player. During his 1924-31 peak, Goslin reliably produced 5.2-7.5 WAR with 102+ RBI and a .308+ AVG every year (except for an off-year in 1929) and was a dangerous clutch hitter. There was more chameleon than goose in his HR totals which bounced between nine in 1923 (his first year as an everyday player) and 37 in 1930. His CVI was hurt by his defensive deficiencies (-4.7 dWAR), including his circuitous arm-flailing pursuit of flyballs, which resembled a goose flapping its wings and earned him his colorful nickname. Goslin never won an MVP, but played in the 1936 All-Star game at age 35. CVI ranks Goslin 10th among LF and at the 1.00 percentile overall.

George Sisler was so highly regarded by his peers that he was among the initial HOF inductees in 1939. Sisler, whose .128 ISO, 10.5% 3TO rate, and .116 SO/H, would not have seemed out of place next to Nap Lajoie or even Cap Anson, is a special case since his productive years straddled the Deadball and Classical eras. During a six-year period in 1917-22, he was considered one of baseball's brightest superstars, a speedy slick-fielding 1B, who hit .377/.420/.541 (162 OPS+) and averaged nearly 300 TB per year, while his WAR ranged from 5.7 to 9.8. Sisler hit over .400 in 1920 and 1922; his 257 hits in 1920 stood as the all-time record until Ichiro Suzuki came along with 262 in 2004. But after winning the first modern AL MVP award in 1922, a severe sinus infection stopped him in his tracks at age 30, leaving him with lasting optic nerve damage.[33] Although he returned in 1924 and played through 1930, he was no longer the same player. Although his 65.2 CVI still ranks 16th among 1B and at the 1.05 percentile overall, Sisler could have climbed far higher had his vision not been impaired.

Terry and Medwick both benefited from the high-offense environment of this era but were legitimately strong hitters, Terry's claim to fame is that in 1930 he became the last NL player to hit over .400 in a season. Medwick was a doubles machine, whose 540 career doubles tied him with Dave Winfield for 39th on the all-time leaderboard, but in 3400 fewer AB). Medwick was also a 10-time All-Star, who starred for the 1934 Gashouse Gang Cardinal World Series champions. CVI ranks Terry and Medwick at the 1.26 and 1.48 percentile, respectively, which put them in HOVG territory.

Beyond the Numbers

- Heilmann was an outstanding and popular broadcaster in Cincinnati from 1933 until his death from lung cancer in 1951.[34]

- Paul Waner and younger brother Lloyd earned the nicknames Big Poison and Little Poison, originally a corruption of a Brooklyn announcer, who called them "the big person" and "the little person," but the nicknames stuck because they were indeed poison to opposing pitchers. Lloyd was a good (but not great) player who rode Paul's coattails all the way to the HOF.

- In 1924, Goslin was the offensive star of a Senators team that won its first AL pennant and its only World Series. Goslin was the hitting star of the 1924 Series, hitting .344 with 3 HR, 4 R, 7 RBI, and a hefty .656 SLG, and won Game 4 almost single-handedly by going 4/4 with 2 HR and 4 RBI.

- By the time Goslin reached Detroit in 1934, he was only a complementary player on a team led by the likes of Greenberg and Gehringer. Still, it was Goslin who delivered the decisive walk-off Game 7 hit against the Cubs that brought the Tigers their first World Series championship in 1935.

- Before his illness, Sisler had begun to adapt to the new longball paradigm in 1919-21 by reaching double digits in HR and raising his isolated power to a robust .225 in 1920, while still averaging 40 SB annually.

- Sisler began his MLB career as a pitcher and once outpitched Walter Johnson 2-1 in a memorable August 1915 duel.[35] However, his bat and his brilliant defensive play convinced Browns management that his future was at 1B.

- Terry managed the Giants for 10 years, compiling an 823-661 record, with a World Series championship in 1933 and another pennant in 1936. However, he is better remembered for a wisecrack about the Dodgers in 1934 ("Are they still in the league?") that came back to bite him when the Dodgers swept them in a season ending two-game series, thereby handing the 1934 NL pennant to St. Louis.[35]

Cream of the Infield Crop

Arky Vaughan (SS):
93.8 CVI – Pittsburgh NL (66.3),
Brooklyn NL (10.0)

Lou Boudreau (SS):
73.7 CVI – Cleveland AL (61.6)

Joe Cronin (SS):
67.2 CVI – Washington AL (36.7),
Boston AL (27.2)

Luke Appling (SS):
85.8 CVI – Chicago AL (77.1)

Joe Gordon (2B):
69.2 CVI – New York NL (36.8),
Cleveland AL (19.0)

Billy Herman (2B):
57.7 CVI – Chicago NL (35.6),
Brooklyn NL (12.7)

With the striking exception of Honus Wagner, shortstop had been a position where defense was paramount, and offense was an afterthought. The same was true to a lesser extent of 2B and 3B. While Appling, Boudreau, and Gordon were also excellent defenders, these six middle infielders (as well as Hornsby, Gehringer, and Frisch, who were covered earlier) were strong offensive contributors, exhibiting strong on-base skills and some power.

Arky Vaughan, one of baseball's most overlooked stars, was the most dangerous hitter of the bunch. His WAR ranged between 5.7-9.7 from 1933-40, when he hit .326/.421/.480 (144 OPS+), and he averaged 9 HR, 83 RBI, 100 R, and 7.4 WAR per season. Starting in 1934, he was chosen for nine consecutive ASG, starting in six. He had doubles power but never hit more than 19 HR. He was a speedy and smart baserunner but stole few bases. In 1935, his best season, he was named NL MVP by the Sporting News but finished only third in the BBWAA voting. But Vaughan is best remembered (if he is remembered at all) as the guy who quit baseball for three prime years because of a clash with manager Leo Durocher. He returned to the Dodgers after Durocher was suspended in 1947, but by then, he was past his prime. Because Vaughan's career was relatively short, and he played mostly with non-contending Pirates teams, 33 years would pass before his posthumous HOF election in 1985; the recognition was long overdue. CVI ranks him fourth among SS and 60th among all HOF-eligible players.

Seven-time All-Star Luke Appling was Mr. White Sox before Ernie Banks was Mr. Cub. He was an on-base machine with minimal power (.088 ISO) who (like Banks) spent his entire 20-year career with a perennial also-ran, never sniffing a pennant. Often called "Old Aches and Pains" for his frequent hypochondriacal complaints, he nevertheless racked up 10,254 PA and could seemingly rise from his sickbed and go 4-for-4. Starting in 1933, Appling hit over .300 in 15 of 16 consecutive seasons. At his peak in 1935-37, he hit .337/.439/.445 (122 OPS+) and averaged 98 BB and 101 R per season, while accruing 20.5 WAR. His highest WAR (7.3) came in 1943, but his 7.2 WAR 1936 season (age 29), with the AL at full strength, was more impressive, with career highs in AVG (.388), OBP (.474), SLG (.508), H (204), R (111), and RBI (128). Appling also became a very capable SS, with 19.0 dWAR for his career. The BBWAA elected him to the Hall of Fame in 1964—his final chance on the ballot. His 85.8 CVI ranks fifth among SS and at the 0.47 percentile overall.

I will always think of Lou Boudreau as the cerebral Cubs radio color man in the 1960s, who always seemed to be several steps ahead of the managers on the field and seemingly could tell you what they were thinking before they even thought it. But before that, he was a seven-time All-Star who led the Indians to the World Series championship as an MVP SS and manager at age 30 in 1948. Boudreau had to manage very skillfully that year, dealing with players far older than himself, incorporating newly-signed African American players Larry Doby and Satchel Paige into a wary veteran team, and enduring constant second-guessing from owner Bill

Veeck and general manager Hank Greenberg to win a tight three-team race that ended in a playoff.

From 1940-48, Boudreau hit .301/.386/.427 (128 OPS+) with 8.1 WAR seasons in 1943-44 in addition to his 10.3-WAR career year in 1948. In 1946, he was the first manager to deploy an extreme defensive shift, moving all players to the right side of the field against Ted Williams. Boudreau was also outstanding defensively, despite chronically sore ankles (a residue of his basketball days); his 23.4 dWAR ranks 17th among all SS. He managed the Red Sox, Athletics and Cubs in 1952-60, and served as the Cubs color commentator from 1961-88. His 73.7 CVI ranks 14th at SS and at the 0.73 percentile overall.

Joe Gordon

Joe "Flash" Gordon was a rare power-hitting 2B and a sparkling defender, who ranked second (22.4), respectively, among all 2B in dWAR. The nine-time All-Star was a 3TO hitter, with 253 HR (eighth among all 2B) and 0.46 SO/H. If one interpolates the average of his 1942-43 and 1946-47 seasons into the missed 1944-45 seasons, the additional 4.8 dWAR and 38 HR he might have accrued in those two wartime years could have brought his career totals to 25.2 dWAR (tops among all 2B) and 291 HR (tied with Craig Biggio for fourth among all 2B).

From 1939-43, Gordon posted 31.7 WAR (6.3 per year) and 11.8 dWAR, while hitting .282/.368/.478 (128 OPS+) and averaging 23 HR, 95 RBI, 95 R, and 273 TB for the Yankees. He won the MVP award in 1942. During this run and in 1938, the star-studded Yankees, with Gordon at 2B, won five AL pennants and four World Series. Gordon, a licensed pilot, joined the Air Force in 1944 but did not see combat. Noting the erosion of his skills after he returned in 1946, the Yankees traded him to Cleveland for SP Allie Reynolds. Gordon became a cornerstone of the Indians' 1948 World Series champions, teaming with Boudreau to form a peerless keystone combination, while Reynolds went on to star for the Yankees dynasty of the early 1950s. Gordon's 69.2 CVI ranks 12th at 2B and at the 0.90 percentile overall. But Gordon, whose wartime military service shortened his career to 11 seasons, had to wait until 2009 to receive posthumous HOF recognition via the VC.

Joe Cronin was a baseball lifer whose distinguished career spanned all aspects of the game. In his prime (and even past it), Cronin was widely viewed as the best SS in the AL (although CVI ranks others higher), and he started in seven ASG. He was solid both defensively (14.3 dWAR) and offensively (119 OPS+). Although 1930 was his best year statistically, 1933 was the most rewarding. That year as player-manager, he led the Senators to a pennant and became the youngest man ever to manage in the World Series; he finished second in the AL MVP voting. The Giants beat the Senators 4-1 in the World Series, but Cronin hit .318 in 22 AB.

Cronin went on to a long career as the manager and general manager of the Red Sox, where he was constantly sabotaged by prima donna veteran players like Wes Ferrell, Lefty Grove, and Bill Werber, who were cozy with owner Tom Yawkey and GM Eddie Collins. Finally, he served as AL president for 15 years. He had only five 5-WAR seasons and modest power, and his career stats fall short of all-time leaderboards. His 67.2 CVI ranks 18th among SS and at the 0.97 percentile overall. Still, the breadth of his career makes him a solid Hall of Famer.

Herman was a 10-time All-Star 2B who was solid but not spectacular on both offense (112 OPS+) and defense (12.4 dWAR) and played for four NL pennant winners for the Cubs (1922, 1935, 1938) and Dodgers (1941) but no World Series champions. CVI ranks him at the 1.28 percentile. His career is on a par with that of Willie Randolph, making him a better candidate for the HOVG, than for the HOF. Non-HOF 2B Bobby Grich and Lou Whitaker are more deserving of HOF recognition.

Beyond the Numbers

- Vaughan was initially a clumsy SS and made 46 errors as a rookie. He worked hard to improve under Honus Wagner's tutelage and finished with a respectable 12.0 dWAR.

- Vaughan's life was cut short at age 40 when he and a friend drowned after their fishing boat capsized. Reportedly, Vaughan was trying to save his friend, who could not swim.[37]

- Appling was known (and loathed by opposing pitchers) for his knack for fouling off pitches to extend counts and eventually draw walks.[38]

- Boudreau starred as a playmaking guard in basketball at Thornton Township High School in the Chicago area. Then at the University of Illinois, he was an All-American in basketball and turned down a contract offer to play professionally.[39]

- Gordon was musically gifted and played violin with the Portland (OR) Symphony Orchestra at age 14.[40]

Beyond the Numbers (cont'd)

- Gordon was the first Indians player to reach out and welcome the AL's first African American, Larry Doby, who signed in 1947.

- Gordon had a mixed record as a manager with the Indians, Tigers, Athletics, and Royals. His most successful and strangest managerial stint was with the Indians under GM Frankie "Trader" Lane in 1958-60. Gordon could not stand Lane's constant meddling as he managed the Indians to a close second place finish in 1959 and announced that he would not return to manage the Indians in 1960. Lane moved to fire him but relented in the face of hundreds of telegrams demanding Gordon's reinstatement. Lane did fire him four days later after the White Sox clinched the pennant., but at a news conference the next day, he announced Gordon's successor – none other than Gordon himself. Then, in 1960, Lane and Tiger GM Bill DeWitt traded managers – Joe Gordon for Jimmy Dykes – the only trade of its kind in baseball history. And if that wasn't enough, when Gordon left the Tigers after the season to manage the Kansas City Athletics under new owner Charley Finley, who should turn up as the new KC general manager, like a bad horror movie, but Frankie Lane again! Unsurprisingly, that arrangement did not survive the 1961 season.[41]

- The toxic atmosphere in the Red Sox clubhouse during Cronin's tenure as player-manager may have cost him a few WAR. For example, when Wes Ferrell refused to pitch until the Red Sox pitcher warming up in the bullpen sat down, Cronin fined him $1000, earning a threat from Ferrell to punch him in the jaw.[42] Ownership failed to enforce the fine.

- When Cronin was promoted to replace Eddie Collins as Red Sox general manager in 1947, he hired Joe McCarthy as his manager and immediately traded for SS Vern Stephens and RP Ellis Kinder to solidify the Sox as contenders. However, the Sox narrowly lost out to the Indians and Yankees in 1948 and 1949 and declined thereafter. Cronin continued his predecessor's policy of not signing black players, famously passing on Willie Mays in 1949. No African American ever wore a Red Sox uniform during Cronin's tenure.[43]

- As AL president, Cronin oversaw the expansion of the AL to 12 teams, the introduction of the DH rule, and the hiring of the first African American umpire, Emmett Ashford. Ashford praised Cronin, saying "Jackie Robinson had his Branch Rickey; I had my Joe Cronin."[44] Perhaps Cronin was just following team policy when he did not integrate the Red Sox, but in any case, this helped even the score.

Masters of Deception

Carl Hubbell (SP):
75.7 CVI – New York NL (68.2)

Stan Coveleski (SP):
74.2 CVI – Cleveland AL (53.0),
Washington AL (9.1)

Red Faber (SP):
70.4 CVI – Chicago AL (60.4)

Hubbell, Coveleski, and Faber relied heavily on deception rather than power to carve out HOF-caliber careers. Hubbell relied on his devastating screwball, a descendant of Christy Mathewson's fadeaway pitch of the preceding generation. Coveleski and Faber were among the 17 spitball pitchers who were grandfathered when the pitch was outlawed in 1920. While Hubbell had almost half as many SO as hits allowed (still well below Feller, Newhouser, and Vance), neither of the two spitballers had more than 0.36 SO/H.

"King Carl" Hubbell was the NL's best pitcher of the mid-1930s. From 1932-36, he compiled a 111-53 W-L with a 2.40 ERA (154 ERA+) and 1.065 WHIP and 37.4 WAR_p and won MVP awards in 1933 and 1936. In his first MVP year, 1933, Hubbell posted 10 shutouts en route to 23 wins, a 1.66 ERA, and 9.0 WAR_p. He then outdid himself in 1936, with a 26-6 record and 9.7 WAR_p. His most memorable achievement came in his second of nine All-Star games in 1934, when he struck out Ruth, Gehrig, Foxx, Simmons, and Cronin consecutively and finished with three shutout innings. He also won three ERA titles and was the ace of three pennant winners in 1933 and 1936-37 and a World Series champion in 1933. He pitched brilliantly in six postseason starts, including two complete game shutout victories in Games 1 and 4 of the 1933 World Series. His 75.7 CVI ranks 39th among SP and at the 0.66 percentile overall.

Stan Coveleski relied on his spitball and pinpoint control to keep hitters off balance. Connie Mack buried him in the minors, where he won 127 games in seven seasons, until the Indians rescued him in 1916.[45] Then from 1917-22 in Cleveland, he averaged 22-13 and 7.8 WAR_p with a 2.56 ERA (139 ERA+) and 1.170 WHIP, but only 111 SO in 300 IP. Although his peak WAR_p (9.9) came in 1918, Coveleski is best remembered for his 8.7-WAR_p 24-W 1920 season as the ace of the Indians team that won its first AL pennant and defeated Brooklyn 5-2 in the World Series. Coveleski won Games 1, 4, and 7 (all complete games) of that World Series, giving up only 2 ER, 15 hits, and 2 BB in 27 IP. After declining in 1923-24, he had a last hurrah for the Washington Senators, helping them win their second consecutive pennant. Coveleski's 74.2 CVI ranks 41st among SP and at the 0.70 percentile overall. He had to wait until he was 79 for the VC to put him in the HOF, but the honor was well deserved.

Red Faber injured his arm in the minor leagues and finally achieved success by mastering the spitball, which he threw from a variety of arm angles. He was a reliable but unspectacular workhorse pitcher for 17 of his 20 years in the major leagues, persevering through injury, World War I, a life-threatening bout of influenza, the Black Sox scandal, and years of laboring for mediocre White Sox teams.[46] His 25 wins in 1921 comprised a "Carltonesque" 40% of his team's 62 wins. Faber did pitch for some very good teams early in his career and won three games in the 1917 World Series, including the Series-clinching complete game 4-2 victory in Game 6. However, it was one brief outstanding stretch in 1920-22 at ages 31-33, in which he went 69-45 with a 2.76 ERA (145 ERA+) and 1.215 WHIP in 1001.2 IP and accrued 26.7 WAR_p—40% of his career total — that propelled him to the HOF. Faber's 70.4 CVI ranks 46th among SP and at the 0.83 percentile overall.

Beyond the Numbers

- Hubbell began his MLB career in Detroit, but manager Ty Cobb would not let him throw the screwball. Without his signature pitch, Hubbell lost confidence and effectiveness and languished in the minor leagues. Fortunately, John McGraw, perhaps remembering Mathewson, allowed Hubbell to use the pitch and flourish in New York.[47]

- Hubbell was the Giants' farm director from 1944-1977, moving with the team to San Francisco in 1958.

- Coveleski's older brother Harry was also a fine major league pitcher for nine years with the Phillies, Reds, and Tigers.

- After spending most of 1918 in wartime military service, Faber was a near victim of the deadly "Spanish Flu" pandemic in 1919. He missed the 1919 World Series, which was probably just as well.

The First Great Catchers

Bill Dickey (C):	**Gabby Hartnett (C):**
71.0 CVI – New York AL (57.3)	60.7 CVI – Chicago NL (55.9)

Dickey, Hartnett, and Cochrane (covered earlier) were MLB's first three CVI-Plus catchers and the first three catchers elected by the BBWAA to the HOF. Dickey and Hartnett were strong defenders (10.2 and 13.3 dWAR, respectively) and solid hitters (127 and 126 OPS+). Each was considered the best catcher in his league from 1933-38, winning 11/12 ASG selections during these six years. Dickey (who was eight years younger than Hartnett) went on to play in six more ASG in 1939-46 after Hartnett faded from the scene. However, Hartnett won an MVP in 1935, while Dickey finished no higher than second (to Foxx in 1938).

Although he played in the shadow of Ruth, Gehrig, and DiMaggio on teams that won eight pennants and seven World Series from 1929-43, Bill Dickey was outstanding in his own right. From 1929-39, he hit .320/.386/.510 (131 OPS+) in 499 PA and 122 games per season, while averaging 16 HR and 91 RBI. He played in 11 ASG (including the first one in 1933) and finished in the top 10 in the MVP voting four times. His .313 AVG ranks second among catchers; he also ranks fourth in 3B, fifth in OBP, and sixth in SLG. Dickey's 71.0 CVI ranks seventh among catchers and at the 0.80 percentile overall.

With no Ruth, Gehrig, or DiMaggio to overshadow him, Hartnett was a big fish in a smaller pond during his 19 years in Wrigley Field. His

Gabby Hartnett, 1933

Cubs won four pennants but lost all four World Series decisively. Hartnett's iconic moment was his late September "Homer in the Gloaming" that capped the Cubs' unlikely comeback from seven games down to overtake the Pirates for the 1938 pennant. His 236 HR set the standard for catchers at the time but has since been surpassed by 15 others. However, his .489 SLG still ranks fourth, behind only Piazza, Campanella, and Javy Lopez. His 60.7 CVI ranks him at the 1.19 percentile overall – just below my dividing line between the HOF and the HOVG. However, as the 13th best catcher, he's close enough for me.

Beyond the Numbers

- Dickey took over for Joe McCarthy as Yankee manager in 1946 and rallied the team to finish third but did not return in 1947. However, he returned as a coach under Casey Stengel from 1949-59 and mentored Yogi Berra and (later) Elston Howard on the fine points of catching.[48]

- Like Forrest Gump, Hartnett was at the scene of three of baseball's iconic moments. He was behind the plate for Babe Ruth's called-shot HR in the 1932 World Series, for Carl Hubbell's five consecutive strikeouts in the 1934 ASG, and for Earl Averill's line drive in the 1937 ASG that broke Dizzy Dean's shin and derailed his career.[49]

Out of Control

Wes Ferrell (SP):
69.6 CVI – Cleveland AL (36.1), Boston AL (23.1)

Wes Ferrell had the proverbial million-dollar arm and 10-cent head. His 60.0 career WAR and 69.6 CVI have garnered little HOF support. His 4.04 lifetime ERA is higher than that of any pitcher in the HOF, but his 116 ERA+ indicates that his ERA was 16% better than the inflated league-average ERA of the 1930s. His relatively brief eight-year career peak contained two 8-WAR_p seasons (1930 and 1935) and four other 6-WAR_p seasons. He played in two ASG. His 9.4 WAR (8.3 WAR_p) in 1930 and his 8.0 WAR (6.2 WAR_p) in 1931 each ranked fourth in the major leagues (behind only Ruth, Gehrig and Lefty Grove), and his 7.2 WAR (6.9 WAR_p) in 1932 was third among AL pitchers, behind only Grove and Ruffing. Ferrell's ERAs in those three years, 3.31, 3.75, and 3.66 were not particularly impressive, except in the context that the major league ERA was 4.81, 4.12, and 4.18 in 1930-32. So his ERA+ was a more than respectable 133. After a sore arm and declining effectiveness led to a trade to the Red Sox, Ferrell came back to produce 10.6 WAR in 1935 (tops in MLB), when he finished second to Hank Greenberg in the AL MVP vote, and 7.7 WAR in 1936 (tied for fourth with Mel Ott behind Grove, Hubbell, and Gehrig).

On the downside, Ferrell was a hothead and a troublemaker, whose rages detracted from his performance and poisoned his clubhouse.[49] In one game in 1934, when his manager tried to remove him after he had nearly blown a 10-1 lead in the third inning, he refused at first to leave the game and then punched himself in the jaw and banged his head against the wall once he reached the dugout. Twice within a five-day period in 1936 he pulled himself out of a game in anger over errors made by his teammates, and he threatened manager Joe Cronin physically when he suspended him. It is perhaps no accident that Ferrell never played for a winning team. He may have been a HOF-caliber pitcher, but how can anyone be a Hall of Famer when he may have been a net detriment to his own team?

Beyond the Numbers

- The ingredient that elevated Ferrell's CVI to HOF territory was his bat. He hit .280/.351/.446 (100 OPS+) in 1344 PA, adding 38 HR with 175 R and 208 RBI over the course of his 15-year career. By contrast, his brother Rick, a dubiously qualified HOF catcher hit .281/.378/.363 (95 OPS+) with only 28 HR and 29.8 WAR. Without his 11.1 WAR_H, Wes Ferrell's CVI would have been 60.7.

Perseverance

Ted Lyons (SP):	Red Ruffing (SP):
67.6 CVI – Chicago AL (70.4)	62.81 CVI – New York AL (56.8), Boston AL (9.8 12.6)

Ruffing and Lyons had the two highest career ERAs in the Hall of Fame until Jack Morris was inducted in 2018, but Lyons's 119 ERA+ indicates that he at least was well above league average. Ruffing has a more complicated story. Both fall in the "near great" category of Hall of Famers with CVI at the 0.96 and 1.14 percentile, respectively.

The affable, soft-tossing Ted Lyons, who loved to tell tall tales that mixed self-deprecating humor with Bunyanesque exaggeration of his hitting prowess, toiled bravely for 26 years (1923-48) as a pitcher, then manager for a hapless White Sox team. After struggling in 1923-24, Lyons emerged as one of the AL's top pitchers in 1925-27, compiling a 3.02 ERA (133 ERA+) and 1.275 WHIP (well under the league average) in 854 IP, with 73 CG, 61 W (including a 1926 no-hitter), and 18.3 WAR$_P$ over three seasons. After nearly 300 IP and 22 W in 1930, Lyons developed shoulder troubles and added the knuckleball to his repertoire. Then, in 1934, when Sox manager Jimmy Dykes cut back his workload to one start per week, usually in Sunday doubleheaders, Lyons thrived for the next eight years as "Sunday Ted" but never again exceeded 4.9 WAR$_P$.[51] After serving for three years as a military fitness instructor, Lyons returned in 1946 to pick up his 260th win and extend his string of complete games (starting in 1941) to 28.

In 1930, Red Ruffing was 25 years old, and after more than five years with the perennial cellar-dwelling Red Sox, his career was going nowhere. His career W-L was a horrific 39-96 after he lost 25 games in 1928, 22 in 1929, and his first three decisions in 1930, and it wasn't just bad luck. Even in a high-scoring era, his 4.57 ERA (92 ERA+) and 1.50 WHIP were poor, he walked more men than he struck out, and he yielded 1194 hits in 1098.1 IP. About all he was good for was eating innings and pinch hitting. In fact his hitting was so good and his pitching so bad that the Sox considered moving him to the OF. But an early-season trade to the Yankees in 1930 turned his career around and put him on an unlikely path to Cooperstown. The contrast is stark:

Table 5.2: Red Ruffing's Stats Before and After His Trade to the Yankees

Years	ERA/WHIP	ERA+	W-L	SHO	CG	IP	SO	BB	WAR$_P$	WAR$_H$
1924-30*	4.61/1.501	92	39-96	5	73	1122.3	450	459	9.8	2.8
1930-46	3.47/1.282	119	231-124	40	261	3168.7	1526	1066	46.5	10.4

*Includes first three games of 1930 (before trade to the Yankees)

When Ruffing was traded to the Yankees in 1930, he suddenly had a good defense behind him and powerful offensive support. Although his W-L improved immediately, he did not emerge as a star until 1932, when he co-anchored the Yankee pitching staff that seized the AL pennant back from Connie Mack's A's.

After three middling years in 1933-35, Ruffing and the Yankees returned to prominence with four consecutive World Series Championships. Ruffing was their go-to guy, averaging 20-8 with a 3.29 ERA (137 ERA+) and 1.278 WHIP, compiling 19.7 WAR_P, and winning all four of his starts in the 1937-39 World Series. He was 7-2 overall with a 2.63 ERA and 1.179 WHIP in seven World Series. Ruffing also contributed to Yankee pennants in 1941-42 and to their victory over Brooklyn in the 1941 World Series. Ruffing was among MLB's best hitting pitchers. His CVI would have been only 52.2 without his 13.2 WAR_H. His 36 HR are one shy of Wes Ferrell's record. Ruffing enlisted in the military at age 38 (despite having lost four toes in a mining accident at age 11) and returned to MLB in 1945, but a line drive shattered his kneecap and ended his comeback in 1947.[52]

Beyond the Numbers

- Although Lyons never threw hard, even in his heyday, he was one of the strongest men in the game, who used to arm wrestle regularly with Lou Gehrig. Lyons claimed that he was the first to notice that something was wrong with Gehrig when he began to beat him too easily in 1938, a year before ALS ended Gehrig's career.[53]

- The Yankees' storied history features many of MLB's most luminous hitting stars but is short of elite pitchers. Ruffing's 56.9 career WAR as a Yankee is second only to Whitey Ford (57.1).

Hall of the Very Good

George Uhle (SP):
56.0 CVI – Cleveland AL (*38.0*), Detroit AL (*19.3*)

Urban Shocker (SP):
54.4 CVI – St. Louis AL (*41.3*), New York AL (*17.5*)

Burleigh Grimes (SP):
53.4 CVI – Brooklyn NL (*32.6*), Pittsburgh NL (*12.4*), St. Louis NL (*6.9*)

Bucky Walters (SP):
53.2 CVI – Cincinnati NL (*43.8*), Philadelphia NL (*10.0*)

Bobo Newsom (SP):
53.0 CVI – Detroit AL (*16.3*), St. Louis AL (*10.2*), Philadelphia AL (*7.4*), Washington AL (*7.4*)

These five pitchers, whose CVI rank between 208th and 235th on the list of HOF-eligible players, were barely candidates for the HOVG, let alone the Hall of Fame. Although Grimes, who was eventually elected by the VC, received 34% of the BBWAA votes in 1960 and finished fourth in the voting, none of the others ever received as much as 25% of the BBWAA votes or finished in the top 10 candidates.

Uhle had only one outstanding 8.9-WAR_p, 27-win season (1926) in a solid but otherwise unremarkable 17-year career. His claim to fame is that he is said to have invented the slider (in 1930).[54] Uhle was also quite a good hitter, with a lifetime .289 AVG – the highest of any post-1900 pitcher with at least 1000 AB. However, his 10.5 WAR_H is well below Red Ruffing (13.2), Walter Johnson (12.7), and Wes Ferrell (11.1), who had far more power. Uhle never received more than 1.5% of the BBWAA HOF vote.

Spitballer Urban Shocker had his best years with the St. Louis Browns in 1920-23, when he averaged 23-13 with a 3.18 ERA (132 ERA+) and a 1.242 WHIP. The aftermath of a broken finger suffered in 1913 forced Shocker to grip the ball in a way that imparted maximum spin and enhanced his effectiveness.[55] He had an uncanny knack for beating the Yankees, his original team, who had traded him to St. Louis in 1917. He is probably best remembered as one of the two left-handed aces (18-6, 2.84 ERA) of the legendary 1927 Yankees, who had reacquired him in 1925. Less than a year later, he died of congestive heart failure and pneumonia, likely caused by rheumatic heart disease. Like Uhle, he never received more than 1.5% of the BBWAA HOF vote.

Grimes, who is best remembered as the last of the legal spitballers, had an unimpressive 108 ERA+ in 19 years and has little to recommend him for the HOF other than his 270 career wins. He was one of six players the VC elected to the HOF in 1964 and owes his election more to the VC's generosity in the 1960s than to merit.

As the co-ace of back-to-back Cincinnati pennant winners in 1939-40, Walters' credentials are more impressive than the others in this grouping, but his relatively modest win total (198) probably doomed his candidacy. His BBWAA support peaked at 23.7% in 1968.

Bobo Newsom, who never received more than 9.4% of the BBWAA vote, is an unlikely player to find even at the bottom of the CVI-Plus list – especially given his mediocre 3.98 ERA (107 ERA+) and 1.464 WHIP over his 20-year MLB career. He got there mainly by virtue of a two-year run 15.6 WAR_p run as the second best pitcher in the AL (behind Feller) in 1939-40, in which he went 41-16 with a 3.22 ERA (149 ERA+) and 1.319 WHIP. He also added seven other above average seasons with 3.0-6.1 WAR_p to counterbalance the mediocrity of his 11 other MLB seasons.

It is interesting to compare the WAR trajectories of Newsom (who barely made the cut for CVI-Plus) and Dizzy Dean, the ex-Cardinal ace and one of MLB's most

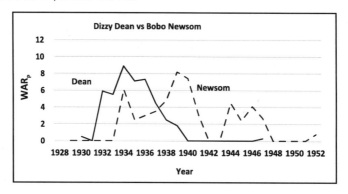

colorful stars of the 1930s (who barely missed the cut). Although Dean was elected to the HOF by the BBWAA in his 11th try despite his injury-shortened 150-win career while Newsom never came close, the two had essentially equivalent careers. But the truth is that neither had statistical records worthy of the HOF. We should be debating the HOF candidacies of superior players like Stieb (63.6 CVI) versus Early Wynn (60.6 CVI), who rank 168th and 180th among HOF-eligible players, not players like Newsom and Dean with the 235th versus the 238th best CVI.

Other Hall of Famers

As in Chapters 3-4, I will provide capsule comments here on the 28 CVI-Minus Hall of Famers (22 hitters and six pitchers) from the Classical Generation listed in Table 5.3 on the next page. This table contains far more players than comparable lists for other generations, thanks to the profligate activity of the VC in 1964-76. The list partly reflects cronyism and partly reflects the statistical illusion that players who hit for a 300+ AVG with no power in an era when the MLB-wide AVG hovered between .275 and .300 were superior to players of the 1950s and 1960s who hit .275-.300 with power in an era when the MLB-wide AVG ranged between .240 and .260.

Three of the players – **Dean**, **Pennock** and **Traynor** – were elected by the BBWAA. One could make a case for **Dean**, the Cardinal icon who averaged 24-13 with a 3.04 ERA (130 ERA+) and 1.210 WHIP and compiled 34.8 WAR_p from 1932-36, before suffering a broken shin in the 1937 All-Star Game that caused him to alter his delivery and sunk his career. It is harder to justify the election of **Pennock** or **Traynor**. **Pennock**'s 51.2 CVI is not that far below **Dean**'s, but he had only a 106 ERA+ (versus 131 for **Dean**) and did not suffer the misfortune of a career-shattering injury. Modern metrics suggest that **Traynor**, whose CVI lies outside the top 2%, was overrated as a defensive 3B (2.0 dWAR) and that his offensive stats were inflated by the high-octane offensive environment of his era. Perhaps, the BBWAA felt pressured to place a 3B in the HOF to keep Jimmy Collins company.

Table 5.3: CVI-Minus Hall of Famers

A) Players (Position)	MidCareer	HOF	AVG/OBP/SLG	OPS+	WAR$_{II}$	CVI
Averill, Earl (CF)	1934	VC	.318/.395/.534	133	51.1	50.4
Doerr, Bobby (2B)	1946	VC	.288/.362/.461	115	51.1	49.7
Klein, Chuck (RF)	1932	VC	.320/.379/.543	137	46.0	49.6
Sewell, Joe (SS)	1926	VC	.312/.391/.413	108	53.9	49.5
Bancroft, Dave (SS)	1921	VC	.279/.355/.358	98	49.1	48.5
Rice, Sam (RF)	1924	VC	.322/.374/.427	112	53.4	45.7
Lazzeri, Tony (2B)	1930	VC	.292/.380/.467	121	47.3	44.2
Manush, Heinie (LF)	1929	VC	.330/.377/.479	121	47.2	43.8
Cuyler, Kiki (RF)	1929	VC	.321/.386/.474	125	47.0	43.2
Wilson, Hack (CF)	1929	VC	.307/.395/.545	144	38.2	39.6
Combs, Earle (CF)	1929	VC	.325/.397/.462	125	43.9	39.0
Jackson, Travis (SS)	1929	VC	.291/.337/.433	102	43.7	38.9
Roush, Edd (CF)	1920	VC	.323/.369/.446	126	45.1	38.2
Lombardi, Ernie (C)	1938	VC	.306/.358/.460	126	39.5	36.1
Traynor, Pie (3B)	1928	BBWAA	.320/.362/.435	107	37.3	31.0
Bottomley, Jim (1B)	1927	VC	.310/.369/.500	125	35.0	30.6
Youngs, Ross (RF)	1921	VC	.322/.399/.441	130	32.3	29.8
Lindstrom, Freddie (3B)	1929	VC	.311/.351/.449	110	27.5	26.2
Ferrell, Rick (C)	1935	VC	.281/.278/.363	95	31.1	26.2
Hafey, Chick (LF)	1930	VC	.317/.372/.526	133	31.1	25.4
Waner, Lloyd (CF)	1932	VC	.316/.353/.393	99	27.9	23.4
Kelly, High Pockets (1B)	1924	VC	.297/.342/.452	109	24.9	22.5

B) Pitchers	MidCareer	HOF	ERA/WHIP	ERA+	WAR$_P$	CVI
Dean, Dizzy (SP)	1935	BBWAA	3.02/1.206	131	43.9	52.6
Rixey, Eppa (SP)	1923	VC	3.15/1.272	115	57.4	52.1
Pennock, Herb (SP)	1924	BBWAA	3.60/1.348	106	44.9	51.2
Gomez, Lefty (SP)	1935	VC	3.34/1.352	125	43.2	49.2
Hoyt, Waite (SP)	1927	VC	3.59/1.340	112	54.2	46.3
Haines, Jesse (SP)	1927	VC	3.64/1.350	109	35.7	29.1

The other 25 Hall of Famers in Table 5.3 were all active after 1925 but were elected by the VC despite failing in the BBWAA voting. Thirteen of them (**Doerr, Gomez, Bancroft, Hoyt, Manush, Jackson, Bottomley, Youngs, Lindstrom, Hafey, Haines, Kelly,** and **Waner**) benefited from having one or more ex-teammates as advocates on the VC. Frankie Frisch (5), Bill Terry (4), and Waite Hoyt (3) were the biggest offenders.[56]

While I would not regard any of these players as worthy Hall of Famers, **Doerr, Gomez, Bancroft,** and **Jackson** were not horrible selections. **Doerr** was a good (but not great) offensive and defensive 2B (13.5 dWAR), whose career ended early (age 33) due to back problems; he might otherwise have finished with a CVI in the upper 50s. Seven-time All-Star **Lefty Gomez** also had physical issues but had a 125 ERA+ when he was healthy and was the co-ace of some great Yankee teams. He was also one of baseball's most memorable and quotable characters. **Bancroft** (23.5 dWAR, 16th among SS) and **Jackson** (22.9 dWAR, tied for 20th among SS) were excellent defensive SS (not quite as good as Tinker or Maranville) and league-average hitters. **Youngs** is a special case, since he was on track for a CVI-Plus career before he was

Chuck Klein, 1936

stricken with Bright's Disease (nephritis) at age 28 and died two years later. But the rest of these picks are indefensible.

The most deserving of the 12 players in Table 5.3 who made it to the HOF without a little help from their friends are **Klein** and **Wilson,** two defensively-challenged sluggers who terrorized NL pitchers circa 1930. **Klein** hit .340/.397/.594 with 246 HR and 950 RBI in 1929-36 before fading. **Wilson,** who played with Frisch in New York but was not elected to the HOF until five years after Frisch's death, set the NL HR record with 56 in 1930, and his 191 RBI that year is still an MLB record. Wilson hit .331/.419/.612 with 177 HR and 708 RBI in 1926-30, before losing his battle with the bottle.

High-AVG hitters **Sewell, Lazzeri, Averill, Lombardi, Rice, Cuyler, Combs,** and **Roush** (like Traynor) all benefited from the stats inflation of the 1920s and 1930s, when a .300 AVG was cheap. **Rick Ferrell** was an odd HOF selection. He was a good but not great defensive catcher (9.4 dWAR), and his 95 OPS+ was outstripped by his brother Wes (100 OPS+). And Wes could pitch.

Bottom of the Pile

It is pretty crowded at the bottom of the Classical Era pile, but I have awarded this dubious distinction to the "Frankie Frisch Wing" of the HOF, which includes three of his ex-teammates – **Chick Hafey, Jesse Haines,** and **High Pockets Kelly** – and another player – **Lloyd Waner** – who played for him when he managed the

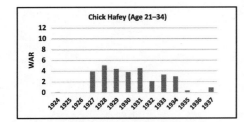

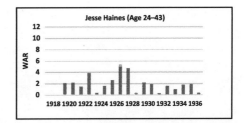

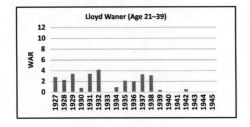

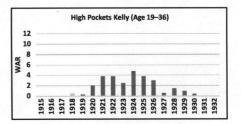

Pirates. All were elected to the HOF during Frisch's tenure (1967-72) on the VC, despite their shocking lack of HOF credentials (CVI <30).

Haines and **Hafey**, members of the St. Louis Gashouse Gang, were good but not great players. **Haines's** 35.7 WAR_P was exceeded by 208 pitchers; Mark Gubicza (37.4) and Jake Peavy (37.2) are recent examples. **Hafey's** 31.1 WAR_H was exceeded by 522 hitters; Shane Victorino (31.5) is a recent example.

Lloyd Waner and **High Pockets Kelly** were even worse selections. Neither had even a single 5-WAR season. **Waner's** 27.9 WAR_H was exceeded by 609 hitters (including Denard Span's 28.1), and **Kelly's** 24.9 WAR_H was exceeded by 712 hitters (including John Kruk's 25.1). **Waner** was an extreme contact hitter, whose 7.8 3TO% was the lowest of any major league hitter with at least 7500 PA. His WAR never exceeded 3.6 in any season, and his 99 OPS+ was mediocre. His empty .316 lifetime AVG (accompanied by a meager .077 ISO) was entirely due to stats inflation. Although he played until 1945, he made only one ASG appearance. Some may have conflated him with his older brother, but Paul's .333 lifetime AVG came with a respectable .140 ISO, a 134 OPS+, and four ASG selections. **Lloyd Waner** (-2.1 dWAR) wasn't even a strong defensive OF, although he was better than Paul (-9.6 dWAR). **Kelly** didn't even have a famous brother or a .300 AVG, and his 148 career HR and .452 SLG were meager for a 1B.

CHAPTER 6

THE BOOM GENERATION (1947-1972)

The Game

April 15, 1947, the date when Jackie Robinson took his position at 1B in Ebbets Field, was a watershed moment in baseball history. The informal Color Line (Chapter 3) had been in place since 1889, enforced by a "gentlemen's agreement" among team owners, with the tacit support of league presidents and Commissioner Kenesaw Mountain Landis.[1] The lack of an explicit policy enabled Landis to proclaim disingenuously, "There is no rule, formal or informal, or any understanding — unwritten, subterranean, or sub-anything — against the hiring of Negro players by the teams of organized ball."[2] Although baseball maverick Bill Veeck's allegation that Landis scuttled his attempt to purchase and integrate the Phillies in 1943 was probably exaggerated, Landis clearly did not use his power to promote integration during his nearly 25 years in office.[3]

Integration of MLB gained traction only after Landis died in November 1944 and was succeeded by former Kentucky Senator Albert "Happy" Chandler, who proclaimed that "if they (Negroes) can fight and die in Okinawa, Guadalcanal, and in the south Pacific, they can play baseball in America."[4] When Brooklyn Dodger GM Branch Rickey signed Jackie Robinson in 1946 and promoted him to Brooklyn in 1947, integration of MLB finally became a reality.[5,6]

Integration began slowly. Only five of MLB's 16 teams had integrated by 1950, led by Branch Rickey's Dodgers (Jackie Robinson, Dan Bankhead, Roy Campanella, Don Newcombe) and Bill Veeck's Indians (Larry Doby, Satchel Paige, Minnie Minoso, and Luke Easter).[7] Although the Dodgers entered the new era full bore, building a contending team around African American stars, other teams either dragged their feet or signed aging Negro League legends to boost gate receipts. Most teams did nothing at all. Three of the 12 Black players (Campanella, Doby, and Robinson) who reached MLB by 1950 are in the HOF based on their MLB careers. Three others – Willard Brown (Browns), Monte Irvin (Giants), and Paige – were elected to the HOF based on their Negro League careers. The two other pre-1950 black players were Hank Thompson (Browns and Giants) and Sam Jethro (Braves).

At first, most black players continued to play in the Negro Leagues. However, the success of the Dodgers on the field and at the gate inspired imitators. Starting in 1951 with Willie Mays and continuing with Henry Aaron, Ernie Banks, Roberto Clemente, Frank Robinson, etc., MLB began bringing in young relatively unknown black players with the potential to grow into superstars. By 1959, all 16 teams were integrated. By 1973, 17.4 % of players, including many of the biggest stars, were African Americans.[8] On September 1, 1971, just over 24 years after Jackie Robinson broke the color barrier, the Pittsburgh Pirates fielded MLB's first all-minority lineup: 2B Rennie Stennett, CF Gene Clines, RF Roberto Clemente,

Jackie Robinson, 1945

LF Willie Stargell, C Manny Sanguillen, 3B Dave Cash, 1B Al Oliver, SS Jackie Hernandez, SP Dock Ellis.[9] What would have been shocking in the 1940s and 1950s had become so commonplace that it was barely noticed.

The Boom Era was characterized not only by tapping into a rich new talent pool of players of color but also by unprecedented growth, fueled by the post-War economic boom and the advent of television. MLB, which had been confined to one race and 10 metropolitan areas in the northeast quadrant of the US, burst from these confines to Milwaukee, Baltimore, Kansas City, Los Angeles, San Francisco, Minneapolis, Houston, Atlanta, Montreal, San Diego, Seattle (briefly), and Dallas. The first expansion in 1961-62 arose from an abortive attempt by Branch Rickey and several other prominent sports executives (Jack Kent Cooke, Bob Howsam) to establish a new league, to be called the Continental League.[10] The AL and NL preempted them by expanding to three of the eight cities that would have received Continental League franchises (Houston, Minneapolis, and New York) and adding a second franchise in Los Angeles. By 1969, the number of teams had expanded by 50% from 16 to 24, and baseball had a strong foothold on the west coast and in the south, with an outpost in Canada. MLB's postseason also expanded from two to four teams in 1969.

As MLB teams grew more prosperous, players began demanding a larger share of the pie. While the best players of the 1960s could pull down $100,000 in their primes, most players were paid more modestly and worked off-season jobs to supplement their salaries. The MLPBA was formally certified as a Union in 1966, and Marvin Miller, a seasoned negotiator from US Steel, was appointed as Executive Director.[11] Three years later, St. Louis CF Curt Flood refused to report to Philadelphia when he was traded for Dick Allen after the 1969 season and sued MLB, claiming infringement on his right to decide where he worked. Although the US Supreme Court ruled 5-3 against Flood in 1972, this was the opening shot in what was to become a revolution.[12] As the Boom Era drew to an end in 1972, the MLPBA staged its first in-season strike; it lasted 14 days and won them the right to binding arbitration in salary disputes.[13]

After a lull during World War II, baseball in the Boom Era built on the longball paradigm of the Classical Era with increasing emphasis on 3TO. Mickey Mantle (1951-68) dethroned Babe Ruth as the all-time 3TO king with 3TO in 40.3% of PA, and Sam McDowell (1961-75) dethroned Bob Feller with 3TO in 37.7% of BF. After falling during the Classical Era, strikeout rates began to rise in the 1950s, and leaguewide 3TO rates climbed to 27% by 1970. The ratio of strikeouts per hit (SO/H) is a useful inverse index of the frequency of effective contact. MLB-wide SO/H climbed as high as 0.48 in 1909 at the height of the Deadball Era, then fell below 0.3 through the 1920s, before starting to inch up in the 1930s. It finally approached 0.4 in the early 1940s and took off after the War, reaching 0.5 in 1955, 0.6 in 1962, and 0.7 in 1967, before settling back at 0.68 in 1972 as the Boom Era drew to a close. The strikeout kings at the end of the Boom Era were Willie Stargell (1962-82) with 0.867 SO/H (leaving Jimmy Foxx's 0.495 SO/H in the dust) and Sandy Koufax with 1.366 SO/H (surpassing the venerable Rube Waddell's 0.941 SO/H).

Despite the continued advance of the longball style of baseball, some neglected elements of smallball that had fallen out of favor in MLB but were popular in the Negro Leagues — aggressive baserunning and stealing bases (as exemplified by Maury Wills' 104 SB in 1962) — re-emerged in MLB in the Boom Era.[14] The concomitant infusion of Latino talent, particularly speedy acrobatic middle infielders like Luis Aparicio, also infused new panache.

Scoring remained steady from 1947-62, hovering mostly between 4.0 and 4.6 runs/team/game, but began to decline precipitously starting in 1962, reaching a nadir in 1968, dubbed the "Year of the Pitcher" (Figure 6.1).[15] Scoring dropped more than a run per team per game from 4.5 in 3.4 in 1961-68, reaching its lowest level since 1908. This was mirrored by a 25% rise in SO/H from 0.60 to 0.75 (Figure 6.2), a drop in the MLB slash line from .258/.328/.399 to .237/.299/.344, and a fall in HR per team per game from 0.95 to 0.61. In 1968, Carl Yastrzemski's .301 AVG led the AL, the lowest AVG ever to win a batting title.

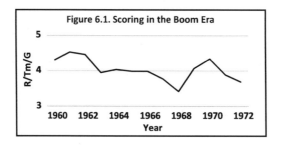

The reasons behind this offensive "mini ice age" are many, but one may have derived from the spate of dominant hard-throwing pitchers (Koufax, Gibson, McDowell) who replaced the finesse pitchers (Spahn, Roberts, Wynn, Ford) of the 1950s. Alarmed by the hitting drought, baseball reacted by lowering the height of the pitcher's mound and contracting the vertical dimension of the strike zone in 1969. These changes, along with a four-team expansion that year, produced a brief rebound in offense in 1969-70, but then scoring fell off again in 1971-72, setting the stage for implementation of the designated hitter rule in 1973. Whatever caused this downturn, one must judge the offensive stats of players who peaked in 1963-68 more leniently (and pitching stats more skeptically) than those of players who peaked in 1920-62 and after 1972.

The dominant team of 1947-64 was the Yankees (who else?), who won 15 of 18 AL pennants, interrupted only by the Indians (1948 and 1954) and White Sox (1959), and 10 World Series before finally crashing and burning in 1965. During the decade-long respite from Yankee dominance in 1965-75, the Orioles and Athletics ruled in the AL, with cameos by the Twins, Tigers, and Red Sox. The Dodgers were by far the most successful NL team of this era with eight pennants and four World Series championships, followed by the Cardinals (three pennants and two World Series championships) and the Giants (three pennants and one World Series championship). The Braves, Pirates, Reds, and Mets also won championships.

The Players

The Boom Generation included 51 CVI-Plus players – 36 hitters and 15 pitchers (Table 6.1). Of the 39 players with CVI ≥62, all but five (Allen, Bando, Boyer, Tiant, and Wood) are in the HOF; Joe Torre was elected as a manager. Five of the 12 CVI-Plus players with CVI <62 are also in the HOF. As in Chapters 3-5, the careers and HOF credentials of these players, partitioned into thematic groupings, are presented below.

Table 6.1: CVI-Plus Players

A) Hitters (Position)	MidCareer	HOF	AVG/OBP/SLG	OPS+	WAR$_{II}$	CVI
Mays, Willie (CF)	1962	BBWAA	.302/.384/.557	156	156.2	232.3
Williams, Ted (LF)	1948	BBWAA	.344/.482/.634	190	121.9	199.5
Aaron, Henry (RF)	1963	BBWAA	.305/.374/.555	155	143.1	187.5
Musial, Stan (LF)	1950	BBWAA	.331/.417/.559	159	128.3	178.1
Mantle, Mickey (CF)	1958	BBWAA	.298/.421/.557	172	110.2	143.0
Robinson, Frank (RF)	1964	BBWAA	.294/.389/.537	154	107.2	118.8
Mathews, Eddie (3B)	1959	BBWAA	.271/.376/.509	143	96.2	116.7
Clemente, Roberto (RF)	1966	BBWAA	.317/.359/.475	130	94.8	110.9
Yastrzemski, Carl (LF)	1969	BBWAA	.285/.379/.462	130	96.4	110.8
Robinson, Jackie (2B)	1951	BBWAA	.311/.409/.474	132	61.7	106.8
Kaline, Al (RF)	1962	BBWAA	.297/.376/.480	134	92.8	99.0
Santo, Ron (3B)	1966	VC	.277/.362/.464	125	70.5	88.1
Banks, Ernie (SS)	1959	BBWAA	.274/.330/.500	122	67.8	83.8
Rose, Pete (LF)	1971	Banned	.303/.375/.409	118	79.7	83.6
Robinson, Brooks (3B)	1967	BBWAA	.267/.322/.401	104	78.4	82.2
Reese, Pee Wee (SS)	1949	VC	.269/.366/.377	99	68.2	78.3
Snider, Duke (CF)	1954	BBWAA	.295/.380/.540	140	66.0	76.8
Berra, Yogi (C)	1954	BBWAA	.285/.348/.482	125	59.5	74.1

(continued)

Table 6.1 (cont'd)

A) Hitters (Position)	MidCareer	HOF	AVG/OBP/SLG	OPS+	WAR$_H$	CVI
McCovey, Willie (1B)	1967	BBWAA	.270/.374/.515	147	64.5	69.4
Boyer, Ken (3B)	1960	No	.287/.349/.462	116	62.9	69.2
Ashburn, Richie (CF)	1954	VC	.308/.396/.382	111	64.6	67.4
Allen, Dick (1B)	1968	No	.292/.378/.534	156	58.8	66.5
Bando, Sal (3B)	1972	No	.254/.352/.408	119	61.5	65.1
Torre, Joe (C)	1967	MGE	.297/.365/.452	129	57.6	65.0
Campanella, Roy (C)	1951	BBWAA	.276/.360/.500	126	35.6	63.1
Slaughter, Enos (RF)	1947	VC	.300/.382/.453	124	57.0	62.8
Williams, Billy (LF)	1967	BBWAA	.290/.361/.492	133	63.7	62.7
Minoso, Minnie (LF)	1955	No	.298/.389/.459	130	50.2	60.5
Wynn, Jim (CF)	1969	No	.250/.366/.436	129	55.8	59.4
Davis, Willie (CF)	1969	No	.279/.311/.412	106	60.8	57.0
Killebrew, Harmon (1B)	1966	BBWAA	.256/.376/.509	143	60.4	56.3
Stargell, Willie (LF)	1971	BBWAA	.282/.360/.529	147	57.5	55.5
Kiner, Ralph (LF)	1949	BBWAA	.279/.398/.548	149	47.9	55.2
Pinson, Vada (CF)	1963	No	.327/.442/.769	111	54.2	54.1
Doby, Larry (CF)	1952	VC	.283/.386/.490	136	49.3	54.0
Freehan, Bill (C)	1969	No	.262/.340/.412	112	44.7	53.1

B) Pitchers	MidCareer	HOF	ERA/WHIP	ERA+	WAR$_P$	CVI
Spahn, Warren (SP)	1953	BBWAA	3.09/1.195	119	92.5	114.4
Gibson, Bob (SP)	1968	BBWAA	2.91/1.188	127	81.7	103.5
Perry, Gaylord (SP)	1972	BBWAA	3.11/1.181	117	93.0	100.7
Roberts, Robin (SP)	1954	BBWAA	3.41/1.170	113	83.0	100.1
Jenkins, Fergie (SP)	1972	BBWAA	3.34/1.142	115	82.2	86.2
Marichal, Juan (SP)	1965	BBWAA	2.89/1.101	123	61.8	76.1
Wood, Wilbur (SP)	1972	No	3.24/1.232	114	52.2	74.7
Wilhelm, Hoyt (RP)	1961	BBWAA	2.52/1.125	147	49.7	74.3
Bunning, Jim (SP)	1964	VC	3.27/1.179	115	60.4	73.1
Koufax, Sandy (SP)	1963	BBWAA	2.76/1.106	131	53.1	70.2
Drysdale, Don (SP)	1962	BBWAA	3.30/1.199	114	61.3	65.8
Tiant, Luis (SP)	1972	No	2.95/1.148	121	65.6	65.0
Wynn, Early (SP)	1954	BBWAA	3.54/1.329	107	51.5	60.6
McDaniel, Lindy (RP)	1965	No	3.45/1.272	110	29.0	56.1
Kaat, Jim (SP)	1970	No	3.45/1.259	108	45.2	53.3

What Greatness Looked Like

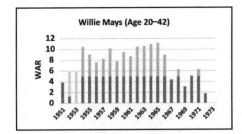

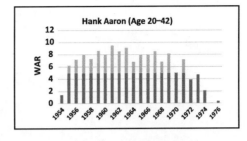

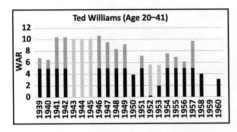

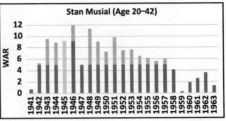

The Boom Era was blessed with four of the top ten players of all time, as ranked by CVI. Mays and Aaron epitomized the new wave of young Black stars who debuted in the early 1950s and were annual MVP contenders for more than a decade. Williams and Musial represented the best of the old guard who debuted before World War II and whose greatness – especially for Williams – was interrupted by wartime military service. Their CVI totals reflect the interpolation (light gray bars) for the seasons they missed.

The New Wave

Willie Mays (CF):
232.3 CVI – New York/San Francisco NL (*154.6*)

Henry Aaron (RF):
187.5 CVI – Milwaukee/Atlanta NL (*142.6*)

Frank Robinson (RF):
118.8 CVI – Cincinnati NL (*63.8*), Baltimore AL (*32.4*), California AL (*8.2*)

Roberto Clemente (RF):
110.9 CVI – Pittsburgh NL (*94.8*)

The arrival of Mays, Aaron, Robinson, and Clemente in 1951-56 brought a new level of excitement that MLB had not seen since Babe Ruth arrived in New York and began setting home run records. These elite and memorable stars (and others covered later) not only demonstrated that players of color belonged in MLB but re-introduced a level of speed, daring, and élan that had been largely missing since the Deadball days of Cobb et al. In addition to their exceptional talents, Mays and Clemente brought charisma and verve, Robinson brought competitive fire, and Aaron brought a quiet dignity to the game. Like Jackie Robinson, each had to endure racial taunts and discrimination on the way to the majors. But unlike Jackie Robinson, who had already reached baseball middle age by 1951, these four players arrived in MLB with their entire careers ahead of them and had ample time set the standards for those who followed. All four are elite Hall of Famers.

Willie Mays

The "Say Hey Kid" Willie Mays was a truly dazzling player, whose tough-guy ex-manager Leo Durocher wrote about him, "If somebody came up and hit .450 and stole 100 bases and performed a miracle in the field every day, I'd still look you right in the eye and tell you that Willie was better. He did the five things you have to do to be a superstar: hit, hit with power, run, throw, and field. And he had the other magic ingredient that turns a superstar into a super superstar, charisma. He lit up a room when he came in. He was a joy to be around."[16]

There is a good deal of truth amidst Leo's hyperbole. Although Ruth and Barry Bonds were both fine defensive OF, neither could match the speed and brilliant athleticism that Mays brought to the party. His back-to-the-plate catch of Vic Wertz's fly ball to the deepest part of the Polo Grounds at a full run in the Game 1 of the 1954 World Series, followed by a superhuman throw to prevent any runners from scoring and preserve a 2-2 tie is the stuff of legends and was the turning point of that 4-0 sweep over the heavily favored Indians.[17] Although Ruth, Bonds, and Ted Williams may have been superior pure hitters, even they never matched Mays's four-year stretch of 10+ seasonal WAR in 1962-1965. And these four seasons were only a fraction of 13 consecutive seasons (1954-66) with 7.6-11.2 WAR, bookended by MVP awards in 1954 and 1965, in which he led the NL in at least one major offensive category.

In 1965, Mays also joined Ruth, Foxx, Kiner, and Mickey Mantle as the fifth man to hit 50+ HR in more than one season. The ASG was Mays's personal playground; he played in 24 of them (including both ASG in 1959-62), batting .307 in 75 AB with 3 HR and 20 R, and sparking the NL to 18 victories. Mays played on four NL pennant winners – the 1951, 1954, and 1962 Giants and the 1973 Mets (when he was just a shadow of his former self); only the 1954 team won the World Series. Mays' 6066 TB ranks third behind only Aaron and Musial, and his 660 HR ranks fifth on the career leaderboard. CVI ranks Mays first in CF and second overall, behind Ruth. This is consistent with the outcome of a 1999 poll to choose baseball's top 100 players and the judgment of the BBWAA when they elected him to the HOF in 1979.

Hammerin' Hank Aaron never had a 10-WAR or a 50-HR season and was not known for spectacular catches or tape-measure HR. He stood only 6'0 and weighed only 180 pounds, but he could generate tremendous bat speed with his quick and powerful wrists. His WAR was consistently between 5.0 and 9.4 for 17 consecutive years (1955-1971). One could liken Aaron to an improved version of Mel Ott, himself one of the top 25 players of all-time. But to get from Ott's to Aaron's 17-year peak, one would have to add an extra 1.4 WAR, 28 H, 60 TB, 8 HR, 5 R, 8 RBI per year to Ott's totals, while adding .010 to his AVG and .033 to his SLG but ceding .039 in OBP.

In 1955-71, Aaron hit .315/.379/.574 (162 OPS+) and averaged 185 H, 337 TB, 37 HR, 108 R, 111 RBI, and 7.7 WAR. He won only one MVP award — for his contributions to the first and only Milwaukee Braves World Series championship in 1957— but neither that season nor his 9.5-WAR season in 1961 stand clearly above the rest. Indeed, Aaron's career highs in the various statistical categories were spread over multiple seasons – 132 RBI in 1957, 223 H, 46 2B, 400 TB, and a .355 AVG in 1959, 47 HR in 1971, 121 R in 1963, a .669 SLG and .410 OBP in 1971, and 92 BB in 1972. He had eight 40-HR seasons plus two 39-HR and a 38-HR season. but never struck out more than 96 times. Aaron played in 25 consecutive ASG in 21 years. Aaron's uninterrupted all-around excellence through age 39 was what put him in position to surpass Babe Ruth's long-standing career home run record where seemingly stronger men had failed. His dignity and quiet strength of character

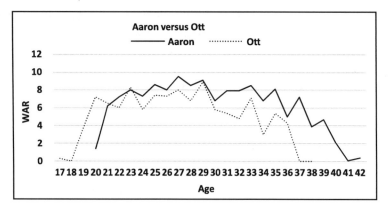

helped him persevere through a barrage of hate mail for daring to threaten Ruth's cherished record and to finally hit number 715 in April 1974 in Atlanta.

It is indicative of Aaron's innate decency that he offered warm congratulations to Barry Bonds without mentioning steroids when Bonds hit his 756th HR in 2007 to supplant Aaron as MLB's home run king. Aaron still tops all players in RBI (2297) and TB (6856) and is tied with Ruth for fourth in R (2174). His 187.5 CVI ranks second to Ruth in RF and eighth overall.

Perhaps MLB's most intense competitor since Ty Cobb, Frank Robinson was raised by his mother in the ethnically mixed tenements of Oakland, CA and brought an urban edge to his game. His desire and competitiveness were perhaps rooted in his parents' early divorce and his absentee father's rejection.[18] Robinson was known for crowding the plate, frequently being hit by pitches, and retaliating by running the bases aggressively and sliding hard into whoever got in his way. When Reds GM Bill DeWitt traded him to Baltimore in mid-career, after 10 seasons as the heart and soul of a good Cincinnati team, calling him "an old 30," Robinson (no doubt reminded of his father's early rejection) responded by winning the 1966 AL triple crown (.316 AVG, 49 HR, 122 RBI) and providing the final piece in the great Orioles team that won four pennants and two World Series in six years from 1966-71, where he earned more renown than in his 10 years in Cincinnati. In 1956-71 in Cincinnati and Baltimore, he hit .302/.393/.550 (156 OPS+) and averaged 31 HR, 100 R, 97 RBI, 291 TB, and 6.0 WAR per year.

Robinson played in 14 All-Star games and is the only player to win the MVP in each league and play in six ASG in each league. Although he had only one 40-HR season, Robinson's 586 HR ranked fourth on the MLB leaderboard when he retired in 1976 but has now fallen to 10th in the aftermath of the Steroid Era. Robinson never had >8.7 WAR in a season but had 14 seasons with at least 4.8 WAR. Robinson's 118.8 CVI ranks fourth in RF and 29th among all HOF-eligible players.

When Roberto Clemente was killed in a plane crash trying to bring aid to Nicaraguan earthquake victims on the last day of 1972 and was swept into the HOF in a special election a few months later, he was lionized as MLB's first African Caribbean superstar and an American and Puerto Rican national hero. But Clemente was not always viewed that way and had to overcome not only the racial animus directed against other black players, but the even bigger burden of the prevalent ethnic stereotypes of Latino players as moody, lazy, hot-headed, and unreliable. The Dodgers originally signed Clemente in 1954 but lost him to Branch Rickey and the Pirates in the Rule V draft. The Pirates had to keep the raw "toolsy" 20-year-old on their major league roster or return him to the Dodgers. He showed flashes of brilliance but lacked plate discipline and consistency. He was a notorious bad-ball hitter, who too often gave away at-bats and baserunning outs.

Furthermore, the man who ended his career and his life as one of the most beloved and heroic leaders in the sport, with his name attached posthumously to baseball's annual humanitarian award, was often viewed as hypersensitive and hypochondriacal. Clemente did indeed have chronic back pain due to an injury suffered in Puerto Rico, and his broken English made it difficult to for him to communicate or be taken seriously. It was not until 1961 at age 26, that Clemente finally broke out to win his first of four batting titles with a .351 average; he never hit below .290 for the rest of his career.

Roberto Clemente

As he matured and acclimated to the language and culture, he blossomed into the great all-around player and role model we all remember so fondly. In 1964-71 (ages 29-36), he hit .334/.383/.514 (152 OPS+) and averaged 7.5 WAR per season. He played in 15 ASG, teaming with Aaron and Mays to form an unbeatable OF that dominated the AL (which was slower to integrate) in the 1960s and won the MVP award in 1966. But what set Clemente apart was his brilliant defense in RF, particularly his powerful and accurate throwing arm, honed by throwing the javelin in high school, which deterred baserunners from taking an extra base or scoring from 3B on a fly ball. Clemente played with two Pirates World Series champions in 1960 and 1971.

He was the MVP of the 1971 World Series, blistering a dominant Orioles pitching staff that featured four 20-game winners for a .414/.452/.759 slash line, and led the underdog Pirates' comeback from a 1-3 deficit to win the Series, hitting the decisive HR in Game 7. A year later, he got his 3000th and final hit in his last full game. Clemente's 110.9 CVI ranks fifth in RF and 36th among all HOF-eligible players.

Beyond the Numbers

- Mays remained humble and approachable and could often be seen playing stickball with neighborhood children in the street after a day game at the Polo Grounds.[19]

- After his military service in 1952-53, Mays accrued at least 5.2 WAR in all but two seasons until 1972, when he was 41 and nearing the end.

- Aaron was the first of three black MLB superstars in this chapter hailing from Mobile, AL; McCovey and Billy Williams are the others. Ozzie Smith was also born in Mobile but grew up in Los Angeles. Negro League Hall of Famer Satchel Paige also hailed from Mobile.

- Aaron was named to MLB's All-Century Team in 2000 and received the Presidential Citizens Medal (2001) and Presidential Medal of Freedom (2002).[20]

- Robinson's 38 HR in 1956 tied Wally Berger's NL rookie record and helped him win Rookie of the Year honors. That record stood until Cody Bellinger hit 39 HR in 2017.

- Robinson became MLB's first black manager in 1974. He was not terribly successful in 16 years of managing in Cleveland, San Francisco, Baltimore, Montreal, and Washington, compiling a 1065-1176 record, and never finishing higher than second.

- Robinson's #20 has been retired by the Reds, Orioles, and Indians; his statue stands in front of each of their ballparks. He received the Presidential Medal of Freedom in 2005.[21]

- Clemente, who was selected by the Pirates from the Dodgers organization in the 1954 Rule 5 draft, is by far the most successful Rule 5 draft pick of all time.

- Clemente credited the genes of his mother, Luisa Walker de Clemente, who (like Roberto) threw the javelin in high school, for his powerful throwing arm.[22]

The Old Guard

Ted Williams (LF):
199.5 CVI – Boston AL (*121.9*)

Stan Musial (LF):
178.1 CVI – St. Louis NL (*128.3*)

Williams and Musial were two historically great stars who straddled the Classical and Boom Eras. Both were .330 hitters with power. Musial's 22% 3TO rate and 0.19 SO/H resembled DiMaggio more than his Boom Era contemporaries. Williams brought more power than Musial and walked and struck out more frequently (though never more than 64 SO after his rookie season), but his 34% 3TO was less than Ruth or Foxx, and his 0.27 SO/H was not much higher than Hornsby. Both are elite Hall of Famers and on the short list of the best of all time.

Ted Williams was a larger-than-life Hemingway-esque character, an expansive and intellectually curious "man's man," full of opinions and passions.[23] A 19-time All-Star, he was arguably the second best pure hitter of all-time behind Babe Ruth, ranking first in career OBP (.008 ahead of Ruth), and second only to Ruth in career SLG and OPS+. He is also MLB's last .400 hitter (1941). Although he amassed his highest WAR (10.6), won the MVP, and played in his only World Series in 1946, his 10.4-WAR 1941 season was even more memorable, featuring not only that .406 AVG, but career highs in OBP (.553), SLG (.735), and OPS+ (235), as well as 37 HR, 120 RBI, 135 R, 147 BB, and 335 TB, but Joe DiMaggio was named AL MVP on the strength of his 56-game hitting streak and a Yankee pennant. However, that 1941 OBP ranks at the top of all non-steroid seasons in MLB history. Sixteen of the top 22 seasons in OPS+ belong to Ruth (eight), Bonds (four), and Williams (four).

Williams hit the ground running in his first season, when he set the rookie record of 145 RBI, and never stopped, except for his nearly five seasons of military service. Although 1941 and 1946 were his best seasons, his 9.7-WAR 1957 season was the best ever by any 38-year-old not on steroids, and his 9.1-WAR 1949 season won him his second MVP. He also posted 10.4, 9.5, and 8.3 WAR in 1942, 1947, and 1948. Take your pick.

Williams was famously temperamental and thin-skinned, alienating reporters and damaging his popularity with fans. This behavior reflected his obsessive perfectionism, rather than malice. Indeed, he was a generous man, always willing to spend hours mentoring anyone asking for his advice on his favorite topic — hitting. In his final public appearance at the 1999 All-Star Game, players flocked around his wheelchair to talk hitting with him one last time. Williams's 199.5 CVI ranks second to Barry Bonds among LF and fifth overall.

Unlike the brash and opinionated Williams, Stan "the Man" Musial was modest and understated. His unorthodox closed batting stance with his neck turned sharply toward the pitcher, his back elbow held high, and his bat pointing almost straight up was instantly recognizable. The 24-time All-Star was a devastating all-around hitter and a key contributor to Cardinals World Series championships in 1942, 1944, and 1946, plus another NL pennant in 1943.

Stan Musial

He played at a very high level from 1942-58, with seven seasons of WAR ≥8 and six more with WAR ≥5.0, and ranks high on virtually every significant offensive leaderboard except SB. He had more TB (6134) than anyone but Aaron. He even had 177 career 3B, despite his lack of speed. His 725 2B and 3630 H also rank third and fourth best of all time. Among his 13 outstanding years, his MVP season in 1948, when he led the NL in almost every offensive category and fell just one HR short of the Triple Crown, stands out. He was also the NL MVP in 1943 and in 1946, after returning from a one-year stint in the Navy. Musial's 178.1 CVI ranks third in LF behind Bonds and Williams and 10th overall.

Beyond the Numbers

- Military service as a marine pilot in World War II and Korea deprived Williams of his age 24-26 and age 33-34 seasons. Unlike many celebrities, who were deployed in safe sinecures during their service, Ted Williams was a genuine war hero, who served as a flight trainer in World War II and flew 39 combat missions in the Korean War. As sports journalist Bob Costas once told him, "You are the guy John Wayne played in all those movies."[24]

- Williams's HR in his final AB in 1960 was immortalized by John Updike in his New Yorker article "Hub Fans Bid Kid Adieu," in which he wrote of Williams's refusal to come out for a curtain call, "Gods do not answer letters."[25]

- In his 1966 HOF induction speech, Williams made an impassioned plea for the recognition of former Negro League stars in the Hall of Fame, a plea that soon bore fruit with the election of Satchel Paige in 1971. He later served on the VC himself.

- Williams managed the expansion Washington Senators from 1969-72—a match many thought would clash explosively with his strong personality — and led them to a surprising fourth place 86-76 finish in 1969, before eventually (and inevitably) running out of patience.

- Musial started out as a pitcher-OF but an arm injury while making a tumbling catch ended his pitching career.

Beyond the Numbers (cont'd)

- The affable Musial made a slew of friends in and out of baseball. Among them were Jackie Robinson, who singled out Musial and Hank Greenberg as the two opposing players who encouraged him in his difficult rookie year, and Presidents John Kennedy and Lyndon Johnson, for whom he served as national fitness advisor.[26]

- Musial was the general manager of the 1967 Cardinals World Series champions, but resigned because he thought himself unqualified. He remained in the Cardinals front office for many years as an advisor.

Golden Boy

Mickey Mantle (CF):
143.0 CVI – New York AL (*110.2*)

One of baseball's most charismatic players, 20-time All-Star and three-time MVP Mickey Mantle, who was named after his father's idol Mickey Cochrane, was the classic five-tool player. It was love at first sight for Yankee Manager Casey Stengel in 1951 when he watched his blond Adonis in spring training and effused, "He has more speed than any slugger that I have ever seen, and more slug than any speedster — and nobody has ever had more of both of 'em put together. This kid isn't logical. He's too good. It's confusing."[27]

It was also love at first sight for Yankee fans, who invested their hopes in Mantle after Joe DiMaggio announced that 1951 would be his final season. However, Mantle's path was not smooth. He slumped early and had to return to the minors briefly to regain his footing. Then, he tore two knee ligaments in the 1951 World Series when he stepped on a drainpipe after stopping short on a Willie Mays line drive to avoid colliding with DiMaggio. Although he was good to go in 1952 after knee surgery, he sustained chronic damage, which tempered his speed and led to the nagging knee problems that would shorten his career.

However, Mantle was terrific in his prime (1952-62), hitting .311/.433/.589 and averaging 36 HR, 99 RBI, 116 R, 110 BB, 297 TB, and 8.1 WAR in 619 PA. Although he lacked the longevity of Mays, Aaron and other superstars of his era, Mantle was every bit the equal of Mays in those prime years. Indeed, Mantle's best years in 1956 (11.2 WAR, 52 HR, MVP, and triple crown), 1957 (11.3 WAR, personal bests in AVG, OBP, and BB, and another MVP), and 1961 (10.4 WAR, 54 HR) are among the best offensive seasons ever put together by anyone not named Ruth, Bonds,

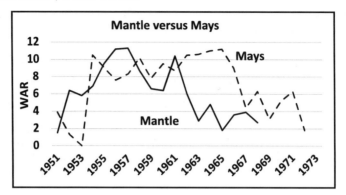

or Williams. But Mantle declined rapidly in his early 30s and was done at age 35 (1967), while Mays remained a superstar well into his 30s and was still very productive at age 40.

Mantle was renowned for his many "tape measure" home runs (the longest being a 540-565 foot blast off Senators lefty Chuck Stobbs in Griffith Stadium in 1953), and for his 1961 duel with Roger Maris to break Babe Ruth's home run record. Mantle faltered due to illness and exhaustion late in the season, while Maris got the record-breaking 61.

On the flip side, Mantle was not shy about striking out. He whiffed 1710 times in his career, and his 0.71 SO/H far surpassed Foxx, Ruth, or any of his predecessors. His SO and his 536 HR and 1730 BB made him MLB's first 40% 3TO player. Mantle played for 11 pennant-winners in his first 14 seasons (1951-3, 1955-8, 1960-4), seven of which won the World Series, and holds the all-time record with 18 postseason

Beyond the Numbers

• Mantle's father, grandfather, uncle, and many other male family members were lead and zinc miners, whose lives were shortened by heart and lung ailments from chronic inhalation of toxic dust. Mantle assumed that he would share their fate and was determined to cram as much as living possible into his allotted 40-45 years.[28,29] His escapades with soul mates Billy Martin and Whitey Ford were notorious. His drinking probably shortened his career and definitely led to his early death from cirrhosis and liver cancer at age 63.

• As a 14-year-old high school freshman, Mantle suffered a football injury that nearly ended his career before it began. He developed a potentially life-threatening leg infection, osteomyelitis, and faced amputation. However, injections of a new antibiotic called penicillin, developed during the War, cured the infection and saved his leg.[30]

HR, three more than Ruth. His 172 OPS+ ranks seventh on the career leaderboard. Mantle's 143.0 CVI ranks fourth among CF, behind Mays, Cobb, and Speaker, and 19th overall. He is an elite Hall of Famer.

The Trailblazers

Jackie Robinson (2B):
106.8 CVI – Brooklyn NL (*61.7*)

Roy Campanella (C):
63.1 CVI – Brooklyn NL (*35.6*)

Minnie Minoso (LF):
60.7 CVI – Chicago AL (*41.4*),
Cleveland AL (*10.7*)

Larry Doby (CF):
54.0 CVI – Cleveland AL (*43.2*),
Chicago AL (*6.7*)

Robinson, Campanella, Minoso, and Doby, who were among MLB's first black players in the late 1940s, belong in the HOF, for their historical significance if nothing else. But they were also great ballplayers. Robinson and Campanella (who had been playing in the Negro Leagues since his teens) were in their late 20s when they received their first major league opportunities. Minoso and Doby were only 23 when they debuted but were 25 when they finally received the opportunity to play every day. At first glance, only Robinson's career appears to be HOF-caliber, but the picture changes when we consider the belated start of their MLB careers.

MLB recently recognized seven Negro Leagues, which operated in 1920-48 as major leagues and have now been incorporated in the official records in Baseball-Reference.com.[31] Unfortunately, these "official" statistics capture only a fraction of the pre-integration Black baseball experience. Many of the greatest Black players before Jackie Robinson played much or all of their careers before 1920 and/or in Cuban, Mexican, or other leagues that are not among the seven recognized by MLB (see Chapter 11, Table 11.3). Moreover, even in the "official" Negro Leagues, teams played fewer than 100 official games per season, and many exhibition games were scheduled (including all-star games against White competition). Statistical records are incomplete even for league games. Although we lack sufficient data

Table 6.2: The Trailblazers – Official Negro League Stats

Player (Years)	PA	AVG/OBP/SLG	HR	RBI	R	SB	WAR
Campanella (1937-45)	832	.322/.382/.491	18	161	144	9	6.2
Doby (1942-47)	603	.329/.412/.574	20	130	124	16	7.2
Minoso (1946-48)	510	.313/.366/.484	9	70	89	11	3.5
Robinson (1945)	137	.375/.449/.600	4	27	25	3	2.1

to properly evaluate their Negro League careers, let alone to calculate CVI, Table 6.2 provides up-to-date official Negro League statistics for these four players as of July 2021.

Even for Campanella (who also accrued 479 Mexican League PA in 1942-1943), documentation currently exists for only 832 PA (the equivalent of less than two MLB seasons) over the course of nine Negro League seasons, starting at age 15. We also have documentation of only about one MLB season's worth of PA for Doby and Minoso, who started at age 18 and 20, respectively, and only 37 PA for Robinson, a world-class college athlete and three-year military veteran who was 26 years old when he reached the Negro Leagues. Rather than try to do something with these sparse data, I have taken an alternative statistical approach (see Appendix A2), which compares their career WAR trajectories to those of other HOF-caliber players to adjust their CVI values to compensate for the years in which they were denied access to MLB. With this rather conservative adjustment (which may underestimate the toll of their early exclusion), Robinson grades out as an elite Hall of Famer, while the others are at the near-great to very good level. Their unadjusted CVI are provided in Table A2.12.

As the man who broke baseball's infamous "color barrier," Jackie Robinson's #42 adorns the uniform of every major leaguer every April 15 to commemorate the anniversary of his 1947 debut. But he was also a great player in his own right — a six-time All-Star and the sparkplug of a team that won six NL pennants and a World Series during his 10-year career — who created a generation of hardcore Dodger fans among people of color and lovers of the underdog.

The youngest son of poor Georgia sharecroppers, Robinson grew up in Pasadena, CA, where his mother Mallie brought her family after her husband deserted them.[32] She supported her family by working as a domestic servant and feeding them leftovers from the houses of her employers. With the help of a welfare agency, Mallie purchased a house in a white neighborhood and had to fend off bigotry and harassment from their neighbors for years. After starring in football, basketball, and track, as well as baseball at UCLA, Jackie was drafted into the army and admitted to Officer Candidate School. He successfully fought a court martial after refusing a driver's order to move to the back of the bus and received an honorable discharge in 1944.

At that time, Dodgers GM Branch Rickey was seeking to integrate baseball and sought a black player who was mature, well-educated, and used to a racially mixed environment, but who also had the self-discipline not to respond in kind to the provocations he was certain to receive as a major league player. When he spotted Robinson playing for the Kansas City Monarchs of the Negro American League in 1945, he knew he had his man. Robinson spent 1946 with the Dodgers' AAA affiliate in Montreal, a racially cosmopolitan city. When Robinson reported to spring training with the Dodgers in 1947, a cadre of disgruntled players, led by Dixie

Walker, circulated a petition to keep Robinson off the team, but Manager Leo Durocher quickly suppressed that rebellion. Robinson then had to endure nearly unbearable racial abuse by fans and opposing teams, but with the support of his teammates, he put together a 4.0-WAR rookie season, hitting .297/.383/.427 (112 OPS+) with 125 R and 29 SB, to earn Rookie of the Year honors at age 28.

From the beginning, he was an exciting player, who used his speed as a disruptive force on the base paths, like a Ty Cobb or Rickey Henderson, but in an era when base stealing had fallen out of fashion. But he was just getting started. Over the next six years (1948-1953), Robinson hit .324/.419/.496 (141 OPS+) and averaged 15 HR, 91 RBI, 108 R, 23 SB, 267 TB, and 7.9 WAR per season. Robinson played in six ASG and won the 1949 MVP. Diabetes (which he hid from the public during his playing career), led to his early decline and retirement at age 37 and eventually to his near blindness and early death at age 53 in 1972. Robinson's 106.8 CVI ranks fifth at 2B and 43rd among all HOF-eligible players.

Roy Campanella (with Willie Mays), 1961.

Barred from MLB because of his mixed Italian and African American parentage, Campanella spent the first 9 years of his professional career in the Negro Leagues, starting at age 15, and was a star there before he reached MLB in 1948. His MLB career was also truncated at the other end by a 1957 automobile accident that left him paralyzed at age 36 after only 10 major league seasons.

Despite only five 4-WAR MLB seasons, Campanella's accomplishments were impressive. As the clean-up hitter on five pennant winning Dodger teams, including the 1955 World Series champion, he won three MVP awards, matching Stan Musial for the most MVPs up to that point. He ranks second in SLG only to Mike Piazza among all catchers and hit 242 HR in the equivalent of half a career. He was also viewed as an elite defensive catcher, leading all NL catchers in range factor nine times, throwing out 57.4% of baserunners attempting to steal (tops among all catchers); he had 5.7 dWAR in 10 seasons. His modest 35.6 career WAR and 63.1

adjusted CVI (which places him at the 1.13 percentile) really just scratch the surface of his career.

Although he lacks the historical import of Jackie Robinson, the Cuban Comet Minnie Minoso was the first Black Latino to play MLB. He was also a nine-time All-Star and brought speed, excitement, and extra base power with a 130 OPS+, almost as high as Robinson's 132. In his nine-year prime (1951-59), Minoso hit .306/.400/.476 (137 OPS+) and averaged 16 HR, 88 RBI, 100 R, and 19 SB, and was the sparkplug of Chicago and Cleveland teams that contended for but never won the AL pennant. Although his 60.6 CVI (1.21 percentile) falls slightly below my line, I believe he belongs in the HOF.

Although Doby's 54.0 CVI (1.49 percentile) falls well below my usual HOF benchmark, I have no problem with his selection by the VC in 1998. He deserves recognition if only because he was the AL's first black player and MLB's second black manager. However, he was also a feared slugger (136 OPS+) and a fine defensive CF. Although segregation delayed his debut until age 23, he hit 253 HR with 970 RBI in his 13-year career and was an important cog of two Cleveland AL champions.

Beyond the Numbers

- Robinson's older brother Mack was an Olympic track star in 1936, finishing second to Jesse Owens in the 200-yard dash.[33]

- Although Robinson did not shine in six World Series, he had a signature moment in Game 1 of the 1955 World Series when he stole home at age 36; the Dodgers lost the game but won the Series.

- Robinson was active in supporting black businesses and civil rights after his baseball career ended, but his conservative politics and support for Richard Nixon put him out of step with others in the movement.

- Although Minoso's career really ended in 1964, Bill Veeck brought him to the White Sox for cameo appearances in 1976 and 1980 (at age 54) to make him the first player to appear in MLB in five decades. It would have been better for Minoso to have received a real opportunity when he was 20 rather than as a publicity stunt in his 50s.

Franchise Icons

Carl Yastrzemski (LF):	Al Kaline (RF):
110.8 CVI – Boston AL (*96.4*)	99.0 CVI – Detroit AL (*92.8*)

Yastrzemski (or "Yaz" to spelling-challenged fans and journalists) and Kaline were closely identified with the franchises with whom they spent their entire careers. While neither could match the sustained excellence of a Williams, Musial, Mays, or Aaron, they were elite players who left a lasting mark on the game.

Following in the footsteps of a legend like Ted Williams is no easy task, but Yaz pulled it off with aplomb. He stepped into Ted Williams's newly vacated LF spot in 1961 and gave the Red Sox another two decades of stellar performance without missing a beat, before handing off the position to another eventual Hall of Famer, Jim Rice, winning three batting titles, seven Gold Gloves, and 18 ASG selections.

Yastrzemski's most remarkable accomplishment by far was his Triple Crown MVP performance in 1967, the season of the "Impossible Dream," when the Red Sox won a close four-team pennant race on the season's final day and took the Cardinals to World Series Game 7 before Bob Gibson finally shut them down. Yaz hit .326/.418/.622 (193 OPS+) with 44 HR, 121 RBI, 112 R, and 360 TB that year in the midst of MLB's offensive drought of the sixties. His 12.5 WAR_H was the third highest ever recorded, behind only Ruth's 1923 and 1921 seasons, and 1.9 WAR higher than Ted Williams's career best. Yaz also far outdid Williams in postseason play, hitting .400/.500/.840 with 3 HR and 5 RBI in 1967, destroying Oakland to the tune of .455/.500/.818, in the 1975 ALCS, and hitting .310/.382/.381 in the close 1975 World Series loss to Cincinnati. Yaz had only two other 8-WAR seasons, in 1968 and 1970, and was only a 3-6-WAR player after 1970, but played for 23 years, long enough to make the top 10 on career leaderboards in BB, 2B, and TB. His 110.8 CVI ranks fifth in LF and tied for 37th among all HOF-eligible players.

Al Kaline was 18 and barely out of high school when he arrived in the major leagues in 1953 and became a star by age 20. His statistical accomplishments were limited by injuries, which caused him to miss the equivalent of 2.5 seasons during his career, and were overshadowed by those of contemporary OF like Mays, Aaron, Mantle, Robinson, and Clemente. He won a batting title in 1955 but never hit 30 HR in a season and fell just short of 400 career HR. He never won an MVP award but did finish second to Yogi Berra in 1955 and to Elston Howard in 1963. He finished with 3007 H, but 30 players have more.

Kaline was an outstanding defensive RF with a powerful arm, winning 10 Gold Gloves, but was not spectacular like Clemente. Kaline played in 18 All-Star games, but his last 4-WAR season (1967) came at age 32. The following year, when the Tigers won the World Series, Kaline was part of a four-man OF rotation with Willie Horton, Mickey Stanley, and Jim Northrup, and also spent time at 1B. He hit .379/.400/.655 in that World Series but never played in another. Kaline served the Tigers as a TV color commentator and spring training instructor from 1975-2002, and then as special assistant to the GM. CVI ranks the venerable "Mr. Tiger" sixth in RF and 55th among all HOF-eligible players.

Beyond the Numbers

- The Yankees and Red Sox courted Yaz as a high school senior but would not meet his father Karol's $100,000 asking price. When the Yankee scout flippantly tossed his pencil, Karol threw him out of his house. Carl accepted a scholarship at Notre Dame, but changed his mind when the Red Sox relented and offered him $108,000 plus tuition and expenses.[34]

- Yaz's grandson Mike currently plays LF for the Giants.

- Kaline taught himself to run on the side of his left foot to overcome the removal of a bone that had been damaged by osteomyelitis. He wore orthopedic shoes throughout his career.[35]

- When Kaline was a high school senior, he was Tiger farm director John McHale's second choice behind pitcher Tom Qualters. When Qualters chose the Phillies, the Tigers signed Kaline and never looked back.[36]

Aces of the 1950s

Warren Spahn (SP):
114.4 CVI – Boston/Milwaukee NL (*99.4*)

Robin Roberts (SP):
100.1 CVI – Philadelphia NL (*71.8*),
Baltimore AL (*11.6*)

Early Wynn (SP):
60.6 CVI – Cleveland AL (*39.8*),
Chicago AL (*10.7*), Washington AL (*10.6*)

While the 1960s were dominated by power pitchers, the 1950s aces were finesse pitchers like Spahn, Roberts, and Wynn, who followed Spahn's motto, "Hitting is timing. Pitching is upsetting timing."[37] They relied on inducing soft contact, not strikeouts. They all could help themselves with a bat, too. None had 3TO rates above 26% or SO/H above 0.55. All benefited from long careers, ranging from 19 years for Roberts to 25 for Wynn.

Warren Spahn ranks sixth in career wins, behind only Young, Walter Johnson, Mathewson, Alexander, and Galvin, despite not winning his first game until age 25. His hallmark was consistency at a high level for a very long time. With guile and a great overhand curve, he won 20-23 games 13 times over his 22-year career, including 23 at age 42 in 1963.

From 1947-63, he averaged 20-12, with a 2.96 ERA (124 ERA+) and 1.176 WHIP. Spahn won the Cy Young award as the ace of the 1957 Milwaukee Braves, who won consecutive NL pennants and beat the Yankees in the 1957 World Series, and played in 17 ASG. Spahn was a strong hitter, too, accruing 7.3 WAR$_H$ over his career.

His career was almost derailed by torn tendons in his pitching shoulder and a broken nose before he reached the major leagues in 1942, Then, before he had won a major league game, World War II intervened. Spahn saw action as an Army combat engineer in 1943-45, while serving as a staff sergeant in France and Belgium. He fought in the Battle of the Bulge and received a battlefield promotion to second lieutenant, plus a Bronze Star, a Purple Heart (he took some shrapnel in his foot), and a Presidential medal.[38] Unlike Bob Feller, Spahn never complained about how many wins his service time cost him, pointing out that military experience gave him the maturity and stamina that allowed him to thrive until age 42.

Robin Roberts

Spahn is one of only 30 pitchers to throw two or more no-hitters in his career — in 1960 and 1961. The second, coming on a snowy April night in Milwaukee against a stacked Giants lineup, which featured three Hall of Famers (Mays, McCovey, and Cepeda), was especially impressive for a 40-year-old finesse pitcher, who could no longer "miss bats." Finally, Spahn's modest and engaging personality and humor, leavened by his military experience, made him a natural leader. Spahn's 114.4 CVI ranks 11th among all SP and 33rd among all HOF-eligible players.

Seven-time all-star Robin Roberts made his mark as the hard-throwing ace of the Phillies Whiz Kids team, surprise winner of the 1950 NL pennant before getting swept by the Yankees in the World Series. He reigned from 1950-55 as the NL's top right-handed pitcher, winning at least 20 games every year and averaging 23-13 with 161 SO, 59 BB, 323 IP, 27 CG, and 7.8 WAR$_P$ with a 2.93 ERA (135 ERA+) and 1.094 WHIP.

The Phillies made only one World Series appearance in this period, a 0-4 sweep by the Yankees in 1950, but Roberts pitched valiantly in defeat, going to-to-toe with Allie Reynolds in Game 2 for nine innings before yielding a game-winning HR to Joe DiMaggio in the 10th to lose 2-1, and pitching a scoreless ninth inning in relief in the 5-2 Game 4 loss. A true workhorse, Roberts relied primarily on a rising fastball and pinpoint control. Because he refused to brush hitters back from home plate, home runs were his Achilles heel.

Over the course of his career, he yielded 505 HR, more than any pitcher until Jamie Moyer surpassed him in 2010. Roberts could not sustain his peak performance into his 30s as his fastball lost several ticks. From 1956-66, his WAR_p exceeded 4.4 only once – in 1958. However, he remained an effective mid-rotation starter through age 38, providing veteran leadership and 250 innings of solid pitching to an up-and-coming Orioles team that was a surprise contender in 1964. At the end of his career, he mentored young future Hall of Famers Jim Palmer in 1965 and Ferguson Jenkins in 1966. His 100.1 CVI ranks 19th among SP and 54th among all HOF-eligible players.

Early Wynn, whose 60.6 CVI ranks at the 1.16 percentile, sits in the border region between Hall of Fame and HOVG. After laboring in futility to a 72-87 record in nine years with the lowly Senators, he suddenly found himself on a strong Cleveland team at age 29, where he joined a staff that included future Hall of Famers Bob Feller and Bob Lemon. He arrived a year too late for their 1948 World Series championship, but won 20 games four times and compiled a 163-100 record in nine years there.

Although Wynn was never a true ace, he was a key contributor to the 111-win 1954 Cleveland team, which broke the string of five consecutive Yankee championships but was swept by the Giants in the World Series. Later, he won his only Cy Young Award with the 1959 "Go-Go" White Sox, who broke yet another string of four Yankee pennants and lost in the World Series after Wynn pitched an 11-0 shutout in Game 1. Although Wynn managed to win 300 games, he had to suffer through seven beatings and an unconditional release over portions of two seasons to get it. I would like him better if he had stopped at 299 W.

Beyond the Numbers

- Like Grover Alexander, Spahn was named after a sitting president—Warren Harding.

- Spahn kept his teammates loose with pranks and practical jokes, while entertaining the media with his wry and self-deprecating wit. For example, when he played for Casey Stengel's Mets in 1964, he remarked, "I'm the only guy to play for Casey Stengel before and after he was a genius." He also joked about the HR he yielded to struggling rookie Willie Mays, which was his only hit in his first 26 MLB AB, "I'll never forgive myself. We might have gotten rid of Willie forever if I'd only struck him out." When the Mets signed Yogi Berra in 1965, Spahn quipped, "I don't know whether we'll be the oldest battery in baseball, but I know we'll be the ugliest."[39]

Beyond the Numbers (cont'd)

- Spahn had a rare off season in 1948, winning only 15 games, the year Boston won the NL pennant by relying on "Spahn and Sain, then two days of rain." Actually, Sain was the ace that year.

- Roberts's MVP "snub" in 1952, when he was 28-7 with a 2.59 ERA and a 1.021 WHIP yet finished second to Hank Sauer, convinced Commissioner Ford Frick that pitchers needed their own award. He created the Cy Young award in 1956.[40]

- Roberts was active in the Players Association through much of his career, representing the Phillies and then the NL in negotiations with the owners on minimum salary and the Players Pension Fund. He and fellow future Hall of Famer Jim Bunning (later a U.S Senator) hired Marvin Miller as the full-time executive director of the Players Association in 1966. However, Roberts never envisioned the advent of free agency and was upset when Miller engineered baseball's first work stoppage in 1972.[41]

- Wynn is the only CVI-Plus player of American Indian heritage.[42]

Aces of the 1960s

Bob Gibson (SP):
103.5 CVI – St. Louis NL (*89.2*)

Juan Marichal (SP):
76.1 CVI – San Francisco NL (*63.5*)

Jim Bunning (SP):
73.1 CVI – Philadelphia NL (*30.8*),
Detroit AL (*30.1*)

Sandy Koufax (SP):
70.2 CVI – Brooklyn/Los Angeles
NL (*48.9*)

Don Drysdale (SP):
65.8 CVI – Brooklyn/Los Angeles
NL (*67.1*)

Luis Tiant (SP):
65.0 CVI – Boston AL (*35.4*), Cleveland
AL (*26.2*)

Unlike their predecessors, the pitching aces of the 1960s dominated by power. Koufax's 1.37 and Gibson's 0.95 SO/H ratios left the pitchers of previous eras (except Rube Waddell) in the dust. Even less extreme pitchers like Bunning (0.83), Drysdale (0.81), and Tiant (0.79) had SO/H ratios at least as high as Feller's (0.79), and Marichal (0.73) wasn't that far behind. All six far outstripped Spahn et al. Just like Mantle on the offensive side, Koufax was an unprecedented "three true outcomes" pitcher whose 36% 3TO rate far surpassed Bob Feller's previous 29% 3TO standard.

Bob Gibson was MLB's greatest post-Negro League African American pitching star. A nine-time All-Star, he had pinpoint control of a devastating mix of fastballs and hard sliders. Because of his intense competitiveness and aggressiveness in moving hitters off the plate, he was the guy hitters — especially right-handers — most hated to face. He never fraternized with his opponents, even at the All Star Game, and was standoffish with the press. His longtime catcher Tim McCarver described his mound presence as follows: "For my money, the most intimidating, arrogant pitcher ever to kick up dirt on a mound is Bob Gibson... If you ever saw Gibson work, you'd never forget his style: his cap pulled down low over his eyes, the ball gripped – almost mashed – behind his right hip, the eyes smoldering at each batter almost accusingly... He didn't like to lose to anyone at anything."[43]

Gibson would have taken that as high praise. In his signature year, 1968, he was nearly unhittable and won both the Cy Young and MVP awards. Gooden (13.3 in 1985), Carlton (12.5 in 1972), Clemens (12.1 in 1997), and Newhouser (12.1 in 1945) are the only pitchers since 1920 who have topped Gibson's 11.9 combined WAR in 1968. Also, his microscopic 1.12 ERA (258 ERA+) and 13 SHO that year rank as the best since 1920. Gibson was just as good in three World Series, winning seven games, racking up 92 SO, and winning two MVPs. Gibson was also a strong hitter with 24 HR and 144 RBI over his 17-year career; his 7.5 WAR$_H$ contributed to his career WAR of 89.2.

Juan Marichal

Gibson's path to greatness was not easy. Although more than a decade had elapsed since the debut of Jackie Robinson, he experienced racial discrimination in the minor leagues and under his first major league manager, Solly Hemus, who relegated him to mop-up duty in his first two years. It was only when Johnny Keane became the Cardinals manager in 1961 that Gibson received a full opportunity.[44] Gibson gradually rose to stardom in 1962-66, earning his first national recognition when he won MVP honors in the 1964 World Series by dominating a still potent Yankee lineup with two wins (including the decisive Game 7) and 31 SO in 27 innings. He won a second World Series MVP in 1967 by beating the Red Sox three times, while allowing only three runs in 27 innings with 26 SO.

However, Gibson's best was yet to come. His 33.2 combined WAR in 1968-70 is surpassed only by Walter Johnson's 43.4 WAR in 1912-

14, since 1900. During those three years, Gibson went 65-29 with 811 SO, a 2.13 ERA (166 ERA+), and a 1.047 WHIP and won his second Cy Young award in 1970. He also started strong in the 1968 World Series against Detroit, posting a World Series record 17 SO in a complete game shutout in Game 1 and adding another 10 SO in a 10-1 victory in Game 4, but he was finally bested 4-1 by Mickey Lolich in Game 7. Because his World Series exploits are not captured by WAR, Gibson is probably underrated by CVI, which still ranks him 16th among SP and 45th among all HOF-eligible players.

The enduring image of Juan Marichal, the first great Dominican pitcher, is his unmistakable windup, left leg raised high over his head, from which he threw a dazzling assortment of pitches that hitters were all but helpless to pick up until it was too late. His career peaked in 1963-1966, coinciding with Koufax's peak. During those four years they were widely viewed as the two best pitchers in baseball. Although he was not overpowering like Koufax, the difference between them was really quite small, with Marichal amassing 33.5 WAR_p versus 36.3 for Koufax. Marichal, who had two additional excellent years in 1968-69 after Koufax retired, eventually amassed more career WAR_p and a higher CVI than his Dodger rival.

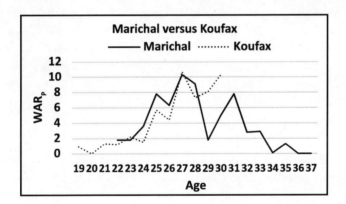

Yet Marichal, whose last really good year came at age 31, is often an afterthought when the great pitchers of the 1960s are remembered. In 1963-69, he posted a remarkable 2.34 ERA and 1.001 WHIP and averaged 22-9, 215 SO, 5 SHO, 23 CG, and 6.9 WAR_p per season (despite a 1.8-WAR_p off-season in 1967). While this was an extreme low-scoring period in which the MLB average ERA ranged from 2.98 to 3.61 and average WHIP ranged from 1.19 to 1.32, Marichal's 146 ERA+ indicates that his flashy stats were more than a mere byproduct of his environment. In 1965, his best season (10.3 WAR_p), Marichal also racked up 10 shutouts, a number exceeded by only three pitchers since 1920. Marichal could not match Koufax's postseason resume; in his only World Series start (1962), he had to leave after four scoreless innings when he injured his hand.

Unfortunately, Marichal's reputation was badly tarnished by an incident in August 1965, when he exploded in rage after Dodger catcher John Roseboro whizzed a return throw to Sandy Koufax past his ear; he opened a two-inch gash on Roseboro's forehead with his bat, starting a brawl. This incident was uncharacteristic of the usually unflappable Marichal and brought him a $1750 fine and nine-day suspension. Roseboro later forgave Marichal, and the two became close friends until Roseboro's death in 2002. This incident delayed Marichal's HOF election for three years, but a press release by John Roseboro in 1983, in which he urged BBWAA members to forgive and vote for Marichal, turned the tide.[45] Marichal's 76.1 CVI ranks 38th among SP and at the 0.64 percentile overall.

Jim Bunning was a tough customer on the mound, where he used his hard slider, pinpoint control, and a propensity for backing hitters off the plate to achieve stardom. Success came slowly, perhaps because his father insisted that his contract stipulate that he would miss the beginning of every season to attend Xavier college until he completed his bachelor's degree in Economics.[46]

Bunning struggled for eight years in the minors and at age 25 was on the verge of quitting if he did not make the Tigers' major league roster in 1957. He not only made the Tigers, he also made the AL All-Star team, going 20-8 with a 2.69 ERA (144 ERA+) and 1.070 WHIP and 6.3 WAR_p. Bunning had never had a season remotely as good in the minors. He then compiled 3.1-6.6 WAR_p in each of the next five seasons, before slumping to 1.5 WAR_p in 1963. When the Tigers traded the 32-year old Bunning to the Phillies after the season, it seemed that the best years of a solid but unspectacular career were behind him.

In fact, the best was yet to come. From 1964-67, Bunning became one of the elite pitchers in the NL, averaging an 18-12 record with 248 K and only 59 BB per season, with a 2.48 ERA (141 ERA+) and 1.039 WHIP. Although his low ERA and WHIP must be viewed in the context of the MLB-wide scoring drought of the sixties, his 30.2 WAR_p in those four years transformed his career from merely good to one worthy of HOF consideration. Although Bunning posted his best WAR_p (9.0) in 1966, his most memorable season was 1964 (5.5 WAR_p), when he pitched MLB's fifth perfect game — the first since 1922—and was the veteran ace of a young and exciting Phillies team, which led the NL almost wire-to-wire, building a 6.5-game lead with 12 games left to play, which dissolved in a Cubs-worthy collapse. This was the closest Bunning ever came to pitching in a World Series.

Bunning never won a Cy Young award, although he did finish second in 1967. He was also a nine-time All-Star for the Tigers in 1957-63 and the Phillies in 1964 and 1966. He is also one of 30 pitchers to pitch two or more no-hitters and one of five pitchers to throw no-hitters in both leagues. Bunning's 73.1 CVI ranks 42nd among SP and at the 0.74 percentile overall. Nevertheless he had to wait until 1996 to be elected by the VC to the HOF.

Although CVI ranks Sandy Koufax only 47th among SP, anyone who watched him pitch in his brief heyday would put him on the short list of baseball's greatest pitchers. He not only threw harder than anyone one else, but he had a devastating curveball that made him all but unhittable. Ernie Banks described Koufax as "... frightening. He had that tremendous fastball that would rise and a great curveball that started at the eyes and broke to the ankles. In the end you knew you were going to be embarrassed ... He was the greatest pitcher I ever saw. Most of the time we knew what was coming ... but it didn't matter."[47]

In 1963-66, his peak years, Koufax averaged 24-7 with 9.1 WAR_p, 307 SO and only 65 BB in 298 IP with a 1.86 ERA (172 ERA+) and 0.909 WHIP, won three Cy Young Awards and an MVP, was named MVP of the 1963 and 1965 World Series, threw three of his four career no-hitters (only Nolan Ryan threw as many or more, but took 27 years to do it), and put up historically high strikeout totals including 382 in 1965 (a record, surpassed in 1973 by Ryan's 383). His outstanding 1.37 SO/H attests to his mastery; the five players ahead of him – Randy Johnson, Ryan, Kershaw, Scherzer, and Pedro Martinez – all pitched more recently when strikeouts were more frequent. Koufax ranks 11th in WAR_p through age 30 among pitchers whose career midpoints came after 1920, despite the fact that he didn't blossom until age 25. If Koufax had been able to continue pitching through 1970 (age 34), allowing for a moderate 10% annual attrition in his 9.1 average WAR_p in 1963-66, he could perhaps have attained a final CVI of 103.4 (see Appendix 2, Table A2.10), which would have placed him just behind Bob Gibson among the elite SP. But it was not to be, and Koufax's actual 70.2 CVI ranks only at the 0.84 percentile. Still, the BBWAA treated Koufax as an elite Hall of Famer, electing him in 1972 with 344/396 votes, more votes than any of his illustrious predecessors had received.

Don Drysdale was the junior partner in the Koufax-Drysdale lefty-righty tandem that pitched the Dodgers to three pennants and two World Series championships in 1963-66. Although he could not quite measure up to Koufax, Drysdale was an intimidating fastballer in the mold of Bob Gibson, who was not afraid to pitch right-handed batters high and tight. He was also a nine-time All-Star and won the Cy Young award in 1962.

Unlike Koufax, Drysdale pitched effectively from the get-go as a 19-year-old swing man starter-reliever, going 5-5 with a 2.64 ERA and contributing to a Dodger pennant in 1956. From 1957-68, Drysdale remained at or near the top of the Dodgers rotation. He peaked in 1959-64, compiling a 2.90 ERA (127 ERA+) and 1.118 WHIP, while averaging an 18-13 W-L, 232 SO vs 75 BB, and 6.0 WAR_p per season. He posted his best WAR_p (7.8) in 1964 but drew the most recognition with his 5.4-WAR_p Cy Young award-winning 1962 season, when he went 25-9 with a 2.83 ERA (128 ERA+), a 1.113 WHIP, and 232 SO. Ironically, the Dodgers did not win the pennant in either year. However, Drysdale pitched well in five

World Series, most memorably in a 1-0 three-hit 11-SO shutout in Game 3 of the Dodgers four-game obliteration of the Yankees in 1963. Drysdale set a record (surpassed by Orel Hershiser in 1988) for consecutive shutout innings (58) in 1968, his final full season. Unfortunately, Drysdale tore his rotator cuff 12 games into the 1969 season and was forced to retire at age 32. Drysdale's 65.8 CVI ranks at the 1.03 percentile.

The charismatic Tiant, a three time All-Star, will be remembered forever in Boston as the mustachioed character with the dazzling repertoire of diverse pitches and deliveries, puffing shirtless on a celebratory cigar in front of his Red Sox locker after a clutch victory. But in spring 1972, the 31-year-old veteran's career was hanging in the balance. In Cleveland, he had put together four solid years culminating in a spectacular 1968 season, when he went 21-9 with a 1.60 ERA (186 ERA+) and 0.871 WHIP. His 8.5 WAR_p in that "year of the pitcher" was second only to Gibson. But then he plummeted to 9-20 in 1969 and was traded to Minnesota, where he missed the last half of the 1970 season with a sore shoulder and was released the following spring.

When the Red Sox took a flyer on Tiant in mid-June 1971, he was terrible. After Tiant suffered a five-run shelling in his first Red Sox appearance, Boston Globe columnist Cliff Keane compared the investment in Tiant to "taking a bagful of money and throwing it off Pier 4 into the Atlantic."[48] But Tiant showed enough in September to get one more chance in 1972. He began the season as a middle reliever and spot starter but caught fire in August to finish 15-6 with a 1.91 ERA (169 ERA+) and 1.078 WHIP to win Comeback of the Year honors. He also became the darling of Boston fans, a status he would not relinquish for the next seven years.

The Sox had long been known for their fractured clubhouse culture (25 players, 25 cabs), but all that changed with Tiant. An incorrigible jokester who did not spare Yaz or other Red Sox stars, he kept his teammates laughing and loose. Teammate Dwight Evans said later, "Unless you have played with him, you can't understand what Luis means to a team."[49] From 1972-76, Tiant compiled a 3.12 ERA (125 ERA+) and 1.170 WHIP, while averaging a 19-12 W-L and 5.7 WAR_p. He won 20+ games in 1973, 1974, and 1976. His 1975 season was the weakest in this period, but he won several key games down the stretch, shut out defending champion Oakland in Game 1 of the ALCS, and won two World Series games against the Reds, before the Sox fell in Game 7.

Tiant began to fade in 1977-78 and was no more than rotation filler when he left to pitch for the Yankees in 1979. Tiant's 65.0 CVI (1.07 percentile) should put him in the HOF, all things considered. However, after receiving 31% of the votes in his BBWAA ballot debut, he never again polled more than 18%. The VC considered him as recently as December 2017, but he lost out to Alan Trammell and Jack Morris. Tiant was far better than Morris and deserves a better fate.

Beyond the Numbers

- Gibson was a sickly child, who suffered from rickets, asthma, and a heart murmur and almost died of pneumonia.[50] After his father died, Gibson's older brother Josh, a Creighton graduate and the director of the local YMCA youth program, became his father figure. Josh insisted that he get a college degree and arranged a scholarship for him at Creighton University.

- In his youth, Gibson's favorite sport was basketball. He was good enough to be the first man inducted into Creighton's sports hall of fame and to tour with the Harlem Globetrotters the winter before his first spring with the Cardinals.[51]

- Marichal grew up in poverty in the Dominican Republic. He was so malnourished that when he was ten, he fell into a coma for nine days and nearly died. The Alou brothers were among his childhood playmates. Juan knew early on that he wanted to play baseball in the US when he grew up, but there were no Dominican ballplayers in the US at that time.[52]

- Bunning may be best known for his uneven 24-year career as a Republican Congressman and Senator from Kentucky in 1986-2010.[53] However, it is his baseball legacy that is most worth remembering and honoring.

- Koufax was MLB's second great Jewish star. His stepfather Irving Koufax wanted Sandy to become an architect and once told him, "a baseball player you will never be." However, he became Sandy's biggest fan after he saw him pitch.[54]

- Koufax was an outstanding basketball player and fierce rebounder, who could dunk despite standing only 6'2" tall. Cincinnati Bearcat coach Ed Jucker thought he was good enough to play in the NBA.[55]

- In 1966, Koufax and Drysdale staged a joint holdout in spring training, auguring more than two decades of labor unrest that would begin six years later. They settled for the then astronomical sum of $240,000 per season, $130,000 for Koufax and $110,000 for Drysdale.

- In 2007, at age 71, Koufax was the final draft choice of the Modi'n Miracle of the fledgling Israeli baseball league. Miracle Manager Art Shamsky (another Jewish ex-major leaguer) remarked, "It's been 41 years between starts for him. If he's rested and ready to take the mound again, we want him on our team."[56] That is perhaps the best way to think of the man who rode off into the sunset in 1966.

- The telegenic Drysdale went directly into broadcasting after he retired, working for the Expos, Rangers, Angels, White Sox, NBC, and ABC, before joining Vin Scully and Ross Porter in the Dodger broadcast booth in 1988. There, Drysdale had the bittersweet pleasure of broadcasting the 1988 game in which Orel Hershiser broke his consecutive scoreless innings record.[57]

- Tiant is the son of legendary Cuban lefty Luis Eleuterio Tiant, had starred in Cuban and American Negro Leagues a generation earlier. Hall of Famer Monte Irvin thought he could have been an MLB star.[58]

Charlie Hustle

Pete Rose (LF):
83.6 CVI – Cincinnati NL (78.1)

Never has a nickname been more fitting than Pete Rose's "Charlie Hustle." Rose was the consummate hustler in the best and worst sense of the word. On the _baseball field, Rose played baseball full-tilt, and by sheer effort and perseverance and hustle surpassed the far more gifted Ty Cobb as MLB's all-time hit king. There is no doubt about his considerable baseball accomplishments or his HOF credentials. Teammate Joe Morgan once said of him, "Pete played the game, always, for keeps. Every game was the seventh game of the World Series."[59]

But unfortunately, Rose was also a shameless con artist who disregarded rules and norms and used his charm to get his way. It was this kind of hustle that led Rose to break baseball's clear and absolute rules against associating with gamblers and betting on baseball, while rationalizing that it was really OK as long as he didn't bet against his own team. Evidently, Rose's gambling habit did not manifest itself until the late stages of his career, and the idea of stepping onto a baseball field and giving less than his best effort to win does not seem to be in his DNA. But Rose's gambling was a ticking time bomb, which put him in a position to be coerced into game-fixing. Banning him from employment in MLB was not only justified but necessary. Rose was playing with fire, and it was just a matter of time until MLB got burned.

Rose is actually a bit overrated. His all-time records for G, H, PA, AB and his second position on the doubles leaderboard attest to longevity as much as skill. He was a versatile but subpar defender at multiple positions (-13.4 dWAR) and stole playing time from younger, better players in pursuit of personal goals as he neared the end. Still, Rose was an essential cog in Cincinnati's "Big Red Machine," which won five NL West titles, three NL pennants, and the 1975-76 World Series. He was an outstanding postseason performer and the MVP in the Reds' thrilling 4-3 triumph over the Red Sox in 1975. He played in 17 ASG. CVI ranks him sixth among LF and at the 0.50 percentile overall — making him a great, but not quite elite, player. While Rose may be a scoundrel, it seems harsh to ban him from the HOF and thereby negate his hard-earned accomplishments on the field.

Beyond the Numbers

- Rose's father Harry was an outstanding semi-pro athlete who taught Pete to switch hit before he was eight. Pete was a poor student, who had to repeat the ninth grade because Harry would not allow him to attend summer school and miss summer baseball. Baseball always came first in the Rose household.[60]

- Rose's late-career gambling habits are documented in a meticulous report by investigator John Dowd.[61] Rose has earned considerable income at memorabilia shows, where he shamelessly signs copies of the Dowd Report on request.[62]

The Grease Man

Gaylord Perry (SP):
100.7 CVI - San Francisco NL (*34.4*), Cleveland AL (*28.8*), Texas AL (*15.5*), San Diego NL (*6.6*)

Gaylord Perry was best known for his spitball and its cousin the greaseball, thrown five decades after these pitches were outlawed. The five-time All-Star pitched for 21 years but was no mere compiler, with a dominant 13-year stretch from 1964-76 (except for off-years in 1965 and 1971) in which he posted a 2.86 ERA (125 ERA+) and 1.119 WHIP in 3740.1 IP and averaged 17 W, 20 CG, 200 SO, and 5.9 WAR_p per season. In 1972, his peak year, Perry posted a 24-16 record for the Cleveland Indians at age 33 with a 1.92 ERA, a 0.978 WHIP, and 234 strikeouts in 342.2 IP, and won a well-deserved AL Cy Young Award. He also added a second NL Cy Young award in 1978 with San Diego, which probably should have gone to Phil Niekro, who had 10.0 WAR_p that year versus Perry's 4.3. His 100.7 CVI ranks 17th among SP and 52nd among all HOF eligible players, putting him in the elite category.

The thornier issue about Perry's legacy is that he built his career on an illegal pitch, which he learned from Giants teammate Bob Shaw in 1963 at age 24, while he was struggling to stick in the major leagues as bullpen filler.[62] Mastering the spitball helped make Perry an entirely different pitcher. It was virtually impossible to catch Perry in the act of throwing it. Many baseball executives (including Commissioner Ford Frick) were ready to throw up their hands and legalize it, but they were loath to risk exacerbating the alarming scoring decline of the 1960s. In 1968, the Baseball Rules Committee, outlawed the practice of pitchers bringing their hands to

Gaylord Perry

their mouth while on the mound, but that didn't stop Perry and others from applying Vaseline and other foreign substances to the ball to achieve the same effect.

Perry was always coy about whether he threw illegal pitches, claiming at times that he was merely using batters' suspicions to play mind games and that he didn't really have to throw many spitballs or greaseballs to reap the benefits. He even primed his five-year old daughter to answer reporters' questions about the spitball by saying, "It's a hard slider."[63] In a 1974 book, he admitted to having "doctored" the ball in the past, but he later recanted, claiming that the book too was a just a ploy in his mind games.[64] Although a handful of BBWAA members refused to vote for him, there was far less resistance to Perry's HOF candidacy than there is to steroid users today. But one can argue that Perry benefited far more from cheating than did Clemens. After all, Clemens was a great pitcher before he ever used performance enhancing drugs, while Perry was a middling reliever until he learned the spitball, while at the same time developing better speed and command on his fastball.

Beyond the Numbers

- Perry's older brother Jim was also a fine major league pitcher, with 42.0 WAR in 17 years with the Indians and Twins.

- Perry had an exaggerated reputation as an inept hitter, prompting Giants manager Alvin Dark to quip that a man would walk on the moon before Perry hit a home run. Sure enough, Perry hit his first career HR on July 20, 1969, moments after Neil Armstrong's "giant step for mankind."[65]

Masters of Third Base

Eddie Mathews (3B):
116.7 CVI – Boston/Milwaukee/Atlanta
NL (*94.1*)

Brooks Robinson (3B):
82.2 CVI – Baltimore AL (*78.4*)

Ken Boyer (3B):
69.2 CVI – St. Louis NL (*58.1*)

Sal Bando (3B):
65.1 CVI – Kansas City/Oakland AL
(*52.1*), Milwaukee AL (*9.4*)

For whatever reason, 3B is the most underrepresented position in the HOF. As of 2020, only thirteen 3B have plaques in Cooperstown (or fifteen if you count Edgar Martinez and Paul Molitor, who appeared more at DH.) In 1951, when Eddie Mathews debuted with the Boston Braves, Jimmy Collins and Pie Traynor, both CVI-Minus players, were the only 3B in the HOF, and Home Run Baker (who had not yet been elected) was the only CVI-Plus 3B in MLB annals. So Mathews, Robinson, Boyer, Bando, and Santo (covered later in this chapter) represented a new flowering of 3B talent. Unfortunately, only Mathews and Robinson had an easy path to the HOF; Santo was honored belatedly and posthumously, and Boyer and Bando are still on the outside looking in.

Eddie Mathews is best remembered as the senior partner of the lefty-righty Mathews-Aaron slugging duo of the outstanding Braves teams of 1954-66, which won NL pennants in 1957-58 and came from a 1-3 deficit to beat the Yankees in the 1957 World Series. He is the only man who played for the Braves in Boston, Milwaukee, and Atlanta. Mathews' career trajectory featured 13 years of sustained excellence (1953-65) when he hit .277/.385/.528 (150 OPS+) and averaged 35 HR, 98 RBI, 100 R, 96 BB, 287 TB, and 6.9 WAR per season, but no seasonal WAR totals higher than 8.2. Mathews won no MVP awards, but finished second in 1953 and 1959 and played in 12 ASG. Since his prime lasted only 13 years, Mathews is not prominent on MLB's leaderboards, but his 116.7 CVI still ranks second at 3B and 32nd among all HOF-eligible players. He is an elite Hall of Famer.

Brooks Robinson was only 5% above average offensively, but the metrics and "eye test" agree that he is indisputably baseball's best defensive 3B. Robinson's 39.1 career dWAR beats runner-up Adrian Beltre's 27.2 by 44%. The dWAR leaderboard is dominated by SS, since more balls are hit there than any other position, but only Ozzie Smith (44.2) and Orioles teammate Mark Belanger (39.5) have more career dWAR than Brooksie. He also won 16 consecutive Gold Gloves from 1960-75. If you need further convincing, check out the 1970 World Series highlights on YouTube and watch Robinson make one of his signature backhanded plays going well into foul territory behind 3B followed by a perfect throw to 1B retire Lee May on what should have been a double.[66]

Robinson's path to becoming a major league hitter was arduous; it took him four years after his 1955 debut to make the starting lineup, another 1.5 seasons for his AVG to top .250, and two more years to reach 20 HR in 1962, his first 5-WAR season. But starting in 1962, he maintained a consistent .284-.303 AVG with moderate power, topped by his 1964 MVP season when he hit .317/.368/.521 (145 OPS+) with 28 HR and a league-leading 118 RBI, as the young Orioles challenged the aging Yankees and the White Sox down to the wire, before settling for third place at 97-65. Although Robinson would never hit above .290 after 1965 (paralleling the general offensive decline in baseball), he still provided timely 20-HR power and remained a perennial All-Star, playing in 18 consecutive ASG from 1960-74.

His defensive stature at 3B grew from elite to iconic; his 4.5 dWAR in 1968 and 4.2 dWAR in 1967 are the top two dWAR totals ever posted at 3B and were the seventh and twelfth (tied) best dWAR totals of all time at any position. Following the abrupt disintegration of the Yankee dynasty in 1965 and the acquisition of Frank Robinson from Cincinnati in 1966, Brooksie was a cornerstone of the Orioles ascent to the top of the AL in 1966-71. The Orioles won four pennants and two World Series with Brooks batting cleanup between Frank Robinson and Boog Powell to spearhead the offense, supplemented by outstanding pitching and historically good defense. The pinnacle of his career probably came in the 4-1 victory over Cincinnati in the 1970 World Series, when he hit .429/.429/.810 with 2 HR, made at least four head-turning plays at 3B, and was named World Series MVP.[66] CVI ranks Brooks Robinson eighth at 3B and at the 0.54 percentile overall.

Ken Boyer was the sort of player who usually gets elected to the HOF. He was an 11-time All-Star in the interim between Mathews and Santo. Although he was not a superstar and did not play long enough to accumulate gaudy career stats, he peaked with 8.0 WAR in 1961, and was voted the NL MVP as the clean-up hitter for the World Series Champion Cardinals in 1964. From 1956-64, Boyer hit .299/.364/.491 (124 OPS+) and averaged 25 HR, 96 RBI, and 93 R.

Boyer was also an outstanding defensive 3B (10.7 dWAR), with five Gold Gloves, but was overshadowed in that department by younger brother Clete of the Yankees. A strong silent type who was well respected throughout the game, Boyer managed the Cardinals in 1978-80. Perhaps it was his early death from lung cancer at age 52 and his utter lack of flamboyance that allowed his memory to fade quickly. CVI ranks him 11th at 3B and at the 0.91 percentile overall, which should be good enough to put him in the HOF. However, Boyer never received more than 25.5% of the BBWAA HOF vote. He has been considered by the VC from time to time but has not made the cut. The VC could do (and has done) a lot worse than elect Boyer the next time his name comes up.

When one recalls the best baseball teams of the 1970s, the Big Red Machine and the Bronx Zoo Yankees come to mind before the Oakland Athletics. But that rollicking bunch with the frugal eccentric owner, the 19th century coifs, and nicknames like "Catfish" and "Blue Moon" won three consecutive World Series in 1972-74 and reigned supreme in the first half of the decade. Sal Bando was one of their core players and team lead-ers — a solid 3B and middle-of-the-order hitter whose patience at the plate and em-phasis of OBP and power over AVG were a harbinger of the future, rather than a relic of the past.

Sal Bando

The A's and Bando probably owe their relative obscurity to the fact that they were the first team to be decimated by free agency in the mid-1970s; indeed, two of their biggest stars, Reggie Jackson and Catfish Hunter, came to be more iden-tified with the Yankees. Bando himself moved to Milwaukee as a free agent in 1977, but his best years were in Oakland. In 1969-78, his 10-year peak, Bando hit .259/.364/.428 (127 OPS+) and averaged 22 HR, 88 RBI, 81 R, 87 BB, and 5.7 WAR with 0.8 dWAR per season. In 1969, his best season, Bando hit .281/.400/.484 (153 OPS+) with 31 HR, 113 RBI, 106 R, and 8.3 WAR.

He was not a superstar but still played in four ASG and finished in the top five in the MVP voting three times. He was the glue that held the fractious A's clubhouse together through their five consecutive postseason appear-ances in 1971-75. Bando's 65.1 CVI ranks 14th at 3B and at the 1.06 percentile overall. He received only three votes in his lone year on the 1987 BBWAA HOF ballot and little or no consideration from the VC since then. Although he is only a borderline HOF candidate, the underappreciated Bando is more deserving than many who have been elected.

Beyond the Numbers

- Ty Cobb said of Mathews, "I've known only 3 or 4 perfect swings in my time, and this lad has one of them."[67]

- Mathews had a quiet but tough demeanor (think John Wayne) and never shied away from a fight (including a memorable dust-up with Frank Robinson in 1960 after an aggressive Robinson slide into 3B).

- Mathews managed the Braves briefly and unsuccessfully in 1972-74 and was criticized for benching Henry Aaron in Cincinnati so that he could break Ruth's career HR record at home in Atlanta. But Mathews' careful use of Aaron during those years helped Aaron manage injuries and the intense pressure he was under.

- Robinson joined the Orioles broadcast team when he finished playing.[68]

- After serving as a special assistant to Brewer GM Harry Daulton from 1982-91, Bando succeeded him as GM in 1992 and held that position until 1999, a difficult period in which the small-market Brewers struggled to keep pace with soaring free agent salaries and could not retain their best players.[69]

Yogi

Yogi Berra (C):
74.1 CVI – New York AL (59.5)

Yogi Berra was not only one of baseball's most beloved and colorful stars, but he was also an institution, ranking sixth among all catchers in CVI (0.71 percentile) and an uncontested first among its philosophers. The 18-time All-Star and three-time MVP was a notorious bad ball hitter, who didn't walk much (704 BB) but struck out even less (414 SO) in more than 8300 career plate appearances. He was a key member of 10 World Series champions plus four additional AL pennant winners and was a strong postseason clutch performer. He leads all catchers with 1430 RBI and ranks third in R, fourth in HR, and sixth in SLG and TB. He also went 484-444 and won two pennants in seven seasons managing the Yankees and Mets. From 1950-59, Yogi hit .287/.356/.490 (130 OPS+) and averaged 26 HR, 100 RBI, 85 R, 256 TB, and 4.8 WAR in 581 PA per season, while hitting mostly in the cleanup spot behind Mantle. But it was his pithy homespun aphorisms and malapropisms, each with a kernel of wisdom at the core, that endeared him to everyone, not just baseball fans.

Berra's boyhood friend Joe Garagiola, a gifted storyteller and prominent broadcaster and TV personality, was largely responsible for creating the "Yogi" persona. Berra himself was a quiet, serious man who most often didn't realize that what he said was funny. Yogi-isms became generic like "Kleenex" and "Xerox" and often included clever quotes that just sounded like something Yogi could have said. For example, "It's tough to make predictions, especially about the future" originated with Danish physicist Nils Bohr but is often attributed to Yogi.[70] As Yogi himself admitted, "I really didn't say everything I said."[71] Still, he said enough of them to feed the legend. Other famous Yogi-isms include, "I want to thank everyone for making this night necessary" and "Always go to other people's funerals, otherwise they won't come to yours, and "Nobody goes there anymore. It's too crowded."[72]

Beyond the Numbers

- Yogi got his nickname from boyhood friends, who thought he waddled when he walked like the Indian fakir in a movie they saw.[73]

- Berra enlisted in the Navy at age 18 in 1943 and served as a machine gunner aboard a rocket boat deployed off the Normandy coast on D-Day, as soldiers assaulted the beach.[74]

- Berra began his Yankee career as an OF/C but was inadequate at both positions. However he worked hard under the mentorship of Bill Dickey and became a good defensive catcher (9.2 dWAR). At the end of his career, Berra moved to LF to make room for young African American star Elston Howard behind the plate.

- Berra had trouble maintaining discipline in his first managerial stint in 1964 and was replaced after the Yankees lost the World Series. He managed the Mets to a pennant in 1973 but again lost in the World Series. George Steinbrenner brought Berra back to manage the Yankees in 1984. Despite a strong second place finish, the impetuous Steinbrenner fired him 16 games into the 1985 season, leading to a 14-year rift between Yogi and the Yankees. He finally reconciled with the contrite Steinbrenner in 1999. Altogether, Berra compiled a 484-444 record with two pennants in seven years managing the Yankees and Mets.

The Boys of Summer[75]

Pee Wee Reese (SS):	Duke Snider (CF):
78.3 CVI – Brooklyn/Los Angeles NL	76.8 CVI – Brooklyn/Los Angeles NL
(*68.2*)	(*65.4*)

The Brooklyn Dodgers, or "Dem Bums" to their frustrated fans, were a doormat team from 1901-46 with only two pennants (1920 and 1941) and no World Series championships. They were constantly outdone by their arch rivals from the Polo Grounds, and both played in the shadow of their uber-successful AL neighbors from the Bronx. But integration suddenly brought the Dodgers to the forefront as one of the iconic teams of the 1950s, as they added Jackie Robinson and Roy Campanella (discussed earlier) and other black stars like Don Newcombe, Joe Black, and Junior Gilliam while most other teams were still clearing their throats. They blended with white stars Snider and Reese and complementary players like Gil Hodges, Carl Furillo, and Johnny Podres to make the Dodgers the national favorites for lovers of the underdog — especially Black fans — whose appeal extended far beyond New York. That final decade in Brooklyn brought the Dodgers six pennants and their first World Series championship in 1955.

The Dodgers' peerless SS and captain Pee Wee Reese provided sterling defense and timely hitting. From 1942-55, interrupted by military service in 1943-45, Reese hit .278/.379/.395 (107 OPS+) while averaging 17 SB (in 24 attempts), 97 runs scored, 5.5 WAR, and 1.8 dWAR. His seasonal WAR was always between 4.1 and 7.4, and his defense was always stellar. His 25.6 career dWAR, achieved despite missing three years in wartime military service, ranks 12th among all SS. He was selected for nine ASG in 1942 and 1946-54. In the 1960s, Reese became the broadcast partner of Dizzy Dean on CBS's Game of the Week. He moved with Game of the Week to NBC as Curt Gowdy's partner in 1966-69 and then spent two years in Cincinnati broadcasting Reds games. Reese's 78.3 CVI ranks ninth at SS and at the 0.58 percentile overall.

Once upon a time, New York ruled baseball, and three sterling CF — Willie, Mickey, and the Duke — ruled New York. Now, in truth, although Duke Snider was a major force in 1953-56, he was almost five years older than Mays and Mantle, who continued to rack up 7-10-WAR seasons long after Snider had passed from relevance. However, while Mays and Mantle were kings, whose careers far surpassed Snider's, the Duke was still royalty. From 1949-57 — the glory years that closed out the Dodgers tenure in Brooklyn — Snider was the team's most feared slugger, hitting .305/.387/.568 and averaging 35 HR, 109 RBI, 107 R, 320 TB, and 6.4 WAR per season. He was also solid in CF except for a hesitancy to charge groundballs, which often enabled batters to take an extra base.

Snider was an outstanding postseason performer and was the Dodgers' top hitter in the 1955 World Series, hitting .320/.370/.840 with 4 HR and 7 RBI, including 2 HR in the 5-3 Game 6 victory that brought the Dodgers back from the brink of defeat. Snider was a seven-time All-Star during this period, plus an "honorary" selection in 1963. He never won an MVP award, but finished second in 1955, third in 1953, and fourth in 1954. However, he declined rapidly after the Dodgers moved to Los Angeles, although he was only 31 years old. His early decline left fans and writers with a lingering sense of unfulfilled promise concerning his career. Although Snider's 76.8 CVI ranks eighth among CF and at the 0.62 percentile overall, the BBWAA did not elect him until his 10th year on the ballot. His contentious relationship with the press may have factored into this delay.

Beyond the Numbers

- The nickname "Pee Wee" came not from Reese's stature, but from his second-place finish in the Louisville Courier peewee marbles competition as a teen.[76]

- Although it is not clear that this really happened, Coney Island commemorates Reese publicly draping his arm on Jackie Robinson's shoulder in Crosley Field (just across the Ohio River from his native Kentucky) to symbolically shield him from the racial abuse he was taking from the fans.[77]

- Snider got the nickname "Duke" from his father for his self-assured swagger.[78]

- In his rookie year, Snider took a liking to fellow rookie Jackie Robinson and refused to sign the petition circulated by Dixie Walker and other Dodger veterans in spring training protesting Robinson's presence on the team.[79]

- Snider spent many years in the broadcast booth for the Padres and Expos after his playing career ended.

The Greatest Team That Didn't Win[80]

Ron Santo (3B):
88.1 CVI – Chicago NL (*72.1*)

Ferguson Jenkins (SP):
86.2 CVI – Chicago NL (*54.9*), Texas AL (*21.9*), Boston AL (*6.9*)

Ernie Banks (SS):
83.8 CVI – Chicago NL (*67.8*)

Billy Williams (LF):
62.7 CVI – Chicago NL (*61.8*)

Not many teams have four still-productive Hall of Famers on their roster at the same time, and most of those teams win pennants. The 1969 Cubs are a painful exception for Cubs fans like me who came of age at that time. The Cubs, who had last appeared in a World Series in 1945 and last won one in 1908, were dismal in the 1950s, with only the great Ernie Banks providing a ray of hope. The early 1960s brought Santo and Williams, but Cubs eccentric owner P.K. Wrigley implemented a system of "rotating head coaches" that made the Cubs a leaguewide laughingstock.

In the meantime, Ernie Banks's prime began to slip away, and the Cubs lost two promising prospects — 2B Ken Hubbs in a plane crash a year after he had won the NL Rookie of the Year award at age 20, and future HOF LF Lou Brock, in a misbegotten trade for sore-armed SP Ernie Broglio.

Finally, in 1966, Wrigley brought in no-nonsense manager Leo Durocher to build a champion, and the Cubs hit rock bottom, finishing last, behind even the two recent expansion teams. But this was the dawn of a new era, in which Santo and Williams flowered, smart trades brought in Fergie Jenkins and Bill Hands, and homegrown players like Glen Beckert, Don Kessinger, and Ken Holtzman made their mark. The Cubs were on their way to a pennant in 1969 when the wheels fell off in late August and early September and the Mets blew by them, as a nine-game Cubs lead turned into an eight-game deficit. The Cubs re-enacted this scenario (albeit less gruesomely) in 1970-72 — building an early lead, and then losing — as the clock ran out on their aging stars. The careers of the four CVI-Plus Cub Hall of Famers of that era are revisited below. Only Williams got the opportunity to play in a postseason, as a DH in Oakland in the 1975 ALCS.

Ron Santo was the Cubs' emotional leader. He was the guy who got the key hit or made the key play, who jumped for joy when they won and hung his head when they lost. The shortening of his career (and his life) by diabetes curtailed his counting stats. Furthermore, because Santo's career peaked during the exact period (1963-72) when MLB offense cratered, Santo's career slash line of .277/.362/.464 was underappreciated, and his HOF candidacy was doomed to languish until after his death in 2010. For example, in Santo's peak year (1967), his solid .300/.395/.512 slash line looks far more impressive when compared to the 1967 MLB average .242/.306/.357. Santo's 153 OPS+ in 1967 and 125 OPS+ for his career give a more accurate picture of his worth.

From 1963 to 1969, Santo averaged 7.7 WAR (ranging from 5.5-9.8) and hit .292/.380/.502 (144 OPS+), averaging 29 HR, 104 RBI, and 92 R per season. He also displayed a sharp batting eye, averaging 86 BB versus 97 SO per season. As well as being a nine-time All-Star, Santo was also a fine defensive 3B with 8.7 career dWAR and five Gold Gloves. In a just world, Santo, whose 88.1 CVI ranks seventh at 3B and at the 0.44 percentile overall, would have been elected to the HOF 20 years earlier, while he was alive to appreciate it.

Fergie Jenkins is indisputably the greatest African American Canadian baseball player of all time, as well as the third best post-Negro League Black pitcher (behind Pedro Martinez and Gibson). A three-time All-Star, Jenkins had seven 20-game-winning seasons during an eight-year span from 1967-74, topped by a 24-win Cy Young award season in 1971 at age 28. Among all pitchers since 1920, only Dwight Gooden (13.3 in 1985), Steve Carlton (12.5 in 1972), and Bob Gibson (11.9 in 1968) surpassed Jenkins' 11.8 combined WAR that year. Jenkins also won 25 games with a 2.82 ERA for Texas in 1974. He was a workhorse, who perennially led the league in starts and complete games, but like his mentor Robin Roberts, his willingness to challenge hitters in the strike zone made him vulnerable to the home run. Jenkins is third behind Roberts and Jamie Moyer with 484 HR allowed in his career.

From 1967-74, Jenkins compiled a 3.07 ERA (123 ERA+) and 1.077 WHIP while averaging 6.6 WAR$_p$ and a 21-14 W-L, 22 CG, 236 SO, and 60 BB in 304 IP per season. Like Gibson, Jenkins knew how to help himself with his bat and glove, accruing 13 HR and 84 RBI over the course of his career and fielding 1.000 in four seasons. His 86.2 CVI ranks 27th among SP and at the 0.47 percentile overall.

Ernie Banks was blessed with a sunny, optimistic temperament, one which, in the words of Kipling's poem "If," could "meet with triumph and disaster and treat those two impostors just the same."[81] That was fortunate, because Ernie Banks's Cubs knew more disaster than triumph. Banks would never have described himself as unlucky, but his timing was off. Not his timing at home plate, which was impeccable. He could turn on a pitch and send it soaring onto Waveland Avenue behind Wrigley Field with seemingly no more than a flick of his strong and supple wrists. But as shown in the table below (which includes only the seasons when he played at least 130 games), he spent his twenties playing SS and hitting like Henry Aaron on an inept team, even winning back-to-back MVP awards in 1958-59, then he spent his thirties playing 1B but hitting more like a SS on a team that had several legitimate but ultimately futile shots at the NL pennant. Moreover, he was a solid defensive SS but a subpar 1B.

Table 6.3: Ernie Banks Before and After Age 30

Years	Position	AVG/OBP/SLG	OPS+	HR/YR	RBI/YR	R/YR	TB/YR	dWAR	WAR
1954-61	SS	.290/.353/.552	138	37	106	94	320	12.3	54.6
1962-69	1B	.260/.307/.450	107	25	91	66	250	-6.5	13.6

Still, the relentlessly positive "Mr. Cub" was always ready to come back the day after a loss to the "friendly confines" of Wrigley Field and proclaim "It's a beautiful day for baseball. Let's play two." So, for better or worse, he came to personify the Cubs' image as "lovable losers." Banks's 83.8 CVI ranks seventh at SS (the position where he accrued the most WAR) and at the 0.49 percentile overall.

Six-time All-Star Billy Williams was the quiet Cubs star, the yang to Ron Santo's yin. His manager Leo Durocher spoke of him as follows: "Billy Williams never gets excited. Never gets mad. Never throws a bat. You write his name down in the same spot every day, and you forget it. He will play left. He will bat third. Billy Williams was a machine."[82] Not literally, but let's just say he never jumped and clicked his heels. Pirate Hall of Famer Willie Stargell once called him the best left-handed hitter he ever saw.

From 1963-72, Williams hit .300/.366/.519 (141 OPS+) and averaged 31 HR, 101 RBI, 101 R, 325 TB, and 5.3 WAR per season. He had his best offensive season at age 34 in 1972, when he hit .333/.398/.606 (171 OPS+) with 37 HR and 122 RBI to win the NL batting and slugging championships and finish second in the MVP voting. However, he had lost so much range by then that his dismal -1.9 dWAR held him to 6.2 WAR. Williams was never more than passable in the OF (and often a lot worse), with -18.0 dWAR over his career; had he been just an average defender, his CVI would have exceeded 70. He posted his best WAR (7.7) at age 27 in 1965 when he was still an adequate OF. Williams's 62.7 CVI ranks 11th in LF and at the 1.15 percentile overall.

Beyond the Numbers

- In 1969, Santo began leaping and clicking his heels when leaving the field after Cub victories. This probably alienated Cubs opponents and their fans and may have subsequently diminished his HOF support.

- As a Cubs broadcaster for 20 years, Santo was the polar opposite of his cerebral predecessor Lou Boudreau and provided little analysis but lots of emotion as he voiced the hopes and frustrations of Cubs fans. Fortunately, his partner Pat Hughes, an excellent even-keeled broadcaster, was there to smooth the rough edges. Deteriorating health from diabetes (which cost him both legs) and bladder cancer (which eventually cost him his life) denied Santo the opportunity to broadcast the Cubs' 2003 postseason run.[83] One can only imagine how he might have reacted to the Cubs collapse in Game 6 of the 2003 NLCS or to the last out of the 2016 World Series.

- Jenkins was a natural athlete who excelled at track, hockey, and basketball, as well as baseball. He toured with the Harlem Globetrotters in 1966-67, as Bob Gibson had done a decade earlier.[84]

- The Cubs signed Banks away from the Kansas City Monarchs, who were managed by Negro League legend Buck O'Neill, in 1950. He served in the Army from 1951-53 before reporting to the Cubs at age 22.

- Leo Durocher unsuccessfully sought to remove the aging Banks from the starting lineup several times, starting in 1966.[85] But Banks kept smiling and never said a bad word about Durocher. Banks remained an everyday player through 1969.

- President Obama awarded Banks the Presidential Medal of Freedom, as "the first black player to suit up for the Cubs and one of the greatest hitters of all time… known as much for his 512 HR as for his cheer and optimism, and his eternal faith that someday the Cubs would go all the way… He is just a wonderful man and an icon of my hometown."[86] The Cubs eventually did go all the way in 2016 — a year after Banks died. Bad timing again.

Beyond the Numbers (cont'd)

- Williams encountered so much bigotry and abuse in AA San Antonio in 1959 that he left the team and went home. The Cubs sent Buck O'Neill to Whistler, AL to persuade him to return.[87]

- Williams broke Stan Musial's NL consecutive games record of 895 in a June 1969 double-header.

The Knuckleballers

Wilbur Wood (SP):	**Hoyt Wilhelm (RP):**
74.7 CVI – Chicago AL (*50.1*)	74.4 CVI – Chicago AL (*16.0*), Baltimore AL (*13.9*), New York Giants NL (*11.0*)

Before Wilhelm, pitchers who threw knuckleballs were curiosities. With a few notable exceptions (like Eddie Cicotte), most were old guys trying to hang on for a year or two before they retired. Wilhelm and Wood both learned the knuckleball as teenagers and relied on it through the best part their MLB careers. Both were successful in a starting and relief role, but Wilhelm earned his fame as a reliever, while Wood's best years were as a starter.

So what is Wilbur Wood doing here? He never received more than 7% of the vote in seven years on the BBWAA ballot, and the Veterans Committee has never given him a serious look. As far as I know, there is no "Wilbur Wood for Hall of Fame" committee pushing his candidacy. Yet this guy was a workhorse, a throwback to an era long past, who had a pretty spectacular seven-year peak — three years as a multi-inning reliever and four years as a 320-380-inning starter, including an 11.8-WAR_p season in 1971 (fourth best after 1920) and a 10.7-WAR_p season in 1972. His CVI is the third highest (behind Bobby Grich and Jack Glasscock) of any HOF-eligible player who was passed over by the BBWAA and remains outside the Hall of Fame.

Knuckleballers just don't get any respect, not even the best lefty knuckleballer of all time. Wood, who learned the knuckleball from his father in junior high school but abandoned it in high school, enjoyed no major league success until he reached Chicago in 1967, where he re-invented himself as a knuckleballer under the tutelage of Hoyt Wilhelm.[88] He became a bullpen stalwart for a good White Sox team in 1967-70, highlighted by a 5.4-WAR_p (10.2 leveraged WAR) 1968 season, when he went 13-12 with 16 saves and a 1.87 ERA in a whopping 159 innings and 88 appearances, all but two of them in relief.

Wilbur Wood

Then, in 1971 new White Sox manager Chuck Tanner and pitching coach Johnny Sain moved Wood to the starting rotation, where he far exceeded expectations. From 1971-74, Wood posted a 2.86 ERA (127 ERA+) and 1.144 WHIP and averaged a 22-17 W-L record, 348 IP, 21 CG, 5 SHO, 193 SO, 77 BB, and 8.9 WAR$_p$ (including his historic 11.8 WAR$_p$ in 1971) for a so-so team. Wood's 24-20 record in 1973 made him the first pitcher since Walter Johnson to win and lose 20 games in the same season, a feat he nearly repeated with a 20-19 record in 1974. Wood appeared in the 1971-72 and 1974 All-Star games and finished first, second, and fifth in the AL in WAR$_p$ in 1971-73., but never finished better than seventh in the Cy Young award voting. Unfortunately, Wood's career was permanently derailed in 1975 when his knee was shattered by a line drive through the box.

Wood's 74.7 CVI ranks at the 0.67 percentile, which ought to be good enough to make him a Hall of Famer. Before you dismiss this idea as preposterous, please consider that Wood's 35.7 WAR$_p$ in 1971-74 is only slightly less than Koufax's 36.4 in 1963-66 and that his 164 career W (held down by years in the bullpen) is only one less than Koufax. Of course, I would not dare to suggest that Wood was as good as Koufax. But would it be so bad for the HOF to make room for an obscure, short, chubby, hard-working, soft-tossing lefty knuckleballer named Wilbur, who for a few years stood tall among the best in the game?

No other player is quite like Hoyt Wilhelm, the first career knuckleballer and the first reliever in the HOF. Unlike most of his predecessors, who used the knuckler as a secondary pitch, Wilhelm threw it on almost every pitch. Wilhelm also stood out because of the advanced age at which he broke into the major leagues (29) and at which he retired (49), a pattern emulated later by knuckleballers like Phil Niekro and Charlie Hough. Before his career was half over, he had earned the nickname "Old Folks."

But most of all, Wilhelm stands out because he was so difficult to hit and score against. In 2254.3 IP, his 147 ERA+ is tied with Walter Johnson as the sixth best of all time, and he is ninth in H9. Wilhelm's 0.92 SO/H ranks fourth among pitchers who completed their careers by 1972. Wilhelm was anything but an overnight success. He spent six years in the minors after his 1945 army discharge and did not reach the major leagues until 1952. Before the invention of the closer, when

RP were used in multi-inning stints rather than exclusively in save situations, Wilhelm's 228 career save total may seem unimpressive, but his CVI (which considers the leverage of situations when he entered a game) better indicates his true value. In his rookie year, Wilhelm got into 71 games, all in relief, pitched a remarkable 159 IP, finished 15-3 with 11 saves, and led the NL with a 2.43 ERA (the first and only time a RP has done this). He even finished fourth in the NL MVP voting, although he lost to Joe Black for NL Rookie of the Year. Two years later, Wilhelm was a valuable cog of the 1954 Giants World Series champions, pitching 2.3 scoreless innings in what would be his only postseason appearance. From there, Wilhelm moved from team to team, making his longest stops with the Orioles (1958-61) and the White Sox (1963-68). His career best 7.6 WAR$_p$ came in 1959 as a starter in Baltimore, when he went 15-11 with a league-leading 2.19 ERA (173 ERA+) and a 1.128 WHIP in 226 IP. He returned to the bullpen in 1960 and starred through the decade, including a 6-year stretch from 1963-68 in which he averaged 110 IP and had an ERA below 2.00 every season. Wilhelm appeared in eight ASG. Wilhelm's 74.3 CVI ranks fourth among RP and at the 0.70 percentile overall.

Beyond the Numbers

- Although Wood enjoyed considerable success in high school without the knuckleball, scouts viewed him as a non-prospect — small and chubby with an indifferent fastball. The Red Sox signed him only to capitalize on his local celebrity as a three-sport high school athlete.[89]

- Wilhelm taught himself the knuckleball in high school from a picture of Emil "Dutch" Leonard, who dug his index and middle fingers (not his knuckles) into the seam. He began using the pitch in high school games, with encouragement from his coach.[90]

- Wilhelm spent three years in the army, saw combat in Europe, and (like Warren Spahn) received the Purple Heart for wounds suffered in the Battle of the Bulge.[91]

Three True Outcomes

Willie McCovey (1B):
69.4 CVI – San Francisco NL (*59.4*)

Jim Wynn (CF):
59.4 CVI – Houston NL (*41.5*),
Los Angeles NL (*12.4*)

Harmon Killebrew (1B):
56.3 CVI – Washington/Minnesota AL (*60.5*)

Willie Stargell (LF):
55.5 CVI – Pittsburgh NL (*57.5*)

Ralph Kiner (LF):
55.2 CVI – Pittsburgh NL (*43.3*)

Even after the Deadball Era gave way to the Babe Ruth and the new breed of HR sluggers, hitters took pains to make contact and avoid striking out. The five players in this group, along with Mickey Mantle and Dick Allen (who are profiled under their own headings), were the vanguard of a new breed of sluggers who swung for the fences, even if it meant striking out at rates that even Babe Ruth and Jimmy Foxx (the most strikeout-prone pre-1950 hitters) never dreamed of. While Ruth and Foxx had fewer than half as many strikeouts as hits, the SO/H ratios of Stargell (0.87), Wynn (0.86), Allen (0.84), Killebrew (0.81), McCovey (0.70), and even Kiner (0.52) easily surpassed them. Each of them had strikeouts, walks, HBP, or HR (3TO) in 34.4% (Kiner) to 39.4% (Killebrew) of their PA, more than any pre-1972 players, except for Mantle (40.3%) and Ruth (39.1%). Unlike Mantle, these were all one-dimensional players with no speed and subpar defense, which helps explain why they do not rank higher in WAR or CVI.

Six-time All-Star Willie McCovey didn't hit more HR than everyone else – he just hit them harder. A classic 3TO slugger along the lines of Mantle and Dick Allen, with 36% 3TO and 0.70 SO/H, the 6'4" lefty-hitting gentle Giant, was known and feared for his wicked line drives and was as famous for hitting the fearsome line drive snared by a leaping Bobby Richardson to end the 1962 World Series (immortalized in a classic Peanuts cartoon, where Charlie Brown laments, "Why couldn't McCovey have hit the ball just three feet higher?") as for any of his 521 HR.[92] Among those 521 HR were 18 grand slams, an all-time NL record.

McCovey made an early and spectacular MLB debut in the last two months of the 1959 season, going 4-4 with two triples against future Hall of Famer Robin Roberts in his major league debut and finished his rookie season hitting .354/.429/.656 (188 OPS+) with 13 HR and 38 RBI in two months.[93] But he was blocked from regular playing time for five years by the presence of another equally young HOF 1B, Orlando Cepeda, on the Giants roster. The Giants tried to accommodate both players by platooning and playing Cepeda at 3B or McCovey in LF, but both men were fish out of water at any position but 1B. Finally, the logjam was broken when a knee injury sidelined Cepeda in 1965 and he was traded to St. Louis in 1966.

When McCovey, who also suffered from chronically arthritic knees and ankles, finally had the Giants 1B job to himself, he overcame his early inconsistency and emerged as a star. In 1965-70, he hit .291/.405/.578 (174 OPS+) and averaged 38 HR, 106 RBI, 88 R, 290 TB, and 6.4 WAR per season, despite worsening chronic knee and ankle pain. In 1968, the "Year of the Pitcher," McCovey simply didn't get the memo; he hit .293/.378/.545 (174 OPS+), and his 36 HR and 105 RBI led the NL. He did even better in 1969, hitting .320/.453/.656 (209 OPS+) with 45 HR,

126 RBI, 101 R, 322 TB, and 8.1 WAR to take NL MVP honors. McCovey's 69.4 CVI ranks 13th at 1B and at the 0.87 percentile overall.

Wynn, Killebrew, Stargell, and Kiner all seem to fall squarely in HOVG territory (1.23 to 1.42 percentile), but the BBWAA elected the latter three to the HOF. So, why were they treated so well, while Wynn (who had the highest CVI of the lot) received not a single HOF vote? The short answer is "black type" – i.e., HR titles, ASG selections, MVP awards, etc., and Wynn's offensive stats were greatly supressed by playing in the Astrodome and Dodgers Stadium. Although Killebrew hit only .256, he was an MVP and 13-time All-Star, whose 573 HR ranked fifth on the career leaderboard before the Steroid Era. Stargell, who hit 475 HR and played in seven ASG, won the 1979 NL co-MVP award based more on his leadership of the close-knit Pirates team than on his 139-OPS+, 2.5-WAR performance.[94] Kiner's CVI was held down by back problems, but his abbreviated 10-year career, mostly with dismal second-division teams included some spectacular highs. He had three 8-WAR seasons, led the NL in HR for seven consecutive seasons (1946-52), and is one of five pre-Steroid Era players with two or more 50-HR seasons.

Wynn, on the other hand, played in only three ASG, finished in the top 10 in MVP voting only once (fifth in 1974), never led the NL in anything except BB and SO, hit only .250 (but with a .366 OBP), and played in only one postseason (for the 1974 Dodgers, hitting only .192/.450/.423). However, he did have 30-HR power (topping out at 37 in 1967) and once stole 43 bases (1965). Although Wynn was only a so-so defender (-6.4 dWAR), he was better than Kiner (-10.7) and far better than Killebrew (-18.7 dWAR) or Stargell (-19.5 dWAR). Thus, Wynn was arguably the best all-around player of the four. However, Killebrew, Stargell, and Kiner were more memorable and did more to impress HOF voters.

Beyond the Numbers

- Kiner spent many years as a broadcaster for the Mets and hosted a popular post-game TV show called Kiner's Korner. While he was no Yogi Berra, he was known for "Kinerisms" like "Bruce Sutter's injury will keep him out of action for the rest of his career." and "If Casey Stengel were alive today, he'd be spinning in his grave."[95]

Confronting the Old Guard

Dick Allen (1B):
66.5 CVI – Philadelphia NL (35.4), Chicago AL (15.4)

Long before Manny was Manny, there was Dick Allen. Allen was an enigma — an immensely gifted hitter, who unfortunately is also remembered for the repeated clashes with managers and teammates that marred his career, especially in Philadelphia, than for his impressive accomplishments on the field.[96]

As a Black man who grew up in the shelter of a large close-knit family in a racially tolerant small Pennsylvania town, Allen had a rude awakening when in 1963 the Phillies sent him to Arkansas for AAA seasoning. There he encountered racial taunts, harassment, and threats that nearly made him quit. So when he reached Philadelphia – a city with a history of poor treatment of Black athletes – in 1964, he was already on his guard. Unlike players like Mays and Aaron, who grew up in the Jim Crow rural south and were conditioned not to draw attention to themselves, and players like Frank and Jackie Robinson, Bob Gibson, and Joe Morgan, who grew up in urban environments and channeled their anger into aggressive play, Allen was ill-equipped to cope with the Philly boo-birds and MLB's stubbornly conservative culture despite the changes going on in society beyond baseball. He could not understand why fans booed him and teammates disliked him or why he met with resistance when he said he wanted to be known as "Dick" instead of "Richie." (his preferred nickname).

So Allen frequently rebelled and drove his old-school managers Gene Mauch, Bob Skinner, and Danny Ozark crazy. Examples include:

- As a rookie, he punched out veteran teammate Frank Thomas (not the Hall of Famer) for calling him "Muhammad Clay." When Thomas was released, the fans booed Allen.

- Later that season, he professed indifference to the Rookie of the Year award because it carried no monetary value.

- In 1969, he was late for a night game after spending the day at the racetrack and refused to meet with manager Bob Skinner for nearly a month after learning that he was suspended. Phillies owner Bob Carpenter finally intervened to end the standoff.

- Things improved in 1972 under White Sox manager Chuck Tanner, who hailed from New Castle, PA, not far from Allen's hometown of Wampum, and gave Allen a lot of latitude. But this relationship soured two years later when an injured Allen tearfully announced his retirement in September 1974, refused a trade to Atlanta, and then shockingly requested a trade – to Philadelphia of all places – a few months later.

- In his second stint with the Phillies in 1976, Allen left the team without permission to consult his own doctor after an injury. Later that season, he refused to pinch hit after being benched during a slump, publicly criticized Ozark's handling of young black players, and skipped the Phillies' celebration of their East Division title clinching. After a slow start in 1977, Allen was released.

In short, Allen's problems in Philadelphia were like a bad marriage in which both sides shared blame. He was treated poorly at times, especially by fans and the press, but his inflexibility and self-absorption undoubtedly played a role.

Still, through all the turmoil, Allen was a terrific hitter in his nine-year prime. His 51.5 WAR in 1964-72 ranked sixth among all MLB hitters, trailing only Clemente (64.7), Aaron (62.1), Santo (59.4), Yastrzemski (59.1), and Mays (58.3). During this period, Allen appeared in seven ASG, hitting over .300 seven times, slugging 29 or more HR seven times, and leading his league in OBP twice and SLG and OPS+ three times. His two best years – in 1964 and 1972 – were impressive bookends to this dominant period. In his 8.8-WAR Rookie of the Year season in Philadelphia, he hit .318/.382/.557 (162 OPS+) with 29 HR, 91 RBI, and a league-leading 125 R and 352 TB. In his 1972 8.6 WAR MVP season with the White Sox, he hit .308/.420/.603 (199 OPS+) with 37 HR, 113 RBI (all league-leading figures and career highs, except AVG). Were it not for the Phillies' epic September collapse that cost them the pennant, Allen might have won the 1964 MVP award as well.

Allen's 66.5 CVI (1.01 percentile and 15th at 1B) makes him a strong HOF contender, but not a shoo-in. Allen's indifferent defense at 3B and 1B (-16.3 dWAR) kept his CVI from being higher. So, what did the HOF voters do with an enigma like Allen, whose misadventures at times overshadowed and undermined his prodigious talent? Allen remained on the BBWAA ballot for 15 years but never received more than 19% of the vote. He has appeared periodically on the VC ballot and fell just one vote short of election in 2014. He was among the ten finalists on the 2020 VC "Golden Age" ballot, but the Covid-19 pandemic forced postponement of the vote (which was to have taken place a day before his death). He will likely be honored posthumously in 2021.

Dick Allen

Beyond the Numbers

- In October 1969, Allen was part of the fateful trade that would have brought Cardinals CF Curt Flood to Philadelphia. Flood's unsuccessful court challenge to this trade and to the Reserve Clause set the ball rolling toward free agency six years later.

- Pursuant to the bad marriage metaphor, Allen's reunion with Philly in May 1975 came five months before the re-marriage of Richard Burton and Elizabeth Taylor and had about as much chance of success.[97] After a terrible 1975 season, Allen got off to a good start in 1976 before re injuring his shoulder on July 25 (the day of the second Burton-Taylor divorce). That injury triggered a cascade of events (described above) that culminated in Allen's release the following spring. At least, the second Allen-Phillies marriage outlasted the second Burton-Taylor marriage 22 months to 10.

- Like Burton and Taylor, Allen and the Phillies grew closer after their second divorce. The Phillies invited him to throw out the first pitch of the 2009 NLDS, and he was inducted into the Philadelphia Sports Hall of Fame in 2010. In a final gesture of affection, the Phillies retired his number in September 2020, shortly before his death.

The Speed Game

Richie Ashburn (CF):
67.4 CVI – Philadelphia NL (*58.2*)

Enos Slaughter (RF):
62.8 CVI – St. Louis NL (*52.2*)

Willie Davis (CF):
57.0 CVI – Los Angeles NL (*54.6*)

Vada Pinson (CF):
54.1 CVI – Cincinnati (*47.7*)

The stolen base never really disappeared from baseball, but it slowly fell out of favor as scoring rose after the transition from deadball to longball. From 1930 through 1958, only George Case (four times), Ben Chapman, Wally Moses, and Snuffy Stirnweiss had more than 40 SB in a season, and no one had more than 61 SB. That is not to say that speed and aggressive baserunning – as exemplified by Jackie Robinson and Enos Slaughter – were not valued; it was more that the risk of getting thrown out outweighed the chance to gain an extra base when base hits were so easy to come by. However, as hitting and scoring waned in the 1960s, the calculus changed, and players like Maury Wills, Lou Brock, Bert Campaneris, and Willie Davis began taking more liberties on the basepaths to manufacture more runs.

The CVI-Plus players in this section reflect this transition. All were aggressive and effective baserunners, but Slaughter, who debuted in 1938, never stole as many as 10 bases in a season. Ashburn, who debuted in 1948, stole 234 bases, peaking with an NL-leading 32 SB in his rookie season, and was an excellent CF (5.4 dWAR). Both were contact hitters with little power, who bucked the 3TO trend of the Boom generation. Pinson, who debuted in 1958, stole 305 bases (but never more than 32 in any season) brought more power (256 HR) to the mix. Davis, who debuted in 1960, stole 398 bases, peaking at 42 in 1964, and was the only elite defender (11.1 dWAR) in this grouping.

Six-time All-Star Richie Ashburn was a speedy leadoff hitter and offensive catalyst of the 1950 Whiz Kids Phillies, who won a surprise pennant in 1950. His .396 OBP and .074 ISO (82% of his hits were singles) would have made him feel at home in the Deadball Era. He began his career as a small speedy lefty hitting catcher with a weak throwing arm, but quickly switched to CF for obvious reasons. In his prime (1951-58), when he hit .319/.406/.400 (118 OPS+) and averaged 193 H, 98 R, 86 BB, 17 SB. Except for 3.4 WAR in 1952, his WAR remained between 5.4 and 7.1 (averaging 6.0). He led the NL in AVG in 1955 and 1958 and in OBP in both years plus 1954. Despite his 7.1 WAR in 1954, his best overall season may have been 1958 (7.0 WAR), when he also led the NL in H, 3B, and BB. He had one more good season with the Cubs in 1960, leading the NL with a .415 OBP and 116 BB, before finishing with the 1962 Mets.

Ashburn may be even better known and more beloved by Phillies fans for his long and successful 34-year career in broadcasting, paired with Harry Kalas, which kept him in the public eye long after his playing career had become a distant memory.[98] Although Ashburn never got more than 42% support from the BBWAA in 15-years on the HOF ballot, his colorful radio persona and anecdotes kept his memory fresh until the VC finally (and deservedly) honored him in 1995. His 67.4 CVI ranks 12th in CF and at the 0.97 percentile overall.

Although his ex-teammate Stan Musial helped get him elected, 10-time All-Star Enos Slaughter, a .300 hitter with .382 OBP and 124 OPS+, is a defensible HOF selection. He played 13 seasons for the Cardinals, despite losing three years to World War II, and went on to play six more seasons in the AL, mostly as a platoon player and clutch pinch hitter for the Yankees. Known for his aggressive baserunning, he is best remembered for his "mad dash" to score the winning run from 1B on a single against the Red Sox in the Game 7 of the 1946 World Series.[99] He played in five World Series overall — two with the Cardinals and three with the Yankees and came out on the winning end in four of them. His 62.8 CVI ranks at the 1.14 percentile overall.

Davis (1.31 percentile) and Pinson (1.48 percentile) fall in the HOVG category. Davis, who played in the shadows of more celebrated teammates on the 1963-66 Dodgers, who won three pennants and two World Series, was underappreciated at the time, although his sterling defense probably saved Koufax and Drysdale a few runs over the years. His career offensive numbers, which include 2561 hits and 182 home runs, were greatly curtailed by his playing nearly his entire career in cavernous Dodgers Stadium. Still, he left no milestone achievements behind to attract HOF support. He received no HOF votes from the BBWAA and has never gotten any attention from the VC.

As Frank Robinson's teammate on the strong Cincinnati teams of the early 1960s, Pinson appeared to be on the HOF fast track with his mixture of power and speed and his five 5-WAR seasons by the age of 26. But his career fizzled early, and he never had more than 2.4 WAR after his age 28 season, as he bounced around among four teams. He received modest HOF support in his 15 years on the BBWAA ballot (peaking at 15.7%) and subsequently from the VC, but has never come close to election.

The Skipper

Joe Torre:
65.0 CVI – Milwaukee/Atlanta NL (*33.3*), St. Louis NL (*22.5*)

Torre never played for the Yankees and never played a postseason game in his 18-year career with the Braves, Cardinals and Mets. It was his managerial success with the Yankees, where he absorbed the constant turmoil emanating from George Steinbrenner and provided a sense of calm confidence in the clubhouse, that got him into the HOF and could have earned him a Nobel Peace Prize if Sweden cared about baseball. But before all that, Torre was a CVI-Plus player, who began as a catcher, then switched to 3B in mid-career. His best position was hitter. In his prime (1963-71), Torre was a middle-of-the-order hitter, who played in nine ASG and averaged .308/.372/.483 (139 OPS+) with 21 HR, 91 RBI, 74 R, 4.7 WAR, and -0.1 dWAR per season. He won the NL MVP award as a 3B in 1971, when he hit .363/.421/.555 (171 OPS+) with 24 HR and 5.9 WAR (slightly below his 1966 WAR) and led the NL in AVG, H (230), RBI (137), and TB (352). His 65.0 CVI ranks 10th among catchers and at the 1.07 percentile overall. That could easily have been enough to make him a Hall of Famer, but his excellence as a player was greatly underappreciated by HOF voters.

Beyond the Numbers

- In 12 years at the Yankee helm (1996-2007), Torre posted a 1173-767 record, winning 10 AL East pennants, going to six World Series, and winning four of them. It was his first managerial success after 15 lackluster seasons (1977-95) with the Mets, Braves, and Cardinals.

Hall of the Very Good

Lindy McDaniel (RP):
56.1 CVI –St. Louis NL (*11.0*), New York
AL (*9.8*), Chicago NL (*5.8*)

Jim Kaat (SP):
53.3 CVI – Minnesota AL (*35.6*),
Chicago AL (*15.3*)

Bill Freehan (C):
53.1 CVI – Detroit AL (*44.4*)

While Kaat (no doubt because of his 283 career wins) was the only one of these players to garner significant HOF support and none really belongs in the HOF, it is worth pausing for a moment to remember how good forgotten men McDaniel and Freehan were. McDaniel's heyday came before the closer role and the save were invented, so he has only 174 saves (but 141 wins) to show for his remarkably consistent 21-year career. He compiled a 3.19 ERA (110 ERA+) and 1.272 WHIP, and remained productive into his late 30s, long after many RP have given up the ghost. He posted 12.3 and 9.1 leveraged WAR in his two best seasons, 1960 and 1970, spaced 10 years apart. His 56.1 CVI (1.37 percentile) places him seventh among RP between Trevor Hoffman and Lee Smith.

Freehan was an 11-time All Star who was recognized as the premier catcher in the AL from 1966-72, and was a core contributor to the Tigers' 1968 World Series Championship and 1972 AL East Division title. He was a solid two-way catcher (112 OPS+ and 12.0 dWAR) with 200 HR in his 15 years in Detroit. His 53.1 CVI (1.54 percentile) places him 16th among all catchers, not high enough for the HOF perhaps, but still very respectable.

Kaat was a fine pitcher in both a starting and relief role for 25 years. His two best years were 1974 and 1975 with the White Sox when he went 21-13 and 20-14 with a combined 3.02 ERA (127 ERA+) and a 1.246 WHIP and compiled 14.8 WAR$_p$. He finished a distant fourth in the AL Cy Young voting in 1975. He was also named AL Pitcher of the Year by the Sporting News when he won 25 games in 1966 (with only 4.5 WAR). He also won 16 Gold Gloves with a career BA of .185 (with 16 HR), contributing to 5.6 oWAR. In 15 years on the BBWAA ballot, he never received as many as 30% of the HOF votes. He was considered on the VC ballot as recently as 2015. His 53.3 CVI places him at the 1.53 percentile.

Other Hall of Famers

Table 6.4: CVI-MINUS HALL OF FAMERS

A) Hitters (Position)	MidCareer	HOF	AVG/OBP/OBS	OPS+	WAR$_H$	CVI
Perez, Tony (1B)	1972	BBWAA	.279/.341/.463	122	54.0	51.4
Rizzuto, Phil (SS)	1949	VC	.273/.351/.355	93	42.0	48.7
Fox, Nellie (2B)	1957	VC	.288/.348/.363	93	49.5	47.1
Aparicio, Luis (SS)	1964	BBWAA	.262/.311/.343	82	55.9	46.4
Cepeda, Orlando (1B)	1963	VC	.297/.350/.499	133	50.1	45.7
Brock, Lou (LF)	1968	BBWAA	.293/.343/.410	109	45.4	42.3
Schoendienst, Red (2B)	1953	VC	.289/.337/.387	94	44.2	39.8
Kell, George (3B)	1950	VC	.306/.367/.414	112	37.6	30.2
Mazeroski, Bill (2B)	1963	VC	.260/.299/.367	84	36.5	30.1

B) Pitchers	MidCareer	HOF	ERA/WHIP	ERA+	WAR$_P$	CVI
Ford, Whitey (SP)	1960	BBWAA	2.75/1.215	133	53.6	52.8
Lemon, Bob (SP)	1952	BBWAA	3.23/1.337	119	37.6	40.9

The 11 CVI-Minus Hall of Famers listed in Table 6.4 (nine hitters and two pitchers) is far more reasonable that the 28 such players in Table 5.3 and reflects the tighter rules and selection criteria under which the VC operated after 1980. Still, six of these 11 questionable HOF selections were made by the VC. Although the impact of cronyism was far less than in the Classical era, only one of the six VC selections (Fox) got in without an ex-teammate or close associate among their electors.[100] As in Chapter 3-5, capsule comments on these 11 players are provided below.

Whitey Ford's 52.8 CVI ranks 237th among HOF-eligible players and just missed the CVI-Plus cut. I personally am surprised that Ford is ranked so low. This may be because Yankee manager Casey Stengel coddled him in his 20s, only once allowing him to pitch more than 225.7 IP until 1961 (his age 32 season) in an era when most aces logged 270-300 IP. Also, Ford's unimpressive 52.8 CVI does not consider his reputation as a big-game pitcher and his outstanding postseason record, including 10 World Series wins and a World Series record 33 consecutive scoreless innings in 1960-62 (breaking Babe Ruth's record of 29.2, which had stood since 1918). While Ford's HOF qualifications do not quite measure up to the all-time greats, he is far from the worst pitcher in the HOF.

Soft-hitting middle infielders Aparicio (31.0 dWAR), Mazeroski (24.0 dWAR), Rizzuto (22.9 dWAR), Fox (21.0 dWAR), and Schoendienst (15.2 dWAR) were all elected based on their undeniable defensive prowess. Mazeroski, who leads all 2B in dWAR and hit a memorable walk-off HR in Game 7 of the 1960 World Series, and Aparicio, whose dWAR ranks fifth at SS, are in the Rabbit Maranville tradition of good-field-no-hit HOF middle infielders; both had OPS+ <85. The three others were less elite on defense and a little better on offense. Rizzuto was a key contributor to the Yankee championship dynasty of 1949-53 and was named AL MVP in 1950. Fox's contact skills were legendary; only Willie Keeler, Joe Sewell, and Lloyd Waner had fewer SO/H. Schoendienst was a fine player and manager for many years. I personally would reserve the HOF for players with more well-rounded skill sets, but these selections are consistent with the Maranvilles and Tinkers of earlier eras.

Brock compiled 3023 hits (passing the magic 3000) and held the career stolen base record (938) before Rickey Henderson came along, so I understand why the BBWAA elected him. But I don't agree with that decision. Brock was a weak defender (-16.8 dWAR) with middling on-base skills and an 0.57 SO/H that was acceptable only for a power hitter. And his CVI was not even in the top 2%. Perez and Cepeda were strong RBI men with otherwise thin HOF creden-

Bill Mazeroski

tials. Perez was an important cog of the Big Red Machine. Cepeda was the 1967 NL MVP at age 29, but was unproductive afterwards. Lemon was a good but not great pitcher and manager.

Bottom of the Pile

Although his CVI was 0.1 higher than Mazeroski's, I have placed George Kell at the bottom of the pile. While Mazeroski was perhaps the best ever defensive 2B, Kell

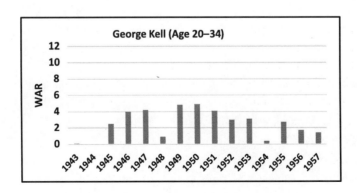

was nothing more than a good but unmemorable player, with a .306 lifetime AVG, but no power, only passable defense (1.6 career dWAR), and no 5-WAR seasons. Scott Rolen, Ken Boyer, Graig Nettles, Buddy Bell, and Sal Bando were all far better 3B than Kell, yet are not in the HOF. Indeed, 386 hitters have more than Kell's 35.7 WAR – including 34 who played at least 75% of their games at 3B. Bill Madlock (38.2 WAR) – no one's idea of a Hall of Famer – is perhaps the most similar to Kell, and Madlock won four batting titles to Kell's one.

CHAPTER 7

THE FREE AGENT GENERATION (1973-1993)

The Game

The racial integration and geographic expansion of the Boom Era made MLB a truly national enterprise and created unprecedented opportunities for revenue growth. As late as 1962, MLB's annual TV revenue totaled only $16.2 million 75% of which was generated locally and benefited mostly the teams in major media markets.[1] By 1983, thanks to big national TV contracts, MLB's annual TV revenue had increased almost tenfold to $153.7 million and total revenues had grown to $500 million annually.[2] Yet player salaries of the 1960s and early 1970s lagged far behind this growth. Before 1975, when arbitrator Peter Seitz declared that star pitchers Dave McNally and Andy Messersmith, who had played the 1975 season without signing contracts, were free agents, thus effectively ending the 96-year reign of the Reserve Clause, no player earned more than Henry Aaron's $240,000 annual salary.[3,4] Five years later, Nolan Ryan received MLB's first million dollar contract. When this era closed in 1993, Bobby Bonilla's contract paid him over $6 million annually.

Seitz's decision set off an acrimonious 20-year labor war, peppered by several work stoppages – one causing cancellation of the middle third of the 1981 season and the last (and most brutal) causing cancellation of the last third of the 1994 season and the entire post season.[5-7] In 1997, MLB players and owners finally achieved a lasting (if uneasy) compromise, in which owners retained some measure of player control over the early portion of their careers, but players were permitted to move freely and earn free-market value thereafter.

From its inception in 1879, proponents of the Reserve Clause system had argued vehemently that this system was absolutely essential to maintaining competitive balance and that without it, rich teams would buy up all the top talent, while poor teams, bereft and unable to compete, would be squeezed into irrelevance or even non-existence.[8,9] Eventually, they argued, fan interest for even the wealthy teams would die without real competition, and MLB itself would die. Of course, this self-serving argument flies in the face of the empirical evidence that the Reserve Clause did not prevent the Yankees from winning 29 AL pennants and 20 World Series in 44 years from 1921-64, while sad sack teams like the Browns, Senators, Red Sox, Phillies, and White Sox rarely fielded competitive teams. Surprisingly, far from destroying competitive balance, the advent of free agency brought unprece-dented competitive parity by multiple objective measures.[10] The gap between good and bad teams narrowed, and the upward mobility of bad teams and downward mobility of good teams increased. Although George Steinbrenner's Yankees were able to leverage the new free agency system into a brief a run of success in 1976-81 with four AL pennants and World Series wins in 1977-78, it was the Yankees who became irrelevant in 1982-94, trading away prospects, fielding poorly constructed rosters with bloated payrolls, and winning nothing. Thirteen of the 26 MLB teams won at least one World Series in this era — three for the Athletics and Reds, two for the Blue Jays, Dodgers, Twins, and Yankees, and one for the Cardinals, Mets, Orioles, Phillies, Pirates, Royals, and Tigers. Five other teams — the Braves, Brewers, Giants, Padres, and Red Sox — appeared in at least one World Series but didn't win. Five other teams — the Angels, Astros, Cubs, Expos, and White Sox — made postseason appearances without reaching the World Series. Only three teams — the Indians, Mariners, and Rangers — were shut out. Competitive balance remains far greater today than at any time during the long reign of the Reserve Clause.

While the overthrow of the Reserve Clause revolutionized baseball off the field, the 1970s and 1980s were a time of remarkable stability on the field. Scoring generally remained between 4.0 and 4.5 runs per team per game (with a slight upward trend on the eve of the Steroid Era) — well below the heights of the 1890s and 1930's, but well above the drought levels of the Deadball Era and the 1960s. HR rates stabilized at about 0.75 per team per game, interrupting the steady climb from 1920-1972 (which resumed in the 1990s). The mix of players was eclectic, drawing from all previous eras.

Looking for 3TO sluggers? How about Mike Schmidt (the new 3TO king at 39.9%) and Reggie Jackson (the new whiff king with 1.005 SO/H)? Looking for elite contact hitters who were a threat to hit .400 and would look at home playing alongside the smallballers of old? Meet Wade Boggs, George Brett, Rod Carew, and Tony Gwynn. Looking for elite base stealers, who could stack up with Cobb, Collins, and Billy Hamilton? Rickey Henderson, Tim Raines, Joe Morgan, and Vince Coleman are your guys. Looking for guys who knew how to draw walks? Henderson, Morgan, Schmidt, and Boggs fill the bill. Looking for power pitchers? How about Nolan Ryan, who led all pitchers to that point with 39.8% 3TO and 1.46 SO/H, Tom Seaver, and Steve Carlton. Looking for finesse and trickery? How about knuckleballer Phil Niekro?

This era produced only one player (Schmidt) who cracked the all-time Top 20 in CVI but produced 21.1% of all players with CVI >100 (12/57) and 19.7% of all players with CVI ≥60 (40/203). It also produced two consensus #1 players at their positions – Schmidt at 3B, and Johnny Bench at C—and perhaps the top defensive player of all time, Ozzie Smith.

The Free Agent Era did bring two significant changes in the game itself. The AL introduced the designated hitter rule in 1973 to stimulate scoring. The new rule created an ERA disparity of about 0.4 between the two leagues (which has shrunk since the advent of interleague play) as well as differences in-game strategy. It also provided a haven in AL lineups for aging and defensively challenged players who could still hit.

The second change was the popularization of specialized bullpen roles. After a decade of workhorse pitchers like Phil Niekro, Nolan Ryan, Gaylord, Perry, Don Sutton, and Steve Carlton, who rank among the top 10 of all time in IP, the 1980s saw the rise of the relief pitcher, starting with guys like Richard "Goose" Gossage, Dan Quisenberry, and Bruce Sutter and evolving under A's manager Tony LaRussa to the deployment of Dennis Eckersley exclusively in the ninth inning in 1988. In the ensuing decades, closers (and their shady statistical companion, the save) would attain outsized prominence. In the meantime, complete games dropped, and 300-inning starters vanished (see Appendix 1, Figures A1.8-11).

Significant demographic changes in MLB also gained momentum. Through the mid-1980s, baseball had appeared to reach a stable equilibrium with about 70% Whites, 18% African-Americans, and 12% Latinos.[1] But starting in 1987, the prevalence of Latinos in MLB began to rise as baseball became an increasingly international sport, while the prevalence of African Americans began to drop. In 1993 the prevalence of Latinos (16.9%) exceeded the prevalence of African Americans (16.8%) for the first time since integration. The prevalence of Whites declined slightly to 66%. These trends have accelerated since then.

The Players

Table 7.1: CVI-Plus Players

A) Hitters (Position)	MidCareer	HOF	AVG/OBP/SLG	OPS+	WAR$_{11}$	CVI
Schmidt, Mike (3B)	1980	BBWAA	.267/.380/.527	147	106.9	142.0
Henderson, Rickey (LF)	1988	BBWAA	.279/.401/.419	127	111.2	134.9
Morgan, Joe (2B)	1974	BBWAA	.271/.392/.427	132	100.5	120.6
Ripken, Cal (SS)	1989	BBWAA	.276/.340/.447	112	95.9	113.3
Bench, Johnny (C)	1974	BBWAA	.267/.342/.476	126	75.2	111.7
Boggs, Wade (3B)	1988	BBWAA	.328/.415/.443	131	91.4	110.8
Carter, Gary (C)	1982	BBWAA	.262/.335/.439	115	70.1	103.1
Brett, George (3B)	1980	BBWAA	.305/.369/.487	135	88.6	101.3
Carew, Rod (2B)	1975	BBWAA	.328/.393/.429	131	81.3	88.7
Yount, Robin (SS)	1983	BBWAA	.285/.342/.430	115	77.3	83.9
Fisk, Carlton (C)	1978	BBWAA	.269/.341/.457	117	68.5	82.8
Jackson, Reggie (RF)	1974	BBWAA	.262/.356/.490	139	74.0	80.7
Grich, Bobby (2B)	1976	No	.266/.371/.424	125	71.1	77.9
Molitor, Paul (DH)	1988	BBWAA	.306/.369/.448	122	75.7	77.8

(*continued*)

Table 7.1 (cont'd)

A) Hitters (Position)	MidCareer	HOF	AVG/OBP/SLG	OPS+	WAR$_H$	CVI
Smith, Ozzie (SS)	1987	BBWAA	.262/.337/.328	87	76.9	74.6
Trammell, Alan (SS)	1986	VC	.285/.352/.415	110	70.7	74.5
Sandberg, Ryne (2B)	1989	BBWAA	.285/.344/.452	114	68.0	74.3
Dawson, Andre (RF)	1982	BBWAA	.279/.323/.482	119	64.8	71.1
Raines, Tim (LF)	1987	BBWAA	.294/.385/.425	123	69.4	69.5
Gwynn, Tony (RF)	1989	BBWAA	.338/.388/.459	132	69.2	68.3
Nettles, Graig (3B)	1976	No	.248/.329/.421	110	68.0	67.0
Whitaker, Lou (2B)	1986	No	.276/.363/.426	117	75.1	66.9
Bell, Buddy (3B)	1980	No	.279/.341/.406	109	66.3	66.2
Winfield, Dave (RF)	1981	BBWAA	.283/.353/.475	130	64.2	65.3
Simmons, Ted (C)	1976	VC	.285/.348/.437	118	50.3	65.0
Murray, Eddie (1B)	1984	BBWAA	.287/.359/.476	129	68.7	64.0
Evans, Dwight (RF)	1982	No	.272/.370/.470	127	67.1	61.9
Hernandez, Keith (1B)	1982	No	.296/.384/.436	128	60.3	61.2
Munson, Thurman (C)	1974	No	.292/.346/.410	116	46.0	60.6
Evans, Darrell (3B)	1978	No	.248/.361/.431	119	58.8	58.6
Smith, Reggie (RF)	1973	No	.287/.366/.489	137	64.6	58.4
Randolph, Willie (2B)	1983	No	.276/.373/.351	104	65.9	57.4
Bonds, Bobby (RF)	1973	No	.268/.353/.471	129	57.9	56.4
Cedeno, Cesar (CF)	1975	No	.285/.347/.443	123	52.8	54.2
Clark, Will (1B)	1991	No	.303/.384/.497	137	56.5	53.9

B) Pitchers	MidCareer	HOF	ERA/WHIP	ERA+	WAR$_P$	CVI
Seaver, Tom (SP)	1974	BBWAA	2.86/1.121	127	106.0	120.5
Niekro, Phil (SP)	1976	BBWAA	3.35/1.268	115	97.0	108.4
Blyleven, Bert (SP)	1977	BBWAA	3.31/1.198	118	96.1	104.2
Carlton, Steve (SP)	1975	BBWAA	3.22/1.247	115	84.1	100.6
Gossage, Rich (RP)	1980	BBWAA	3.01/1.232	126	41.6	90.6
Ryan, Nolan (SP)	1979	BBWAA	3.19/1.247	112	83.6	79.9
Eckersley, Dennis (RP)	1982	BBWAA	3.50/1.161	116	62.2	75.9
Palmer, Jim (SP)	1975	BBWAA	2.86/1.180	125	67.6	69.3
Reuschel, Rick (SP)	1978	No	3.37/1.275	114	68.1	67.0
Saberhagen, Bret (SP)	1989	No	3.34/1.141	126	58.9	66.5
Stieb, Dave (SP)	1984	No	3.44/1.245	122	56.5	63.6
Hiller, John (RP)	1974	No	2.83/1.268	134	31.0	60.7
Sutton, Don (SP)	1976	BBWAA	3.26/1.142	108	68.3	58.7

(*continued*)

Table 7.1 (cont'd)

B) Pitchers	MidCareer	HOF	ERA/WHIP	ERA+	WAR_p	CVI
Hershiser, Orel (SP)	1988	No	3.66/1.270	112	51.4	56.8
Tanana, Frank (SP)	1978	No	3.48/1.261	106	57.1	56.5
Gooden, Dwight (SP)	1987	No	3.51/1.256	111	48.2	55.8
Smith, Lee (RP)	1986	VC	3.03/1.256	132	29.3	55.4
Fingers, Rollie (RP)	1977	BBWAA	2.90/1.156	120	25.0	55.0
Langston, Mark (SP)	1990	No	3.97/1.354	107	50.0	54.5
Koosman, Jerry (SP)	1975	No	3.36/1.259	110	57.0	53.7

The Free Agent Generation contains a bumper crop of CVI-Plus players, including 35 hitters and 20 pitchers (Table 7.1), of whom 33 are in the Hall of Fame. All but three of the Hall of Famers (Trammell, Simmons, and Lee Smith) gained entry via the BBWAA. No players from this era remain on the BBWAA ballot, but the VC, which has only recently begun to consider this era, may still add to this total. As in Chapters 3-6, the careers and HOF credentials of the players in Table 7.1, are presented below in thematic groupings.

What Greatness Looked Like

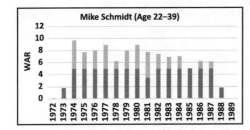
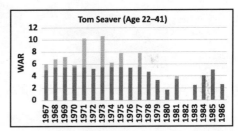

Mike Schmidt and Tom Seaver were the best hitter and pitcher of the Free Agent Era. Though not quite as impressive as the top players of previous eras. Each put together more than a decade of five-WAR seasons and was recognized via multiple MVP and Cy Young awards as the best of their time.

New Kings of Three True Outcomes

Mike Schmidt (3B):
142.0 CVI – Philadelphia NL (*106.9*)

Reggie Jackson (RF):
80.7 CVI – Kansas City/Oakland AL (*48.1*), New York AL (*17.2*)

Schmidt and Jackson continued the trend of 3TO sluggers that had reached unprecedented heights with Mantle, Killebrew, et al in the preceding generation. Indeed, Jackson (41%) not only surpassed Mantle's career record 40% 3TO rate but became the first CVI-Plus player to have more career SO (2597) than hits (2584). He still holds the career SO record, and his 1.01 (SO/H) is still the sixth highest of all time among qualifying hitters, behind only Adam Dunn, Mike Cameron, Jim Thome, Curtis Granderson, and Jose Canseco. Schmidt ranks 18th on this list. Offensively, Schmidt, who struck out in 22.5% (1883/8352) of his AB) was almost a clone of Harmon Killebrew, with similar OBP, slight advantages in AVG (.001) and SLG (.020), but 15 fewer HR. Of course, Schmidt's superb defense at 3B elevated him far above Killebrew (who was awful at 3B and not much better at 1B); his CVI is more than twice Killebrew's.

Mike Schmidt, with permission from the National Baseball Hall of Fame and Museum

Mike Schmidt's combination of slugging, speed, and brilliant defense (18.4 dWAR and 10 Gold Gloves — more than any 3B except Brooks Robinson) make him the consensus pick for the best 3B of all time. Schmidt catapulted to stardom in 1974, hitting .282/.395/.546 (158 OPS+) with a league-leading 36 HR plus 116 RBI, 108 R, 310 TB, 23 SB and 2.4 dWAR and posting a career-high 9.7 WAR.

Thus began a run of 14 consecutive seasons (1974-87) with at least 5.0 WAR, including four 8-WAR seasons, 12 ASG selections, and three MVP awards. He hit >30 HR in all but one of these seasons, topped by 48 HR in 1980, and drove in 100 or more runs in nine seasons. Meanwhile, the Phillies, heretofore one of MLB's most hapless franchises, finished above .500 every year, won six NL East Division titles. two NL pennant, and the 1980 World Series. Schmidt's back-to-back MVP seasons in 1980-81, when he hit .298/.402/.632 (182 OPS+) and posted 16.6 WAR, were arguably even better than 1974. He posted career bests in HR (48) and RBI (121) in 1980 and hit .381/.462/.714 with two HR, seven RBI, and six R to earn MVP honors in the 4-2 win over the Royals in the World Series and bring the Phillies their first championship. Schmidt then set career highs in AVG (.316), OBP (.435), SLG (.644), and OPS+ (198) in the strike-shortened 1981 season, where he amassed 7.7 WAR and would likely have exceeded 10 WAR had the season not been interrupted.

Schmidt sacrificed contact for power and struck out at least 100 times every year except 1981 from 1973-1988 (topped by 180 in 1975). He struck out 1883 times overall (12th on the all-time list), and his lifetime AVG was only .267. However, he also walked 1507 times in his career, and his OBP was a robust .380. Schmidt has garnered many awards and honors, including selection by fans as the Phillies' greatest player of their first 100 years, the *Sporting News* Player of the Decade in 1990, election by the BBWAA in 1997 as baseball's all-time best 3B, and being ranked 28th on the Sporting News Top 100 players of the 20th century in 1999.[5] His 548 career HR ranked seventh on the all-time leaderboard when he retired on the eve of the Steroid era and still ranks 16th through 2019. CVI ranks him first among 3B and 20th overall, making him an elite Hall of Famer.

Reggie Jackson was Muhammad Ali in cleats, a larger-than-life player with the massive ego to (allegedly) call himself "the straw that stirs the drink" and to embrace the nickname "Mr. October" and with the skill and nerve to back it up. Nearly 90 players outrank Reggie in CVI, but only Babe Ruth himself had his flair for drama. From 1968-80 with the Athletics and Yankees, Jackson was one of the most feared sluggers in the AL, hitting .275/.366/.518 (152 OPS+) and averaging 31 HR, 94 RBI, 87 R, and 5.4 WAR per season, topped by his 7.8-WAR 1973 MVP season in Oakland.

However, he saved his best for the big stage, i.e., his 11 postseasons and 14 ASG. Highlights included his mammoth HR off the Tiger Stadium light tower in the 1971 ASG and his three-HR obliteration of the Dodgers in Game 6 of the 1977 World Series as cheers of "Reggie! Reggie! Reggie!" rained down from the stands to clinch the Series for the Yankees and earn the Mr. October nickname. Reggie was an outstanding postseason player throughout his career, especially in his five World Series, hitting .357/.457/.755 with 10 HR and 24 RBI in 116 PA. He also hit the two-run, third-inning HR that gave the A's a lead they would never relinquish in Game 7 of their 1973 World Series victory over the Mets to earn Series MVP honors. On the downside, despite his speed (in his early days) and a powerful throwing arm, Jackson was a subpar OF, whose defensive shortcomings forced a move to DH when he was 34. Jackson is also remembered for better or worse for his clashes with Manager Billy Martin after he signed a $3 million contract – one of the richest of that time – to join George Steinbrenner and the Yankees in 1977. Jackson's 563 HR put him sixth on the pre-steroid leaderboard and 14th overall. CVI ranks Jackson ninth in RF and at the 0.55 percentile overall.

Beyond the Numbers

- Jackson attended Arizona State University (ASU) on a football scholarship and was a starting defensive back who could run a 60-yard dash in 6.3 seconds. Baseball coach Bobby Winkles encouraged him to play summer baseball to refine his relatively raw skills. He quickly improved to the point where he became ASU's starting CF.[11]

Speed-Power Combinations

Rickey Henderson (LF):
134.9 CVI – Oakland AL (*72.7*),
New York AL (*30.9*)

Joe Morgan (2B):
120.6 CVI – Cincinnati NL (*57.9*),
Houston NL (*30.7*)

Rickey Henderson

The stolen base, which had been mostly dormant in MLB since the days of Ty Cobb and Eddie Collins, returned with a vengeance in the 1970s and 1980s. Henderson, Morgan, and Raines (covered later) were the cream of the crop, but players like Lou Brock, Vince Coleman, Ron Leflore, and Omar Moreno also joined Maury Wills (1962) in passing or flirting with Cobb's previous 20th century record 96 SB. Although Morgan's best SB total was "only" 67, both he and Henderson brought 20-HR power into the mix, to create a species not really seen before.

Rickey Henderson is one of baseball's most unforgettable characters and the greatest leadoff hitter of all time. Who else besides this 10-time All-Star was equally capable of starting a game with a home run or with a walk and three SB? He was a disruptive force that opponents could do little or nothing to stop. He not only leads all MLB players with 1406 SB and 2295 R, but hit 297 HR, 81 of them leading off a game (also a major league record), just to keep opposing teams off balance. His 2190 BB rank second among the all-time leaders, even though pitchers knew that walking Henderson was like spotting their opponent a man in scoring position. He and Morgan stick out like sore thumbs among the array of sluggers (Bonds, Ruth, Williams, Yastrzemski, Thome, Mantle) who populate the BB leaderboard. Henderson not only holds the modern seasonal record for SB with 130 in 1982, but he also posted three of MLB's eight 100-SB seasons since 1900, with 108 (fifth) in 1983 and 100 (eighth) in 1980.

In 1979-84 with the A's, Henderson was basically Lou Brock 2.0 with improved on-base skills, hitting .291/.400/.408 (132 OPS+) and averaging 5.7 WAR, 82 SB, 98 R, 87 BB, but only 8 HR per season. His isolated power was only .117. However, after being dealt to the Yankees in 1985, he traded some SB for more HR and a higher SLG and hit .290/.410/.466 (145 OPS+) while averaging 6.8 WAR, 67 SB, 111 R, 98 BB, and 19 HR in 1985-93. His 9.9 WAR season in 1990, which matched his 9.9 WAR in 1985, earned him his only MVP award.

Rickey continued to play until 2003, long after his prime but often still productive, and bounced from team to team as a "hired gun" for the pennant chase and postseason. Henderson played in eight postseasons with five different teams in his 24-year career; he hit .284/.389/.441 with 5 HR, 47 R, and 33 SB, and was named MVP of the 1989 ALCS. CVI ranks him fourth in LF and 21st overall, making him an elite Hall of Famer.

Joe Morgan stood only 5'7", but he was the ignition of the Big Red Machine in 1972-76, a remarkable five-year span in which he accrued 47.8 WAR, hit .303/.431/.499 (163 OPS+) and averaged 22 HR, 85 RBI, 113 R, 62 SB, and 118 BB per season. For comparison, Henry Aaron's best five-year run in 1959-63 produced only 43.7 WAR. Morgan won consecutive MVP awards for the World Series champions of 1975-76 and finished fourth in the MVP voting for the 1972 NL champions and 1973 NL West champions. His 11.0 WAR in 1975 is second only to Hornsby's 12.2 WAR in 1924 among all MLB 2B. When you add Morgan's 5.6 and 5.8 WAR sea-

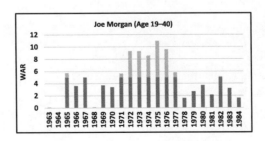

sons on either side of this five-year run, the 1971-77 seasons account for 71% of Morgan's CVI (as shown in his career trajectory plot). No other player of Morgan's caliber crammed so much of his career value into such a small portion (less than one-third) of his career. Morgan had three other 5-WAR seasons in 1965, 1967, and 1982, but his other 12 seasons were not special. Morgan played in 10 ASG but struggled in seven postseasons, hitting. 182/.323/.348. Morgan's 126.4 CVI ranks fourth at 2B and 26th among all HOF-eligible players. He is an elite Hall of Famer.

Beyond the Numbers

- Henderson was born Rickey Nelson Henley in the back seat of a Chicago taxi on Christmas Day 1958. He took the surname Henderson from his stepfather.[12]

- Morgan came to Cincinnati in 1972 after a controversial trade sending two of Cincinnati's most popular players (Lee May and Tommy Helms) to Houston. His manager in Houston, Harry Walker, considered Morgan a troublemaker, but Reds HOF manager Sparky Anderson, considered him the smartest player he ever managed.[13]

- After his playing career, the articulate and insightful Morgan had a long successful career in broadcasting, most notably as the analyst on ESPN Sunday Night Baseball from 1990-2010, and served on the HOF Board of Directors until his death in 2020.

The Aces

Tom Seaver (SP):
120.5 CVI – New York NL (*78.7*), Cincinnati NL (*19.5*), Chicago AL (*9.7*)

Phil Niekro (SP):
108.4 CVI – Milwaukee/ Atlanta NL (*88.5*)

Bert Blyleven (SP):
104.2 CVI – Minnesota AL (48.9), Cleveland (*20.1*), Texas AL (*11.1*), Pittsburgh NL (*8.3*)

Steve Carlton (SP):
100.6 CVI – Philadelphia NL (*69.4*), St. Louis NL (*22.1*)

Nolan Ryan (SP):
79.9 CVI – California AL (*40.6*), Houston NL (*23.5*), Texas AL (*15.2*)

Jim Palmer (SP):
69.3 CVI – Baltimore AL (*68.5*)

The common denominator among this otherwise eclectic group of aces — which ranges from knuckleballer Niekro to extreme strikeout pitcher Ryan — is their endurance and longevity. Indeed, Niekro, Ryan, Carlton, Blyleven, and Seaver rank 4th, 5th, 9th, 14th, and 19th in IP among all MLB pitchers of every generation, and 1st,

2nd, 6th, 8th, and 10th of all post-1920 pitchers. Even Palmer (who ranks 43rd in IP and 21st since 1920) pitched more innings than any pitcher in the Classical Era or any of the hard-throwing aces of the 1960s.

Seaver, the cerebral, hard-throwing 12-time All-Star and three-time Cy Young winner is the single player most responsible for transforming the New York Mets from a laughingstock into a World Series champion in 1969 and changing forever how the Mets franchise would be viewed. The transformation can be pinpointed to a near perfect game against the East Division-leading Cubs on July 8, 1969. Although that game only narrowed the Cubs' NL East lead from four to three games, it gave the Mets credibility as a genuine contender. During his peak (1967-77), Seaver posted a 2.48 ERA (142 ERA+) and 1.057 WHIP while averaging an 18-10 W-L, 230 SO, 271 IP, and 7.2 WAR_p and earning the nickname "Tom Terrific." He led the league five times in SO, three times in ERA and WHIP, twice in W, and once in SHO and CG during this period.

Although Seaver received the most acclaim for his 25-win, 165-ERA+, 7.2-WAR_p tour de force for the 1969 "Miracle Mets," which earned him his first Cy Young Award, his two best years were in 1971 (20 wins and 10.2 WAR_p) and 1973 (19 W, 175 ERA+, 10.6 WAR_p, and his second Cy Young Award). He also won a third Cy Young award in 1975 (22 W, 146 ERA+, 7.8 WAR_p). Seaver ranks sixth on the career SO leaderboard (3640) and tied for seventh in shutouts (61). Seaver's 120.5 CVI ranks ninth among SP and 27th among all HOF-eligible players, making him an elite Hall of Famer. The BBWAA concurred and gave him 98.8% of their votes in 1992, a record that stood until the elections of Ken Griffey Jr. in 2016 and Mariano Rivera (unanimously) in 2019.

It is the sad plight of knuckleballers, especially those who pitch until age 48, to be remembered as paunchy middle-aged men trying to scrape by in a young man's game on guile and a trick pitch. We often forget how good they were in their prime. Niekro was a truly great pitcher for a six-year stretch in 1974-1979 at ages 35-40, averaging 18-16 with a 3.21 (125 ERA+), a 1.263 WHIP, and 205 SO in 309 IP. He averaged 7.9 WAR_p per season, leading the NL in 1978 (10.0) and 1979 (7.4), but never garnered more than 15% of the Cy Young Award votes. It didn't help that his team, the Braves, finished last in most of his best seasons.

Niekro was also pretty good during the seven years leading up to that peak and into his mid-40s. He compiled 330+ IP in three seasons (1977-9) and 250+ IP in eight other seasons, and won 20+ games three times, topped by 23 in 1969. He played in five ASG, led the NL in ERA in 1967, and pitched a no-hitter against the Padres in 1973. However, nothing comes easily for knuckleballers. He spent 1959-64 in the minors (interrupted by military service in 1963) and two more years shuttling between the Braves and AAA bullpens before receiving an opportunity to join the Braves starting rotation in 1967 at age 28. He played mostly for losing Braves teams, except for the 1969 and 1982 NL West champions, who were each swept in the NCLS. Even when he was a mid-rotation starter for decent Yankee teams in 1984-85, they did not win their division. Niekro's 108.4 CVI ranks 13th among SP and 40th among all HOF-eligible players, making him an elite Hall of Famer. The BBWAA elected Niekro to the HOF in 1997, his fifth year of eligibility.

With his 96.0 WAR_p and his 106.2 CVI, Bert Blyleven would seem a no-brainer first-ballot HOF selection. So why did he receive only 17.5% of the BBWAA votes in his ballot debut in 1998, and why did almost 20 years elapse from the end of Bert Blyleven's 23-year career until he finally crossed the 75% threshold for HOF election in 2011?

Bert Blyleven

For that matter, why did a player who posted ten 5-WAR_p seasons appear in only two All-Star games and never come close to a Cy Young award? Perhaps it is because he pitched for mediocre teams for most of his career and struggled to win more games than he lost. Perhaps his outspoken criticism of fans and management with the Twins and Pirates soured some BBWAA voters. Yet these factors notwithstanding, Blyleven's eight-year peak from 1971-78, in which he averaged 16-14 with a 2.79 ERA (134 ERA+) and 1.136 WHIP and 222 SO in 278 IP and 6.5 WAR_p per season was among the best of his time. And a series of injuries and clashes with management did not prevent him from putting up several more very good seasons in his 30s, including for the 1987 World Series champion Twins. Blyleven ate innings but was no mere innings-eater; he pitched for 23 years but was no mere compiler. His 3701 SO total is exceeded only by Ryan, Randy Johnson, Clemens, and Carlton. His 104.2 CVI ranks 15th among SP and 44th among all HOF-eligible players, making him an elite Hall of Famer.

Ten-time All-Star Steve Carlton, aka "Lefty," was just different. An avid student of Eastern philosophy and practitioner of meditation since his teens, Carlton was a perfectionist, who was uniquely able tune out distractions and had no problem zigging when everyone else zagged.[14] His career was also different. Unlike most great players, who build gradually to a peak, sustain it for several years, then gradually decline, Carlton's WAR trajectory plot looks like a few California redwoods scattered in an apple orchard — a lot of pretty good seasons, punctuated by a few spectacular ones.

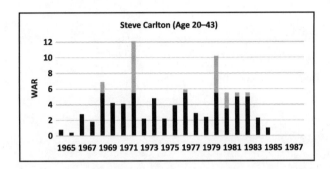

His best season was achieved with a dreadful last-place Phillies team in 1972 at age 27, when he went 27-10 with a 1.97 ERA (182 ERA+) and 0.993 WHIP and 310 SO in 346.1 IP, while the rest of the team went an abysmal 32-87. His 12.1 WAR_p was the second highest (behind Dwight Gooden's 12.2 in 1985) since 1920. Future Pirate Hall of Famer Willie Stargell compared hitting Carlton's wicked slider that year to "drinking coffee with a fork."[15] However, the control problems that plagued Carlton in this early career returned in 1973-75 as his BB9 increased from 2.3 to 3.8. Although Carlton's 23-W 5.9-WAR_p 1977 season won him a second Cy Young award, It was not until 1980 that the Carlton of 1972 re-emerged with a 10.2-WAR_p 24-W season that won him his third Cy Young award and sparked the Phillies to their first World Series championship. He won his fourth and final Cy Young award in 1982. Due in part to his longevity, Carlton ranks fourth in career SO (4136) and second in BB (1833) although his 30% 3TO rate is not extreme. Carlton's 100.6 CVI ranks 18th among SP and 53rd among all HOF-eligible players, making him an elite Hall of Famer.

Texas icon Nolan Ryan is baseball's undisputed strikeout king. The 839 SO (17%) gap between the eight-time All-Star and runner-up Randy Johnson is almost as large proportionally as the 94-win (23%) gap between Cy Young and runner-up Walter Johnson. Ryan struck out >300 batters six times in his career, including the all-time record 383 in 1973 and 301 16 years later, in 1989, at age 42. Ryan was also baseball's hardest pitcher to hit, yielding only 6.56 H9 (topping the MLB leaderboard), and threw seven no-hitters — three more than runner-up Sandy Koufax. Combining these two areas of dominance, Ryan racked up 1.4565 SO/H, second (by a hair) to Randy Johnson among pitchers with >7500 BF.

Ryan's best run came with the Angels in 1972-77 (at ages 25-30), when he averaged 5.6 WAR_p, a 19-16 W-L, with a 2.91 ERA (118 ERA+) and a 1.281 WHIP (despite 173 BB per season), and an unprecedented 322 SO per year. Only six other pitchers — Randy Johnson (five times), Sandy Koufax, Rube Waddell, Bob Feller, Gerrit Cole, and Sam McDowell — have ever exceeded 322 strikeouts in a single season, let alone *averaged* 322 SO over six seasons. Other highlights included nine shutouts in 1972 and no-hitters in 1973 (2), 1974, and 1975, but no Division titles. Ryan remained a very good pitcher with the Astros and Rangers for another 15 years after 1977, including no-hitters in 1981, 1990, and 1991 at age 44 (becoming the oldest man to throw a no-hitter) and led the league in SO in 1978-79 and 1987-92.

So why did Ryan never earn a Cy Young award, appear in only one World Series, and win only 32 more games than he lost (324-292) during his 28-year career? Bases on balls were his bane — 2795 for his career, a whopping 0.52 BB9. Indeed, he laps the field in career BB even more extremely than he does in SO, with 962 (52%) more BB than runner-up Steve Carlton. So, his career 3.19 ERA, 112 ERA+, and 1.247 WHIP are unremarkable, and his CVI is "only" 79.9 (33rd among SP and at the 0.57 percentile overall) rather than the elite 135 it might have been had he been able to harness his command as Randy Johnson did in the 1990s. Still, the BBWAA elected Ryan to the HOF with 98.8% of the votes in 1999.

Palmer was the AL's top pitcher of the 1970s, the perennial ace who pitched 3948 innings and won 268 games for Oriole teams that won seven AL East championships, six AL pennants, and three World Series from 1966-83. In his prime (1969-78), Palmer compiled a 2.52 ERA (139 ERA+), and 1.135 WHIP and averaged 19-10 with 162 SO, 88 BB, 18 CG, 5 SHO, and 5.6 WAR$_p$), despite a 7-12 injury-marred 1974 season. He won 20 or more games eight times, pitched in six ASG, and won Cy Young awards in 1973 and 1975-76. Palmer's best year was probably 1975 when he went 23-11, with 10 SHO, a miniscule 2.09 ERA (169 ERA+), a career-low 1.031 WHIP, and a career high 8.4-WAR$_p$. He was also one of three 20-game winners on the Orioles 1970 World Series champions and one of the record four 20-game winners on the 1971 AL Champions.

Palmer was at his best in the postseason, going 8-3 with a 2.61 ERA and 1.214 WHIP in 124.1 IP for eight playoff teams, three of whom won the World Series. An intelligent, articulate player who had his own ideas about pitching, Orioles fans also remember his love-hate relationship with his fiery manager Earl Weaver, the oddest couple since McGraw and Mathewson 70 years earlier. Palmer and Weaver bickered like an old married couple, with Weaver trying to tell Palmer how to pitch, and Palmer trying to tell Weaver how to manage. Neither made much headway, but there was always an underlying mutual respect. It was always Palmer whom Weaver relied on to win the biggest games. Palmer's 69.3 CVI ranks 52nd among SP and at the 0.90 percentile overall, good enough to make him a solid Hall of Famer.

Beyond the Numbers

- It was the Braves, not the Mets, who jumped on Seaver in the 1966 amateur draft. However, when Seaver signed before the college season ended, in violation of MLB rules, Commissioner Kuhn voided the contract. The Mets won the lottery for Seaver's service among the three teams willing to match the Braves' $51,000 bonus offer.[16]

- When Seaver and the Mets had a falling out in 1977, he was traded to Cincinnati. The trade ruined the Mets, but the reign of the Big Red Machine had also begun to decline. Seaver pitched his only no-hitter for Cincinnati in 1978. No Met pitched a no-hitter until Johan Santana in 2012.

- Phil Niekro's younger brother Joe was also a fine knuckleball pitcher, who was 221-204 (29.8 WAR) in 22 seasons (1967-88) with the Astros and six other teams. In 1979, Phil and Joe co-led the NL in wins by combining for 42 wins (21 each), with Phil's coming for the hapless 66-win Braves. Phil and Joe's combined total of 539 career wins is the highest for any pair of brothers in major league history (beating 529 by Gaylord and Jim Perry) and represents 28 more wins than fellow Ohioan Cy Young won all by himself.

- Blyleven is the first of 11 MLB players — and the only Hall of Famer — born in the Netherlands. He and his parents emigrated to Saskatchewan in 1954 and finally settled in Garden Grove, CA in 1957.[17]

- Although Blyleven's trade to Pittsburgh gave him a long-awaited opportunity to pitch for a good team and win a World Series ring in 1979, he resented manager Chuck Tanner's quick hook and was a disgruntled dissenter in the close-knit Pirate's family.

- Blyleven thrived as a popular Twins TV color commentator from 1996-2020. Though often brash and an unabashed "homer," he came across as fun-loving and playful rather than entitled and disgruntled, as in his worst moments as a player.

- Carlton was generally shy and introverted but could also be brash. When he approached veteran catcher Tim McCarver as a rookie and told him he needed to call for more breaking balls when behind in the count, this elicited a "who the hell are you" response from the incredulous McCarver. Carlton would remain very stubborn about how he wanted to pitch throughout his career no matter who was catching him.[18]

- Carlton began with the Cardinals but was traded to the Phillies in 1971 for Rich Wise, another outstanding young SP with a similar record to Carlton, after a salary dispute. His anger at being traded may have been a prime motivator of the 12.1-WAR_P 1972 season that was the crown jewel of his career.

Beyond the Numbers (cont'd)

- Ryan was Seaver's teammate on the 1969 "Miracle Mets" as a RP/spot starter. It was not until his trade to the Angels (for SS Jim Fregosi) in 1972 that Ryan blossomed.

- Ryan became a successful minor league baseball executive in Texas after he retired, and more recently served as president of the Texas Rangers and a senior advisor to the Houston Astros.[19]

- Palmer was adopted when he was two days old by Moe and Polly Wiesen, of New York City. Palmer played catch in Central Park as a boy. Moe died when Jim was nine, and Polly moved to Beverly Hills and married an actor, Max Palmer, who adopted him and gave him his name.[20]

- Palmer made his first big splash at age 20, winning 15 games for an upstart Orioles team that surprised the AL and swept the defending champion Dodgers in the World Series. Palmer pitched a 6-0 shutout in Game 2, besting Sandy Koufax in his final major league appearance. However, arm problems laid him low in 1967-68. The Orioles did not even protect him in the 1969 expansion draft, but the Royals and Pilots passed.

The Throwbacks

Wade Boggs (3B):
110.8 CVI – Boston AL (*71.9*),
New York AL (*18.3*)

George Brett (3B):
101.3 CV I – Kansas City AL (*88.6*)

Rod Carew (2B):
88.7 CVI – Minnesota AL (*63.8*),
California AL (*17.4*)

Tony Gwynn (RF):
68.3 CVI – San Diego NL (*69.2*)

Here are four players, all members of the "3000-hit club," who bucked the relentless historic march toward hit-or-miss 3TO sluggers. Boggs (.328), Brett (.306), Carew (.328), and Gwynn (.338) were all lifetime .300 hitters, and none had more than 21.4% 3TO. Indeed, Gwynn's 13.5% 3TO is near the bottom of hitters with at least 7500 PA; only five of the 31 hitters below him played after 1950. These four players combined for 16 seasons in which they hit .350 or more, and Carew (1977), Brett (1980) and Gwynn (1994) each flirted with becoming MLB's first .400 hitter since Ted Williams in 1941.

Brett (.182 ISO) had some power, but none of the others had ISO >.121. Similarity scores for these players on Baseball-Reference.com, show that apart from each other, Boggs, Carew, and Gwynn were most similar to Paul Waner, Zach Wheat, and Sam Rice, who played at least 50 years earlier in a far better offensive environment. Brett's greater power made Al Kaline his closest comp, but 1920s stars Goose Goslin and Al Simmons were not far behind. All four modern players had superior CVI to their 1920s comps, since similarity scores use unadjusted raw stats.

Wade Boggs stands out from his peers as an on-base machine, who started strong as a rookie and never posted an AVG <.325 or an OBP <.400 until he was 32 years old. Boggs had a lot of naysayers in the Red Sox organization and spent six years (1976-81) in the minors before receiving a major league opportunity. Since he lacked speed or power and played mediocre defense, most scouts viewed him as a one-dimensional non-prospect. From 1983-1989 (ages 25-31), his WAR stayed between 6.3 and 9.4 (averaging 8.0), and he hit .352/.446/.483 (152 OPS+), while averaging 211 H, 110 R, 289 TB, 43 2B, and 103 BB. He won AL batting titles in 1983 and 1985-88 and led the AL in OBP all those years plus 1988. He played in 12 consecutive ASG and finished fourth in the MVP voting in 1995, his best season. He worked hard to become a good 3B and even won Gold Gloves in 1994-95; he finished with 13.9 dWAR for his career. Boggs had little HR power, hitting only 118 over his career, 24 of them concentrated in one season (1987). Boggs's 110.8 CVI ranks third at 3B and tied with Carl Yastrzemski for 37th among all HOF-eligible players. He is an elite Hall of Famer.

George Brett has been "Mr. Royal" for more than 40 years, first as a player and then in management. While Boggs walked more and had a far higher lifetime OBP, Brett was a middle-of-the-order hitter who hit 20 or more HR eight times and drove in 100 or more runs four times. Brett played in 13 ASG, nine times as the starting 3B, beating out Boggs in 1982-85 while their careers overlapped. During his peak years from 1975-85, he hit .320/.381/.521 (148 OPS+) and averaged 6.3 WAR per season, with his best seasons coming in 1980 (9.4 WAR) and 1985 (8.3 WAR).

In his 1980 MVP season, Brett flirted until September 19 with becoming the first man since Ted Williams to hit .400, but a 4-27 slump knocked him down to .384, and he "settled" for .390/.454/.664, while leading the Royals to their first World Series. In 1985, he hit .335/.436/.585 (179 OPS+) with a career high 30 HR, 112 RBI, 108 R, and 322 TB and finished second in the AL MVP voting. He then hit .348/.500/.826 with 3 HR in the comeback ALCS win over Toronto, earning him MVP honors, and .370/.452/.407 in the World Series to lead the Royals to their first championship. Brett's 101.3 CVI ranks fourth among 3B and 51st among all HOF-eligible players, making him an elite Hall of Famer. He received 98.5% of the BBWAA votes in 1999, more than any predecessor except Seaver, Ryan, and Cobb.

Rod Carew, 1975

Carew combined the contact skills of Brett and Boggs with the baserunning skills of Morgan and Henderson, but without power or elite on-base skills. Early in his career, he showed a particular flair for stealing home, probably baseball's most exciting play, falling only one short of Ty Cobb's 1912 record with seven steals of home in 1969. Curiously, he stole home only 10 more times during the rest of his career.

For 15 consecutive years (1969-84) Carew hit at least .300, winning seven batting titles in 1969, 1972-75, and 1977-78. In his peak years (1972-77), Carew hit .352/.414/.473 (150 OPS+) and averaged 93 R, 33 SB, and 7.4 WAR. This peak culminated in his 9.7-WAR 1977 season, when he made his remarkable run at a .400 AVG (falling just short at .388), attained career highs in R (128), 3B (16), and RBI (100), and easily won the AL MVP award. Carew played in 18 consecutive ASG from 1967-84. Although his defensive limitations forced a move to 1B in 1975, he accrued 52% of his WAR at 2B, despite playing 54 more games at 1B, mostly with the Angels. Carew's 88.7 CVI ranks seventh at 2B and at the 0.42 percentile overall. Carew was the only Panamanian Hall of Famer until Mariano Rivera's election in 2019.

No player was more beloved and more closely identified with his franchise than "Mr. Padre" Tony Gwynn. Gwynn excelled in just one thing — delivering base hits. He hit over .300 in 19 of his 20 major league seasons, won eight NL batting titles, and played in 15 ASG. His .338 career AVG was the highest by far of the post-integration era, and his .394 AVG in the strike-shortened 1994 season was the highest since Ted Williams hit .406 in 1941.

Gwynn struck out only 434 times in 10,232 AB over the course of his career, less often than Ty Cobb. In the entire post-integration era, only Nellie Fox, Vic Power, Felix Millan, Bobby Richardson, and Glenn Beckert struck out less often. Like Ted Williams before him, Gwynn was an avid student of the science of hitting and pioneered the study of video in the pursuit of his craft. To be sure, Gwynn was not a perfect player. He possessed little home run power, and his increasingly rotund physique (5'11" and 225 pounds) limited his range in RF. Although he won five Gold Gloves in six years in 1986-91, his dWAR was only 1.0 during this period and -7.6 for his career; this held down his career WAR and CVI. But he was almost unstoppable with a bat in his hands. Gwynn's CVI ranks 14th in RF and at the 0.93 percentile overall.

Beyond the Numbers

- Boggs was known as a lover of routines and rituals (perhaps stemming from his military childhood) and was nicknamed "Chicken Man" because he ate chicken every day.[21]

- Boggs had a four-year extramarital affair, which came to light in 1987, and faced a messy palimony suit. Fortunately, he and his wife Debbie were able to weather the scandal and stay together.[22]

- Apart from his batting exploits, Brett is remembered for a bad case of hemorrhoids that sidelined him briefly in 1981 (he quipped after his surgery that his troubles were now behind him) and for the notorious "pine tar incident" in 1983, when he went ballistic after his go-ahead two-run ninth inning HR against the Yankees was disallowed because he had pine tar too high on his bat.[23] The decision was overturned by the league president, and the Royals won.

- Brett's older brother Ken (who was considered the family's star athlete in his youth) was a journeyman pitcher for 10 MLB teams from 1967-81.

- Carew was born on the crowded "colored-only" rear coach of a train en route from his parents' rural Panama home to the maternity hospital. He was named after Dr. Rodney Cline, the physician-passenger who delivered him. Margaret Allen, the nurse who assisted him, became his godmother, and sponsored his mother to move her family to New York to escape her abusive alcoholic husband.[24]

- Carew received a heart and kidney transplant after a near-fatal heart attack in 2015. He established the Heart of 29 Campaign (after his old uniform number and his donor's age) to raise awareness of heart disease prevention.[25]

- Gwynn starred in basketball (as a point guard) as well as baseball at San Diego State University and was drafted by the NBA Clippers, as well as the Padres.

- After his retirement from MLB, Gwynn became the head baseball coach at his alma mater San Diego State University. He was a natural coach and a superb teacher. Stephen Strasburg was his best known protégé. But Gwynn, who had a long-term oral tobacco habit as a player, was stricken with salivary gland cancer in 2000 and ultimately succumbed in 2014 at age 54.[26]

- In 35 games and 103 PA against Greg Maddux, Gwynn hit .429/.495/.538 and NEVER struck out.[27]

Catching Greats

Johnny Bench (C):
111.7 CVI – Cincinnati NL (*75.2*)

Gary Carter (C):
103.1 CVI – Montreal NL (*55.8*),
New York NL (*11.4*)

Carlton Fisk (C):
82.8 CVI – Boston AL (*39.5*),
Chicago AL (*28.9*)

Ted Simmons (C):
65.0 CVI – St. Louis NL (*45.0*),
Milwaukee AL (*6.1*)

Thurman Munson (C):
60.6 CVI – New York AL (*46.0*)

Through 1972, MLB had only six CVI-Plus catchers, topped by Yogi Berra (74.1 CVI). This number nearly doubled in the Millionaire Era, including the catchers with the first, second, and fifth highest CVI. Bench's power, superb throwing and receiving skills, and leadership made him #1 at this position, at least until the physical demands and repeated injuries wore him down in his early 30s. Carter, a good hitter and elite defender, and Fisk who caught until he was 45 were also among the best to ever play the position. Simmons, who was completely overshadowed by Bench in his peak years, was elected by the VC to the 2020 HOF class. Thurman Munson, who was on a HOF trajectory when he was killed in a tragic plane crash at age 32, is not in the HOF but probably should be.

Johnny Bench combined power and superlative defense and played in 14 ASG. His powerful throwing arm enabled him to control the running game, and his unusually large hands enabled him to wear a flexible catcher's glove and to make defensive plays that no other catcher of his era could and to set the "Bench-mark" for future catchers. From the time he stepped on a major league field at age 19, he was a team leader and instant star, winning Rookie of the Year honors in 1968. Despite a major health scare in 1972, when a benign tumor was removed from his right lung, Bench hit .270/.346/.485 (130 OPS+) during his peak (1968-79), while averaging 28 HR, 99 RBI, 78 R, 1.7 dWAR, and 5.8 WAR in 600 PA per season in the cleanup spot. He was the chief power source for the Big Red Machine, which won six NL West Division championships, four NL pennants, and two World Series during this period, and still holds the all-time Reds franchise record in career HR and RBI. He won NL MVP awards in 1970 (when he led the NL with 45 HR and 148 RBI) and 1972 (40

HR and 125 RBI) and finished fourth in the MVP voting in 1974 (33 HR and 129 RBI) and 1975 (28 HR and 110 RBI).

Bench was also a postseason force, hitting at least one HR in nine of 10 series. He was named MVP of the Reds' 1976 World Series sweep of the Yankees, hitting .533/.533/1.133 with 2 HR, 6 RBI, and 4 R. Bench ranks second among all catchers in HR (389), third in RBI (1376) and fifth in R (1091) and TB (3644). Bench also accrued 21.5 dWAR while winning 10 Gold Gloves in 14 seasons behind the plate, trailing only Ivan Rodriguez, Gary Carter, Bob Boone, Yadier Molina, and Jim Sundberg. But his -1.8 dWAR as a 3B/1B/OF in his last three seasons, after a series of broken foot bones, two broken thumbs, arthritic hips (which would later require bilateral hip replacement surgery), and various back and shoulder injuries from collisions, made it impossible for him to continue as a catcher, knocked him down to 19.7 dWAR. In 1999, Bench was named the #1 catcher on MLB's All-Century team. CVI ranks Bench first among catchers and 35th among all HOF-eligible players, making him an elite Hall of Famer.

Gary Carter, aka "The Kid," is one of baseball's most underappreciated superstars, ranking second only to Johnny Bench on the all-time catchers list by WAR and by CVI. The 11-time All-Star was a dangerous hitter and superior defensive catcher on some outstanding Expos and Mets teams, finishing second in the NL MVP voting for the 1980 Expos and third for the 1986 World Series Champion Mets. During his 10-year peak (1977-84 with the Expos and 1985-86 with the Mets), he hit .274/.347/.474 (128 OPS+) and averaged 25 HR, 89 RBI, 75 R, and 6.1 WAR per season.

His best season (8.6 WAR) came in 1982 when he hit .293/.381/.510 with 29 HR, 32 2B, 97 RBI, and 91 R. His 26.1 career dWAR not only ranks second to Ivan Rodriguez among catchers, but ranks 14th among players at all positions. He was also a team leader, relentlessly sunny and optimistic. Like Bench, Carter's time as an everyday catcher was cut short by the wear and tear of the position, which ruined his knees by age 34, although he played until age 38 as a part-time C/1B. Carter's 103.1 CVI ranks 46th among HOF-eligible players. He is an elite Hall of Famer.

The image of Carlton Fisk waving and gesticulating to guide his towering flyball over Fenway's Green Monster and inside the foul pole for a walk-off Series-tying HR against the Reds in the 12th inning of Game 6 of the 1975 World Series endures as one of baseball's iconic moments. But the 6'3" Fisk (who was nicknamed Pudge as a chubby eighth-grader) was no mere one-hit wonder. The 11-time All-Star caught 2226 major league games in 24 big league seasons, surpassed only by another Pudge (Ivan Rodriguez). He also ranks second among all catchers in R (1276) and TB (2999), third in H (2356), and fifth in 2B (421) and SB (128).

Carlton Fisk

Fisk's 7.3-WAR rookie season in 1972, when he hit .293/.370/.538 (162 OPS+) with 22 HR, and 61 RBI and was the unanimous choice for AL Rookie of the Year, was probably his best. He even led the AL with nine triples — a total outlier for his career. But he also had a very nice 17.2-WAR three-year stretch in 1976-78 and played in 15 ASG in his 24-year career, the last at age 43. He even put up a 4.9-WAR season in 1990 at age 42. The BBWAA elected Fisk to the HOF in 2000, his second year of eligibility. CVI ranks him fifth among catchers and at the 0.52 percentile overall.

Switch-hitting catcher Ted Simmons was an eight-time All-Star and ranks second among catchers in H (2472) and RBI (1389) and third in TB (3793). From 1971-80, he was the second best catcher in the NL behind Johnny Bench, hitting .301/.367/.466 (131 OPS+), averaging 17 HR, 90 RBI, 71 R, 32 2B, 253 TB, and 4.5 WAR, and finishing in the NL Top 10 in WAR_H five times. In 1975, his .332 AVG was second in the NL behind Bill Madlock's .354, and he finished sixth in the MVP balloting. Simmons was traded to Milwaukee in 1981 after feuding with Cardinals manager Whitey Herzog and was a key member of the Brewers Harvey's Wallbangers team that won the 1982 AL pennant before falling to the Cardinals in a closely contested World Series. While known mostly for his offense, his 9.1 dWAR as a catcher in 1968-83 was solid. Unfortunately, his subpar defense during his final year behind the plate in 1983 and when he bounced between 1B, OF, and DH in 1984-88 dragged his career dWAR down to 5.2. CVI ranks Simmons ninth among catchers and at the 1.07 percentile overall.

Munson was very similar to Carlton Fisk. Both were tough, hard-nosed catchers and team leaders, who were solid at the plate and excellent behind it. Munson became a regular in 1970 at age 23, and Fisk became a regular in 1972 at age 24. Their WAR trajectories through 1979 (the year of Munson's death) were strikingly similar. At age 33 (after 10 seasons as a regular), Munson (46.0 WAR) actually had 3.7 more WAR than Fisk (42.3); Fisk did not pass Munson until 1983, when he was 35 and in his 12th full season. So one can only imagine what Munson's career might have been had he not crashed his small plane in August 1979. If you prefer to consider conventional stats, look at Table 7.2.

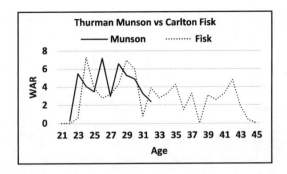

Table 7.2: Thurman Munson versus Carlton Fisk Through Age 33

Player	PA	AVG/OBP/SLG	OPS+	HR	RBI	R	dWAR	WAR
Munson (1969-79)	5905	.292/.346/.410	116	113	701	696	11.9	46.0
Fisk (1969-81)	4747	.283/.356/.471	125	169	613	671	10.2	42.3

Fisk had the higher OPS+ and hit more HR, but Munson played more, hit for a higher AVG, and was a slightly better defender As it is, Munson was the 1976 AL MVP and appeared in seven ASG—three times as a starter over Fisk. I am not trying to argue that Munson would have matched Fisk's career value had he survived; no other catcher remained as productive as Fisk into his 40s. However, I would argue that it would have been reasonable to expect Munson to attain a CVI in the upper 60s given his trajectory up to his death. Thus, I believe Munson's 60.6 CVI in a truncated career, which ranks 14th among catchers and at the 1.20 percentile overall, warrants inclusion in the HOF. However, he only once received more than 10% of the BBWAA vote in 15 years on the HOF ballot and has gotten little support from the VC.

Beyond the Numbers

- Bench, who grew up in tiny Binger, OK and idolized fellow-Oklahoman Mickey Mantle, knew he wanted a career in baseball by the second grade. He narrowly escaped death when brake failure sent his high school team bus rolling down a 50' ravine, killing two of his teammates and knocking him unconscious.[27]

- Off the field, Bench was an instant celebrity, hanging with Bob Hope and Arnold Palmer, appearing on *Mission Impossible*, hosting his own local TV show, and always being photographed with a pretty model or actress on his arm. In 1975, he married a former Miss South Carolina after a whirlwind courtship, but the marriage ended very publicly within a year, and he returned to bachelor life.[28]

Beyond the Numbers (cont'd)

- Carter won the NFL Punt, Pass, and Kick competition in 1961 at age seven and reached the finals again two years later.[29]

- Although Carter posted only 3.4 WAR during the Mets' 108-win 1986 season, his two Game 4 home runs brought the Mets a World Series-tying victory. However, his biggest hit may have been his two-out single in the 10th inning of the infamous (for the Red Sox and Billy Buckner) Game 6, which started the improbable three-run rally that brought the Mets back from the brink of defeat.

- Fisk attended the University of New Hampshire on basketball scholarship and led the freshman basketball team to an undefeated season.[30] But he gave up basketball when the Red Sox drafted him, realizing that there was no NBA future for a 6'3" power forward.

- Fisk was known for his strength, combativeness, and intolerance for anything less than best effort. He often called on his pitchers to throw high and tight and frequently skirmished with rival teams, including incidents with Frank Robinson and Thurman Munson. He was unsparing about calling out lackadaisical play. He even publicly criticized Red Sox icons Carl Yastrzemski and Reggie Smith for poor leadership and lack of hustle before backing off and saying that he meant nothing personal.[31]

- Although Fisk is most closely identified with the Red Sox, with whom he spent 11 seasons, he actually played more seasons (13) with the White Sox.

- The trade that brought Simmons to Milwaukee also brought 1982 ace SP Pete Vuckovich and HOF bullpen ace Rollie Fingers. However, one of the players sent to St. Louis, Sixto Lezcano, was used in the trade that brought Ozzie Smith to St. Louis.

- Simmons served as general manager of the Pirates in 1992 but stepped down after a heart attack. He has held a variety of jobs in player development since then.[32]

When the Orioles Lost Their Way

Cal Ripken Jr. (SS):
113.3 CVI – Baltimore AL (*95.9*)

Eddie Murray (1B):
64.0 CVI – Baltimore AL (*56.5*),
Los Angeles NL (*8.5*)

From 1966-85, coinciding roughly with HOF manager Earl Weaver's tenure and Cal Ripken Sr.'s leadership in minor league development, the Baltimore organization fostered something they called the "Orioles Way," which emphasized pitching, defense, and sound fundamentals over star quality. When they were blessed with great players like the Robinsons and Jim Palmer, they won championships, but even when they lacked star power, they were always in contention and a pleasure to watch. When Weaver retired after coming within a game of the 1982 AL East pennant, the Oriole Way was alive and well. While Palmer was nearing the end of the line, their pitching was still outstanding, and their lineup was anchored by two young stars, 27-year-old slugging 1B Eddie Murray and 22-year-old budding superstar SS Cal Ripken Jr.

However, when they won the 1983 World Series under new manager Joe Altobelli, that would be the Orioles' last pennant for 37 years and counting. Over the next five years, the Orioles slid into the abyss, losing their first 21 games of the 1988 season and firing Ripken Sr. as the manager. Worse still, Murray was scapegoated shamefully, as the steady play that was once treasured was relabeled "lackadaisical," and jeers and even racial taunts replaced the cheers. Ripken Jr. became the lone vestige of what was once the Orioles way. While the Orioles have had individual stars like Roberto Alomar, Albert Belle, Adam Jones, Manny Machado, Mike Mussina, Rafael Palmeiro, and Miguel Tejada since 1988, and fielded playoff contenders in 1996-97 and 2012-16, they have spent more time near the bottom than the top of the AL East.

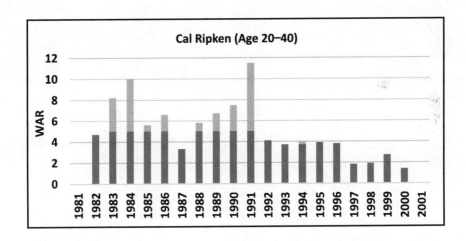

The one salient fact that casual fans know about Cal Ripken Jr. is his signature feat of surpassing Lou Gehrig's 2130 consecutive game streak (once thought unassailable) by 502 games to finish at 2632. If you probe deeper, fans will identify him as the prototype of the modern big power-hitting SS. Ripken was thought of as steady and reliable in the field, as well as at bat, making all the routine plays and rarely making an error. However, the stats and his career WAR trajectory plot tell a somewhat different story. His offensive production was erratic and was concentrated in three outstanding seasons in his 20s — his 8.2-WAR 1983 MVP season, his 10-WAR 1984 season, and his remarkable 11.5-WAR 1991 MVP season, in which he hit .323/.374/.566 (162 OPS+) with 34 HR, 114 RBI, and 99 R at age 30. This season is tied with Honus Wagner (1908) as the best ever by an MLB SS and has been topped only by Babe Ruth (five times), Barry Bonds (twice), Carl Yastrzemski, Rogers Hornsby, and Lou Gehrig among non-pitchers.

However, from 1992-2001, Ripken hit only .271/.329/.424 (97 OPS+) while constantly tinkering with his batting stance, making him a slightly *below* average offensive player in his 30s. On the other hand, Ripken was far more than merely steady and reliable at SS. While he was not flashy or acrobatic like Ozzie Smith, his 35.7 career dWAR ranks behind only Smith and Belanger at SS and better than defensive wizards Aparicio (31.8), Maranville (30.8), and Vizquel (29.5). Ripken was a perennial All-Star through thick and thin, being selected to the AL team for 19 consecutive seasons starting in 1983 and finished with 3184 hits. While Ripken's 78.1 oWAR would have been enough to put him comfortably in the HOF, it was his defense that made him special. Ripken's 113.3 CVI ranks second only to Wagner at SS and 34th among all HOF-eligible players, making him an elite Hall of Famer. He won 98.5% of the BBWAA votes when he was elected to the HOF in 2007.

Switch-hitting 1B Eddie Murray was an eight-time All-Star, who is in the top 40 on six significant career leaderboards and has checked off two of the milestones (3000 hits, 500 HR) that HOF voters most cherish. Murray's production was like clockwork. Until the last season of his 21-year major league career (in which he made only 185 PA), Murray never had fewer than 76 RBI (or more than 124) and 16 times hit 20 or more HR (but never more than 33). Hence the nickname "Steady Eddie." During his peak in 1982-85, Murray hit .306/.394/.529 (154 OPS+), averaged 31 HR, 31 2B, 114 RBI, 102 R, 305 TB, and 6.2 WAR, and finished second in the AL MVP voting in 1982-83. He even won three Gold Gloves in 1982-84, despite dWAR totals near zero.

Although he continued to average .287/.368/.472 with 25 HR and 86 RBI in 1986-88, Murray was scapegoated shamefully for the Orioles decline and was given away to the Dodgers for two journeyman pitchers and George Bell's little brother, Juan Bell. He continued to be moderately productive for the Dodgers and Mets and as DH of the 1995 Cleveland World Series team at age 39. Murray placed 77th on the 1998 Sporting News list of Baseball's 100 greatest players, and Bill James ranked him fifth at 1B in 2001.[33] So why does CVI rank Murray only 17th at 1B and at the 1.10 percentile overall? First, WAR does not consider situational stats like Murray's 1917 RBI and 1627 R. Second, his -11.6 dWAR offset some of his offensive value. Third, Murray had only four 5-WAR seasons, and none with >7.1 WAR, and thus was something of a compiler. Still, he deserves his plaque in Cooperstown.

Beyond the Numbers

- Ripken performed well in his only three postseasons, hitting .336/.411/.455 for the 1983 World Series champions and the 1996-97 teams that lost in the ALCS.

- Ripken has recently been active in baseball as owner of the Orioles' Aberdeen Iron-birds franchise. In 2007, President Bush appointed Ripken as Special Sports Envoy for the State Department, where he recruited former MLB players to hold baseball clinics in China for more than 800 children.[34]

- Murray and Ripken were both Rookies of the Year, in 1977 and 1982, respectively.

- In 1988, in the face of withering criticism by Orioles fans and writers, Murray quietly made a generous donation to the Baltimore City Parks and Recreation Department to establish the Carrie Murray Nature Center in honor of his late mother. Twenty years later, he released a wine called Eddie Murray 504 Cabernet and donated the proceeds to the Baltimore Community Foundation.[35]

Harvey's Wallbangers

Robin Yount (SS):	**Paul Molitor (DH):**
83.9 CVI – Milwaukee AL (*77.3*)	77.8 CVI – Milwaukee AL (*60.0*), Toronto AL (*10.5*)

Yount and Molitor were the sparkplugs of the power-laden Brewers teams that won the 1982 AL pennant under manager Harvey Kuenn and were popularly known as "Harvey's Wallbangers." They were table-setters rather than wallbangers themselves. Both were 21% 3TO hitters, more similar to pre-integration players than most of their contemporaries. Yount struck out more often than Molitor but was superior defensively.

Robin Yount, who arrived in the major leagues in 1974 as a precocious teenage SS, was the face of the Brewers franchise and their best all-around player for 20 years. His best season came in the pennant year of in 1982, when he was the AL MVP, hitting .331/.379/.578 (166 OPS+) with 29 HR, 114 RBI, 129 R, and 367 TB, good for 10.5 WAR. But despite Yount's best efforts (.414/.452/.621 with 1 HR, 6 RBI, and 6 R), the Brewers lost a closely contested seven-game World Series to the Cardinals. The 1982 season was the centerpiece of his five-year run (1980-84) as the finest all-around SS in the AL. After a 1985 shoulder injury forced Yount to move to CF, he had a second lesser run of success on the mediocre Brewer teams

Robin Yount (as coach), 2006

of the late 1980s, capped by a second AL MVP award in 1989, (when his 5.8 WAR ranked only ninth in the AL). Curiously, although Yount played 20 years and had six 5-WAR seasons, he played in only three ASG. Yount's 83.9 CVI ranks sixth at SS and at the 0.48 percentile overall.

Seven-time All-Star Paul Molitor's story is one of multiple setbacks and incredible resilience. Indeed, without the designator hitter rule, Paul Molitor's career would have been over long before he attained 3000 hits or the other achievements that got him into the HOF in 2004. Although Molitor was able to maintain a consistent if unspectacular level of production over his long career, with 3.6 to 6.2 WAR in 13 of his 21 major league seasons, the devil is in the details. He overcame cocaine addiction in 1980, and he was frequently sidelined by serious injuries to his ankle (1981), wrist (1983), elbow (1984), hamstring (1986), and shoulder and forearm (1990). In 1984, he was among the first position players to undergo Tommy John surgery. The pennant-winning 1982 season, when he avoided injury and hit .302/.366/.450 (129 OPS+) with 41 SB and led the AL with 136 R, good for 6.2 WAR, was Molitor's best.

Like Yount, Molitor performed valiantly in the postseason, hitting .316/.381/.684 with 2 HR, 4R, and 5 RBI in the ALCS and .355/.394/.355 with 5 R and 3 RBI in the 1982 World Series, including five hits in Game 1. But injuries continued to plague him until finally, in 1990, when he could no longer throw, he became a full-time DH. Playing a full injury-free season at DH in 1991, he hit .325/.399/.489 (147 OPS+) with a remarkable 133 R and 19 SB, showing us all what we had been missing. Then in 1993, weary of playing for a losing team, Molitor joined the Blue Jays and hit .332/.402/.509 (143 OPS+) with 121 R and 22 SB at age 36, helping them repeat as World Series champions. He was even better in the postseason, hitting .391/.481/.696 with 1 HR, 5 RBI, and 7 R in the 4-2 ALCS victory over the White Sox and a scalding .500/.571/1.000 with 2 HR, 8 RBI, and 10 R in the 4-2 World Series victory over the Phillies. He was named World Series MVP, beating out Joe Carter and his walk-off Series-clinching HR. Against all odds, Molitor continued to play until he was 41 years old, including a three-year sunset before his hometown fans in the Twin Cities. Whether you love or hate the DH rule, its preservation of Molitor's career was a gift to baseball fans. Molitor's 77.8 CVI ranks third at DH and at the 0.60 percentile overall, making him a solid Hall of Famer. He was also voted 99th on baseball's all 20th century team in 1999.

Beyond the Numbers

- Yount was an excellent golfer. He considered leaving baseball to join the PGA tour when he was 22 to join the PGA tour when he grew frustrated after four losing seasons in Milwaukee.[36] Everyone is glad he stayed.

- Yount's older brother Larry was a major league pitcher, who is listed on Baseball-Reference as having made a single appearance without ever facing a batter. He injured his arm while warming up for his MLB debut with the Astros and never returned.

- Molitor was a major baseball star at St. Paul's Cretin High school and at the University of Minnesota, where he was a first team All-American as a sophomore.[37] The university retired his #11 and gave him their Distinguished Service Award when he accepted an $80,000 to sign with Milwaukee after his junior season.

- Molitor began to abuse cocaine while rehabilitating from a midseason injury in 1980.[38] Matters reached a crisis on Christmas Day when he failed to show up at his parents' house because he had passed out after an all-night drug party. When his fiancée threatened to leave him, Molitor turned to religion and overcame his addiction.

- In 2015, Molitor realized his long-delayed ambition to manage the Twins, who had been a perennial loser for a decade after a brief run of one-and-done postseason appearances in the early 2000s. To everyone's surprise, the Twins made an 83-win playoff run in Molitor's first season, then after falling back to 59-103 in 2016, made the playoffs as the second wildcard team in 2017. But the Twins fell back again in 2018 and although they rallied to finish second, it was not enough to save Molitor's job.

Sisyphus

Andre Dawson (RF):	Tim Raines (LF):
71.1CVI – Montreal NL (*48.4*), Chicago NL (*18.7*)	69.5 CVI – Montreal NL (*49.2*), Chicago AL (*16.6*)

The Expos' history in Montreal is reminiscent of the myth of Sisyphus, whose eternal punishment in Hades was to repeatedly push a boulder up a steep hill, only to have it roll down just before it reached the top. Similarly, the onset of free agency, coupled with the team ownership's severe financial constraints, doomed the

Expos to forever watch All-Star players and eventual Hall of Famers like Dawson, Raines, Gary Carter, Larry Walker, Randy Johnson, and Pedro Martinez depart before they could ever get quite over the hump and win a championship. The ultimate kick came in the cataclysmic strike year of 1994, when the Expos compiled the best record in MLB by August, only to have the rest of the season cancelled. By the time play resumed in 1995, star players Larry Walker, Marquis Grissom, and John Wetteland had departed, and so had the Expos chances for a pennant. Dawson, who left the Expos in 1987, and Raines, who left in 1991, were part of this frustrating legacy.

Eight-time All-Star Andre "The Hawk" Dawson was a "five-tool" star who had to hobble through the last half of his career as a one-dimensional slugger after his knees (already damaged while playing high school football) were ruined by Olympic Stadium's unforgiving artificial turf. In his prime years with the Expos (1980-83), Dawson hit .302/.350/.518 (140 OPS+) and averaged 24 HR, 87 RBI, 94 R, 31 SB, 286 TB, 1.6 dWAR, and 7.2 WAR per season, while winning four Gold Gloves in CF. He was widely regarded as one of the best all-around players in baseball. Although his highest WAR_H (7.9) came in 1982 (third best in MLB), his 7.5 WAR_H (with a 157 OPS+) in the strike-shortened 1981 season was even more impressive; he could easily have finished with 10-11 WAR_H in a full 162-game season. As it was, Dawson finished a close second to Mike Schmidt in WAR_H in 1981 and was the runner-up to Schmidt in the MVP voting. He also finished second to Dale Murphy in the 1983 NL MVP vote.

Dawson's only clear weakness, then and throughout his career, was poor plate discipline. He struck out more than 2.5 times as often as he walked, and his low BB rate generally kept his OBP below .360. Bad knees forced Dawson to move to RF in 1984, where he won four more Gold Gloves, despite falling below zero dWAR for the last 10 years of his career. When Dawson earned free agency at the end of the 1986 season, he finally found a soft landing spot for his balky knees on the natural grass of Wrigley Field. He responded by leading the NL with 49 HR and 137 RBI and winning his only MVP award, despite only 4.0 WAR (not even in the NL Top 10). In his six years with the Cubs, Dawson reinvented himself as a pure slugger and veteran leader, hitting .285/.327/.507 (125 OPS+) while averaging 29 HR, 98 RBI, 72 R, and 3.1 WAR per season and leading the Cubs to their second NL East championship in 1989. He moved to the AL as a DH in 1993, when he could no longer play RF, and soldiered on until age 43, long enough to become one of three players (along with Mays and Barry Bonds) to hit 400 HR and steal 300 bases. Dawson's 71.1 CVI ranks 13th in RF and at the 0.70 percentile overall,

During the early part of his career, Tim Raines was often compared to Rickey Henderson because of his outstanding on-base skills and his uncanny success in stealing bases. The comparison is unfair because Henderson was one of a kind, but Raines was still the sparkplug of some very good Expos teams in the 1980s and later settled into a long second career as a utility OF, appearing in four postseasons for the White Sox and Yankees in the 1990s. Raines hit the ground running as a rookie in 1981 — literally. He hit .304/.391/.438 (135 OPS+) with 71 SB in a strike-shortened season and finished second to Dodger pitching sensation Fernando Valenzuela for Rookie of the Year. The Expos won the NL East second half crown that year and defeated the Phillies for the Division title but were stopped by the Dodgers 3-2 in the NLCS. That would be the Expos' only postseason appearance in their 36-year history before moving to Washington in 2005.

From 1981-87, Raines was second only to Henderson among baseball's leadoff men, hitting .310/.396/.488 (135 OPS+) and averaging 72 SB, 103 R, and 5.5 WAR per season, despite fighting cocaine addiction in 1982. His 90 SB in 1983 and 78 SB in 1982 rank eighth and 20th (tied) since 1900. He played in seven ASG, all during this period. Raines had one more outstanding 6.3-WAR season in 1992 after his trade to the White Sox, but gradually declined to a part-time role thereafter, although he was still an important cog for division-winning teams in Chicago in 1993 and World Series champions in New York in 1996 and 1998. Raines averaged .300 in nearly 800 ABs during his three seasons with the Yankees. CVI ranks Raines ninth in LF and at the 0.87 percentile overall. The BBWAA elected him in 2017, his tenth and final year on the ballot.

Beyond the Numbers

- Dawson was a victim of MLB's illegal collusion as a free agent in the winter of 1986, and after receiving only lowball offers, had to offer Cubs ownership a blank check to get a $500,000 contract.[39]

- After returning to his hometown to play out the last two years of his career, Dawson joined the Marlins front office and served as a special assistant through 2017.

- Although Raines lacked Rickey Henderson's power and flair, he did outstrip him in one stat — his 84.7% success rate on SB attempts beats Henderson's 80.8% and is among the best in history. He ranks fifth with 805 SB.

- In 1999, while playing for Oakland, Raines was diagnosed with lupus, a serious and potentially life-threatening chronic auto-immune disease. He returned to Montreal in 2001 after missing most of two seasons.[40] The Expos obliged him by trading him to Baltimore in September so he could join his son Tim Jr. in the OF.

Bullpen Aces

Rich Gossage (RP):
90.6 CVI – New York AL (*18.8*), Chicago
AL (*9.6*), Pittsburgh NL (*6.1*)

Dennis Eckersley (RP):
75.9 CVI – Boston AL (*21.9*),
Oakland AL (*16.0*), Cleveland AL (*13.3*),
Chicago NL (*10.3*)

John Hiller (RP):
60.7 CVI – Detroit AL (*30.4*)

Lee Smith (RP):
55.4 CVI – Chicago NL (*18.6*),
St. Louis NL (*4.3*)

Rollie Fingers (RP):
55.0 CVI – Oakland AL (*12.6*),
Milwaukee AL (*8.0*), San Diego NL (*5.1*)

The 1980s ushered in the age of bullpen specialization and brought us six CVI-Plus RP. Rich "Goose" Gossage and Dennis Eckersley are no-doubt Hall of Famers, Hiller, Smith, and Fingers, were HOVG types, but Smith and Fingers made it to the HOF anyway. Given the limitations of CV or any WAR-based metric to judge the careers of RP, I cannot quarrel too much with those selections. Gossage, Hiller, and Fingers were multi-inning "old-school" late-inning relievers who came into games whenever a high-leverage situation arose and pitched as hard and as long as they could. Eckersley and Smith belonged more to the "new school" of RP popularized by Eckersley's manager Tony LaRussa, in which designated "closers" were held back to preserve ninth-inning leads and earn saves.

Nine-time All-Star Goose Gossage was the quintessential workhorse 1970s reliever, a big, intimidating guy with a blazing fastball who entered games in the middle of jams and blew away opposing hitters for multi-inning stretches. His 1975 season, in which he compiled 8.2 WAR$_p$ and 19.8 Leveraged WAR (the metric used here to evaluate RP) with a 1.84 ERA (212 ERA+) and 1.193 WHIP in 141.2 IP is perhaps the best ever for any RP, despite his modest 26 saves, which nonetheless led the AL. He

Rich Gossage

also posted 31 more strikeouts (130) than hits allowed (99) and yielded only three HR in 141.2 IP.

When old-schooler Paul Richards (who thought that the best arms belonged in the starting rotation) replaced Chuck Tanner as White Sox manager in 1976, Gossage was tried as a starter, but was thoroughly mediocre, going 9-17 with a 3.94 ERA and 1.357 WHIP. Gossage said he didn't have the patience to wait four days between starts, but he probably missed the adrenaline rush of pitching with the game on the line. So Tanner, now managing in Pittsburgh, traded for Gossage and paired him with sinkerballer Kent Tekulve to create a dominant bullpen there. Gossage had his second-best season, going 11-9 with 26 saves, a 1.62 ERA, a 0.955 WHIP, and 6.0 WAR_p (13.1 leveraged WAR).

But the Pirates, with a limited budget and Tekulve already in place, allowed Gossage to move to the Yankees as a free agent that winter, joining 1977 Cy Young award-winning bullpen ace Sparky Lyle, who as 3B Graig Nettles quipped, "went from Cy Young to sayonara."[41] Gossage enjoyed a very successful six-year run with the Yankees in 1978-83, averaging 7-5 with 25 saves, 84 SO, and only 30 BB in 86 IP per season. His workload and leveraged WAR were down from his mid-1970s peak, in part because of age and in part because of the evolution of the closer role. But he cemented his reputation as a big-game reliever and key contributor to three AL East Division titles, two AL pennants and a World Series championship, including a 2.87 ERA, 0.894 WHIP, and 8 SV in four postseasons (the last with the Padres in 1984). Gossage's 310 saves rank 25th on the career leaderboard. CVI is not an especially effective tool for evaluating RP and comparing RP across eras, but Gossage's ranking as second among RP and 62nd among all HOF-eligible players seems about right.

Six-time All-Star Dennis Eckersley, a converted starter, was the prototype of the modern closer for the Athletics in the late 1980s and was the first to be used almost exclusively for one-inning stints in save situations. Whether or not you like the idea of pitcher usage being tailored to optimize a statistic of dubious merit (you can probably sense that I do not), Eck at that stage of his career was the perfect vehicle for this strategy. Fans often forget that Eckersley also had a very successful career as a starter with the Indians, Red Sox, and Cubs from 1975-86. The highlight of those 12 years was a three-game stretch in 1977 (at age 22) in which he pitched 22.1 consecutive hitless innings (including a 1-0 12-SO no-hitter against the Angels), falling barely short of Cy Young's record 23 consecutive hitless innings in 1904. He also won 20 games for the ill-fated 1978 Red Sox in his first year with the team. He was known for exceptional control but was vulnerable to the long ball, yielding 59 HR in 1978-79, his two best seasons as an SP.

But Eckersley's ticket to the HOF was his trend-setting second career as a closer. From 1988-92, Eckersley was the dominant RP in the game, saving 45, 33, 48, 43, and 51 games and producing ERAs ranging from 0.61 to 2.96 and WHIPs from 0.607 to 0.913. Freed from having to conserve his strength to pitch multiple innings, he became an extreme strikeout pitcher, with 1.53 SO/H (378/247). Eckersley had only 0.68 SO/H as a SP before his move to the bullpen. He made up for his awful 1984 postseason as an SP by racking up 15 saves in six postseasons as an RP. He was named MVP of the 1988 ALCS, in which he saved all four victories while allowing no runs and one hit in 6.0 IP. Unfortunately, that success was followed by coughing up Kirk Gibson's epic walkoff HR in Game 1 of the 1988 World Series, initiating a shocking Dodger sweep.

Two Eckersley seasons stand out above the rest. In 1990, he gave up only 5 ER in 73.1 IP and sported an unreal 0.61 ERA and 603 ERA+, making him six times stingier(!) than the average MLB pitcher. Two years later, in 1992, he posted 7 W, 51 SV (without a single blown save opportunity), a 1.91 ERA, and a 0.913 WHIP to sweep the Cy Young and MVP awards. Only nine pitchers have more than Eckersley's 51 SV that season. His 390 SV, which topped the leaderboard when he retired, still rank seventh. Eckersley's 75.9 CVI ranks third among RP and at the 0.65 percentile overall. That and his historical significance add up to a no-doubt Hall of Famer.

Long forgotten Tiger RP John Hiller is an unlikely candidate to appear on any list of baseball's top players. This is a guy who suffered three heart attacks (!)

John Hiller

in the 1970-71 off-season, missed the entire 1971 and half of the 1972 season, and returned to post two of the great RP seasons of all time.[42] In 1973, Hiller went 10-5 with a league-leading 38 SV and an ERA of 1.44 in 155.1 IP. And the following year, Hiller won 17 games as a reliever, with an amazing 150 IP. Hiller's 31 decisions that season and only 13 SV are a testament to his use when games were on the line, not when the Tigers were already winning. His 8.0 WAR_p and 18.2 leveraged WAR in 1973 rank second only to Gossage's 8.2 WAR_p and 19.8 leveraged WAR in 1975 as the best ever by a RP. Hiller collected only 125 SV in his 15-year career. Hiller's 60.7 CVI (1.18 percentile) ranks fifth among RP, well behind Eckersley and Wilhelm but ahead of Hall of Famer Trevor Hoffman, as well as Smith, Fingers, and Sutter. Yet Hiller did not and probably will not receive much

HOF support. While I would not call this a historical injustice, Hiller's unique career is still worth remembering.

Going by CVI, Smith and Fingers, who reside in the 1.41-1.44 percentile range, fall well below my HOF standard. Yet each has something to recommend him. Smith had 478 saves in his 18-year career and still ranks third on the all-time leaderboard behind Rivera and Hoffman. His 132 ERA+ is also tied for 33rd on the career leaderboard. He closed for Division winners in Chicago (1984) and Boston (1988) but was terrible (8.44 ERA) in two postseason defeats.

Fingers (341 in 17 years) ranks 14th on the saves leaderboard despite pitching before the advent of the one-inning closer. Fingers was the ace RP of Oakland's 1971-75 mini-dynasty, surpassed 100 IP in relief for eight consecutive seasons, and (unlike Smith) was outstanding in the postseason, posting 4 wins and 9 saves with a 2.35 ERA and 1.169 WHIP in 57.3 IP for Oakland in 1971-75 and Milwaukee in 1981 (when he won the Cy Young award and MVP in the strike-shortened season). He saved his best for the World Series (1.35 ERA and 1.050 WHIP).

Beyond the Numbers

- Gossage enjoyed playing for the free-spending Steinbrenner, but their relationship deteriorated late in his Yankee tenure. In 1982, he grew his signature Fu Manchu mustache, not only for the intimidation factor, but specifically to tweak "the Boss" by pushing the limits of his facial hair ban.[43]

- Eckersley had barely established himself in Cleveland when his life was disrupted by the dissolution of his marriage after his wife Denise left him to marry his friend and teammate Rick Manning.[44] This messy situation triggered a trade to the Red Sox in March 1978. The Indians would soon grow to regret the deal, since the best player they got back was over-the-hill Rick Wise, who may be remembered as the guy who was traded for two Hall of Famers (Steve Carlton was the other) entering their primes.

- Eckersley, who had a drinking problem as a teenager, nearly went off the rails in 1986, when he began drinking again in 1986 while sidelined by tendinitis in his left shoulder.[45] He checked into a rehab center to get his life back on track and earned a second chance with LaRussa in Oakland in 1987. This turned out to be the turning point of his career — and his life.

- Eckersley is now a popular Red Sox color commentator on broadcasts, and is known and loved for his unsparing candor that earned him the nickname "Honest Eck" and for the colorful "Eck-isms" he first introduced into the baseball lexicon as a player, such as "hard cheese," "yakker," and "punchout."

Just One Thing

Bobby Grich (2B): 77.9 CVI – Baltimore AL (*36.0*), California AL (*35.1*)	**Ozzie Smith (SS):** 74.6 CVI – St. Louis NL (*66.0*), San Diego NL (*11.0*)
Alan Trammell (SS): 74.5 CVI – Detroit AL (*70.7*)	**Ryne Sandberg (2B):** 74.3 CVI – Chicago NL (*68.1*)
Lou Whitaker (2B): 66.9 CVI – Detroit AL (*75.1*)	**Willie Randolph (2B):** 57.4 CVI – New York AL (*34.0*)

Grich, Smith, Trammell, and Sandberg, are four middle IF with very similar CVI, between the 0.59 and 0.69 percentile. All should be solid Hall of Famers, yet they have fared very differently with HOF voters. Smith, a below-average hitter (88 OPS+) but perhaps the greatest defensive player of all time, was an easy first ballot selection. Sandberg, a power-hitting 2B (282 HR) and strong defender (13.5 dWAR) with an MVP award on his resume, won HOF election in his third try on the BBWAA ballot. Trammell, an above average hitter (110 OPS+) and a near-elite defender at SS (22.7 dWAR), was elected by the Veterans Committee in 2018 after being passed over by the BBWAA. Finally, Grich, who had the best CVI and best OPS+ of the bunch and was superior defensively to Sandberg (but not as good as the two SS), has not come close to HOF election, receiving only 2.6% of the BBWAA ballots, and completely ignored by the VC.

Actually, Grich was almost halfway to rivalling Mazeroski (24.0 dWAR) as the best defensive 2B of all time with 11.5 dWAR by the end of his fifth full season (1976). But a herniated lumbar disk suffered at age 28 limited his mobility and forced him to re-invent himself as a slugger, topping out at 30 HR in 1979. So he never left an indelible impression as a particular kind of player. Clearly, HOF voters are most impressed by players like Ozzie Smith, who excel at "just one thing" (as the crusty old cowboy Curly told Billy Crystal's character in City Slickers), and have a harder time integrating the accomplishments of a player like Grich with broadly-based skills and no single defining attribute.[46] This section will also cover two other CVI-Plus 2B who rank a notch or two below these four, Lou Whitaker, who was joined to Trammell at the hip for 19 years, and the underrated Willie Randolph.

As the owner of the highest CVI of any eligible non-Hall of Famer who is no longer on the BBWAA ballot, six-time All-Star Bobby Grich is a sabermetric

darling. Let's face it, Grich's traditional career statistics do not scream "Hall of Fame," particularly his
.266 AVG, his 224 HR and 864 RBI. He was an excellent defensive 2B, especially early in his career, and
won four Gold Gloves, but his 16.8 dWAR places only
12th among 2B. He had excellent plate discipline, but
his .371 OBP, while very good, places him only 26th
among 2B. His bat also had some extra-base pop
with a .158 ISO, but his .424 SLG stands only 53rd
among 2B.

Grich had to serve a five-year minor league apprentice-
ship, since the Orioles major league infield was stacked
with Hall of Famer Brooks Robinson, defensive whiz
Mark Belanger, and solid 2B Davey Johnson. When
he finally got a full major league opportunity, Grich
was among the best 2B in baseball, combining solid
hitting with superlative defense. From 1972-76, he hit

Bobby Grich

.263/.374/.410 (129 OPS+) and averaged 14 HR, 83 R, 59 RBI, 89 BB, and 7.0 WAR
per season. His defense was even better, with four consecutive Gold Gloves and 2.1
dWAR per season. His 4.0 dWAR in 1973 ranks third among all 2B.

Then, after leaving the Orioles to sign with his hometown Angels as a free
agent in 1977, he suffered a herniated lumbar disk trying to lift an air condi-
tioner.[47] He returned in 1978 with more power but limited mobility. Grich led
the AL with 8.3 WAR in 1973, but he never finished higher than eighth in the
MVP balloting. His 5.5 WAR in the strike shortened 1981 season was fourth
best in the AL and could easily have been >8.0 in a 162-game season, but he
still finished only 14th in the MVP voting. He played in five ALCS but hit poorly,
and his teams never advanced. Grich's 71.1 career WAR is not just an oddity of
the Baseball-Reference methodology; his FanGraphs career WAR is 69.2. Grich
was a player with no real weaknesses; every aspect of his game was very good,
but none stood out. Grich may not stand among baseball's giants, but he was
better than many fans realize. His 77.9 CVI ranks eighth at 2B and at the 0.59
percentile overall.

Ozzie Smith's specialty was defense, and he did it better than anyone before or
since. Advanced defensive metrics and the "eye test" are in total agreement on
this point. Ozzie Smith's defense was so spectacularly acrobatic that fans would
come to Cardinal games two hours early to watch "the Wizard of Oz" take infield practice and turn a backflip somersault or two. His 44.2 career dWAR tops
all players and is 4.7 more than second place Mark Belanger. In his rookie year,
he made what some have called the greatest infield play ever, in which he dove

to his left for a Jeff Burroughs groundball, reached up to snag the ball with his bare hand from the prone position when the ball took a bad hop, bounced up to his feet, and threw to 1B in time to nail the runner. You can still see the play on YouTube.[48]

But the point is, not only the many "highlight reel" plays that he made, but that he routinely reached balls that were beyond the reach of other SS and converted them into outs. As former Mets SS Bud Harrelson put it: "The thing about Ozzie is, if he misses a ball, you assume it's untouchable. If any other SS misses a ball, your first thought is, 'Would Ozzie have had it?'"[49]

Ozzie was an anemic hitter at first, posting a miserable 48 OPS+ in 1979 with San Diego, but a 1981 trade to St. Louis, where Whitey Herzog deployed a small-ball offense that utilized Smith's speed and contact skills, was a godsend. After hitting no higher than .258 in 1978-84, Ozzie gradually became a decent hitter and finished second in the MVP voting in 1987 when he hit .303/.392/.383 (105 OPS+). And (unlike the Padres) the Cardinals were a winning team that gave him exposure to showcase his skills nationally. Smith played in four post-seasons and three World Series with the Cardinals, including a 4-3 World Series win over the Brewers in 1982. Although his postseason offensive stats on the whole were underwhelming, he was chosen as the 1985 NLCS MVP when he hit .435/.500/.696 and launched a shocking walk-off HR against the Dodgers' ace RP Tom Niedenfuer in the pivotal Game 5. Smith was also a 15-time All-Star from 1981-96 (missing only in 1993). He was voted the #3 SS on MLB's All-Century team in 1999 and as one of the Top 100 players of the 20th Century by the Sporting News. CVI ranks him 11th at SS and at the 0.68 percentile overall.

Sandberg was one of the best all-around players in the NL from 1984-92, a 10-time All-Star who hit .295/.357/.484 and averaged 24 HR (topped by 40 HR in 1990) to establish new slugging standards for 2B. Sandberg was also an excellent defensive 2B (13.5 dWAR) who won nine consecutive Gold Gloves from 1983-91. From my vantage point as a Cubs fan, Sandberg deserves his spot in the HOF, if only for his 8.6-WAR 1984 MVP season, when he came out of nowhere to hit .314/.367/.520 (140 OPS+) with 19 HR, 19 3B, 84 RBI, 114 R, 331 TB, and 32 SB, and like Moses, led the Cubs to within sight of the promised land after 40 years in the desert. At least, that's what it felt like to legions of Cubs fans who had not even sniffed the World Series since 1945.

As in the biblical story of Moses, it was left to others to complete the tortuous journey and finally enter the promised land, which for the Cubs would not happen until 32 years later. However, Sandberg was stellar (.368/.455/.474) in the 1984 NLCS loss to the Padres and again (.400/.458/.474) in the 1989 NLCS loss to the Giants. On June 13, 1994 with a strike impending, Sandberg, who was off to a slow start following a subpar year in 1993, announced his retirement. He returned in

1996 but could not recapture his old form. Sandberg's 74.3 CVI ranks 10th at 2B and at the 0.69 percentile overall.

How often is a team blessed with a keystone combination like Alan Trammell and Lou Whitaker, who played together for 19 years and provided above average offense and superlative defense for a perennial pennant contender? The 1902-13 Cubs HOF combo of Joe Tinker and Johnny Evers (immortalized in rhyme) comes to mind, but Trammell and Whitaker played together for seven years longer and were significantly better all-around players. Their partnership began in the 1976 Fall Instructional League and continued from 1977 until Whitaker retired in 1995 (a year before Trammell). Whitaker was a slightly better offensive player than Trammell over the course of his career and had the higher career WAR, but Trammell had the higher peak (including a near-MVP season in 1987) and a higher CVI. Trammell peaked in 1983-90, hitting .297/.362/.451 (125 OPS+) and averaging 16 HR, 72 RBI, 83 R, 17 SB, and 5.8 WAR (despite down years in 1985 and 1989). Highlights of this period included MVP honors in the Tigers' 4-1 World Series victory over the Padres in 1984, when he hit .450/.500/.800 with 2 HR and 6 RBI in 23 PA.

Whitaker's hallmark was consistency, with WAR never rising above 6.8 and only once falling below 3.5 from 1978-93, but he fared poorly in his two postseasons. Both were outstanding defenders—Trammell with 22.7 dWAR and four Gold Gloves, Whitaker with 16.3 dWAR and three Gold Gloves. Trammell played in six ASG, one more than Whitaker. CVI ranks Trammell 0.68 percentile) significantly higher than Whitaker (1.00 percentile), but both deserve HOF recognition. Neither was treated well by BBWAA voters, but at least Trammell remained on the ballot for 15 years, while Whitaker inexplicably fell off the ballot after one year. The VC elected Trammell in 2018 but ignored Whitaker until he became a finalist on their December 2019 ballot, where he received only six of the necessary 12 votes. Trammell and Whitaker were inseparable on the playing field and ought to be reunited in the HOF.

As the quiet member of the Yankees Bronx Zoo teams, which logged four AL pennants, two World Series wins, and scores of tabloid headlines in 1976-88, it is no wonder that Willie Randolph was often overlooked. But he was the infield "glue" that held together those boisterous teams with his stellar defense and timely hitting speed and speed (271 SB) at the top of the lineup in good times and bad. His 20.2 dWAR ranks sixth among all 2B – 3.8 less than 2B dWAR leader Bill Mazeroski – and he was a far better hitter. He played in six All-Star games, four times as the starter at 2B. His 57.4 CVI (1.28 percentile) ranks 17th at 2B and places him sqaurely in HOVG territory, but he ranks higher than Hall of Famers like Billy Herman, Bobby Doerr, Nellie Fox, Mazeroski, and others. He received only five HOF votes in his one year on the BBWAA ballot.

Beyond the Numbers

- Bobby Grich was no shrinking violet, even as a rookie. In 1970, 34-year-old future Hall of Famer Frank Robinson approached Grich when he was discussing hitting with a teammate in the clubhouse, and asked, "What does a rookie like you know about hitting?" Grich told the fiery Robinson, "Tell you something pal. I'll be hitting for 10 years around here after you're gone."[50] Evidently, Grich lived to tell the tale.

- Sandberg came to the Cubs as an unheralded throw-in in a 1982 trade of incumbent SS Ivan De Jesus for veteran Phillies SS Larry Bowa.

- Sandberg compiled a 119-159 record as the Phillies manager in 2013-15.

- Smith was born Mobile, AL, a hotbed of African American baseball talent, but grew up in the Watts section of Los Angeles. One of his earliest memories was sleeping on the floor during the 1965 Watts riots to avoid stray bullets when he was 10.[51]

- When the Cardinals traded Garry Templeton, another slick fielding SS who was a far better hitter, to get Smith, many thought at the time that the Padres had won the trade.

- Trammell had the misfortune of managing the Tigers in 2003 when they fielded one of the worst teams in history. Trammell was helpless to stem the tide of a near-historic 119-loss season. The team improved in 2004-05, but a late-season collapse in 2005 cost Trammell his job, which went to Jim Leyland. It's too bad that Trammell couldn't have stayed a year longer, as many of the young players he helped develop came of age in 2006 and surprisingly won the AL pennant. Perhaps, Leyland was a better field manager than Trammell, whose forte was teaching, or perhaps Trammell was just unlucky.

- Whitaker is one of only three 2B to accumulate at least 2000 H, 200 HR, 1000 RBI, and 1000 R. Hornsby and Morgan are the others — pretty good company. His career 117 OPS+ is good but not extraordinary for a 2B.

Brooks Robinson Lite

Graig Nettles (3B):
67.0 CVI – New York AL (*44.4*),
Cleveland AL (*17.5*)

Buddy Bell (3B):
66.2 CVI – Texas AL (*36.3*),
Cleveland AL (*24.5*)

From a CVI perspective, the 3B position was a desert until Mathews, Santo, Robinson, Boyer, and Bando, all of whom debuted in 1951-60, joined Home Run Baker as CVI-Plus 3B. Schmidt, Boggs, Brett, Nettles, and Bell joined the club during the 1970s and 1980s — and that doesn't count DH Paul Molitor, who played twice as many innings at 3B as at any other position on the field. Although neither Nettles nor Bell was a great hitter, they were superb defenders, ranking fifth and third respectively in dWAR at 3B and winning eight Gold Gloves (Nettles in 1977-78 and Bell in 1979-84) between them after Brooks Robinson released his stranglehold on that honor. Unfortunately, Nettles fell off the BBWAA HOF ballot after four tries, and Bell was one and done.

If the HOF can accommodate a myriad of outstanding CVI-Minus defensive middle IF (Aparicio, Bancroft, Fox, Maranville, Mazeroski, Reese, Rizzuto, Schoendienst, Tinker) who could not even muster a 100 career OPS+, why should it summarily dismiss two great defensive CVI-Plus 3B like Nettles (110 OPS+) and Bell (109 OPS+)? This disparity helps explain why the Hall of Fame currently includes 24 SS and 20 2B, but only 13 3B. When one further considers how long it took Ron Santo to be elected to the HOF and the lukewarm support Scott Rolen received from the BBWAA in his first two years on the ballot, one could call 3B the "Rodney Dangerfields" of the diamond — they get no respect! Nettles and Bell belong in the HOF and deserve a closer look from the VC.

If six-time All-Star Graig Nettles, a 27% 3TO hitter with 390 HR but only a .248 career AVG, were elected to the HOF, he would displace Ray Schalk (.253) as the owner of the lowest AVG of any non-pitcher in Cooperstown. But it would be a shame if that prevents him from getting there. We know that OPS+ is a far better metric of offensive prowess than AVG and that Nettles began his career in a period when the MLB-wide AVG was below .250. From 1970-78, Nettles was a model of consistency, hitting .254/.332/.432 (115 OPS+), averaging 26 HR, 84 RBI, 78 R, 2.4 dWAR, and 5.4 WAR per year, while making the AL All-Star team in 1975 and 1977-78.

Nettles's career 110 OPS+ is quite respectable, especially for a defensive star with 21.4 dWAR at 3B. When compared with HOF 3B Pie Traynor, who hit .320 in an era when league batting averages were 40-50 points higher than in the 1970s, Nettles had a longer career and a higher WAR at almost every age. He also had a slightly superior OPS+ (110-109) and ran rings around Traynor (2.1 dWAR) at 3B. Don't take my word for it; check out the 1978 World Series highlights yourself online.[52] Unfortunately, Nettles was eclipsed by Reggie Jackson in the 1978 World Series and by Brooks Robinson in the Golden Glove competition. CVI ranks Nettles 12th at 3B and at the 0.98 percentile overall.

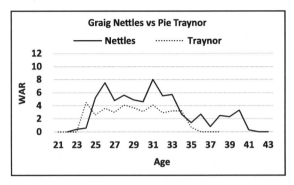

Buddy Bell did not carry the albatross of a sub-.250 career AVG, and his 23.8 dWAR is even better than Nettles. In his six peak years (1979-84), Bell hit .301/.358/.445 (123 OPS+) and averaged 14 HR, 77 RBI, 72 R, 2.5 dWAR, and 6.0 WAR per season, while playing in four ASG and winning six consecutive Gold Gloves. Bell's HOF case resides primarily in this six-year stretch of excellence. But Bell lacked many of the "extras" that make the difference between Hall of Famers and the near-misses. Despite his respectable .279 AVG, Bell (201 HR, .127 ISO) lacked Nettles' pop at the plate. Furthermore, unlike Nettles, who was a key player on several championship teams, Bell never appeared in a postseason. CVI ranks Bell 13th at 3B and at the 1.02 percentile overall, but without those extras, he is less likely than Nettles to get there. However, he surely deserved more than the eight HOF votes he received in his only year on the BBWAA ballot.

Beyond the Numbers

- Nettles led all major league position players with 7.5 WAR in 1971 and 8.0 WAR in 1976 but received virtually no MVP support in either year, since so much of his value was as a defender.

- Nettles' 3.9 dWAR in 1971 is tied with Matt Chapman (2019) as the third highest ever achieved at 3B. Only Brooks Robinson (4.5 in 1968 and 4.2 in 1967) was better.

- Bell belongs to one of MLB's great multigenerational families. His father Gus was a four-time All-Star OF for the Reds. His son David was a 12-year major league IF and is the current Reds manager, and his son Mike played 19 games with the Reds in 2000.

- Bell managed the Tigers in 1996-98, the Rockies from 2000-2002, and the Royals in 2005-07 with little success, compiling 519 wins and 724 losses in nine years. He is now a vice president and senior advisor to the GM of the Reds.

Mr. May and the Boss[53]

Dave Winfield (RF):
65.3 CVI – San Diego NL (*32.0*), New York AL (*27.1*)

This book is about MLB players and their quantifiable achievements, rather than MLB executives, but the story of Dave Winfield cannot be told without George Steinbrenner, the mercurial Yankee "Boss," with whom he was locked in a hellish 10-year embrace spanning the 1980s and who scornfully dubbed him "Mr. May" (a snide comparison to Reggie Jackson). Winfield was a chiseled 6'6" 220 pound athlete who played basketball well enough to be drafted out of the University of Minnesota by the NBA and ABA and looked enough like a tight end to be drafted by the NFL, despite never having played college football. But he chose the San Diego Padres, who selected him fourth overall in the 1973 amateur draft and immediately brought him to the major leagues. By 1977, he was an All-Star (his first of 12 consecutive ASG appearances), and by 1979 he hit .308/.395/.558 (166 OPS+) with 34 HR and 118 RBI and 97 R, led the NL with 8.3 WAR, and finished third in the NL MVP voting (an award he would have won easily if the Padres were a contending team). Going into free agency at the end of the 1980 season, he seemed to be on the fast track to the HOF.

Dave Winfield

But Winfield made the near-fatal mistake of signing with Steinbrenner and the Yankees as a free agent. Steinbrenner, who viewed Winfield as the natural heir to Reggie Jackson's Mr. October mantle, had buyer's remorse before the ink on the contract was dry, when he learned that it included a cost-of-living escalator clause that would cost him $7 M over the contract's 10-year duration. Steinbrenner reluctantly accepted a compromise that involved donating the disputed money (plus $4 M of Winfield's own money) to Winfield's charitable foundation, as had been done to resolve a similar salary dispute in San Diego three years earlier. By the end of the 1981 season, when Winfield disappointed in the ALCS and got only one single in 27 World Series AB, the truce was over. He would never get a chance to redeem himself in the Boss's eyes, since that would be the Yankees' last postseason appearance until 1995, long after Winfield's departure.

Steinbrenner did his best to get rid of Winfield over the remaining nine years of his contract, but Winfield was too expensive to trade and after five years had full no-trade protection. So, he resorted to ordering manager Lou Piniella to bench Winfield (he refused) and to accusing Winfield of misappropriating foundation funds, while withholding his required payments (three courts ordered him to pay). Then, in 1988, Steinbrenner paid professional gambler Howard Spira $40,000 to misrepresent a $15,000 check that Winfield had written as a gambling debt. After an investigation, the Commissioner absolved Winfield and banned Steinbrenner for life from participation in the operation of the Yankees in 1990. Unfortunately, the ban (which was lifted in 1993) was a mere slap on the wrist for infractions (consorting with a professional gambler, suborning perjury) that were perhaps as bad as anything Pete Rose was accused of.

Winfield soldiered on for eight tumultuous years in New York, hitting .291 / .357 / .497 (135 OPS+) and averaging 25 HR, 102 RBI, 89 R, and 3.4 WAR per season from 1981-88—not exceptional, but very good under the circumstances. Then, after missing the entire 1989 season with a herniated lumbar disk, Winfield was finally traded to the Angels in 1990. Although Winfield was never great defensively, despite his seven Gold Gloves (which are often given to players who look better than they play), the back injury limited his mobility in RF and eventually forced a move to DH. However, he enjoyed a long and productive sunset, including a 4.1-WAR season with the World Series champion Blue Jays, when he obtained some vindication for his 1981 failures by hitting 2 HR with 6 RBI in the postseason, including the decisive two-run 11th-inning double that decided Game 6 and clinched the World Series. He also joined the 3000-hit club with his hometown Twins in 1993. Winfield's 65.3 CVI ranks 16th in RF and at the 1.05 percentile overall. His CVI was held down by his unsightly -22.7 dWAR (despite all those Gold Gloves).

As a sidebar, it is appalling that Steinbrenner's name continues to crop up for HOF consideration. Does the "character clause" apply only to players? As far as I can tell, Steinbrenner's main talent was writing checks – including illegal checks to the Nixon campaign in 1972 and to Spira. Crimes and misdemeanors aside, Steinbrenner doesn't even merit HOF consideration on pure baseball grounds. He took over a franchise with unmatched resources, and after some short-term success in leveraging the new free agency rules in 1976-78, he misspent those resources on bloated contracts for overrated veterans, while trading away prospects, and overseeing the Yankees's longest postseason drought since the Deadball Era in 1982-94. The foundation for the Yankee dynasty of 1996-2001 was laid not by Steinbrenner, but by GM Gene Michaels and his young assistant Brian Cashman *in Steinbrenner's absence while he served his suspension.* Jeter, Pettitte, Posada, and Rivera were all signed in 1991-92 while Steinbrenner was banned. To be fair, Steinbrenner's checkbook brought in several important veteran stars (Clemens Cone, Wells, etc.) to build around the young core. But without the intervention of Michaels and Cashman, Steinbrenner would have traded Mariano Rivera for SS Felix Fermin (thereby burying Jeter), and there might have been no dynasty. George Steinbrenner is no Hall of Famer.

Beyond the Numbers

- A powerful rebounder, Winfield helped lead the Gophers to their first Big 10 championship in 35 years and a berth in the NCAA tournament as a freshman and to an NIT berth as a senior.

- When Winfield established the David M. Winfield Foundation for Underprivileged Youth in 1977, it set the stage for more than 40 years of charitable works, which earned him the Branch Rickey and Roberto Clemente Awards in 1992 and 1994 and served as a model and inspiration for future stars, including Derek Jeter. As of 2020, Winfield serves as an executive in the Players Association under Tony Clark.and an eloquent spokesman for the MVP program, which supports personalized treatment plans for multiple myeloma.

Close Calls – Pitchers

Rick Reuschel (SP):
67.0 CVI – Chicago NL (*49.1*), Pittsburgh NL (*11.8*), San Francisco NL (*7.1*)

Bret Saberhagen (SP):
66.5 CVI – Kansas City AL (*40.7*), New York NL (*11.7*), Boston AL (*6.4*)

Dave Stieb (SP):
63.6 CVI – Toronto AL (*56.8*)

Don Sutton (SP):
58.7CVI – Los Angeles NL (*48.9*)

Orel Hershiser (SP):
56.8 CVI – Los Angeles NL (*39.6*),
Cleveland AL (*8.6*)

It is easy to see why Sutton is in the HOF and the others are not. Sutton was the only one to pitch long enough to check off the career milestones – 300 W, 3000 SO – that impress HOF voters. But really, there is more to like about Reuschel, Saberhagen, and Stieb than Sutton as HOF candidates. There is even a case to be made for Hershiser, whose shoulder woes turned him from an ace to a journeyman after his 30th birthday.

Three-time All-Star Rick "Big Daddy" Reuschel was a strapping 6'4" 225-pound Illinois farm boy who carved out a nice career as the unsung ace of a drab Cubs team that was neither good enough nor bad enough to be interesting or to do more than occupy space in the bottom half of the NL East in the post-Durocher decade.[54] Reuschel anchored the Cubs pitching staff from 1972-80, compiling a 3.43 ERA (116 ERA+) and 1.301 WHIP and averaging 14-13 with 140 SO and 65 BB and 5.2 WAR_p in 232 IP per season. However, other than his 20-win 9.5-WAR_p 1977 season, when he finished third in the Cy Young voting, his peak years with the Cubs passed almost unnoticed.

He seemed to be finished after the Cubs dropped him from their 1984 postseason roster and released him at age 35, but like one of those horror film villains who never stays dead, he resurrected his career with a 6.2-WAR_p 1985 season with the Pirates, going 14-8 with 2.52 ERA (159 ERA+) and 1.057 WHIP. After flopping in 1986 and getting dumped by the Pirates, he added two more excellent seasons with the Giants (36-19) in 1988-89. So he wound up as a credible (but totally overlooked) 214-W HOF candidate. His 67.0 CVI ranks 56th among SP and at the 0.98 percentile overall, but he had no awards nor signature moments to excite HOF voters. While Reuschel's HOF omission represents no great miscarriage of justice, most players with CVI in the top 1% and many with lesser CVI are in the HOF.

Bret Saberhagen's career consisted of stretches of disappointing performance, due mainly to a succession of career-threatening injuries, punctuated by periods of sheer brilliance (including two Cy Young Awards). He had enough of the latter to put his CVI at the 1.01 percentile, but enough of the former to leave an overriding sense of regret for what might have been. Saberhagen's most memorable year was 1985 at age 21. Showing the poise and control of a veteran, he went 20-6 with a 2.87 ERA (143 ERA+), 1.058 WHIP, and a 4.16 SO/BB ratio and anchored the young staff that brought the Royals their first-ever World Series championship over their cross-state rivals from St. Louis. He easily won the Cy Young Award and followed by winning the World Series MVP award for giving up only one run and 11 hits in 18 IP including a 6-1 CG victory in Game 3 to prevent the Royals from going down 0-3 and an 11-0 CG shutout in Game 7.

Saberhagen then established a peculiar pattern of excelling in odd years and failing in even years, which would hold through 1992, as his WAR_p inexplicably bounced from 7.1 to 2.0 to 8.0 to 3.8 to 9.7 (second Cy Young award) to 3.6 to 5.1 to 1.5. Through it all, pinpoint control was his trademark; his 3.64 SO/BB ranks 24th on the all-time career list. His 11.00 SO/BB in 1994 ranks second on the all-time single-season list behind only Phil Hughes's 11.62 in 2014. After the Royals traded him, he gave the Mets a good half-season in 1994 and gave the Red Sox two nice seasons in a late-career comeback in 1998-99. Saberhagen played in three ASG (in 1987, 1990, and 1994), but not in his two Cy Young seasons. He lasted just one year on the BBWAA HOF ballot, garnering only seven votes in 2007, and has received no support from the VC. He deserved better, since he was a great pitcher at his best, but there were more mediocre years than great ones. He finished with only 167 W. His 65.5 CVI places him 58th among SP and at the 1.01 percentile overall. Like Reuschel, he is a borderline HOF candidate.

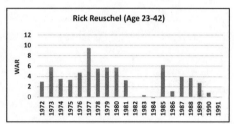

The first ace of the expansion Toronto Blue Jays, seven-time All-Star Dave Stieb was the poster boy for hard-luck pitchers who keep losing close games, while lesser pitchers for better teams rack up wins. The seven-time All-Star, who mixed a variety of fastballs and a devastating slider and relied more on inducing soft contact than missing bats, never won more than 18 games in a season, even after the Blue Jays became a competitive team, despite posting ERAs of 3.04 in 1983 (17 wins), 2.83 in 1984 (16 wins), 2.48 in 1985 (14 wins), 3.04 in 1988 (16 wins), and 2.93 in 1990 (18 wins). He led the AL in WAR_p in 1982-84.

Although the Cy Young award almost always went to 20-game winners in those days, Stieb finished in the top 10 in the AL Cy Young award voting in 1982 and 1984-85. He also lost three no-hitters in the ninth inning (two of them in consecutive starts in 1988) before finally completing one against the Indians on September 2, 1990 – still the only no-hitter in Blue Jay history. Despite his hard luck, Stieb's 140 wins ranked second for the 1980s behind Jack Morris's 162. Unfortunately, shoulder tendinitis and a herniated disk in 1991 effectively ended his career at age 31, although he kept trying to come back as late as 1998. Stieb's 63.6 CVI ranks 64th among SP and at the 1.11 percentile overall. Although he is a borderline HOF candidate, his shortened career, 176 W, absence of awards or 20-win seasons, and lack of a postseason resume make it unlikely that he will ever get to Cooperstown.

Don Sutton was a classic complier, who pitched in the major leagues for 23 years but played in only four ASG, never finished higher than third in the Cy Young award voting, and peaked at only 6.6 WAR$_p$ in 1972. He began his career as the fourth starter on the 1966 Dodgers of Koufax and Drysdale and was a rotation stalwart (but rarely an ace) through 1980. His best year was in 1972, when he went 19-9 with a 2.08 ERA (144 ERA+) and 0.913 WHIP. He remained a solid starter for the Astro, Brewers, Athletics and Angels though 1987 before finishing his career with the Dodgers in 1988. Although his 60.1 CVI ranks only at the 1.17 percentile, his 324 W, his top 10 standing on the career leaderboards in SO, SHO, and IP, and his postseason excellence put him in the HOF. Sutton went on to enjoy a long career in broadcasting.[55]

Orel Hershiser was among the best pitchers in the game in 1987-89, particularly in 1988, when he went 23-8 with a 2.26 ERA (149 ERA+), a 1.052 WHIP, 8 SHO, and 7.2 WAR$_p$, set a still unbroken record of 59 consecutive scoreless innings, and won the NL Cy Young award. He followed by going 3-0 with a 1.05 ERA, 0.891 WHIP, and 32 SO in 42.2 IP in the postseason and winning MVP honors in the Dodgers' NLCS and World Series victories. A shoulder injury derailed him in 1990, but he came back to put together nine solid years with the Dodgers, Indians, and Mets and finished with 204 W. Although his 56.8 CVI (1.32 percentile) falls well below my HOF standard, he was among the 10 finalists on the VC ballot in December 2018 and could get in eventually.

Close Calls – Hitters

Dwight Evans (RF):
61.9 – Boston AL (66.5)

Darrell Evans (3B):
58.6 CVI – Atlanta NL (*22.9*),
San Francisco NL (*21.5*), Detroit AL (*14.5*)

Keith Hernandez (1B):
61.2 CVI – St. Louis NL (*34.4*),
New York NL (*26.6*)

Reggie Smith (RF):
58.4 CVI – (*34.2*), Los Angeles NL (*19.4*),
St. Louis NL (*8.3*)

None of these four outstanding players, whose CVI rank in the 1.17-1.26 percentile is in the HOF, but a case can be made for each of them.

Three-time All-Star Dwight Evans was the least heralded of the young OF trio (which also included Fred Lynn and Hall of Famer Jim Rice) that sparked the Red Sox 1975 AL pennant, but he had the best career. A succession of injuries curtailed Lynn's MLB career, which had begun with a 7.4-WAR season that earned him Rookie of the Year, Gold Glove, and MVP honors. Rice had a fine career but was never more than a one-dimensional slugger. Evans, on the other hand, was a solid hitter (127 OPS+) and an outstanding RF (eight Gold Gloves) with a rifle arm, who played for 20 years and eventually overtook his more celebrated teammates in WAR and CVI.

He even out-homered Rice and Lynn 386-382-309. Although Evans lacked the signature achievements or milestones that might have prevented him from falling off the BBWAA ballot after three years, he has recently begun to attract support from the VC and received eight of the 12 votes required for election on the December 2019 VC ballot. His 61.9 CVI (1.17 percentile) would make him a credible Hall of Famer.

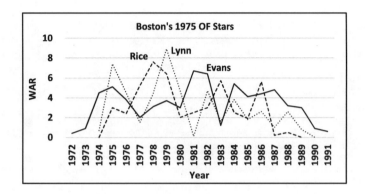

Keith Hernandez was a slick fielding solid hitting 1B, who enjoyed an excellent 17-year career for Whitey Herzog's Cardinals and Davey Johnson's Mets, two of the iconic NL teams of his era. He is a borderline HOF candidate whose best arguments for recognition are his 11 Gold Gloves at 1B, his 1979 NL batting title and co-MVP award, his five ASG, and his contributions to two World Series champions. However, he was elected to start only one ASG and topped out with 7.6 WAR in 1979. His 61.2 CVI ranks 18th at 1B and at the 1.17 percentile overall.

Bill James has called two-time All-Star Darrell Evans (no relation to Dwight) "the most underrated player in baseball history."[56] I wouldn't go that far, but he certainly deserves more consideration than he has gotten from the BBWAA (one and done) or from the VC so far. Evans was basically Graig Nettles with a few more HR (414) and BB (1605), but with more SO (1410) and, most significantly, without the elite defense. His 58.6 CVI places him 15th at 3B and at the 1.25 percentile overall. I see him more as an HOVG than an HOF type.

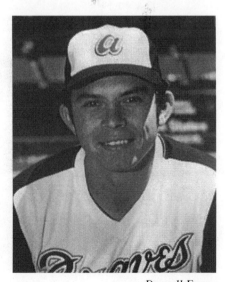

Darrell Evans

Seven-time All-Star Reggie Smith, who played on four pennant winners and a World Series champion in his 17-year career, was a consistently strong hitter (137 OPS+) and a solid OF (3.0 dWAR) but never exceeded 6.7 WAR in a season and achieved no career milestones that might have commended him to HOF voters. Although he was considered a star in his day with fourth place finishes in the 1977-78 NL MVP voting, he lasted only a year on the BBWAA ballot and has been ignored by the VC. With a 58.4 CVI (1.26 percentile), he falls a bit short of my standard for the HOF, but like Darrell Evans, he is not that far away.

Squandered Promise

Bobby Bonds (RF):
56.4 CVI – San Francisco NL (*38.1*),
California AL (*7.2*)

Dwight Gooden (SP):
55.8 CVI – New York NL (*46.4*)

We come now to two players with HOF talent whose promising careers were ruined by alcohol and substance abuse. Three-time All-Star Bobby Bonds was more than just Barry's father. He was the premier power-speed player of the 1970s, with 332 HR and 461 SB in his 14-year career. He and Barry are the only MLB players with 300 HR and 400 SB. After starring with the Giants from 1968-74, alcoholism ruined the second half of his career as he bounced from team to team. Even so, his 56.4 CVI ranks 24th in RF and at the 1.34 percentile overall.

Four-time All-Star and 1985 Cy Young award-winner Dwight Gooden reached even greater heights and fell even more precipitously. After a 17-W 5.5-WAR$_p$ Rookie of the Year campaign in 1984 at age 19, Gooden followed with 12.2 WAR$_p$ in 1985—the best since Walter Johnson in 1913. But starting in 1986, cocaine and alcohol steadily eroded his performance, even as he anchored the Mets World Series champion pitching staff. By 1995, he had fallen so low that he was suspended for the entire season. He made a comeback with the Yankees in 1996-98 in a secondary role (although he pitched a no-hitter in 1996) but relapsed in 1999 and was released in spring training of 2001. He had several relapses after leaving baseball, even spending a year in prison, but has reportedly been sober since 2012.[57] His 55.8 CVI places him at the 1.40 percentile, but oh, what might have been!

Hall of the Very Good

Frank Tanana (SP):
56.5 CVI – California AL (*34.3*), Detroit
(*13.1*), Texas AL (*7.7*)

Mark Langston (SP):
54.5 CVI – California/Anaheim AL (*26.0*),
Seattle AL (*19.2*)

Cesar Cedeno (CF):
54.2 CVI – Houston NL (*49.6*)

Will Clark (1B):
53.9 CVI San Francisco NL (*35.8*),
Texas AL (*15.1*)

Jerry Koosman (SP):
53.7 CVI – New York NL (*36.8*),
Minnesota AL (*11.0*)

The first four of these five players with CVI in the 1.33-1.51 percentile range share a common career pathway. Each started strong enough to be looked at as potential Hall of Famers but for varying reasons could not sustain that level of performance. Tanana began his career as the Angels' flame-throwing lefty complement to Nolan Ryan but injured his shoulder and reinvented himself as a soft-tossing finesse pitcher, carving out a solid 21-year career with the Rangers and Tigers and finishing with 240 W and 2773 SO. Langston, who is perhaps best remembered as the guy the hapless Expo's received for Randy Johnson, amassed 44.6 WAR_p between the ages of 23 and 32, (including four seasons with WAR_p between 5.6 and 8.5) but did nothing afterwards. Cedeno (who had 40.0 WAR by age 26) and Clark (who posted 15.3 WAR in his age 23-24 seasons) appeared to be on HOF trajectories early in their careers but fizzled before they turned 30.) Koosman who gained fame as Seaver's lefty sidekick on the Miracle Mets in his mid-20s, did not quite achieve the early success of the others, but held his value into his 30s, posting a 7.2-WAR_p season at age 36 for the Twins. None of these players lasted more than a year on the BBWAA ballot, and none is a serious HOF contender today, although Clark was among the 10 finalists on the December 2018 VC ballot.

Other Hall of Famers

Table 7.3: CVI-Minus Hall of Famers

A) Hitters (Position)	Midcareer	HOF	AVG/OBP/SLG	OPS+	WAR$_{11}$	CVI
Rice, Jim (LF)	1979	BBWAA	.298/.352/.502	128	47.7	50.5
Puckett, Kirby (CF)	1989	BBWAA	.318/.360/.477	124	51.1	49.9
Baines, Harold (DH)	1988	VC	.289/.356/.465	121	38.7	32.8

B) Pitchers	MidCareer	HOF	ERA/WHIP	ERA+	WAR$_p$	CVI
Sutter, Bruce (RP)	1979	BBWAA	2.83/1.140	136	24.5	53.0
Hunter, Catfish (SP)	1973	BBWAA	3.26/1.134	104	36.3	40.2
Morris, Jack (SP)	1985	VC	3.90/1.296	105	43.6	37.8

There are only six CVI-Minus Hall of Famers (three hitters and three pitchers) from the Free Agent Era. This small number reflects the fact that this era has only recently come under the scrutiny of the VC; there will undoubtedly be more to come, now that the last player from this era (Fred McGriff) has passed the 10-year limit for the BBWAA ballot process.

Four of the players listed in Table 7.3, **Sutter, Rice, Puckett,** and **Hunter** were elected by the BBWAA. Although only Sutter comes close to meeting the CVI standard for even the HOVG, all but **Hunter** placed at least in the top 2% by CVI.

Sutter, the original master of the split-finger fastball, barely missed the cut for CVI-Plus status, ranking 236th on the list of HOF-eligible players with a 53.021 CVI – only a hair behind #235 Boob Newsom's 53.04 CVI. **Sutter** pitched only 12 seasons and was effective in only eight of them. However, he was outstanding in his brief prime; his 136 ERA+ ranks tied for 21st on the career leaderboard. As the relief ace of the 1982 Cardinals World Series champions, **Sutter** posted 2 wins and 3 saves with a 3.00 ERA and 0.750 WHIP in 12 IP in his only postseason opportunity.

Rice and **Puckett** were highly regarded hitters with 18 All-Star appearances (8 for **Rice** and 10 for **Puckett**) and an MVP (**Rice** in 1978), but both (like **Sutter**) had relatively short peaks with only eight 5-WAR seasons between them. **Puckett** might have reached CVI-Plus status if his career had not ended abruptly at age 35 due to glaucoma.

Hunter, on the other hand, was a weak choice for the HOF. He had three really good seasons – 5.7 WAR$_p$ in 1972, 6.9 in 1974, and 8.1 in 1975 – but was pretty much finished by age 29. His 104 career ERA is barely above league average (ERA+ 104). However, he had a colorful nickname pitched for two colorful and successful teams, and had statistics that were enhanced by his having his peak during a pitcher-friendly era.

Jack Morris, whose 3.90 ERA (105 ERA+) is the highest in the HOF, is memorable for pitching one of the most thrilling games in MLB history, a 10-inning 1-0 shutout over the Braves in Game 7 of the 1991 World Series. Only 36 World Series have been decided by winner-take-all games and nine (25%) have been complete game shutouts. Koufax's three-hit, 10-SO, 2-0 shutout of the Twins in 1965 is probably the best of the lot, but **Morris**'s gem was not far behind and provided more drama. But somehow this narrative has expanded to paint him as a big-game pitcher and ace of four World Series champions. The record shows that **Morris** performed well only in the 1984 ALCS (1.29 ERA) and WS (2.00 ERA) and in the 1991 WS (1.17 ERA). He had a 6.75 ERA in the 1987 ALCS, a 4.05 ERA in the 1991 ALCS, a 6.57 ERA in the 1992 ALCS, an 8.44 ERA in the 1992 WS, and did not even make Toronto's postseason roster in 1993. His overall postseason line was nothing special – 7-4 with a 3.80 ERA and 1.245 WHIP.

Morris's 254 career wins (34 fewer than his 2018 VC ballot-mate Tommy John) is tied for 43rd on the career leaderboard, and his 162 wins led the 1980s. But winning 162 games in a 10-year period was not that rare even in that era, as Palmer, Gaylord Perry, Seaver, Carlton, and Niekro all exceeded that amount in the 1970s. Greg Maddux won 180 from 1991-2000, Roy Halladay won 170 from 2002-2011, and Mike Mussina won 163 from 1994-2003. **Morris** was certainly a fine pitcher and a fierce competitor who was an asset to every team he played for. But not a Hall of Famer.

Bottom of the Pile

If the HOF were meant to honor great *people*, Harold Baines, the humble, self-effacing, hard-working, wryly witty longtime MLB fixture, could stand at the head of the line. But the HOF is meant to honor great *players*, and there he simply falls short. Baines was a classic compiler with 2866 H, 384 HR and 1628 RBI in 22 MLB seasons who peaked at 4.3 WAR in 1984. His solid 121 OPS+ was offset by poor

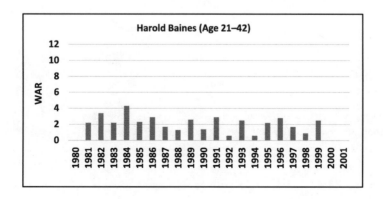

defense (-19.5 dWAR), which soon rendered him a full-time DH. He did play in six All-Star games, once (in 1989) as the starting DH, and earned the Edgar Martinez award as MLB's best DH in 1988 and 1989. His HOF candidacy was undoubtedly helped by the respect and popularity he enjoyed throughout his career and perhaps by the advocacy of his manager Tony LaRussa, White Sox owner Jerry Reinsdorf, ex-Orioles GM Pat Gillick, and ex-Oriole teammate Roberto Alomar on the VC voting panel.[58] However, while Baines was better than some of the Frisch era VC selections, fans in 2070 will look upon the election of Baines as quizzically as we look at those of Frisch's teammates Jim Bottomley (30.6 CVI) and Jesse Haines (29.1 CVI) today.

CHAPTER 8

THE STEROID GENERATION (1994-2011)

The Game

The big story of this 18-year period spanning the turn of the millennium was the prevalence of performance-enhancing drugs, specifically anabolic steroids, which inflated HR totals and scoring and had an outsized impact on the psyche of baseball fans.[1] HR rates peaked at 1.17 per team per game in 2000 (an all-time high at the time) then fell back in 2007-14 (Figure 8.1). Scoring also rose significantly, peaking at 5.14 runs/team/game in 2000, well below earlier peaks in 1894 (7.38) and 1930 (5.55) (Figure 8.2).

Of course, the impact of steroids on individual HR totals is considerably higher since these graphs are diluted by their inclusion of non-users as well as the theoretical offsetting impact of steroid-enhanced pitchers.

Before the catastrophic strike of 1994, there had been eighteen 50-HR seasons by eleven players — Ruth (4), Foxx (2), Kiner (2), Mantle (2), Mays (2), Cecil Fielder, George Foster, Hank Greenberg, Roger Maris, Johnny Mize, and Hack Wilson. Then, in only eight years (1995-2002), 19 more 50-HR seasons were added, including six totals — Sosa (66, 64, 63), McGwire (70, 65) and Bonds (73) — that exceeded Maris's record 61 in 1961. Only the cancellation of the final third of the 1994 season prevented the number of 50-HR seasons from being as high as 25, since six healthy players (Matt Williams, Griffey, Thomas, Bonds, Belle, and McGriff) had at least 34 HR (two-thirds of 50) when the strike began on August 11. The impact of steroids on WAR_H, which includes defense, on-base skills, speed, and other aspects of performance is less extreme.

Steroids, of course, were not new to baseball or to sports. In 1889, Hall of Famer Pud Galvin took part in an experiment involving the "Brown-Sequard elixir," which contained extracts from guinea pig and dog testicles.[2] His ensuing two-hit shutout was undoubtedly nothing more than coincidence, since steroids don't build muscle overnight, but require rigorous training and nutritional supplements, which were clearly foreign to the pudgy Galvin. Even Babe Ruth once received an injection of sheep testicle extract, which did nothing but make him sick.[3] Steroids have been a staple of bodybuilding and weight-lifting, but baseball players long avoided them for fear of becoming "musclebound."

Baseball culture began to change in 1986 when Jose Canseco took a page from the body-builders' handbook and used steroids to develop a massive physique. By 1988,

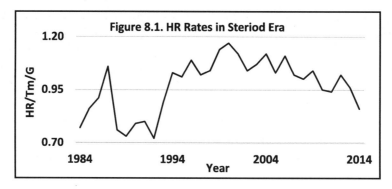

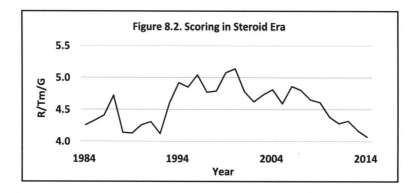

when he became baseball's first 40-HR-40-SB man, Canseco and his well-sculpted body were a sensation. Noted celebrity photographer Annie Leibovitz photographed him shirtless for *Vanity Fair*, and Washington Post columnist Tom Boswell called him "the most conspicuous example of a player who has made himself great with steroids" in a *Nightline* interview with Charlie Rose.[4,5] Although steroid use was still legal in 1986, Boswell's comments on the eve of the 1988 ALCS drew a flurry of denials. The fuss died down quickly as the headlines shifted to Kirk Gibson's game winning home run in Game 1 of the World Series and the Dodgers' subsequent upset of the powerful A's.

Well-muscled teammate and "Bash Brother" Mark McGwire had clearly been body building himself. But Canseco, even on steroids, was always a flawed player, and McGwire was beset with plantar fasciitis and other injuries in the early 1990s. Although Commissioner Fay Vincent issued a memo prohibiting the use of all illegal drugs, including steroids, on June 7, 1991 (shortly after the passage of the Anabolic Steroids Control Act of 1990), this memo was toothless since it lacked any drug testing protocol, specific penalties, or means of enforcement.[6-8] So the steroid issue remained dormant for several years and was not a significant bargaining point in the bitter 1994-95 labor negotiations.

The tipping point came in 1998 when McGwire (70 HR) and Sosa (66 HR) both annihilated Maris's single season home run record (61). Although the five 50-HR seasons in 1995-97 — 50 by Belle in 1995, 52 by McGwire and 50 by Brady Anderson in 1996, 58 by McGwire and 56 by Griffey in 1997 — did not set off alarm bells, the 1998 onslaught by McGwire and Sosa (plus 56 by Griffey and 50 by Greg Vaughn) was just too good to be true. Players who hit "only" 40-45 HR, usually enough to lead their leagues, now looked like slackers. When reporter Steve Wilstein spotted a bottle of androstenedione (an orally administered steroid precursor used commonly by body-builders as a "nutritional" supplement, which had just been reclassified as a controlled substance in 1997) in Mark McGwire's locker, the only outrage this seemed to elicit was against Wilstein, who had invaded McGwire's privacy and thrown cold water on a feel-good story which had helped baseball win back fan support that it had lost during the 1994 strike.[9] McGwire and Sosa were everything fans could want of their heroes — strong, modest, respectful of each other, diverse; they were the new twin faces of baseball. So, MLB leaders — and I include the MLBPA as well as the Commissioner's Office — kept their heads buried firmly in the sand concerning the lurking scandal.

This is where Barry Bonds got into the act.[10] Arrogant, disdainful of public opinion, and with a boulder-sized chip on his shoulder, Bonds would have none of this. He had played clean all his life and had earned the right to be considered the best player in baseball, with perhaps a nod to Ken Griffey Jr, his closest rival. He was incensed to find all the coverage going to two popular steroid-fueled impostors. If McGwire and Sosa could steal the accolades that should have been his, he would show everyone what greatness really looked like. So, he hired Greg Anderson as his trainer and began to juice in 1999. He overdid it at first, nearly ripping his triceps tendon away from his left elbow, which could have ended his career right there, as a first ballot Hall of Famer, no doubt, but without any home run records. He recovered in 2000 and went to Victor Conte at Balco and began using the "cream" and the "clear," two steroid cocktails that were difficult to detect. Reportedly, Conte provided "plausible deniability" by telling Bonds that these were not illegal steroids; this was the basis of Bonds's successful legal defense. But Bonds is too smart not to have known that the cream and the clear were steroids and violated the spirit if not the letter of the law.

So in 2001-2004, Bonds used steroids to turn himself into arguably the best hitter in the history of baseball. It is hard to imagine that even Ruth himself could have been better. Bonds swept by McGwire with 73 HR and seemed poised to march inexorably toward Aaron's sacred 755 career HR record. The baseball establishment, which never liked Bonds in the first place, did not continue to look the other way as it had with McGwire and Sosa, but began to look for ways to incorporate effective drug testing protocols to stop Bonds and his fellow "cheaters," even if it meant throwing erstwhile heroes McGwire and Sosa under the bus too.

Commissioner Selig persistently tried to get Donald Fehr and the MLBPA to accept random drug tests with harsh penalties for violators, but the union resisted on civil liberties grounds. While both sides paid lip service to getting steroids out of the game, neither made it a high enough priority to get a deal done. Finally, both parties agreed to an informational testing protocol in 2003 to assess the prevalence of steroid use in MLB, with a guarantee to keep the results for individual players anonymous. They agreed that non-anonymous random drug testing (with penalties) would take effect in 2004 if the 2003 protocol found that steroid prevalence exceeded 5%. The 2003 testing protocol found a prevalence between 5% and 7%.[11]

Random drug testing began in 2004, but the penalties were relatively light — suspensions of 10 days for the first violation, 30 days for the second, 60 days for the third, and one year for the fourth.[12] Congress intervened in 2005, and pressured MLB to increase the suspensions to 50 games, 100 games, and life for successive violations. (The penalties for the first two violations were further increased to 80 games and 162 games, respectively, in 2014.) Congress also forced a ban of amphetamines and other prescription-only stimulants, which had been widely used throughout baseball (likely by many Hall of Famers) as far back as the 1950s but had been ignored. MLB then commissioned former Senator George Mitchell to investigate, but he got little cooperation from players.[13]

In 2012, MLB added blood testing for Human Growth Hormone (HGH) to the protocol. Though not a steroid itself and of unproven efficacy as a performance enhancer, HGH is often used in conjunction with steroids, and is thought to mitigate some undesirable steroid side effects, like loss of flexibility. In nature, excessive HGH (as produced and secreted by certain pituitary tumors) is associated with gigantism in afflicted children who are still growing or acromegaly (a condition characterized by thickened but brittle bones) in adults. Neither condition is associated with increased strength or athletic ability; in fact, the opposite is true.

The remarkable aspect of the Steroid Era is not that some players cheated to get an edge. Cheating is as old as baseball, whether we are talking about the widespread use of stimulants (including controlled substances like amphetamines) in prior decades, stealing signs, Ty Cobb's intimidation tactics, or Gaylord Perry's greaseball. What is more remarkable and regrettable is the failure of leadership, which created a lawless environment that *incentivized* cheating. MLB owners and executives, the MLBPA, and even baseball journalists and fans were all complicit.

MLB and the MLBPA, bruised and bloodied from 25 years of labor war, did not want to jeopardize the fragile peace or the renewed fan interest (and revenue) stimulated by the surge in home runs and scoring. Journalists and fans loved the excitement of the McGwire-Sosa home run chase and did not want to hear anything negative – at least until the anti-hero Bonds came along. So we can villainize Donald Fehr for resisting random drug testing and Bud Selig for being unwilling to fight for it (as he did for a salary cap), but let's not forget to look in the mirror. Many fans loved the sugar high.

Now that the Steroid Era has receded, leaving only a manageable trickle of drug violators, how should we deal with the legacies of the great players of that era who used steroids during some portion of their careers? Some understandably take a moralistic "throw all the bums out" position. This begs the question of figuring out who the "bums" are. Is a guy who passed all his drug tests but has back acne a bum? What about someone who used steroids to help recover from an injury but never actually played on steroids? What about a one-time steroid user who was caught and punished and never used them again?

I have adopted a pragmatic approach that "adjusts" a player's career stats to estimate what they would have been without steroids. I will focus on distinguishing the genuine superstars who padded their resumes by using steroids from the impostors who would not have been great players without steroids and leave the thorny moral judgments to others.

The simplest example of an empirical adjustment would be to look only at the pre-steroid stats of Barry Bonds; his 138.2 CVI through 1998 would have him in the top 20 players in MLB history. However, I have taken a more nuanced approach, based on comparing Bonds peak steroid years (2001-04) with his pre-steroid performance level (Table 8.1).

Table 8.1: Barry Bonds Before and After Steroids

PED	Years	AVG/OBP/SLG	OPS+	HR/ YR	RBI/ YR	R/ YR	TB/ YR	BB/ YR	SB/ YR	dWAR	WAR
No	1987-98	.294/.416/.565	168	33	97	108	292	108	34	1.1	8.0
Yes	2001-04	.349/.559/.809	256	52	110	122	332	189	9	-0.8	10.8

Steroids obviously immensely boosted Bonds's already impressive power stats, especially HR and SLG, and secondarily his BB rate, since pitchers were afraid to give him something he could hit. But baseball is a game of skill and finesse, not just brute power. Steroids did not prevent the decline in his speed and defense as he aged. The net effect was a roughly 25% increase in WAR from 8.0 to 10.8.

My steroid adjustment undoes this 25% increase in WAR by discounting his steroid inflated WAR totals by 20%, as illustrated in Figure 8.2. In the right panel, I have applied the same 20% discount to Mark McGwire, who probably used steroids throughout his career and whose undiscounted CVI was only 61.0.

The steroid adjustment (dashed line) brings Bonds's 2001-04 WAR totals in line with his pre-steroid peak years and lowers his CVI from 232.3 (second only to Ruth) to 203.8 (still the fourth best of all time). The adjustment for McGwire reduces his CVI from 61.0 to 42.0, indicating that he would not have been a great player without steroids (Figure 8.3).

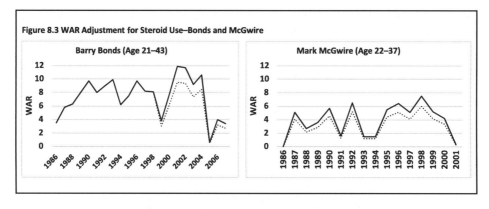

Figure 8.3 WAR Adjustment for Steroid Use–Bonds and McGwire

Barry Bonds, 1993

Since no one (other than Roger Clemens perhaps) trained harder than Bonds, I would argue (without proof) that Bonds represents pretty much the upper limit of how much WAR can be enhanced with steroids. So I have applied a 20% across-the-board discount for all position players for every season in which we have substantial evidence of steroid use. Because pitching is far more dependent on location and deception than sheer power, I have discounted pitching WAR totals by only 10% in each year of presumed steroid use. (The fact that scoring went up during the Steroid Era is empirical evidence that steroids helped hitters more than pitchers.) The player vignettes in this chapter present only "adjusted CVI."

However, Table A2.3 in Appendix 2 provides unadjusted CVI for steroid users and the years to which the steroid adjustment was applied.

Of course, 1994-2011 was about more than just steroids. Once the 1994-95 labor stoppage was settled, the Steroid Era brought labor peace and continued competitive parity. Starting in 1995, the leagues (which each had 14 teams) were each realigned into three divisions with the best of the non-division champions joining the three division champions in the postseason. This change, the introduction of interleague play in 1997, and the addition of two new teams in 1998 helped build baseball's popularity by keeping more teams in postseason contention. In the 17 years (1995-2011) following the "nuclear winter" of 1994, every team except the Pirates, Royals, Blue Jays, and Expos/Nationals made the postseason at least once, 17 different teams went to the World Series, and ten different teams won it. The Yankees still led the way with 17 postseason appearances, seven AL pennants, and five World Series championships in 1995-2012, and the Braves won an unprecedented 14 consecutive NL Divisional pennants (interrupted by the 1994 strike) from 1991-2005. But at least other teams also had a turn to shine.

The growing reliance on relief specialists and decline in complete games was another notable trend. With starters leaving games earlier, an ever-increasing proportion of wins were credited to relief pitchers, rendering the "Wins" statistic nearly meaningless. Also, 3TO and SO continued their inexorable rise. By 2011, 30% of all PA resulted in a 3TO and the MLB SO/H ratio had climbed to 0.816. Adam Dunn now led all hitters with 51.0 % 3TO and 1.459 SO/H, and Randy Johnson led all pitchers with 40.9% 3TO and 1.4570 SO/H (see Tables A1.4-5).

The replacement of the oversized cookie-cutter stadiums of the 1960s and 1970s with cozier "throwback" ballparks with "character," along the lines of Camden Yards in Baltimore (which opened in 1992) was also noteworthy. Also, MLB's demographic trends toward increasing international representation (mainly Latino) and decreasing African American representation, which began in the late 1980s, have continued into the 21st century. As of 2012, 26.9% of all MLB players were Latino and another 1.9% were Asian; meanwhile, only 7.2% of MLB players were African American.[14]

The Players

This chapter, which covers 57 CVI-Plus players from the Steroid Generation (35 hitters and 22 pitchers), differs in several ways from the previous chapters. It is the first chapter that includes active players (Pujols, Cabrera, and Felix Hernandez) and players who are (or will soon be) on the BBWAA ballot. Although it includes 23 Hall of Famers, it is also the first chapter that includes no one who has been elected by the VC and (not coincidentally) no CVI-Minus Hall of Famers. As in Chapters 3-7, the careers and HOF credentials of these 41 players, are presented below in thematic groupings.

Table 8.2: CVI-Plus Players

A) Players (Position)	MidCareer	HOF	AVG/OBP/SLG	OPS+	WAR$_{II}$	CVI
Bonds, Barry (LF)	1996	On Ballot	.298/.444/.607	182	162.8	203.8
Pujols, Albert (1B)	2007	Active	.299/.377/.546	146	100.6	132.7
Rodriguez, Alex (SS)	2003	Ret2016	.295/.380/.550	140	117.5	106.0
Griffey, Ken (CF)	1996	BBWAA	.284/.370/.538	136	83.8	101.8
Beltre, Adrian (3B)	2010	Ret2018	.286/.339/.480	116	93.6	98.8
Martinez, Edgar (DH)	1996	BBWAA	.312/.418/.515	147	68.4	89.7
Jones, Chipper (3B)	2002	BBWAA	.303/.401/.529	141	85.3	88.3
Bagwell, Jeff (1B)	1997	BBWAA	.297/.408/.540	149	79.9	87.8
Thomas, Frank (DH)	1996	BBWAA	.301/.419/.555	156	73.8	87.4
Rodriguez, Ivan (C)	1999	BBWAA	.296/.334/.464	106	68.7	85.3
Piazza, Mike (C)	1997	BBWAA	.308/.377/.545	142	59.6	83.2
Suzuki, Ichiro (RF)	2005	Ret2019	.311/.355/.402	107	59.7	81.9
Utley, Chase (2B)	2008	Ret2018	.275/.358/.465	117	64.4	76.3
Walker, Larry (RF)	1997	BBWAA	.313/.400/.565	141	72.7	75.7
Thome, Jim (1B)	2001	BBWAA	.276/.402/.554	147	72.9	73.8
Beltran, Carlos (CF)	2006	Ret2017	.279/.350/.486	119	70.1	72.6
Cabrera, Miguel (1B)	2011	Active	.313/.391/.540	147	69.3	72.2
Jeter, Derek (SS)	2002	BBWAA	.310/.377/.440	115	71.3	71.3
Rolen, Scott (3B)	2003	On Ballot	.281/.364/.490	122	70.1	70.8
Lofton, Kenny (CF)	1997	No	.299/.372/.423	107	68.4	70.6
Larkin, Barry (SS)	1994	BBWAA	.295/.371/.444	116	70.5	70.4
Jones, Andruw (CF)	2002	On Ballot	.254/.337/.486	111	62.7	69.8
Helton, Todd (1B)	2003	On Ballot	.316/.414/.539	133	61.2	69.7
Mauer, Joe (C)	2010	Ret2018	.306/.388/.439	125	55.3	69.7
Biggio, Craig (2B)	1996	BBWAA	.281/.363/.433	112	65.5	68.6
Alomar, Roberto (2B)	1995	BBWAA	.300/.371/.443	116	67.0	67.7
Ortiz, David (DH)	2008	Ret2016	.286/.380/.552	141	55.3	65.4
Edmonds, Jim (CF)	2001	No	.284/.376/.527	132	60.4	61.0
Abreu, Bobby (RF)	2003	On Ballot	.291/.395/.475	128	60.2	59.8
Guerrero, Vladimir (RF)	2002	BBWAA	.318/.379/.553	140	59.5	58.6
Sheffield, Gary (RF)	2000	On Ballot	.292/.393/.514	140	60.5	57.2
Olerud, John (1B)	1998	No	.295/.398/.465	129	58.1	56.8
Ramirez, Manny (LF)	2001	On Ballot	.312/.411/.585	154	69.3	54.3
Pedroia, Dustin (2B)	2011	Ret2019	.299/.365/.439	113	51.6	53.9
Garciaparra, Nomar (SS)	2000	No	.313/.361/.521	124	44.3	53.8

(continued)

Table 8.2 (cont'd)

B) Pitchers	MidCareer	HOF	ERA/WHIP	ERA+	WAR$_p$	CVI
Clemens, Roger (SP)	1994	On Ballot	3.12/1.173	143	138.7	172.3
Johnson, Randy (SP)	1999	BBWAA	3.29/1.171	135	103.5	144.1
Maddux, Greg (SP)	1996	BBWAA	3.16/1.143	132	104.8	128.2
Martinez, Pedro (SP)	2000	BBWAA	2.93/1.054	154	86.1	118.2
Rivera, Mariano (RP)	2004	BBWAA	2.21/1.000	205	56.3	101.9
Schilling, Curt (SP)	2001	On Ballot	3.46/1.137	127	80.5	97.4
Mussina, Mike (SP)	1999	BBWAA	3.68/1.192	123	82.8	91.1
Halladay, Roy (SP)	2007	BBWAA	3.38/1.178	131	65.4	88.4
Glavine, Tom (SP)	1997	BBWAA	3.54/1.314	118	73.9	78.7
Smoltz, John (SP)	1997	BBWAA	3.33/1.176	125	66.4	71.9
Cone, David (SP)	1994	No	3.46/1.256	121	61.6	70.0
Brown, Kevin (SP)	1997	No	3.28/1.222	127	68.2	67.0
Appier, Kevin (SP)	1994	No	3.74/1.294	121	54.9	63.7
Sabathia, CC (SP)	2008	Ret2019	3.74/1.259	116	62.0	63.4
Santana, Johan (SP)	2006	No	3.20/1.132	136	51.1	62.6
Pettitte, Andy (SP)	2002	On Ballot	3.85/1.351	117	60.7	60.1
Hudson, Tim (SP)	2004	On Ballot	3.49/1.239	120	56.5	57.0
Hernandez, Felix (SP)	2011	Active	3.42/1.206	117	50.3	56.9
Hoffman, Trevor (RP)	1998	BBWAA	2.87/1.058	141	28.1	56.2
Buehrle, Mark (SP)	2007	On Ballot	3.81/1.281	117	60.0	56.0
Rogers, Kenny (SP)	1999	No	4.27/1.403	107	50.5	55.2
Oswalt, Roy (SP)	2006	No	3.36/1.211	127	49.9	55.1

What Greatness Looked Like (Without Steroids)

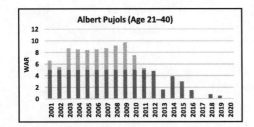

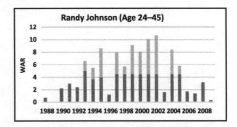

Neither of the two top "clean" players of the steroid era have the consistent procession of MVP- or Cy Young-caliber seasons across their career that we expect to see in this section. Pujols began with 11 consecutive seasons with at least 5.0 WAR, but faded badly in his 30s. Johnson started slowly but built momentum in his late 20s and 30s with 11 out of 13 seasons with at least 5.0 WAR$_P$ topped by four consecutive Cy Young Awards in 1999-2002 at ages 35-38. Nevertheless, Johnson's 144.1 CVI ranks 18th among all HOF-eligible players, while Pujols's 132.7 CVI tops all active players.

The Unholy Trinity

Barry Bonds (LF):
203.8 CVI – San Francisco NL (*112.5*),
Pittsburgh NL (*50.3*)

Roger Clemens (SP):
172.3 CVI - Boston AL (*80.8*),
New York AL (*21.1*), Toronto AL (*20.3*),
Houston NL (*17.1*)

Alex Rodriguez (SS):
106.0 CVI – New York AL (54.0),
Seattle AL (38.1), Texas AL (25.5)

A particularly sad aspect of the Steroid Era is that three men who were on the short list of MLB's greatest players saw fit to cheat the game by using steroids, thereby trashing their legacies and (in the case of Bonds) taking down MLB's most iconic home run records. Their story parallels the Greek myth of Icarus, a youth who fashioned wings out of wax and feathers and flew like a bird. The gods brought Icarus to his tragic end when he had the hubris to try to fly to the sun; he fell into the sea and drowned when the sun's heat melted his wings. The BBWAA voters also hate hubris. Not that any of us wouldn't have been tempted to use them while watching lesser players surpass us by cheating.

The damage that they did to baseball statistics in general and to the HOF has been exaggerated, since one can to some extent statistically remove the impact of steroids from their yearly WAR totals. At least that is true for Bonds, whose steroid use we can pinpoint precisely to have begun after the 1998 season. Clemens's case is more ambiguous, since his steroid use can only be traced back definitively to 1998, one year *after* his major performance uptick in 1997.

Rodriguez's case is nearly impossible to chronicle since he has admitted to using steroids in 2001-03 and in 2010-12, and we cannot pinpoint any discrete upturn in performance related to those periods; he likely used steroids throughout his career. In any case, the damage they did was bad enough. Their achievements would have clearly put them not only in the HOF, but in its inner circle. However, whether they should be honored in the actual HOF is not a statistical question. Bonds's and Clemens's HOF support has stalled at 62% support in 2021 after nine years on the BBWAA ballot, and Rodriguez is unlikely to fare better when he joins the BBWAA ballot in 2022. The VC may be even less receptive than the BBWAA to their candidacy.

As we have seen above (Table 8.1), Barry Bonds basically had two distinct careers. Natural Barry Bonds (1986-98), a supremely gifted player with a superior work ethic, could have retired after the 1998 season with a 138.2 CVI (just behind Mike Schmidt) and with a 168 OPS+, which would have tied him with Ty Cobb for 10th on the all-time list. He would have been a slam-dunk first-ballot Hall of Famer. Instead, he became Steroid Barry Bonds, who terrorized MLB pitchers and soared to greater heights than even Babe Ruth. The transformation was not instantaneous. Steroid Barry Bonds severely tore a triceps tendon and missed much of the 1999 season, but after a solid comeback in 2000, he really took off in 2001, giving us the three best seasonal OPS+ (and the 11th best) of all time. Can you imagine being more than 2.5 times as productive as the major league average hitter over a four-year period? In 2001-04, Bonds played in four ASG, won four consecutive MVP awards, and after years of postseason failure, finally lived up to his billing in the 2002 World Series, where he hit an astounding .471/.700/1.294, including 4 HR, in a seven-game loss to the Angels. Curiously, his record-setting 73 HR in 2001 was his only 50-HR season. Unfortunately, the apt comparison for Steroid Barry Bonds is not Ruth, but Joe Hardy ("Damn Yankees") or Roy Hobbs ("The Natural'), whose feats belong to the realm of fiction.[15,16]

Still, Bonds's place on the short list of baseball's all-time greats is indisputable. In addition to topping the MLB leaderboard in HR, he also ranks first in BB and WAR_H, third in R and OPS+, fourth in TB, and sixth in RBI. Even after adjustment for steroids, his 203.8 CVI ranks behind only Ruth, Mays, and Walter Johnson as the best of all time.

There is also much to admire about Roger Clemens, the hypercompetitive adopted Texan with the work ethic of a Marine and a violent allergy to failure, who willed himself to become one of the best and most durable pitchers in the history of MLB. He pitched for 24 years with no serious injuries, played in 11 ASG, won an incredible seven Cy Young awards plus an MVP in 1986, and amassed more WAR_P than any pitcher in the past 100 years. He led his league in ERA and WAR_P seven times, won 20 or more games and led his league in shutouts six times each, led his league in strikeouts five times, twice struck out 20 batters in a game, and threw two one-hitters (but never a no-hitter). He ranks 11th with 1.116 SO/H and is one of 27 qualifying pitchers with more SO than hits allowed. He also put in a season's worth of work (199 IP) in 11 postseasons and was at his best in six World Series (including champions in 1999-2000), compiling a 3-0 record with a 2.37 ERA and 0.993 WHIP and 49 strikeouts in 49.1 IP.

Clemens established himself as an elite pitcher in 1986 by going 24-4 with a 2.48 ERA (169 ERA+), a 0.969 WHIP, and 238 SO in 254 IP, an 8.9-WAR_P performance that earned him both the Cy Young and MVP awards. The previously mediocre Red Sox came within a booted Mookie Wilson grounder of winning the World Series over the New York Mets. After seven years averaging

19-9 with a 2.66 ERA (160 ERA+) and 1.089 WHIP, 239 SO, and 8.3 WAR_p with the Red Sox in 1986-92, Clemens then suffered a four-year mid-career slump, which led to whispers that he was washed up at age 33.

Clemens proved the doubters wrong with perhaps the best season of his career, going 21-7 with a 2.05 ERA (222 ERA+), a 1.030 WHIP, a career-high 292 SO, and 11.9 WAR_p, earning him his fourth Cy Young award. There is no hard evidence that he used steroids until the following season (which brought him yet another Cy Young award) when Toronto's strength and conditioning coach Brian McNamee testified that he first injected Clemens with Winstrol.[24] Clemens had amassed 92.8 of his 138.7 career WAR_p *before* McNamee was hired. Clemens never tested positive for steroids and was acquitted on charges of lying to Congress. Clemens's 172.3 CVI, which discounts his post-1996 WAR_p by 10%, places him third among SP and 13th overall. Clemens's WAR trajectory with (dashed line) and without (solid line) the steroid adjustment shows no clear inflection point associated with steroid use. Clearly he would have been an elite Hall of Famer even without steroids.

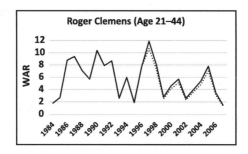

The youngest of the "unholy trinity," Alex Rodriguez (known popularly as "A-Rod") is perhaps even more reviled than Bonds or Clemens. A-Rod's story is all the sadder because he had once been regarded (much like Fernando Tatis Jr. today) as the face of baseball's future. Only three hitters in the history of baseball (Trout, Cobb, and Mantle) accrued more than A-Rod's 63.6 WAR through his age 27 season. A-Rod's popularity nosedived when he and agent Scott Boras negotiated an unprecedented 10-year $252 million contract with the Texas Rangers after the 2000 season, renegotiated an even more lucrative contract three years later after a trade to the Yankees, and then opted out of that contract four years later to extract even more money from the Yankees.[17]

Although A-Rod continued to put up great numbers, fans booed him as a mercenary and for his failure to lead his teams to postseason success. By 2009, when he and his Yankee teammates finally won a World Series, his steroid use during his Texas years had been exposed. The Biogenesis scandal of 2013, in which A-Rod was the headliner among several players obtaining illegal performance-enhancing drugs from a bogus anti-aging clinic operating out of Coral Gables, FL, cemented A-Rod's reputation as a villain.

His adjusted (dashed line) and unadjusted (solid line) WAR trajectory are plotted below. As for Bonds and Clemens, whatever you think of A-Rod the man, he was indisputably one of the elite talents and outstanding players in MLB history. A-Rod was a consistent superstar from 1996-2010, hitting .305/.390/.576 (148 OPS+) and averaging 41 HR, 121 RBI, 116 R, 332 TB, 20 SB, and 7.3 WAR per season for the Mariners, Rangers, and Yankees. He hit >50 HR three times and never hit <30 HR. He also exceeded 100 RBI in every season except 1997. He was a three-time MVP and played in 14 ASG. He is the only player to end his career with at least 3000 H, 2000 RBI, 2000 R, and 300 SB. And of course there are those 696 HR — more than anyone except Bonds, Aaron, and Ruth. A-Rod's 106.0 adjusted CVI places him third among SS and at the 0.28 percentile overall. His unadjusted 156.0 CVI would have ranked 17th on the all-time list.

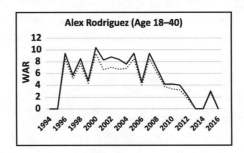

Beyond the Numbers

- Although Bonds led Arizona State to two College World Series finals (losing both) in 1983-84, he routinely skipped practices and ignored rules. His teammates once voted to kick him off the team, but Coach Jim Brock overruled them because the vote was not unanimous.[18]

- Bonds helped lead the Pirates to three consecutive NL East Championships (but no NL pennants) in 1990-92. Although he was played in six of his 14 NL ASG as a Pirate and won the 1990 and 1992 MVP awards, Pirate fans never fully embraced him. He hit only .191/.337/.265 in three losing NLCS as a Pirate. He also seemed to go out of his way to antagonize reporters, whom he reportedly distrusted because he felt that the press mistreated his father when alcoholism ended his career.

- When he signed a mega-contract with his father's and godfather's original team, the Giants, in 1993, he was finally embraced by the fans and local press. He played in six more ASG in 1993-1998 and won another MVP in 1993, but Bonds continued to disappoint in the postseason and there were no championships.

Beyond the Numbers (cont'd)

- After a series of knee surgeries ruined his 2005 season, Bonds hung on long enough to pass Babe Ruth (in 2006) and Henry Aaron (in 2007) on the all-time home run list. But when his contract expired in 2007, the Giants quietly let him go. No one else picked him up, despite the fact that he was still productive.

- Clemens was raised by his oldest brother Randy after his stepfather died. A star athlete himself, Randy taught Roger that "Either you're a winner or a failure" — seven words that foreshadowed Roger's eventual downfall.[19]

- Clemens, who would later be known as "Rocket," did not throw hard in high school; his coach had to pull strings to get him a baseball scholarship to San Jacinto Junior College in 1981. That was the jumping off point for a scholarship at the University of Texas and two trips to the College World Series that made him the 12th pick of the 1983 amateur draft and brought him to the Red Sox in 1984.

- Clemens pitched until he was 44 years old, logging six years with the Yankees (including pennants in 1999-2001 and 2003 and World Series championships in 1999-2000) and three with the Astros (including a pennant in 2005). He won his last two Cy Young awards at age 37 (2001) for the Yankees and at age 40 (2004) for the Astros.

- A-Rod was a good defensive SS, accruing 9.3 dWAR before moving to 3B in 2004 to accommodate Derek Jeter. He accrued an additional 4.0 dWAR as a 3B from 2004-11 before slowing down at ages 36-40.

- When Texas signed A-Rod as a free agent in 2001 they bit off more than they could chew. Although he performed up to expectations, the Rangers could not afford to put good players around him and won only 73, 72, and 71 games in 2001-03. They improved to 89 wins in 2004, after trading him to the Yankees.

- A-Rod also did not bring instant success to the Yankees. He generally underperformed in their four consecutive unsuccessful postseason runs in 2004-07. However, in 2009, A-Rod hit .455/.500/1.000 in the Yankees ALDS victory over the Twins, .429/.567/.952 in their ALCS victory over the Angels and hit a pivotal HR in their World Series victory over the Phillies.

- A-Rod's last six seasons were an ordeal, as his notoriety grew and his skills waned. Unlike Bonds and Clemens, who retired from the public arena before scandal engulfed them, Rodriguez played on and was greeted with derisive chants of "A-Roid" everywhere he performed. He bottomed out in 2013 when he missed most of the season due to hip surgery while the Biogenesis scandal erupted around him and the Yankees sought to void his contract. He accepted a suspension for the entire 2014 season. To the surprise of most, he returned in 2015 to have a pretty good (3-WAR) season as a DH, but he had nothing left in 2016, the final year of his contract.

- A-Rod joined ESPN's Sunday night baseball telecasts in 2018.

La Nueva Ola

Albert Pujols (1B):
132.7 CVI - St. Louis NL (*86.6*),
Los Angeles AL (*14.0*)

Adrian Beltre (3B):
98.8 CVI - Texas AL (*41.2*), Los Angeles NL
(*23.4*), Seattle AL (*21.2*), Boston (*7.8*)

Edgar Martinez (DH):
89.7 CVI - Seattle AL (*68.4*)

Carlos Beltran (CF):
72.6 CVI - New York NL (*31.1*), Kansas City
AL (*24.8*), St. Louis NL (*6.2*)

Miguel Cabrera (1B):
72.2 CVI - Detroit AL (*51.4*), Florida NL (*18.3*)

Going into the 1990s, Clemente, Carew, and Marichal were the only CVI-Plus Latino players in the HOF. That number has already grown to nine and will likely reach 15 within the decade, as Latinos have surpassed African Americans as MLB's preeminent minority. The new wave of Latino stars included Pujols, Beltre, and Rodriguez (Dominican Republic), Martinez and Beltre (Puerto Rico), and Cabrera (Venezuela). Rodriguez and Martinez were actually born in New York; Rodriguez grew up in Miami and Martinez in Puerto Rico. Pujols came to the US at age 16 and finished high school in Independence, MO.[20]

The five players here and A-Rod (see above) won eight MVP awards and appeared in 55 ASG between 2001 and 2015. Only Martinez is in the HOF; Pujols and Cabrera are still active, and the others have not been retired for five years. Several other CVI-Plus Latino players are covered elsewhere in this chapter – Pedro Martinez, David Ortiz, and Vladimir Guerrero (Dominican Republic), Ivan Rodriguez and Roberto Alomar (Puerto Rico), Bobby Abreu and Johan Santana (Venezuela), and Mariano Rivera (Panama).

Albert Pujols has the highest CVI of any active player, ranking second at 1B behind Lou Gehrig and between Rickey Henderson (#21) and Mel Ott (#22) on the all-time list. He is the highest-ranking foreign-born player and was MLB's most consistent superstar during his 11 years with the Cardinals. When he became a free agent in at age 31 in December 2011, more good times seemed to lie ahead. But when the Cardinals wisely (as it turned out) chose not to match the Angels' $254 million 10-year offer to sign Pujols as a free agent, his decline was almost immediate. After 11 years as a Cardinal when his WAR never fell below 5.3, he has never exceeded 4.8 WAR as an Angel. The slight dip to 5.3 WAR in 2011 turned out to be a harbinger of future decline to 4.8, 1.5, 4.0, 3.0, 1.3, -1.8, 0.5, 0.4, and -0.2 WAR in 2012-20.

Moreover, his defense at 1B, for which he received Gold Gloves in 2006 and 2010, declined precipitously to where he is best used as a DH. While he once appeared a threat to catch Cardinal icon Stan Musial at #10 on the all-time CVI list, he is now unlikely to crack the top 20. Pujols still packs power and has climbed to fifth on the career HR list (662) and 15th on the all-time hit list (3236). He also ranks third in RBI (2100), fifth in TB, (5923) and 2B (669 for his career, but his slash line and OPS+ are falling yearly. Still, he was a great player in his prime and will be a deserving first-ballot Hall of Famer.

Adrian Beltre, 2011

Adrian Beltre, who never won an MVP award and played in only four ASG, was the stealth superstar. Unlike his country-man Pujols, Beltre built his HOF resume largely in his 30s, starting in 2010 with Boston and continuing in 2011-16 with the Rangers. When he was installed as the Dodgers' everyday 3B in 1998 at age 19, he was hyped as the jewel of the franchise, but he could not live up to their lofty expectations. So, he was viewed as a disappointment during his first six years, never attaining a WAR as high as 4.0 and only once posting an OPS+ above 102. Then, at age 25, he broke out with a remarkable 9.6-WAR season hitting .334/.388/.629 (163 OPS+) with 48 HR, 121 RBI, 104 R, and 376 TB, far surpassing anything he had done before, and finished second in the NL MVP voting (between Bonds and Pujols). Although he was better from 2005-09 with Seattle than he had been from 1998-2003 with the Dodgers, he never came close to replicating his 2004 success.

Through his age 30 season in 2009 (including 2004), Beltre hit only .270/.325/.453 (105 OPS+) and averaged 21 HR, 76 RBI, 69 R, 238 TB, and 3.7 WAR – solid, but certainly not HOF material. He had never played in an ASG or (except in 2004) received any votes for MVP. But from 2010-16, mostly with Texas, Beltre hit .310/.359/.521 (133 OPS+) and averaged 28 HR, 95 RBI, 86 R, 299 TB, and 6.5 WAR per season. He played in four ASG, added three more Gold Gloves at 3B, and finished in the top 15 in the AL MVP voting every year. One constant throughout his career was his superlative play at 3B, where his 27.2 dWAR ranks second only to Brooks Robinson. He won five Gold Gloves, the last coming at age 37. He retired in 2018 with a 98.8 CVI, ranked fifth among 3B and at the 0.36 percentile overall, making him a certain Hall of Famer.

The eldest of this group, the underrated seven-time All-Star Edgar Martinez, defined the role of designated hitter; like Cy Young, the annual award to the best player at his position now has his name on it. He did not set out to be a DH. He was a fine 3B when he first reached the major leagues but was blocked by power-hitting Jim Presley, an inferior hitter who was at best Edgar's equal at 3B. Then when Martinez finally won the 3B job at age 27, a severe knee injury in 1993 ruined his season and forced him off 3B permanently. He took over at DH in 1995 and had a career year, leading the AL with a .356 AVG, .479 OBP, and 185 OPS+, finishing third in the MVP voting, and winning what later became the Edgar Martinez Award, an award he received five times in his career. He then hit .571/.667/1.000 with 2 HR and 10 RBI to spark the Mariners 3-2 victory over the Yankees in the 1995 ALDS, providing the walk-off two-run double that turned a 4-5 deficit into a 6-5 series-clinching victory. If there were an ALDS MVP award, Martinez would certainly have won it.

From 1995-2001, Martinez was baseball's premier DH and one of the best hitters in the game, hitting .329/.446/.574 (164 OPS+) and averaging 28 HR, 110 RBI, 100 R, 298 TB, and 5.8 WAR per season. Randy Johnson called him the best hitter he has ever seen. The Mariners had shinier stars – A-Rod, Griffey, Johnson, Ichiro – during Martinez's 18-year tenure, but Edgar was their "secret sauce" – the one constant and indispensable ingredient in their success. The Mariners have made the postseason only four times in their 43-year history – 1995, 1997, 2000, and 2001. Edgar Martinez was a key player on all four of those teams. WAR, which systematically downplays the DH position by setting the replacement level very high and assigning a negative dWAR, underestimates his impact. Martinez's 89.7 CVI ranks leads all DH and ranks at the 0.41 percentile overall. Martinez finally won HOF election in his tenth and final year on the BBWAA ballot. It shouldn't have taken that long.

Carlos Beltran's stats don't bowl you over until you take a closer look at how strong he was in every aspect of the game in his 20-year career. Early on, he was known for his outstanding speed and OF defense. After hitting .293/.337/.454 (99 OPS+) with 22 HR, 108 RBI, 112 R, 27 SB, and 4.7 WAR to earn AL Rookie of the Year honors in 1999, he hit a bump in the road in 2000, when his poor plate discipline put him back in the minors. But he bounced back to hit .288/.365/.521 (125 OPS+) and average 29 HR, 102 RBI, and 111 R, 37 SB, and 5.9 WAR in 2001-04. When the financially strapped Royals sent him to Houston for the 2004 pennant run, Beltran almost single-handedly carried them to the World Series, hitting .435/.518/1.022 with 8 HR, 14 RBI, 21 R, and 6 SB in the 3-2 NLDS win over Atlanta and 3-4 NLCS defeat to St. Louis. He single-handedly sunk the Braves in the NLDS clincher, going 4-for-5 with 2 HR and 5 RBI. Although he hit 3 HR against the Cardinals in the 2006 NLCS, his most memorable moment in that series, unfortunately, was taking a called third strike from Adam Wainwright with the bases loaded and two outs in the bottom of the ninth inning to seal a 3-1 Game 7 defeat.

Beltran's peak years came with the Mets in 2006-2008, when he hit .278/.372/.537 (135 OPS+) and averaged 34 HR, 113 RBI, 112 R and 6.9 WAR. In his twenties, Beltran was an elite CF, accruing 10.1 dWAR in 1998-2008, but he backslid to 1.6 dWAR for his career after his knees began troubling him. In his final years, Beltran was a highly sought after complementary piece for contending Giants, Cardinals, Yankees, and Astros teams. Beltran's 72.6 CVI ranks ninth in CF and at the 0.76 percentile overall, which should make him a strong HOF candidate in 2023. However, his involvement in the Astros 2017 sign-stealing scandal, which cost him an opportunity to manage the Mets in 2020, may cost him some support.

In 2013, when 11-time All-Star Miguel Cabrera had just won his second consecutive AL MVP award at age 30 to bring his career WAR up to 54.6, there was little doubt that we were looking at one of the all-time elite 1B and a future first-ballot Hall of Famer. As a 20 year-old rookie in 2003, Cabrera was the catalyst that brought the Wild Card Marlins their second World Series Championship, hitting .268/.325/.468 (106 OPS+) with 12 HR and 62 RBI in a half-season, followed by .265/.311/.471 with 4 HR, 12 RBI and 11 R in 17 postseason games. For the next four years (2004-07), Cabrera was a fixture in middle of the Marlins batting order, pacing the team in HR and RBI. He hit .318/.396/.551 (147 OPS+) and averaged 32 HR, 115 RBI, 102 R, 40 2B, 328 TB, and 4.4 WAR.

After the rebuilding Marlins traded him to Detroit, Cabrera hit .325/.404/.573 (161 OPS+) and averaged 34 HR, 114 RBI, 97 R, 38 2B, 328 TB, and 6.8 WAR, while leading the Tigers to four consecutive postseasons in 2011-14 including a trip to the World Series in 2012. But age and injuries have slowed him down since then to only 9.5 WAR in six years, with -0.5 WAR in 2017-20. Miggy has been a marvelous hitter, combining power, a high AVG, and elite run production. However, he has also been a poor defender (-17.7 dWAR) with below average speed, which made him a less valuable player than say, Trout or Pujols, even at his peak. Now, as an increasingly injury-prone and immobile 37 year-old DH, Miggy is a poor bet for a late-career resurgence. Still his 72.2 CVI ranks 11th at 1B and at the 0.77 percentile overall. His eventual place in the HOF seems secure.

Beyond the Numbers

- Pujols burst onto the major league scene in 2001, posting a 6.6-WAR All-Star season, hitting .329/.403/.610 (157 OPS+) with 37 HR, 130 RBI, 112 R, and 360 TB, and winning Rookie of the Year honors by a unanimous vote.

- From 2001-2011, Pujols hit .328/.420/.617 (170 OPS+) and averaged 40 HR, 121 RBI, 117 R, 354 SB, 89 BB, only 64 SO, and 7.9 WAR. He played in nine ASG and picked up MVP awards in 2005 and 2008-09.

Beyond the Numbers (cont'd)

- Pujols led the Cardinals to seven postseasons in 12 years, with NL pennants in 2004, 2006, and 2011 and World Series championships in 2006 and 2011. He was every bit as good in the postseason as during the season, in a half-season's worth of games (77) spread across 14 series and eight years. He was named MVP of the Cardinals 4-3 win over Houston in the 2004 NLCS, when he hit .500/.563/1.000 with 4 HR, 9 RBI, 10 R, and 28 TB.

- The Dodgers signed Beltre at 15, which is under the minimum signing age.[21] Someone in the Dodgers organization apparently altered his birth certificate to cover his tracks. Beltre's agent Scott Boras filed for free agency when the deception was uncovered in 1999, but MLB let the Dodgers off with a fine and a warning.

- Edgar Martinez's hitting achievements are all the more remarkable because he struggled with strabismus (cross-eyes) which began to noticeably impair his depth perception in 1999.[22] He undertook a rigorous program of daily eye exercises and martial arts training to stay sharp.

- Beltran's 435 career HR place him fourth among all switch hitters, behind Mantle, Murray, and Chipper Jones.

Aces of the Steroid Era

Randy Johnson (SP):
144.1 CVI - Arizona NL (*50.8*), Seattle AL (*39.0*), New York AL (*7.4*)

Greg Maddux (SP):
128.2 CVI - Atlanta NL (*67.3*), Chicago NL (*34.7*)

Pedro Martinez (SP):
108.2 CVI - Boston AL (*53.5*), Montreal NL (*19.0*), New York NL (*7.6*)

Curt Schilling (SP):
97.4 CVI - Philadelphia NL (*36.3*), Arizona NL (*25.3*), Boston AL (*17.8*)

Mike Mussina (SP):
91.1 CVI - Baltimore AL (*47.8*), New York AL (*35.0*)

Roy Halladay (SP):
88.4 CVI - Toronto AL (*48.0*), Philadelphia NL (*16.2*)

Although the Steroid Era mainly conjures up images of muscular sluggers popping mammoth home runs in record numbers, it was also graced by seven of the best 25 pitchers ever to take the mound. CVI ranks Clemens (covered earlier in this chapter), Johnson, Maddux, Martinez, Schilling, Halladay, Mussina as the third, sixth, eighth,

11th, 20th, 23rd, and 25th best SP of all time. From 1991-2002, Clemens, Johnson, Maddux, and Martinez held a virtual stranglehold on the Cy Young award, winning 16 of the 24 awards bestowed in those 12 years. Only in 1996 was this quartet shut out of the Cy Young awards; in 1995, 1997, and 1999-2001 they won in both leagues. Clemens and Halladay also won five Cy Young awards in other years. Schilling and Mussina never won the Cy Young award, but Schilling was a three-time runner up.

Standing 6'10 and weighing 225 pounds, most of it arms and legs, the "Big Unit" Randy Johnson was one of the most intimidating pitchers ever to take the mound. His intense demeanor, gangly frame, and early problems commanding his 98 mph fastball gave the impression of a guy who might just crack your skull with an errant heater. Just watch the video of .300-hitter John Kruk bailing out on three successive Johnson fastballs after watching a wild pitch sail over his head in the 1993 ASG, then taking a comedic bow after striking out.[23]

Of course, much of Kruk's performance was theater, as Johnson was no longer the wild man of 1990-92, who averaged 139 BB and 12 HBP per season. He reduced his BB to 99 in 1993 and would never again walk as many as 90 batters in a season. But still with that memory lingering in the back of the mind, facing Johnson would never become a comfortable at-bat, especially for lefty hitters. And Johnson exploited that discomfort to dominate opposing hitters for more than a decade with his blazing fastball and a slider that he lovingly (and aptly) called "Mr. Nasty" and wound up with a respectable 0.36 BB/IP (in the same neighborhood as Gibson and Carlton and far lower than Ryan).

Randy Johnson, 2008

Johnson leads all qualifying pitchers with a 1.46 SO/H ratio and 41% 3TO and stands second to Nolan Ryan in career strikeouts. He owns five of the all-time top 11 post-1900 seasonal strikeout totals – 372 (3rd) in 2001, 364 (5th) in 1999, 347 (8th) in 2000, 334 (10th) in 2002, and 329 (11th) in 1998. He appeared in 10 ASG and won five Cy Young awards, including four consecutively in 1999-2002. He was also named MVP of the 2001 World Series when he won three games, the last one in relief over Mariano Rivera in Game 7 – Rivera's only postseason defeat. Johnson's 144.1 CVI ranks sixth among SP and 18th overall. He is an elite Hall of Famer.

While Clemens, Johnson, and Martinez were consummate power pitchers, Maddux's calling cards were intelligence and finesse. He looked like Clark Kent, whose glasses and sly smile disguise the Superman beneath. Painting the corners to keep hitters off balance was his *modus operandi* for a seven-year stretch from 1992-98 for the Cubs and Braves, during which he averaged 7.8 WAR_p with an 18-8 W-L, a 2.15 ERA (190 ERA+), a 0.968 WHIP, 184 SO, and a meager 38 walks. His 271 ERA+ in 1994 ranks third on the MLB leaderboard, and his 0.811 WHIP in 1995 ranks fourth. He played in 10 ASG and became the first pitcher to win four consecutive Cy Young awards in 1992-95. His 18.2 WAR_p in 1994-95 could have been 23 if the strike had not cost him the last third of his 8.5-WAR_p 1994 season and the first tenth of his 9.7-WAR_p 1995 season.

Maddux holds the record for most consecutive seasons (17 in 1988-2006) with 15 or more wins. He also fielded his position superbly, winning 18 Gold Gloves, and could help himself with the bat. The only flaw in his resume was his unimposing postseason record; in 198.0 postseason IP, he was 11-14 with a 3.27 ERA and a 1.242 WHIP and won only one World Series ring. His 128.2 CVI ranks eighth among SP and 25th among all HOF-eligible players. He is an elite Hall of Famer.

The best pitcher of the Latino new wave, Pedro Martinez stood only 5'11' and weighed only 170 pounds in his prime, but no one was better than Pedro at his best. In 2000, he posted the best ERA+ (291) and the best WHIP (0.737) of any pitcher in any era with at least 162 IP. While his 11.7 WAR_p in 2000 ranks "only" tied for 10th since 1900, Pedro did it in only 217 IP. Every other pitcher who posted that many WAR_p in a season required at least 264 IP, and all but Clemens (11.9 in 264 IP in 1997) and Gooden (12.2 in 276.2 IP in 1985) required at least 334 IP. And among these elite SP, only Clemens (who used steroids himself) and Pedro had to face steroid-enhanced 60-70 HR sluggers. Thus, one could argue that Pedro's 2000 season was the best inning-for-inning for any SP in baseball history. And Pedro's 1999 season (243 ERA+, 0.923 WHIP, 9.8 WAR_p in 213.1 IP) wasn't far behind.

But Pedro's peak was shorter (nine seasons) than most other great pitchers. He was brought along slowly as a RP early in his career because of his small frame, did not fully blossom as an SP until his fifth season (age 25), and was greatly diminished by shoulder problems after age 33. But the value he packed into his 1997-2005 seasons, when he posted a 2.47 ERA (187 ERA+), a 0.969 WHIP, 10.7 SO9, and 1.61 SO/H (2196/1361) while averaging a 17-6 W-L, 244 SO, and 7.7 WAR_p per season, was enough to make him the 11th best MLB pitcher (and the best Latino pitcher) of all time by CVI. His 37.7 WAR_p in 1997-2000 was especially impressive. Pedro also ranks fourth, behind Randy Johnson, Ryan, and Scherzer in 3TO (37.7%) and fifth in SO/H (1.420). Despite the brevity of his peak, Martinez's 118.2 CVI ranks 30th among all HOF-eligible players, making him an elite Hall of Famer.

Were it not for Twitter, six-time All-Star Curt Schilling would likely have been an HOF shoo-in, like nearly every eligible player with CVI >90. But his inflammatory tweets – particularly his endorsement of a T-shirt "humorously" advocating lynching journalists ("Rope. Tree. Journalist. Some assembly required.") – have been more than many HOF electors can stomach.[24] After all, lynching is no laughing matter, and giving the proverbial middle finger to the HOF electorate of journalists is arrogant and beyond stupid. His recent support for the January 6, 2021 Capitol riot will not help his cause. But should the expression of extreme and obnoxious views disqualify an otherwise great player from the HOF?

Make no mistake, Schilling was a great pitcher. CVI ranks Schilling 20th among SP and tied for 56th among all HOF-eligible players, almost enough to make him an elite Hall

Curt Schilling

of Famer, even without considering his postseason heroics. Do not be fooled by his modest 216 win total (which by the way is 13 more than first-ballot Hall of Famer Roy Halladay). Schilling pitched mostly for losing teams in his first 13 years. When he finally got to pitch for an excellent Diamondback team in 2001-02, Schilling was a worthy co-ace with elite Hall of Famer Randy Johnson, posting a composite record of 45-13 in 516 IP, with 609 SO and only 72 BB, a 3.10 ERA (148 ERA+), a 1.021 WHIP, and 17.4 WAR_p. The Johnson-Schilling tandem finished 1-2 in the Cy Young award voting both years, with Johnson on top, but Schilling was named Pitcher of the Year by the Sporting News. After his 2003 season was ruined by an appendectomy and a broken hand, Schilling moved on to the Red Sox as a free agent in 2004 and led them to their first World Series Championship since 1918, with a 7.8-WAR_p season, featuring a 21-6 record, 316 SO, a 3.26 ERA, and a 1.063 WHIP, finishing second in the AL Cy Young Award voting. He went on to post wins in the ALDS, ALCS and World Series,

Schilling, who was on the winning side in three of four World Series appearances, was also a spectacular postseason pitcher — one of the best ever. In 133.1 IP, he went 11-2 with a 2.23 ERA, 0.968 WHIP, and 120 SO. He started five postseason elimination games, including his iconic "Bloody Sock" performance against the Yankees in Game 6 of the 2004 ALCS, and his team won all five. He was voted the NLCS MVP in 1993 and the World Series co-MVP in 2001. Even if his CVI were 25 points lower, he would have merited HOF recognition.

But there is more. During his career, Schilling was regarded as one of the MLB's most charitable and community-minded players. He received the Lou Gehrig Award in 1995 and the Roberto Clemente, Branch Rickey, and Hutch awards in 2001. Indeed, he was once even celebrated as baseball's "most caring" player.[25] Thus, while Schilling's inflammatory rhetoric is perhaps just symptomatic of the hyperbole and rancor of what currently passes as political discourse, his apparent devolution into a pariah has been especially painful to watch. Although Schilling's support from the BBWAA has slowly grown to 70% in 2020 and 71% in 2021, the opposition of the remaining 30% has hardened. Unless he can somehow repair his reputation, they will continue to block his path to the HOF in his tenth and final scheduled year on the ballot. The point may be moot now that Schilling has asked to be removed from the 2022 ballot, leaving his fate to the VC starting in 2023. Schilling's record and conduct during his MLB career are clearly worthy of the HOF; if that honor is denied to him, it will have been his own doing.

Mike Mussina, the cerebral, introverted pitcher who won over 100 games each for the Orioles and the Yankees over a 17-year career, was the polar opposite of Reggie Jackson, doing his job quietly and efficiently and assiduously shunning the limelight. Almost by design, he was always a bridesmaid, never a bride. He was a five-time All-Star, who finished in the top 10 in Cy Young voting nine times without ever winning the award. He twice took perfect games into the ninth inning but never pitched a no-hitter. He never won 20 games until his final season, then retired 30 games short of the 300 wins that would have sped his HOF election. He initially received lukewarm HOF support but was elected in 2019, his seventh year on the ballot. Mussina's 91.1 CVI ranks 23rd among SP and at the 0.39 percentile overall.

Eight-time All-Star Roy Halladay enjoyed the best of times and endured the worst of times during his 16-year major league career. He took a no-hitter into the ninth inning in his second major league start for Toronto in 1998, before yielding a two-out HR to Bobby Higginson, then hit rock bottom three years later when he was sent to Class A Dunedin. He fought his way back to win the AL Cy Young award in 2003, slipped back to mediocrity in 2004, settled in as Toronto's ace in 2008-09 and the Phillies' ace in 2010-11 (after a trade), then rapidly faded due to injuries in 2012-13. At his peak, from 2005-2011, Halladay averaged 17-8 with a 2.82 ERA (152 ERA+), a 1.086 WHIP, 176 SO, only 34 BB, and 6.4 WAR_p per season. He was especially masterly in 2010-11 with the Phillies when he amassed 8.5 and 8.8 WAR_p, respectively, and finished first (unanimously) and second (to Kershaw) in the NL Cy Young voting. In both seasons, he led all MLB in WAR_p. A highlight of his 2010 MVP season was his perfect game against the Marlins on May 29, the first no-hitter of his career. He added another no-hitter in the NLDS in October. Halladay's 88.4 CVI ranks 25th among SP and at the 0.43 percentile overall.

Beyond the Numbers

- Johnson's 13.41 SO9 in 2001 (372 SO in 249.2 IP) was the highest ever recorded by a qualifying pitcher until Gerrit Cole's 13.82 (326 SO in 212.1 IP) in 2019.

- In 2004, Johnson became the oldest man to pitch a perfect game (against the Braves). In his only other no-hitter, which came in 1990 before he learned control, he issued six BB.

- The Cubs made no effort to re-sign Maddux after his Cy Young award-winning 1992 season, signing Juan Guzman instead.[26] That's what it was like to be a Cubs fan.

- Although Maddux's performance declined markedly at age 37 in 2003 when his ERA+ fell from 159 to 108, he continued as a solid mid-rotation starter for the Cubs, Dodgers, and Padres through 2008. This enabled him to climb the career leaderboards in W, SO and WAR_p, but took some of the shine off his ERA, ERA+, and WHIP. Had he retired after the 2004 season (when he won his 300th game), he would have finished with a 2.95 ERA, 141 ERA+ (tied for 15th on the all-time list), and 1.127 WHIP.

- Maddux's and Martinez's older brothers, Mike and Ramon, both enjoyed fine careers as MLB pitchers.

- Before he joined the Red Sox, Martinez was the ace of the ill-starred Expo team that compiled MLB's best record in 1994 before the strike.

- Schilling struggled early in his career, bouncing from the Red Sox to the Orioles to the Astros in 1988-91 before establishing himself with the Phillies in 1992 at age 25.

- Schilling ranks 19th among all qualifying pitchers with 1.06 SO/H. He had three 300-SO seasons in 1997-98 and 2002. Schilling's 4.38 SO/BB ratio is the best of any post-1900 pitcher with at least 2000 IP.

- Halladay may go down in history as the last practitioner of the complete game. He pitched 67 CG over the course of his career and led his league eight times – typically with 8-9 CG. In 2010, Halladay's 9 CG represented 12.5% of the NL total of 72. In 2019, there were only 18 CG in the *entire* NL—only nine more than Halladay had in 2010 all by himself.

- Mussina grew up in Montoursville, PA, near the home of Little League World Series in Williamsport. He played Little League from age 8-15 and joined their Board of Directors in 2001. He was elected to the Little League Hall of Excellence in 2014.[27]

- Despite joining the Yankees after consecutive championships in 1998-2000, Mussina never got a ring himself. The Yankees lost the 2001 and 2003 World Series, and Mussina retired a year before their 2009 championship.

Kings of October

Mariano Rivera (RP):
101.9 CVI - New York AL (*56.3*)

Derek Jeter (SS):
71.3 CVI - New York AL (*71.3*)

David Ortiz (DH):
65.4 CVI - Boston AL (*52.7*)

The expanded playoffs of the Steroid Era provided unprecedented postseason exposure – as much as a season's worth of PA or IP – to players on winning teams. So, while players of earlier generations like Ruth, Gehrig, Mantle, Ford, Koufax, Gibson, Bench, and Brooks Robinson, earned reputations for their postseason exploits, they were based on modest sample sizes. This section covers three players who were known for their postseason exploits over many more games. If clutch performance represents a real attribute and not just the play of chance, these three players embody it:

Rivera: 141.0 IP, 0.70 ERA, 0.759 WHIP, 42 SV, 8-1 W-L, 110 SO, 1999 WS MVP, 2003 ALCS MVP

Jeter: 158 G, 734 PA, .308/.374/.465, 200 H, 20 HR, 61 RBI, 111 R, 32 2B, 302 TB, 18 SB, 2000 WS MVP

Ortiz: 85 G, 369 PA, .289/.404/.543, 17 HR, 61 RBI, 51 R, 22 2B, 165 TB; 2004 ALCS MVP, 2013 WS MVP

These players are systematically underrated by CVI and other WAR-based metrics, which ignore postseason performance.

Another member of the Latino new wave, 13-time All-Star Mariano Rivera, stands head and shoulders above his peers as the best RP ever by any reasonable metric, including CVI. From 1997-2011, his cool and deliberate walk from the bullpen to the mound in the ninth inning to the doleful strains of Metallica's "Enter Sandman" signaled impending doom to opposing teams hoping to overcome a close Yankee lead. He saved 652 such games, posting a 2.01 ERA (223 ERA+) and 0.966 WHI while averaging 62 SO (versus 14 BB) in 69 IP, Although he never won a Cy Young Award (which are typically given to SP), he finished third in the voting in 1996, 1999, and 2004, and second in 2005.

Rivera is the all-time career leader in saves and in ERA+ and tops all RP in WHIP and leveraged WAR; no other RP is close. He won the Rolaids Relief award five times (1999, 2001, 2004-05, 2009); the AL award is now named after him. He did it all with basically one pitch, a wicked cutter, which rendered batters helpless even though they knew it was coming. Rivera put up eight seasons with 40 or more saves, including two 50-save seasons, 12 seasons with ERA+ >200 (over at least 60 IP), including two seasons with ERA+ >300, and nine seasons with WHIP <1.0 (over at least 60 IP).

How does Rivera compare with other great pitchers? Arguably, he was the best ever, inning-for-inning. Consider that Rivera faced 5103 batters in his 19-year career (not including post-season games) and amassed 56.3 WAR$_p$. That 5103 BF is similar to the number of batters Tim Keefe or Old Hoss Radbourn faced in 2-3 seasons in the 1880s, that Cy Young or Walter Johnson faced in 3-4 seasons, that Sandy Koufax faced in 5 seasons, or that Justin Verlander faced in 6 seasons. So what happens if we cherry-pick the best seasons by WAR$_p$ per 1000 BF for all the great pitchers in MLB history, stopping when we get to 5103 BF, and compare their cumulative WAR$_p$ totals to Rivera? Table 8.3 provides the answer.

There were only 14 pitchers who amassed at least 40 WAR$_p$ in 5103 BF in the best seasons of their careers. There are no flukes on this list, which includes nine of MLB's top 11 SP in CVI and no one with CVI <80. Rivera tops this stellar list, and no one except Pedro Martinez is even close. I am not arguing that Rivera's career was better than that of Walter Johnson or Clemens or Grove or the others, who produced considerable value beyond the 5103 BF constraint of this table, but it does illuminate how great Rivera was within the parameters of the closer role.

Table 8.3: Pitchers With More Than 40 WAR$_p$ per 5103 BF in Their Best Seasons

Player	CumWAR$_p$	Seasons
Mariano Rivera	56.3	1995-2014
Pedro Martinez	54.4	1997, 1999-2001, 2002*, 2003, 2005
Roger Clemens	50.3	1986, 1990, 1992, 1994*, 1997, 2005
Walter Johnson	49.3	1912-13, 1915*, 1919
Randy Johnson	49.1	1995, 1997, 1999*, 2000-02, 2004
Lefty Grove	47.0	1930-31, 1936, 1937*, 1939
Greg Maddux	46.4	1992, 1994-95, 1996-97, 1998*
Clayton Kershaw	43.7	2011, 2012*, 2013-17, 2020
Justin Verlander	42.8	2011-12, 2016, 2018-19, 2017*
Max Scherzer	41.9	2013, 2015, 2016*, 2017-20
Cy Young	41.7	1892*, 1895, 1901, 1908
Tom Seaver	41.1	1969*, 1971, 1973, 1975, 1977
Curt Schilling	41.1	1996, 1999, 2001-04, 2006*
Christy Mathewson	40.4	1901*, 1905, 1907-09

*Prorated season to bring cumulative BF to exactly 5103.

Rivera was even better – if that is possible – in the postseason with everything on the line. His incredible 0.70 ERA and 0.759 WHIP and 42 saves arguably make him the best postseason pitcher of all time. In his lone postseason defeat in 96 appearances — Game 7 of the 2001 World Series — he was undone by an error and two bloop hits. All things considered, Rivera was the most valuable core player on the Yankee teams that appeared in 16 postseasons between 1995 and 2011 (missing only 2008), playing in seven World Series, and winning five (in 1996, 1998-2000, and 2009). ESPN ranked Rivera 49th among the all-time greats; CVI also ranks him 49th among all HOF-eligible players. In 2019, he became the BBWAA's first unanimous selection to the HOF. He is absolutely an elite Hall of Famer.

Derek Jeter was a leader and an exemplary teammate on multiple winning Yankee teams, who had an uncanny knack for coming up with the decisive hit or defensive gem on the big stage. His calling card during his extraordinary 20-

Derek Jeter, 2008

year career was his excellence in an entire season's worth (158 G) of postseason competition. This "extra season," which does not count toward his CVI, included his brilliant iconic game-saving defensive play in Game 3 of the 2001 ALDS versus Oakland when he ran in from SS to pick up a loose relay throw near the first base line and flipped the ball to catcher Jorge Posada in time to nip Jeremy Giambi as he tried to score.[28] There were also his 2000 WS MVP award and his dramatic walk-off 10th inning HR in Game 4 of the 2001 World Series against Arizona, hit just after midnight on November 1, to tie the Series 2-2. This HR made Jeter "Mr. November" to Reggie Jackson's "Mr. October" in the eyes of Yankee fans. His composite postseason stat line is similar to that of his 6.8-oWAR 2001 season (.311/.377/.480 with 21 HR, 72 RBI, and 110 R) – but against the toughest possible competition and championship-caliber pitching. So, his postseason line probably translates to at least 7.5 WAR, which would elevate his CVI from 71.3 to roughly 77.

Jeter's defensive shortcomings are a flashpoint of contention between the traditionalist and sabermetric communities. His career dWAR of -9.4 is pretty awful for a SS, especially since SS have the benefit of a +7 run positional adjustment. He had limited range to his right and compensated by perfecting a signature jump throw to get enough mustard on his throws to 1B. However, an online comparison of plays by Jeter and a top-notch defensive SS, Brendan Ryan, shows that Ryan routinely made plays that were beyond Jeter's range.[29] On the other hand, any casual fan who knew Jeter primarily from his postseason play and the highlight reels understands that he had a unique baseball intelligence/intuition that enabled him to make plays that no one else would make.

So does Jeter's penchant for the exceptional offset his limited range on routine plays? Perhaps not, but it defies credulity that Jeter's Yankee teams could have won so many pennants and played such good team defense with an inadequate defender in the most important position on the field. Infield defense is the most collaborative of all the elements of baseball. Perhaps, Jeter's defensive limitations were mitigated by pairing him with strong defensive 3B like Scott Brosius and converted SS Alex Rodriguez, who had the range to compensate for Jeter's limitations on balls hit to his right. In any case, I can't buy the idea that Jeter's play at SS hurt the Yankees as much as it hurt his WAR, even if he did not deserve his five Gold Gloves (which were probably awarded just to annoy sabermetricians) CVI ranks him only 15th at SS and at the 0.78 percentile overall. Considering his baseball intelligence and postseason resume, this seems too low. Not counting A-Rod, Yount, and Banks, who spent nearly half their careers at other positions, only Wagner Ripken, Vaughan, Appling, and perhaps George Davis were more valuable than Jeter at SS, all things considered.

When one looks at the accomplishments of David "Big Papi" Ortiz as the power-hitting DH and spiritual leader of the Red Sox team that broke the "Curse of the Bambino" in 2004 and added two more championships in 2007 and 2013, it is easy to forget that the Red Sox picked up the 10-time All-Star and 2013 World Series MVP off the scrap heap at age 27 after the Twins declined to tender him a contract for the 2003 season. It was his friend Pedro Martinez, who had given up a big HR to Ortiz in August 2002, who lobbied Theo Epstein to take a flier on the stocky 1B/DH.[30] The reclamation of David Ortiz was a legend-making, curse-breaking personnel move. He began the 2003 season fighting for playing time and ended it as Boston's everyday DH and MVP. At his peak (2004-07), Ortiz absolutely destroyed AL pitching, hitting .304/.408/.616 (159 OPS+) while averaging 44 HR, 135 RBI, 111 R, 352 TB, 42 2B, and 5.4 WAR in 684 PA per season. The fact that he was a full-time DH curtailed his WAR and undoubtedly hurt him in the MVP voting, but he still won the Henry Aaron Award as the AL's best hitter in 2005 and finished in the top five of the AL MVP voting all four years.

In the bookend Red Sox World Series championships of 2004 and 2007, Ortiz was a one-man postseason wrecking crew, hitting a composite .386/.504/.733 with 8 HR, 29 RBI, 29 R, 27 BB, and 72 TB in 131 PA as the Red Sox steamrolled over all opposition. Of particular note, Ortiz was the MVP of the Red Sox comeback from an 0-3 deficit against their nemesis, the New York Yankees, in the 2004 ALCS, including a walk-off 12th inning two-run HR that started the comeback in Game 4, a leadoff HR in Game 5 that started a game-tying rally, and a three-run first inning Game 7 HR that put the Red Sox on their way to a series-clinching 10-3 rout. His postseason dominance continued throughout his career. He saved his best for his three World Series, hitting .455/.576/.795 with 3 HR and 14 RBI in 59 PA in the four-game sweeps over the Cardinals in 2004 and the Rockies in 2007 and the 4-2 win over the Cardinals in 2013. In 2013, he hit .688/.760/1.188 with 2 HR and 6 RBI and was named WS MVP. His .455 composite World Series AVG is the highest in MLB history. Ortiz's 65.4 CVI ranks fourth among DH and at only the 1.04 percentile overall, but his postseason heroics have earned him a loftier place in MLB history.

Beyond the Numbers

- Rivera, a deeply religious man, grew up in abject poverty in a Panamanian fishing village with an abusive father. His autobiography reads as a series of divine interventions:[31]

  o His narrow escape from drowning when his father's fishing boat broke down

  o Earning a tryout with a Yankee scout after being summoned in from SS to relieve his team's best pitcher

  o Overcoming career-threatening elbow and shoulder injuries as a minor leaguer

  o Accidentally discovering his trademark cutter while playing catch in the bullpen

Beyond the Numbers (cont'd)

- In 1995, Steinbrenner nearly traded Rivera for SS Felix Fermin, which would have derailed both his and Jeter's careers and strangled the budding Yankee dynasty in its crib. Fortunately for the Yankees, GM Gene Michaels and assistant GM Brian Cashman dissuaded him.[32]

- When Jeter accepted a full baseball scholarship from the University of Michigan after finishing high school, MLB scouts realized that he would be difficult to sign. Nevertheless, Houston scout Hal Newhouser strongly recommended that the Astros select Jeter with the #1 pick in the 1992 amateur draft. When the Astros instead selected Cal State Fullerton OF Phil Nevin, whom they considered more "signable," Newhouser resigned in protest. So, Jeter fell to the Yankees, who held the #6 pick and were willing to spend whatever it took (which turned out to be $800,000) to persuade Jeter to give up his scholarship.[33]

- In 2017, at age 43, Jeter joined an investment group that put together the winning bid to purchase the Miami Marlins. Jeter now oversees their baseball operations as CEO.

- Ortiz is rumored to be one of the players who tested positive for steroids in the anonymous testing protocol of 2003. Although he never tested positive during his prime years, these unsubstantiated rumors may complicate his path to the HOF.

The Naturals

Ken Griffey Jr. (CF):
101.8 CVI - Seattle AL (*70.6*),
Cincinnati (*12.8*)

Frank Thomas (DH):
87.4 CVI - Chicago AL (68.3)

Jim Thome (1B):
73.8 CVI - Cleveland AL (*48.0*),
Chicago AL (*12.1*), Philadelphia NL (*8.5*)

Although Griffey, Thomas, and Thome were among the most prolific HR hitters of the steroid era, they were conspicuous for the absence of even a whiff of association with steroids.

The son and namesake of the fine 34.5-WAR OF who played for Cincinnati's Big Red Machine in the 1970s, Ken Griffey Jr. broke into the majors at age 19 in 1989 and instantly became one of the most charismatic stars of the game, known and loved for his exuberant play, his ever-present smile, and backward-facing baseball cap. A 10-time All-Star, he was widely regarded as the best all-around player in the AL in the 1990s. From 1990-1999 (ages 20-29), he hit .302/.384/.581 (152 OPS+) and averaged 38 HR, 109 RBI, 100 R, 312 TB, 15 SB, 1.0 dWAR, and 6.8 WAR per season. His WAR exceeded 4.9 in every year except 1995 (when he missed 73 games after breaking his wrist while making a spectacular catch in CF). He led the AL with 9.7 WAR in 1996 and finished second in 1993, 1994, and 1997, when he posted 9.1 WAR and won AL MVP honors. He led the AL in HR four times in 10 years, including consecutive 56-HR seasons (1997-98); his 112 HR two-year total is second only to Ruth's 113 in 1920-21 among players not on steroids. Griffey's 630 career HR total still ranks seventh on the all-time leaderboard.

Griffey was also an outstanding defensive CF, with a penchant for the spectacular, winning 10 Gold Gloves and racking up 11.0 dWAR through age 30 (very high for an OF) before age and leg injuries slowed him down. He even threw in about 20 SB per season in his prime. With Griffey's help, the Mariners attained respectability and appeared in their first postseason in 1995, beating the Yankees 3-2 in the ALDS before falling 2-4 to Cleveland in the ALCS. Griffey was outstanding, hitting .364/.423/.818 in 52 PA with 6 HR, 9 RBI, 11 R, and 3 SB in the two series. Although his HR totals were overshadowed by those of his steroid-enhanced contemporaries, he was doubly appreciated when the steroid scandals left him unsullied.

Unfortunately, chronic lower body injuries slowed him down and sapped his power after age 30. In this respect, his career is the mirror image of late bloomer Adrian Beltre, who disappointed in his 20s and blossomed in his 30s. From 2001-10, Griffey hit only .260/.350/.483 (114 OPS) and averaged 19 HR, 57 RBI, and 50 R in 398 PA and only 0.8 WAR per season, a far cry from his production in the

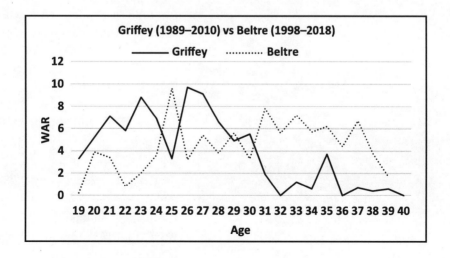

1990s. Still, his 101.8 CVI ranks seventh among CF and 50th among all HOF-eligible players, making him an elite Hall of Famer. His HOF election in 2016 was nearly unanimous.

At 6'5" and 240 pounds, Frank Thomas, the genial giant known affectionately as "The Big Hurt" by White Sox fans, looked more like a defensive lineman than a baseball player. But, man, could he hit! Not only did he have power galore, but his outstanding contact skills and plate discipline (1667 BB versus 1397 SO) placed him 20th on the career OBP leaderboard at .419. His 36% 3TO ranks 27th on the all-time list, but his 0.566 SO/H ranks only 91st. Only 18 players — elite players like Ruth, Bonds, Williams, Gehrig, Mantle, etc. — have career OPS+ higher than Thomas's 156, while Thomas ranks equal to Mays and ahead of guys like Aaron, DiMaggio, Ott, and Frank Robinson. And he did it all without steroids. Indeed, he was an outspoken advocate for more rigorous steroid testing and harsher penalties as early as 1995 and was the only player who volunteered to be interviewed for the Mitchell Report a decade later. Thomas peaked in 1991-97, hitting a Jimmy Foxx-like .330/.452/.604 (182 OPS+) and averaging 36 HR, 118 RBI, 107 R, 313 TB, 119 BB, and 6.4 WAR, despite losing 50 games to the strike in 1994.

Jim Thome, 2008

Thomas made five consecutive All-Star teams in 1993-97 and won back-to-back MVP awards in 1993-94. The Sporting News named him Major League Player of the Year In 1993. He hit .347 in 1997 to win his only batting title. But Thomas cost the White Sox runs defensively at 1B, and eventually played more games at DH than at 1B. His WAR, which penalizes him doubly for poor defense (-22.5 dWAR) and playing half his games at DH, is less impressive than his OPS+, but his 87.4 CVI still ranks second at DH and at the 0.45 percentile overall.

Five-time All-Star Jim Thome was the lefty-hitting counterpart of Thomas, a gentle giant and a prolific but defensively-challenged slugger, who never used steroids and was widely admired throughout baseball. Thomas's superior contact skills made him the better pure hitter, but Thome (who began as a 3B) was not as bad defensively (-16.4 dWAR). With due respect to Rob Deer (whose 50% 3TO in 4513 PA inspired the 3TO concept) and Adam Dunn (whose 51% 3TO leads all players with at least 7500 PA), Jim Thome's 48% 3TO tops all HOF-quality hitters.

Thome is also one of only six qualifying hitters with more strikeouts than hits; his 1.095 SO/H is topped only by Dunn and Mike Cameron. In his prime years in Cleveland (1995-2002) at 3B and then at 1B, Thome hit .293/.426/.588 (159 OPS+) and averaged 38 HR, 104 RBI, 102 R, 290 TB, 113 BB, and 5.5 WAR. He played long enough to become only the eighth player to hit 600 HR in 2011 and finished with 612, eighth on the all-time leaderboard. Thome and Thomas were both in the all-time Top 10 in career BB and had OBP >.400. Thome's 73.8 CVI ranks 10th at 1B and at the 0.72 percentile overall.

Beyond the Numbers

- Griffey's on-field exuberance hid a troubled adolescence, in which he quarreled with his parents, ran wild at night, and grew increasingly angry and depressed. The Mariners almost backed off from drafting him when he failed their standard psychological test but relented when he retook (and passed) the test. He attempted suicide by swallowing a bottle of aspirin in January 1988.[34]

- As he neared eligibility for free agency in 1999, Griffey declined an eight-year $135 M contract extension from the Mariners to play closer to his home and family in Orlando, FL. The Mariners reluctantly traded him to Cincinnati, where he could play for his father's team in the city where he grew up. Griffey signed a nine-year contract for $112.5 million, substantially less than the Mariners' offer he rejected. Sadly, he had only one Griffey-like year in Cincinnati (in 2000), before a succession of injuries sent his career downhill.

- Postseason appearances were scarce for Thomas. He hit .353/.593/.529 in the 1993 ALDS when the Jays beat the Sox 4-2. When the White Sox won the 2005 World Series, Thomas was injured and did not play.

- Like Griffey and Thomas, Thome never played for a World Series champion, but he did play for Cleveland in losing World Series against the Braves in 1995 and Marlins in 1997. He arrived in Chicago in 2006, the year after the White Sox won the World Series.

- Thomas and Thome currently have successful careers as studio analysts for Fox Sports and the MLB network, respectively.

Catchers of the Steroid Era

Ivan Rodriguez (C):
85.3 CVI - Texas AL (*50.0*),
Detroit AL (*14.2*)

Mike Piazza:
83.2 CVI - Los Angeles NL (*32.0*),
New York NL (*24.6*)

Joe Mauer (C):
69.7 CVI - Minnesota AL (*55.3*)

The Steroid Era also gave us the top defensive catcher of all time (Rodriguez) and one of the top offensive catchers of all-time (Piazza) plus a third catcher (Mauer) who was on his way to being on the short list of all-time great catchers until the aftermath of a severe concussion forced him to move to 1B, where he was only a league-average performer. Unfortunately, the accomplishments of Rodriguez and Piazza were tainted by steroid rumors. The rumors are perhaps more plausible for Rodriguez (who was the Texas teammate of several proven users and was fingered in Jose Canseco's tell-all book) than for Piazza, who was guilty only of using andro-stenedione when it was still legal and available over the counter and of surpassing everyone's expectations.[35] It is hard to prove a negative, especially when there was no drug testing until 2003. but neither were mentioned in the Mitchell report or ever failed a drug test. Some have pointed to Rodriguez's 22-pound weight loss in 2005 after Canseco's book came out, but his performance did not decline until two years later. In contrast to Bonds, Sosa, Palmeiro, etc., one can point to no suspicious inflection point in the career WAR trajectory plots of either player.

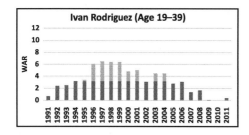

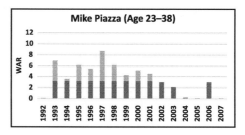

Ivan "Pudge" Rodriguez leads all catchers in G, dWAR, H, R, TB and 2B. His defense and longevity particularly set him apart. His 29.6 dWAR not only leads all catchers but ranks eighth among *all* position players. The "eye test" confirms his lofty defensive ranking. Even a casual fan could marvel at Rodriguez's agility behind the plate and his powerful and accurate throwing arm (which enabled him to throw out 46% of baserunners who attempted to steal against him). He played in 14 ASG and won 13 Gold Gloves, three more than any other catcher.

Although Pudge was initially celebrated mostly for defense, his hitting gradually improved as he gained experience. From 1996-2001, Pudge hit .319/.355/.529 (121 OPS+) while averaging 24 HR, 86 RBI, 92 R, 34 2B, and 5.9 WAR per season, excellent for any position, but stellar for the top defensive catcher in baseball. In his 1999 MVP season, Pudge hit .332/.356/.588 (125 OPS+) with career highs in HR (35), RBI (113), R (116), and TB (335) and 6.4 WAR, as the Rangers (who had never made a postseason appearance in their first 28 years) won their second consecutive AL West Division pennant and their third in four years.

Ivan Rodriguez

He started even stronger in 2000 but broke his thumb on July 24. When the Rangers, struggling under the financial burden of A-Rod's mega-contract, let Pudge go to Florida as a free agent in 2002, he helped bring the Marlins their second World Series championship, hitting .313/.390/.522, with 3 HR, 17 RBI, and 10 R in the postseason and earning MVP honors in the NLCS win over the Cubs, in which he drove in 10 and scored five of the Marlin's 40 runs. When the Tigers, coming off a 43-119 2003 season, acquired him in 2004, they immediately improved by 29 games; by 2006, they won the AL pennant, with Pudge still contributing 2.9 WAR and world-class defense. The fact that teams just seemed to get better when they acquired Rodriguez and to get worse when they lost him speaks volumes. Pudge's 85.3 CVI ranks third among catchers and at the 0.48 percentile overall. Although steroid rumors held his vote total to 76%, he still became only the second catcher (after Bench) to be elected in his first appearance on the BBWAA ballot.

Mike Piazza leads all MLB catchers in SLG (.545) and OPS+ (142) and ranks in the top five in AVG, RBI, and TB. His ascent to the major leagues is a Cinderella story – or at least what Cinderella's story might have looked like had her guardian been Vince Piazza instead of the Wicked Stepmother. Mike's father Vince was a successful and gregarious self-made businessman who could afford to indulge his son's passion for baseball.[39] Although Mike always could hit for high average and power, even as a high school 1B, it took calls from Vince to his buddies, University of Miami baseball coach Ron Fraser and Dodger manager Tommy Lasorda, to open doors for Mike to get a college scholarship (as the Hurricanes backup 1B) and to get the Dodgers to select Mike in the 62nd round of the 1989 amateur draft.

Since Dodgers scout Ben Wade would agree to sign Piazza only as a catcher, a catcher is what he became. Nobody in the Dodger organization expected anything of him. Piazza worked hard to become a competent catcher in 1989-90 but won few converts. Finally, his strong hitting in 1992 at several minor league levels and in a September major league cameo, earned him an opportunity with the Dodgers in 1993. Piazza was a rookie sensation, hitting .318/.370/.561 (153 OPS+) with 35 HR, 112 RBI, 81 R, 307 TB, and 7.0 WAR and earned unanimous acclaim as the NL Rookie of the Year, his first of 12 ASG selections, and ninth place in the NL MVP voting. From 1993-2001 Piazza was one of the top hitters in the NL at any position, hitting .326/.393/.583 (156 OPS+) and averaging 35 HR, 108 RBI, 86 R, 296 TB, and 5.7 WAR per season. He twice finished second in the MVP voting in 1996 (to Ken Caminiti) and 1997 (to Larry Walker) but never won the award.

After announcing his intention to become a free agent at the end of the 1999 season, Piazza was traded to the Marlins and then the Mets, where he starred through 2002 before entering his decline years. Piazza's 83.2 CVI ranks fourth among catchers and at the 0.52 percentile overall. I view the attribution of Piazza's success to steroids by many naysayers, which delayed his HOF election until his fourth appearance on the BBWAA ballot, to be largely sour grapes for having so misjudged his ability. Although I have no inside knowledge of Piazza's habits, I would rather grant this Cinderella the presumption of innocence than believe the "ugly stepsisters."

In MLB's 2001 amateur draft, two college level prospects, both considered nearly major league ready, stood out above all the others – 20-year-old SP Mark Prior of Southern California (viewed then as perhaps the greatest college pitcher ever) and 21-year-old slugging 3B Mark Teixeira of Georgia Tech. So, when the Twins chose an 18-year-old local high school catcher Joe Mauer with the first overall pick, many viewed it as a "signability pick" — a polite way of calling the cash-starved

Twins cheapskates. When Prior won 24 games as the ace of a contending Cubs team in 2002-03 and Teixeira slugged 64 HR for the Rangers in 2003-04 while Mauer was still working his way through the minor leagues, the naysayers and second-guessers had a field day. But the Twins had the last laugh. Prior developed shoulder problems and pitched his last major league game in 2006. Teixeira had a fine 14-year career and finished with a 50.1 CVI, well short of HOF territory.

In the meantime, Mauer put together an HOF caliber career at a premium position, averaging .327/.410/.473 (139 OPS+) with 11 HR, 70 RBI, 76 R, 31 2B, and 5.0 WAR from 2006-13, with six ASG appearances, three Gold Gloves and a well-deserved MVP award in 2009, when he hit .365/.444/.587 (171 OPS+), leading the AL in all four categories, and hit an uncharacteristic 28 HR with 96 RBI and 94 R. He is the only catcher ever to lead the league in all three "slash line" categories, and his 7.8 WAR were the most ever by any AL catcher. After being forced from C to 1B by a concussion in 2013, he played his last five years as the Twins' everyday 1B, where he was only ordinary. Hopefully, this decline and his pedestrian postseason resume will not overshadow his eight stellar prime years as a catcher. Mauer's 69.7 CVI ranks eighth among catchers and at the 0.86 percentile overall, which should land him in the HOF in the mid-2020s.

Beyond the Numbers

- The nickname "Pudge" actually fit the 5'9" 205 pound Rodriguez far better than the 6'3" 200 pound Carlton Fisk, although there was no trace of fat on Ivan's smaller frame.

- Pudge was called up to the Rangers in June 1991 at age 19 when starting C Geno Petralli was injured. The call-up was inconvenient, since Ivan and his fiancée Maribel had to postpone their wedding, which was scheduled for the next day.[40] Ivan hit safely in 10 of his first 11 games and took over as the Rangers everyday catcher for the next 12 years; meanwhile, Petralli joined Wally Pipp as the answer to a trivia question.

- Pudge's son Dereck pitched for the Giants in 2018-19.

- Piazza's most iconic moment with the Mets came in the first game following the 9/11 attack, a game that had no impact on the pennant race, when he hit a game-winning two-run eighth inning HR to turn a 1-2 deficit into a 3-2 lead. His curtain call before cheering fans was an emotional moment that few New Yorkers will ever forget.

- Piazza was never a Gold Glove catcher, but his 1.5 career dWAR suggests that he was better than his reputation. He had a 4.5 dWAR in 1993-2000, and only went into the red in his last seven years. Piazza was an excellent pitch framer and was especially good at keeping errant pitches in front of him and preventing baserunners from advancing.[38]

Beyond the Numbers (cont'd)

- Mauer was a multisport star at St. Paul's Cretin-Derham High School, following in the footsteps of Hall of Famer Paul Molitor.[42] Mauer struck out only once during his four-year high-school career and hit over .500 every year (.605 as a senior). He caught for the Team USA national team in 1998-2000, winning several awards. He also starred in basketball and football, averaging 20 points per game as a point guard and quarterbacking the football team to a state title game appearance in 1998 and a state championship in 1999.

Postseason Problems

Chipper Jones Jr. (3B):	Tom Glavine (SP):
88.3 CVI - Atlanta NL (*85.3*)	78.7 CVI - Atlanta NL (*63.5*), New York NL (*17.1*)
John Smoltz (SP):	Andruw Jones (CF):
71.9 CVI - Atlanta NL (*69.5*)	69.8 CVI - Atlanta NL (*61.0*)

From 1991-2005 (except for the strike-shortened 1994 season), you could count on the annual appearance of the Atlanta Braves and their infernal Tomahawk Chop cheer in the postseason. Although they won only one World Series (1995) and made it to four others (1991, 1992, 1996, 1999), no team – not even the Yankees – can match their record of 14 consecutive postseason appearances. Five core players were at the heart of this unprecedented run – Greg Maddux (profiled earlier) and the four players profiled below. Glavine and Smoltz were there from the beginning during the building years of 1987-90, when the Braves were a perennial bottom-dweller. Maddux joined as a free agent in 1993, coming off a Cy Young award-winning year as a Cub in 1992. The Joneses joined in 1995-96 when the dynasty was entering its peak.

Although the Braves long run as NL East champion was built primarily on starting pitching, eight-time All-Star Chipper Jones was their best hitter and team leader. Like Mauer, Chipper was not considered the best available player in his draft class. When the last-place Braves had the first pick in 1990, the consensus #1 prospect was high school pitcher Todd Van Poppel, who publicly announced that he would not sign with the then-lowly Braves. So, the Braves went in another direction and chose the relatively unheralded Florida high school SS Chipper Jones, while Van Poppel was drafted later in the first round by the defending AL champion Oakland

A's. In a wonderful example of karma, Jones not only enjoyed a far more productive career than the more celebrated Van Poppel (who bounced around for 11 years as a journeyman RP and never pitched in a postseason game), but also played in 12 postseasons in his 19-year career including a World Series championship in 1995.

Chipper was deemed ready for prime time in 1994, but he tore his left ACL in spring training. His debut was delayed until 1995, when he replaced the departed free agent Terry Pendleton at 3B. (He no longer had the mobility to play SS.) Although Chipper had a solid but unspectacular season, finishing second to Hideo Nomo for 1995 Rookie of the Year honors, he was good enough to become a key to the Braves only World Series championship of their 15-year run, hitting .364/.446/.618 with 3 HR, 8 RBI, 10 R and 24 TB in 65 PA in 14 postseason games, including the decisive ninth inning HR in a 5-4 win over the Rockies in Game 1 of the NLDS.

For the next 13 years (1996-2008), Chipper was the bedrock of the Braves offense. He hit .314/.411/.555 (148 OPS+) while averaging 30 HR, 99 RBI, 99 R, 291 TB, 90 BB, and 5.6 WAR. The only knocks against him were durability in his later years (he played in only 109-137 games in 2004-08) and his barely adequate defense at 3B and in a two-year detour to LF in 2002-03. Jones did not have spectacular highs but was consistently excellent. His 6.9 WAR 1999 season, when he achieved career highs in HR (45) and TB (359) won him his only MVP award, but his 7.6-WAR 2007 season and 7.3-WAR 2008 season, when he won his only batting championship and sported a career-high 176 OPS+, were arguably even better. Chipper is among the best switch-hitters of all time and is the only one to compile at least a .300 AVG, a .400 OBP, a .500 SLG, and 400 HR. He ranks first among all retired 3B in SLG and in OPS, second (behind Beltre) in RBI and fourth (behind Schmidt, Mathews, and Beltre) in HR. His 88.3 CVI ranks sixth at 3B and at the 0.43 percentile overall.

Tom Glavine was the lefty in the Braves' triumvirate of HOF pitchers. Although one could argue that Maddux (for sure) and Smoltz (perhaps) were better, Glavine averaged 17-8 with a 3.15 ERA (134 ERA+), a 1.275 WHIP, 144 SO, 77 BB, and 4.6 WAR$_p$ in his 12 prime years in Atlanta (1991-2002). It was usually Glavine, the two-time Cy Young Award winner

Tom Glavine, 1993

and 10-time All-Star, to whom the Braves turned for the Game 1 postseason assignments. However, like Maddux, his postseason resume is notable more for quantity than quality. He went only 14-16 with a 3.30 ERA and 1.273 WHIP in 218.1 IP, although he did win MVP honors in the 1995 World Series, in which he pitched eight one-hit innings in the Series-clinching 1-0 shutout of the mighty Indians in Game 6. He gave the Mets five solid years as a mid-rotation starter in 2003-07 before returning to Atlanta to finish out his career in 2008. He finished with 305 wins. His 78.7 CVI ranks 34th among SP and at the 0.58 percentile overall.

CVI says that John Smoltz was only the third best pitcher on the perennial NL East champion Braves of 1991-2005, in a multifaceted career that included a Cy Young award in 1996 and four years as a closer following Tommy John surgery in 2000. But Smoltz was the Braves' Mr. October every year, ranking up there with Rivera and Schilling as the best postseason pitchers in the era of divisional play. In 13 postseasons with the Braves (plus a 2009 appearance with the Cardinals), Smoltz went 15-4 with a 2.67 ERA, 1.144 WHIP, 199 SO and 4 SV in 209.0 IP and was named 1992 NLCS MVP. When Jack Morris pitched his magnificent 1-0 10-inning shutout in Game 7 of the 1991 World Series, there was Smoltz on the other side matching him zero for zero for seven tense innings. That game was a microcosm of Smoltz's postseason career – brilliant, but ultimately in a losing cause. Atlanta's lone World Series championship in 1995 was the notable exception – on both counts; Cleveland touched him up for 4 ER, 6 H, and 2 BB in 2.1 IP in his 1995 World Series start, but the Braves prevailed in six games.

During the regular season, Smoltz was an eight-time All-Star, who averaged a solid 14-10 W-L with a 3.29 ERA (124 ERA+), a 1.174 WHIP, 187 SO, 67 BB, and 3.9 WAR_p in 214 IP in his prime (1989-99). The highlight of this 11-year stretch was his 24-win 7.4-WAR_p 1996 Cy Young award-winning season. The low point was 1994, when he struggled to a 6-10 record with a 4.14 ERA. After undergoing Tommy John surgery in 2000 and struggling to come back in 2001, he re-emerged as an All-Star closer in 2002-04, posting a 2.47 ERA (173 ERA+) and 1.003 WHIP with 148 saves and 243 SO in 226.1 IP. His 55 saves in 2002 is tied for the fourth highest of all time. He returned to the starting rotation in 2005-07 and averaged a 15-8 W-L with a 3.22 ERA (135 ERA+), a 1.172 WIP, 192 SO, 52 BB, and 5.1 WAR_p per season – pretty remarkable for a guy pushing 40. But by then his elbow was shot, and this time he could not come back successfully. Smoltz's 71.9 CVI ranks 44th among SP and at the 0.77 percentile overall. However, especially when his postseason resume is considered, Smoltz was a no-doubt Hall of Famer, as well as a model of resilience.

Five-time All-Star and ten-time Gold Glove CF Andruw Jones began his MLB career as a 19 year-old 6'1" 170-pound speedster who played CF like a modern-day Tris Speaker, playing shallower than anyone else but gliding back effortlessly to catch flyballs hit over his head. His 24.4 dWAR leads all OF and ranks 22nd for all position players. By the time he was 23 in 2000, he had added 15 muscular pounds and became a legitimate power hitter, hitting .303/.366/.541 (126 OPS+) with 36 HR and 104 RBI and 355 TB, without sacrificing speed or defense. Five years and 25 pounds later, in 2005, he hit a career-high 51 HR with 128 RBI and finished a close second to Pujols for NL MVP but had to dive to make catches that he used to glide to easily. Although he still managed to win a Gold Glove (mostly on reputation), he had become a one-dimensional slugger who represented no threat on the bases. As his weight ballooned to 225 in his 30s, his hitting bottomed out and he could no longer play CF. The transformation from Ferrari to jalopy was complete.

Andruw Jones's 69.8 CVI ranks 11th in CF and at the 0.85 percentile overall, which should be good enough to put him in the HOF. However, the memory of the lumbering, overweight Andruw Jones of 2008-12 has eclipsed the more distant memory of the lithe defensive superstar of 1998-2006. After two years in which he barely exceeded the 5% needed to remain on the ballot, Jones's support rose to 19% in 2020 and 34% in 2021. Perhaps, the BBWAA's selective amnesia is clearing, and Jones will eventually get his due.

Beyond the Numbers

- Young Larry Jones acquired the nickname "Chipper" because Larry senior (a high school baseball coach) and his mother Lynne considered him a "chip off the old block."[40]

- Glavine was an ice hockey star in high school. He was drafted by the Los Angeles Kings in the fourth round of the 1984 NHL Entry Draft, ahead of future NHL Hall of Famers Brett Hull and Luc Robitaille.[41]

- Glavine is also remembered as the intelligent, articulate, and media-savvy Braves representative to the MLBPA, who was a prominent spokesperson during negotiations surrounding the 1994-95 strike.

- Smoltz's parents earned extra money as accordion teachers and playing at polka parties. John could play by age four and joined his parents and two younger siblings in the family business, winning prizes for his musicianship.[42]

- Smoltz received his big break when the Tigers, looking for immediate help in the 1987 pennant race, traded him to rebuilding Atlanta for 36-year-old journeyman SP Doyle Alexander. Although Alexander won nine consecutive games for the Tigers to help them win the AL East pennant and then won 14 more games for the second place Tigers in 1988, the Tigers would regret that trade for the next 15 years.

- Smoltz is one of 27 qualifying pitchers with more SO (3084) than hits allowed (3074).

Beyond the Numbers (cont'd)

- After his playing career ended, Smoltz became a first-rate broadcaster and a regular on Fox national baseball broadcasts, including the World Series. He is articulate and humorous with a natural easy style that wears well and will undoubtedly lead to a long and successful second career.

- Growing up in Curacao, Andruw Jones was a baseball prodigy who excelled at every position. At age 11, he played on a select team that traveled to Japan.[43] At age 13, he hit a mammoth 400-foot HR while playing on his father's team against adults. He later played on Curacao's national team in the Latin American games and was recognized as Curacao's best player by the age of 15. Although Curacao was off the beaten path for MLB scouts, the Braves signed him when he turned 16.

- After hitting only .217/.265/.443 in 113 PA in his first exposure to major league pitching at age 19, Andruw Jones's speed and defense earned him a spot on the Braves' 1996 postseason roster. By the start of the World Series, he was playing every day. In Game 1, he became the youngest player to hit a HR in the World Series and added another for good measure; the resulting 5 RBI powered the Braves to a 12-1 rout of Andy Pettitte. Although the Braves eventually fell to the Yankees 4-2, Jones hit .400/.500/.750 for the Series.

- Andruw Jones's 3.9 dWAR in 1998 is tied with Devon White (1992) for third among all OF, behind only Kevin Kiermaier (4.6 in 2015) and Darren Erstad (4.2 in 2002).

Killer Bs

Jeff Bagwell (1B):	**Craig Biggio (2B):**
87.8 CVI - Houston NL (*79.9*)	68.6 CVI - Houston NL (*65.5*)

Like many expansion teams, the Astros spent their first three decades mostly looking up from the bottom at their competitors, finishing first or second only four times in 32 years. Their postseason forays in 1980-81 and 1986 all ended in first-round defeats. That all changed in 1994, when the Astros began a 13-year run when they finished first or second every year but one (2000) and went to the playoffs six times. The "Killer Bs" Bagwell and Biggio were the heart of those winning teams. Unfortunately, brilliant as they were in regular season play, both struggled in the postseason:

Bagwell: .226/.364/.321, 2 HR, 13 RBI, 11 R, 32 TB in 129 PA

Biggio: .234/.295/.323, 2 HR, 11 RBI, 23 R, 54 TB, 2 SB in 185 PA

Thus, the Astros continued to falter in the playoffs. They did not win their first play-off series until 2004 when they upset Atlanta in the NLDS before falling to the Cardinals in the NLCS. When they finally reached the World Series in 2005, the White Sox swept them. The Astros would have to wait for a new generation of stars and a move to the AL to finally win the World Series in 2017, their 56th year of existence.

No trade in MLB's long history was more lopsided than the August 1990 deal sending minor league 3B prospect Jeff Bagwell from Boston to Houston for 37-year-old journeyman RP Larry Anderson. Anderson gave up 2 ER in 3 IP in Oakland's four-game sweep of the Red Sox in the ALCS, then left as a free agent, while Bagwell went on to become one of the NL's top 1B, and the best player in Astros history. From 1993-2001, Bagwell hit .308/.424/.581 (161 OPS+) and averaged 39 HR, 129 RBI, 128 R, 344 TB, 20 SB, and 6.5 WAR per 162 games. Bagwell's peak was over-shadowed by Mark McGwire's steroid-fueled home run show; he played in only four ASG and won only a single MVP award in 1994, when he hit .368/.451/.750 (213 OPS+) with 39 HR, 116 RBI, 104 R, 300 TB, 15 SB, and 8.2 WAR in a strike-short-ened season. If he had been able to play a full 162 games that season, he might have accrued 11-12 WAR and challenged Roger Maris's record of 61 HR.

Bagwell is somewhat controversial due to steroid rumors, which delayed his HOF election until his seventh year on the BBWAA ballot. Following the 1995 season, Bagwell undertook a rigorous weight-lifting regimen to build up his strength and prevent him from wearing down over the course of the summer.[44] His regimen involved eating lots of red meat and taking supplements like creatine (which was and still is legal) and androstenedione (a steroid precursor that was legally avail-able over the counter in 1995 but was banned in 1997). There is no evidence that Bagwell continued to use androstenedione after 1997 or that he went on to use injectable steroids; he never failed a drug test. It is also noteworthy that Bagwell's best season came in 1994 — before any body-building — that any performance bump he experienced in 1996 or thereafter can be attributed to avoiding the sea-son-ending hand injuries he suffered in 1993-95 (see WAR trajectory plot). Bag-well made nearly 30% more PA (699 versus 542 per season) in 1996-98 (the three years after starting his body-building regimen) than in 1993-95. When normalized to 162 games, his HR (38 v 36), RBI (126 v 129), R (119 v 119), TB (331 v 354), OPS+ (168 v 165), and WAR (6.7 v 7.4) were nearly the same after as before adding the extra muscle. Indeed, many of the "before" numbers were slightly better. It is also clear that Bagwell's overzealous workouts gradually damaged his right shoulder, eventually sapping his power and leaving him unable to throw, and almost certain-ly shortened his career. Therefore, I regard Bagwell's stats as legitimate and have not docked his CVI for using then-legal supplements. His 87.8 CVI ranks eighth at 1B and at the 0.45 percentile overall. He deserves his plaque in Cooperstown.

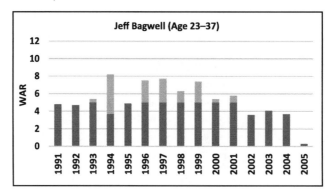

Seven-time All-Star Craig Biggio was the sparkplug leadoff hitter with speed (414 SB) and doubles power, who for 20 years set the table for Bagwell and the other Astros power bats. From 1991-99, he hit .299/.391/.451 (129 OPS+) and averaged 175 H, 15 HR, 67 RBI, 110 R, 38 2B, and 5.6 WAR in 686 PA. His 668 career doubles are the most for any right-handed batter in MLB history and the fifth best all-time. His 1844 R and 3060 H rank 15th and 25th on the career leaderboards. Biggio enjoyed his career year in 1997, posting 9.4 WAR (behind only NL MVP Larry Walker) and finishing fourth in the MVP voting. The following year, Biggio became the first player since Tris Speaker to hit 50 2B and steal 50 bases in a season. While Biggio was not known for sterling defense, he competently played two key up-the-middle positions – C and 2B – and won four Gold Gloves at 2B in 1994-97. His 68.6 CVI ranks 13th at 2B and at the 0.93 percentile overall.

Beyond the Numbers

- Bagwell's unique batting stance, in which he spread his feet far apart and seemed to sit on an imaginary chair, was instantly recognizable. Unfortunately, it left him unable to get away from pitches in on his hands and led to 128 HBP in his career, including season-ending broken hands and wrists in 1993-95.

- Although Bagwell made it to the 2005 World Series, his damaged right shoulder limited him to pinch hitting and DH duties. He retired after the World Series.

- Biggio had a close brush with death while playing 2B in a 1984 summer league game. Lightning struck the field and knocked Biggio and other players to the ground. The SS, who was standing only a few feet away from Biggio and was the only player on the team wearing metal cleats, was killed.[45]

- At Seton Hall, Biggio and teammates Martese Robinson and future Red Sox 1B Mo Vaughn became college baseball legends as the "Hit Men."[46] Seton Hall lost in regional play and did not make the College World Series.

- Biggio's son Cavan currently plays 3B, 2B, and OF for the Toronto Blue Jays and appears to be a rising star in the mold of his dad.

The Coors Effect

Larry Walker (RF):
75.7 CVI - Colorado NL (*48.3*),
Montreal NL (*21.1*)

Todd Helton (1B):
69.7 CVI - Colorado NL (*61.2*)

Since the NL expanded to the "mile-high city" in 1993, baseball writers and fans have been ambivalent on how to view stats accrued in the thin dry air of Denver. Rockies players — even guys like Vinny Castilla and Dante Bichette — seem to have no trouble getting selected to All-Star teams or receiving postseason honors as if their stats could be taken at face value, but when it comes to the HOF, genuinely great players like Walker and Helton are treated as suspect. CVI, which is based on ballpark-adjusted WAR, enables us to sort the wheat from the chaff.

Five-time All-Star and seven-time Gold Glover Larry Walker was a three-time batting champion, a first-rate slugger, and plus RF defender with a powerful arm, who played the majority of his career (9/17 years) for the Rockies. He ought not be conflated with the "Blake Street Bombers," the one-dimensional sluggers who would not have been stars in any other venue. Yes, Walker had some strong years for the Rockies, especially his 9.8-WAR MVP season in 1997, when he led the NL in OBP, SLG, TB, and HR and was the main reason the Rockies played in their first postseason. But before Denver, there was Montreal, where Walker hit .284/.359/.489 (130 OPS+) and averaged 20 HR, 76 RBI, 73 R, 19 SB, and 4.3 WAR in 527 PA in five full seasons. Not as gaudy as his .344/.438/.624 (152 OPS+) and 28 HR, 96 RBI, 102 R, and 5.8 WAR per season in Colorado's thin air in 1997-2003, but still excellent.

The other knock against Walker is that he had trouble staying healthy and averaged only 123 games and 498 PA over his 16 full seasons. That argument is illogical since he achieved his 72.7 career WAR *despite* his injuries; his WAR could only have been *higher* if he had been missed fewer games. Prorated, Walker's 24 HR, 82 RBI, and 84 R per season translate to 32 HR, 108 RBI, and 111 R per 162 games. Walker was a lifetime .313/.400/.565 hitter (141 OPS+), whose career SLG was higher than Wille Mays, Mickey Mantle, and Henry Aaron (to name a few). Walker's 75.7 CVI ranks 11th among RF and at the 0.66 percentile overall, putting him comfortably in HOF territory. He finally achieved HOF recognition in his 10th and final year on the BBWAA ballot.

As a five-time All-Star, three-time Gold Glove 1B, and a .316/.414/.539 lifetime hitter, who ranks in the all-time Top 40 in OBP, SLG, 2B, and BB, Helton would be a shoo-in for the HOF were it not for the fact that Coors Field was his home

Todd Helton, 2013

ballpark for his entire 17-year career. In his prime years (2000-04), Helton hit .349/.450/.643 (160 OPS+) and averaged 37 HR, 123 RBI, 125 R, 50 2B, 108 BB, and 366 TB. Despite the fact that WAR is ballpark-adjusted, he averaged 7.5 WAR per season and finished in the top five in WAR for NL position players all five years. Although he never finished higher than fifth in the MVP voting (which was monopolized by the steroid-enhanced version of Barry Bonds), he received the Henry Aaron Award as the NL's top hitter in 2000, when he won the NL batting championship (.372) and led the league with 8.9 WAR. Unfortunately, Helton's productivity was curtailed by a degenerative back condition, which began to sap his power in 2005 and reduced him to a part-timer in his mid-30s. The fact that most of his value was packed into the first half of his career makes his HOF case weaker than Walker's. Still, Helton's 69.7 CVI ranks 12th at 1B and at the 0.86 percentile overall, which ought to be good enough. His HOF support has increased from 16% to 29% to 45% in his first three years on the BBWAA ballot.

Beyond the Numbers

- Walker has now joined Ferguson Jenkins as the second Canadian in the HOF.

- Helton was a star high school quarterback but played behind Heath Shuler and Peyton Manning at the University of Tennessee. He and Manning remain good friends.[47]

- In 2005, Helton was the subject of false steroid rumors, based on a misconstrual of manager Don Baylor's advice to "get off the juice" in 1998. The "juice" in question was the legal body-building supplement creatine, not steroids. There is no evidence that Helton ever used steroids.[48]

Speed and Defense

Ichiro Suzuki (RF):	Kenny Lofton (CF):
81.9 CVI - Seattle AL (*56.2*)	70.6 CVI - Cleveland AL (*48.6*)

Suzuki and Lofton are two speedy OF who bucked the 3TO trend and the steroid-infused home run boom of their era. Neither really resembled the high-contact hitters of the Deadball Era or even of the Classical Era; both, especially Lofton, struck out far more often. Similarity scores suggest a strong resemblance to each other (831.4). Both players contributed elite defense and base-stealing skills, in addition to the ability to hit for high average.

Ichiro Suzuki is instantly recognizable by his first name alone, which means "most cheerful boy."[49] Ichiro's value was concentrated in high AVG and speed, with few walks and only a .091 ISO. When Ichiro arrived in Seattle after a nine-year career with Japan's Orix BlueWave as the first Japanese position player of any consequence to play in the major leagues, he was greeted with a mixture of anticipation, curiosity, and skepticism. He did not disappoint. In his first season, Ichiro hit .350/.381/.457 (126 OPS+), leading the AL in AVG and leading MLB in H (242), PA (738), AB (692), and SB (56), while posting 7.7 WAR. He also played in his first of 10 consecutive All-Star games and won his first of 10 consecutive Gold Gloves in RF. He was a near-unanimous AL Rookie of the Year selection (CC Sabathia got the only dissenting vote) and was named AL MVP for leading the Mariners to a record-tying 116 wins.

For a decade (2001-2010), Ichiro remained a perennial All-Star, Gold Glover, and MVP candidate, hitting .331/.376/.430 (117 OPS+) and averaging 224 H, 105 R, 38 SB, 291 TB, 0.6 dWAR, and 5.5 WAR. In his best season (2004), he collected 262 H to break George Sisler's 82-year-old record of 257 and posted a league-leading 9.2 WAR and 2.5 dWAR. I have adjusted Ichiro's CVI by the same method I used to adjust the CVI of the great Black players of the 1940s and early 1950s — Jackie Robinson, Roy Campanella, Minnie Minoso, Larry Doby — whose careers straddled the Negro League and the newly integrated MLB (see Appendix, Table A.5), although the circumstances of their delayed MLB debuts were of course very different.

In Ichiro's case, we have complete statistical records that document his greatness in Japan, rather than having to rely on anecdotes and incomplete newspaper archives as was necessary for the Negro League stars of the 1930s and 40s. Thus, we know that Ichiro's Japanese stats were similar to those from his prime seasons in Seattle, except for more HR in Japan. The adjustment raises Ichiro's CVI from 63.8 to 81.9 (see Appendix 2, Table A2.2). His combined 4367 hits (1278 in Japan and

Ichiro Suzuki, 2002

the 3089 in the US) is 111 more than Pete Rose's MLB record 4256 hits. In the US, Ichiro was a unique player and personality, whose example has opened the door for many other Asian players who have followed him to MLB and are making their own marks here. Ichiro's 81.9 adjusted CVI ranks eighth among RF and at the 0.55 percentile overall, which should make him a no-doubt Hall of Famer when his time comes in 2025.

Six-time All-Star CF Kenny Lofton is almost an afterthought when one remembers the 1990s, since he was overshadowed by Ken Griffey Jr., who was widely regarded as the best player in the AL. But Lofton was no slouch. He was an outstanding leadoff hitter and prolific base stealer and was the offensive sparkplug for the outstanding Indians teams of the 1990s. Lofton, unlike Ichiro, was willing to take a walk; his career OBP was 17 points higher than Ichiro's, despite Ichiro's 12-point edge in AVG. After establishing himself as Cleveland's starting CF at age 25, Lofton led the AL in SB for five consecutive years in 1992-96, during which he hit .316/.382/.437 (117 OPS+) and averaged 174 H, 108 R, 65 SB, 6.2 WAR and 1.6 dWAR. He won Gold Gloves in 1993-96 and was the AL's starting CF (over Griffey) in the 1995-96 ASG.

Lofton was a superb CF, ranking seventh among all OF in dWAR. Basically, he was a superior version of Lou Brock (one of his closest comps by similarity score), with about one-third (316) fewer SB (and 147 fewer CS), but with a higher OBP (.372 vs. .343) plus far better defense (+15.5 versus -16.8 dWAR). His WAR surpassed Brock's at virtually every stage of his career. Yet, unlike Brock, Lofton received little support from the BBWAA in his 2013 ballot debut, receiving a scant 18 votes (3.2%), too few to even remain on the ballot. One factor in his lack of HOF support may be that he bounced from team to team in the last six years of his career as a highly sought after "hired gun" for the pennant chase and playoffs. Indeed, Lofton played in 95 games for six different teams in 11 postseasons. Lofton's 70.6 CVI ranks 10th among CF and at the 0.82 percentile overall, which should be enough to earn HOF recognition. He will be eligible for consideration by the VC in 2023.

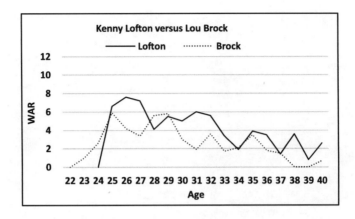

Beyond the Numbers

- When seven year-old Ichiro asked his father to help him become a baseball player, his father required him to commit to rigorous three-hour daily practice sessions year-round without exception. By the time he reached third grade, Ichiro could hit 65 mph pitches from a standard pitching machine. Three years later, he could hit the maximum 80 mph pitches and had to move in closer to challenge himself. When Ichiro was in high school, his father told the coach never to praise him or tinker with his swing.[50]

- In Japan, Ichiro's serene temperament earned him the nicknames "spaceman" and "no-weather" from his teammates. In a research project, the local university measured his brainwaves on the eve of a big tournament and gave him a 91% "super-serene" rating.[51]

- Lofton grew up in the slums of East Chicago. He was abandoned by his mother as an infant and raised by his grandmother Rosie Persons, who was disabled by glaucoma but managed to support her family on her deceased husband's social security.[52]

- Although he stood only 6' tall, Lofton could execute a 360-degree turnaround slam dunk. He was the back-up point guard on a University of Arizona team that went to the Final Four as a freshman and the starting point guard on their Sweet 16 team as a sophomore.[55]

- Lofton now operates his own television production company FilmPool, Inc. He has also made several TV guest appearances and co-wrote the Ruben Studdard song "What If" for the 2006 *Soulful* album.[56]

Infield Stars

Chase Utley (2B):
76.3 CVI - Philadelphia NL (*62.0*)

Scott Rolen (3B):
70.8 CVI - Philadelphia NL (*29.2*),
St. Louis NL (*25.9*), Cincinnati NL (*7.6*),
Toronto AL (*7.4*)

Barry Larkin (SS):
70.4 CVI - Cincinnati NL (*70.5*)

Roberto Alomar (2B):
67.7 CVI - Toronto AL (*22.3*),
Cleveland AL (*20.3*), Baltimore AL (*12.5*),
San Diego NL (*12.2*)

Four other HOF-caliber infielders — Utley, Rolen, Larkin, and Alomar — emerged from the Steroid Era; none was associated with steroids. All were outstanding defenders and key players on championship teams.

Six-time All-Star Chase Utley was the best position player on a Phillies team that appeared in consecutive World Series in 2008-09 (and won it in 2008). In his six-year prime (2005-10), Utley hit .298/.388/.523 (133 OPS+) and averaged 27 HR, 95 RBI, 105 R, 2.4 dWAR, and 7.6 WAR per season, quite remarkable for a 2B. Unfortunately, he was stuck behind Placido Polanco early in his career and did not get the opportunity to play every day until he was 26. He also began to decline at age 32, although he remained moderately productive until age 35. Thus, he fell far short of the career milestones (like 3000 hits) that most impress Hall of Fame voters. Still, his OPS+ in his prime was higher than the career OPS+ of Morgan, Robinson, Gehringer, and Carew. His 18.3 dWAR ranks tied for ninth among all 2B, but he never won a Gold Glove or finished better than seventh in the MVP voting. His career WAR trajectory resembles that of Bobby Grich, but with a three-year delay. (The two 2B have an 882.6 similarity score.) However, Utley (unlike Grich) has a World Series ring. Although Utley's 76.3 CVI ranks ninth at 2B (ahead of Hall of Famers Sandburg and Frisch) and at the 0.63 percentile overall, his path to the HOF may not be easy.

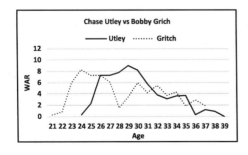

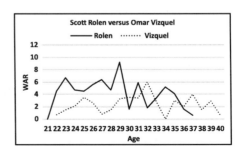

There is no better illustration of the ridiculous disparity in how HOF voters value defense at 3B and at SS than to compare two outstanding defensive players, 3B Scott Rolen and SS Omar Vizquel, who debuted on the BBWAA HOF ballot together in 2018. Rolen's 21.2 career dWAR ranks sixth among all 3B, while Vizquel's 29.5 career dWAR ranks seventh among all SS. The 8.3-win difference mostly reflects Vizquel's longevity and the larger positional bonus dWAR gives to SS than 3B. Both players were Gold Glovers in their heyday — Rolen with eight in 17 years and Vizquel with 11 in 24 years. But Rolen was the far superior hitter. Rolen beats Vizquel 122 to 82 in OPS+, 70.1 to 45.6 in WAR, and 70.8 to 39.1 in CVI. His WAR trajectory plot shows Rolen to be vastly superior in every season through age 29, and roughly equal to Vizquel in his 30s, when he was beset with injuries. From 1997-2004, Rolen hit .287/.379/.524 (133 OPS+) and averaged 28 HR, 102 RBI, 96 R, 36 2B, 279 TB, and 5.8 WAR in 622 PA per season, including winning unanimous Rookie of the Year honors in 1997. Rolen also played in seven ASG (four as a starter), while Vizquel played in only three ASG (none as a starter). Certainly, Vizquel's agility and panache at SS were appealing, but Rolen was undoubtedly the superior all-around player.

Yet somehow, BBWAA voters were slow to warm to Rolen, giving him less than 20% support in 2018-19 — less than half of Vizquel's support. Their primary knock against him is that after tearing the labrum in his left shoulder in 2005, recurring shoulder issues held Rolen to only 108 games per season in 2007-12 and sapped his power even when he played. Still, Rolen's 70.8 CVI ranks Rolen ninth at 3B and at the 0.80 percentile overall, which should make him a solid Hall of Famer. In 2020, Rolen's BBWAA support doubled to 35%, but was still 17% below Vizquel. However, Rolen's support shot up to 53% in 2021 inching ahead of Vizquel and on track to. reach 75% in the next few years.

Barry Larkin, a 12-time All-Star, three-time Gold Glove winner, and 1995 MVP, was a Reds fixture for 19 years. He did everything well but had no single outstanding attribute. He played in the shadow of AL superstars like Ripken in the first half of his career and A-Rod and Jeter in the second half of his career but had the NL to himself. From 1988-99, Larkin hit .304/.383/.461 (126 OPS+) and averaged 13 HR, 61 RBI, 81 R, 26 SB, 5.3 WAR, and 1.2 dWAR.

Larkin stole as many as 51 bases in 1995, his MVP year, and hit as many as 33 HR in 1996, his best overall season by WAR (7.2). He was the star and team leader of the 1990 Reds who swept the heavily favored Oakland Athletics in the World Series. Larkin hit .353/.421/.529 in that World Series and started the two-run eighth inning rally that won the clincher. He was strong on defense (14.4 dWAR) and an above average hitter for a SS (116 OPS+). His career was similar to Alan Trammell, his predecessor by a decade, who played 20 years in another midwestern city (Detroit), but Larkin succeeded with the BBWAA voters, while Trammell had to wait for the VC to elect him to the HOF. Larkin 70.4 CVI ranks 16th at SS and at the 0.83 percentile overall.

Twelve-time All-Star Roberto Alomar was widely regarded as MLB's best 2B of the 1990s. Although his so-so 3.3 career dWAR does not agree with the "eye test," he had great range and versatility in the field and won 10 Gold Gloves between 1991 and 2001. There is no doubt that he was a strong hitter with extra-base power, an outstanding baserunner, and a leader of two World Series champions in Toronto and several postseason contenders in Baltimore and Cleveland. He played in 12 consecutive ASG from 1990-2001, including nine times as the AL starter at 2B. He was on his way to finishing among the top 10 2B of all time when his skills evaporated virtually overnight at age 34.

Alomar's two signature seasons came in 1992-93 with the Blue Jays, who acquired him in the blockbuster trade that also brought Joe Carter to Toronto and sent Fred McGriff and Tony Fernandez to San Diego. Alomar hit .318/.406/.460 (136 OPS+) and averaged 12 HR, 84 RBI, 107 R, 52 SB, and 6.4 WAR. He also hit a composite .354/.418/.495 with 2 HR, 14 RBI, 15 R, and 16 SB in 110 PA over 24 games in four winning postseason series; he was named MVP of the 1992 ALCS. Alomar also starred with the playoff-contending Orioles in 1996-98 and Indians in 1999-2001, where he compiled 20.3 WAR in three years. Alomar fell barely short of election to the HOF in his BBWAA ballot debut but won election in his second try in 2011 with 90% of the votes. As ex-Orioles teammate BJ Surhoff said, "Robbie could beat you with the bunt, with the extra base, with the homer. He could beat you with a stolen base. He could beat you by going from first to third, a base running move. He could beat you by making plays in the field. Robbie's a baseball player. And a damn good one at that."[55] Alomar's 67.7 CVI ranks 14th at 2B and at the 0.95 percentile overall.

Beyond the Numbers

- Utley was an outstanding postseason player with the Phillies in 2007-11, hitting .279/.377/.532 with 10 HR, 25 RBI, 38 R, and 10 SB in 204 PA, including a pivotal HR in Game 3 of the 2008 World Series win over the Rays and 3 HR off CC Sabathia in the 2009 World Series loss to the Yankees. However, in his 54 postseason PA with the Dodgers in 2015-17, he got only four singles and five walks and was hitless in his last 33 AB.

- Rolen was an inconsistent postseason performer. In 2004 with the Cardinals, he went a combined 0-for-27 in the NLDS and World Series, sandwiched around an outstanding NLCS in which he hit .310/.355/.690 with 3 HR (including game-winners in Games 2 and 7), 6 RBI, and 6 R.

Beyond the Numbers (cont'd)

- Larkin attended Cincinnati's Archbishop Moeller High School (1982), the school that gave us Buddy Bell (1969) and Ken Griffey Jr. (1987).[56] His son Shane played in the NBA in 2013-18.

- Alomar's father Sandy Sr. was a utility infielder and major league coach for many years. His oldest brother, Sandy Jr., was an All-Star major league catcher and Roberto's teammate with the Padres and Indians.

- In the last game of the 1996 season, Alomar's reputation suffered when he spat in the face home plate of umpire John Hirschbeck after hearing what he perceived as a racial slur during an argument.[57] Alomar received a five-game suspension but was allowed to participate in the postseason and to serve his suspension at the start of the 1997 season. Alomar immediately apologized to Hirschbeck and even donated $50,000 to ALS research in honor of Hirschbeck's afflicted son, and the two men eventually became friends. However, the incident probably delayed Alomar's HOF election.

Close Calls – Pitchers

David Cone (SP):
70.0 CVI - New York AL (*20.2*) New York NL (*20.2*), Kansas City AL (*14.0*)

Kevin Brown (SP):
67.0 CVI - Los Angeles NL (*19.7*), Texas AL (*17.7*), Florida NL (*14.6*), San Diego NL (*9.1*)

Kevin Appier (SP):
63.7 CVI – Kansas City AL (*47.0*)

CC Sabathia (SP):
63.4 CVI - New York AL (*29.3*), Cleveland AL (*28.0*)

Johan Santana (SP):
62.6 CVI – Minnesota AL (*36.0*), New York NL (*15.7*)

Andy Pettitte (SP):
60.1 CVI – New York AL (*51.1*), Houston NL (*9.0*)

Trevor Hoffman (RP):
56.2 CVI – San Diego NL (*25.8*)

These seven CVS-Plus players all have borderline HOF credentials. Of the six who are HOF-eligible, only Hoffman has been elected, although Pettitte remains a viable candidate after receiving 11.5% and 13.7% of the vote in his first two years on the BBWAA ballot. None of the other four eligible players mustered as many as 4% of the BBWAA votes; all fell off the ballot in one year.

At 6'1 and 180 pounds, the boyish looking David Cone did not conform to anyone's image of a power pitcher, but that is exactly what he was. His 34.2% 3TO and 1.065 SO/H rank 15th and 16th, respectively, among all qualifying pitchers. Cone had short stretches of brilliance but could not sustain them long enough to win BBWAA votes. In 1993-95, Cone was absolutely superb, posting a 3.31 ERA (143 ERA+) and 1.200 WHIP with three different teams while averaging 15-9, with 171 SO and 7.0 WAR_p per season, despite the strike, which wiped out the last third of the 1994 and first tenth of the 1995 season. He won the AL Cy Young award in 1994. Cone also posted 20-win seasons ten years apart (an MLB record) in 1988 (5.5 WAR_p) and 1998 (4.0 WAR_p). He pitched a perfect game against the Expos in July 1999. Cone was also a highly sought after "hired gun" for playoff contenders, going 8-3 in eight postseasons for the Yankees (6), Mets (1) and Blue Jays (1) and winning five World Series rings. What kept him from being regarded as a Hall of Famer was a series of injuries that (along with the 1994 strike) limited him to only eight seasons (out of 18) with 200 or more IP. So, Cone fell short of career milestones — 3000 IP, 3000 SO, 200 W — that might have won him HOF support. Still, Cone's 70.0 CVI, which ranks 48th among SP (just behind Koufax) and at the 0.85 percentile overall, is worthy of the HOF. Although Cone received only 3.9 % of the BBWAA votes in 2009 and dropped off the HOF ballot, the VC should give him serious consideration.

David Cone

Kevin Brown, who featured prominently in the Mitchell Report, was a confirmed PED user. Taciturn and often surly with reporters, Brown may have been unlikeable, but to give him his due, the six-time All-Star with a hard sinking fastball won 211 games and compiled a 3.28 ERA over 19 years, facing sluggers who probably benefited more than he did from PED. Playing for seven teams in both leagues gave him the opportunity to become one of only 18 pitchers to beat all 30 major league teams. Although his steroid use probably dates back to the early 1990s with Texas, Brown was no better than a solid mid-rotation starter with a 3.38 ERA (111 ERA+) and 1.340 WHIP who averaged 12-10, 120 SO, and 3.1 WAR_p per season in 1989-95. But in 1996-2000 with the Marlins, Padres, and Dodgers, Brown posted a 2.51 ERA (164 ERA+) and 1.051 WHIP and averaged 16-8 with 212 SO and 7.3 WAR_p per season. He finished second in the NL Cy Young award voting in 1996 and third in 1998, when he was named the Sporting News Pitcher of the Year. Although applying the 10% discount to his annual WAR_p drops his CVI from 78.6 to

67.0, CVI still ranks him 57th among SP and at the 0.99 percentile overall. However, the steroid adjustment is hardly exact science, and there is no reason to fault BB-WAA voters for summarily dismissing him from HOF ballot in 2011 with only 2.1% of the votes or to urge the VC to reconsider his candidacy in 2021.

Kevin Appier is virtually a forgotten man after getting only a single BBWAA vote in 2011 and dropping off the ballot. However he did have two truly great seasons in Kansas City in 1992 (8.0 WAR_p) and 1993 (9.3 WAR_p) and averaged 13-9 with a 3.22 ERA (140 ERA+), a 1.215 WHIP, and 5.8 WAR_p per season in 1990-97 for some lackluster Royals teams. However, he won only 169 games, played in only one ASG, and was mediocre (5.34 ERA) in two postseasons with Oakland and Anaheim when he was past his prime. He never won a Cy Young award but did finish third in 1993 (when he led the AL in ERA and WAR_p). Although his 63.7 CVI (1.10 percentile) is good enough to put him in the HOF conversation, he probably falls a bit short.

Sabathia, who retired in 2019 and is not yet HOF-eligible, is a six-time All-Star and 2007 AL Cy Young award winner, who was a fixture among the top AL pitchers (though rarely the best) in his prime. From 2006-2011, Sabathia posted a 3.09 ERA (142 ERA+) and 1.163 WHIP and averaged 19-8 with 217 SO and 5.8 WAR_p per season. One highlight of Sabathia's career was going 11-2 with a 1.65 ERA to help Milwaukee win the NL Central pennant after a July 2008 trade from Cleveland. Unfortunately, he was done in by a 5-run second inning in a Game 2 loss to Philadelphia in the NLDS, as Milwaukee made a quick exit. However, Sabathia's in-season excellence earned him a rich free agent contract with the Yankees in 2009 and an opportunity to redeem himself in the 2009 postseason by going 3-1 with a 1.98 ERA in the Yankees run to the World Series championship, winning ALCS MVP honors along the way. Sabathia's 63.4 CVI ranks 65th among SP and at the 1.12 percentile overall. Among the seven HOF-eligible post-1900 SP with CVI between 60 and 65, only Ruffing (273 W) and Wynn (300 W) are in the HOF; Tiant (229 W), Appier (169 W), Stieb (166 W), Santana (139 W), are not, and Pettitte (256 W) is in his third year on the BBWAA ballot. The fact that Sabathia has 251 W and 3093 SO could make him a viable HOF candidate in 2026.

Johan Santana, who garnered only 2.4% is his one chance on the 2018 BBWAA ballot, pitched like a Hall of Famer for five years before shoulder problems diminished his effectiveness and then ended his career. In those five magical years (2004-08), he was arguably MLB's best SP, averaging 17-8 with a 2.82 ERA (157 ERA+), a 1.022 WHIP, 238 SO, and 7.1 WAR_p in 229 IP. He was a four-time All-Star and won the Cy Young award as well as leading MLB in WAR_p in 2004 and 2006. However, he only had only two other 4-WAR seasons as a SP, so his reign was brief. He also pitched the Mets' first no-hitter on June 1, 2012, when he had almost nothing left. His 1.158 SO/H ranks 10th among qualifying pitchers. However, he finished with only 139 W, which puts him 11 wins below two other Hall of Famers with brief but spectacular careers, Sandy Koufax and Dizzy Dean. Santana's 62.6 CVI ranks only at the 1.16 percentile, not as good as Koufax but better than Dean. Although Santana lacked longevity and would have fewer wins than any SP in the HOF, the VC should give him another look when his name comes up again in several years.

Andy Pettitte's strongest HOF credentials are his 256 career wins and his prolific postseason resume. However, although Pettitte leads all MLB pitchers in postseason wins (19) and IP (276.7), his postseason performance — 19-11, 3.81 ERA, 1.305 WHIP — is notable more for quantity than quality. Throughout his 19-year career, he was rarely viewed as one of the AL's top pitchers, playing in only three ASG and only three times exceeding 5.0 WAR_p. He was a serious Cy Young award contender only in 1996, when he finished a close second to Pat Hentgen. His 3.85 ERA (117 ERA+) would be the second highest in the HOF (behind Morris) were he elected. Pettitte's 60.1 CVI places him at the 1.22 percentile, a little short of HOF territory. His dalliance with HGH to help him recover from a 2002 hip injury may hurt his HOF prospects (unfairly, I think). Pettitte received 11% of the votes in his second year on the BBWAA ballot.

Trevor Hoffman's ranks second to Mariano Rivera with 601 saves, but his 56.2 CVI (1.36 percentile) puts him far closer to Lindy McDaniel in the HOVG category than to the great Rivera. His 28.1 WAR_p in 4388 BF in his career, is not even close to Mariano Rivera or even Gossage or Eckersley. On the other hand, while I attach little importance to saves, Hoffman also ranks high on several other career leaderboards with 6.99 H9, 1.058 WHIP, 9.36 SO9, 141 ERA+, which affirm that Hoffman really was among the best in his role. He pitched reasonably well (4 Saves and a 3.46 ERA) in four postseasons with the Padres, although he gave up 2 ER in 2 IP in his only World Series. He is a two-time winner of the NL Rolaids Relief award, which is now named after him. Recognizing the limitations of CVI as a metric for RP, I have no serious problem with Hoffman's inclusion at the low end of the HOF.

Beyond the Numbers

- In spring 1987, the day after Cone had been told he had earned a spot on their major league roster, the Royals traded him to the defending World Series Champion Mets for catcher Ed Hearn. It was probably the worst trade the Royals ever made.[58]

- Cone's HOF candidacy may have been damaged by serious but unsubstantiated allegations of some unsavory off-field allegations, which brought him unwanted notoriety at the time.[59]

- Cone was a vocal leader in the MLBPA during the strike and was one of the prime movers in obtaining an injunction from Judge Sonia Sotomayor against the use of replacement players in 1995.

Beyond the Numbers (cont'd)

- Since 2008, Cone has been a part-time Yankee color commentator on the Yes Network, and has developed a reputation for being sophisticated, outspoken, and funny.

- Brown was not a particularly strong postseason pitcher (5-5 with a 4.19 ERA and 1.310 WHIP in 81.2 IP), but his outstanding performance in the 1998 NLDS and NLCS helped the Padres reach the World Series.

Close Calls – Hitters

Jim Edmonds (CF):
61.0 CVI - St. Louis NL (*37.9*),
California/Anaheim AL (*20.5*)

Bobby Abreu (RF):
59.8 CVI – Philadelphia NL (*47.2*),
New York AL (*7.0*), Los Angeles AL (*6.4*)

Vladimir Guerrero (RF):
58.6 CVI – Montreal NL (*34.7*),
Los Angeles AL (*22.8*)

Gary Sheffield (RF):
57.2 CVI – Los Angeles NL (*17.0*),
Florida NL (*13.2*), Atlanta NL (*11.2*),
New York AL (*8.7*)

Manny Ramirez (LF):
54.3 CVI – Boston AL (*33.2*),
Cleveland (*30.0*), Los Angeles NL (*6.3*)

The five OF in this grouping include one Hall of Famer (Guerrero), one who dropped off the BBWAA ballot after receiving only 2.5% of the vote in his first year (Edmonds), and three who are still under active consideration by the BBWAA.

Notwithstanding his summary dismissal by the BBWAA, Jim Edmonds has the highest CVI of the lot, mainly because he was the only one with defensive as well as offensive value. Edmonds was a four-time All-Star 3TO slugger with 132 OPS+ and a penchant for making the highlight reels in CF. While he was not the slugger that Manny and Vlad were, his .527 SLG was higher than Sheffield's or Abreu's. His 40% 3TO and 0.89 SO/H both rank 11th among all qualifying hitters. Unlike most 3TO sluggers, he is best remembered for his eyepopping catches in CF. He had 7.8 dWAR through age 35, but fell back to 6.4 in his late 30s as he slowed down and played more 1B. Edmonds excelled in seven postseasons, hitting .274/.361/.513 with 13 HR, 42 RBI, 33 R, and 118 TB in 263 PA, including the Cardinals' 2006 World Series championship. His 61.0 CVI ranks 13th in CF and at the 1.18 percentile overall. He is a close call for the HOF, but I think his defense and postseason resume put him over the threshold. He will be eligible for VC consideration in 2026.

Bobby Abreu had outstanding on-base skills and ranks surprisingly high with 59.8 CVI, 20th in RF and at the 1.22 percentile overall. The Tampa Bay Devil Rays stole him from Houston in the 1997 expansion draft but passed him along to the Phillies in a lopsided trade for a nondescript SS named Kevin Stocker. He quickly became a star with the Phillies, hitting .308/.416/.525 (143 OPS+) and averaging 23 HR, 92 RBI, 104 R, and 5.9 WAR in 1998-2004. Although he could not sustain this performance level into his 30s, he continued to provide solid production for the Phillies, Yankees, and Angels through age 37. Abreu hit .284/.392/.418 in 79 PA in four postseasons with the Astros, Yankees, and Angels, but his teams never advanced to the World Series. On the downside, Abreu played in only two ASG, never had >6.5 WAR, and was a subpar defender (-10.9 dWAR). Although it is a close call, I would put Abreu in the HOVG category, rather than the HOF. He received only 5.5% of the BBWAA vote in his 2020 ballot debut but improved to 8.7% in 2021.

Vladimir Guerrero, a nine-time All-Star, was universally regarded as one of the top young players in baseball, with power, speed, and a cannon arm in RF. He hit .328/.395/.600 (153 OPS+) and averaged 37 HR, 112 RBI, 103 R, 19 SB, and 5.5 WAR in 1998-2004. He was a notorious free swinger, but still managed 48 BB per 600 PA. But Olympic Park's unforgiving artificial turf wrecked his knees and turned him into a one-dimensional slugger. He moved to Anaheim in 2004 and won an MVP award, moved to DH at age 33, and was finished at age 36. Despite his speed and powerful arm, he was never a plus defender and finished with -10.0 dWAR. His 58.6 CVI ranks 21st in RF (just behind Abreu) and at the 1.25 percentile overall. I am not convinced that he was quite good enough to be a Hall of Famer, but the BBWAA was convinced and elected him on the second ballot. His son Vlad Jr, who broke in with Toronto in 2019, has become one of MLB's biggest stars.

Sheffield and Ramirez were HOF-quality sluggers, but their candidacies have been badly damaged by their steroid history. Sheffield's steroid involvement when he trained with Barry Bonds in 2002 may have been inadvertent. I docked his CVI only for that single season; this adjustment reduced his CVI only from 57.9 to 57.2 It is his atrocious defense (-27.7 dWAR) more than this small steroid adjustment that puts him in HOVG territory. Still, the HOF includes several one-dimensional sluggers with CVI in the mid-50s (Killebrew, Stargell, Kiner), so it would not be that surprising to see Sheffield get in. He received 41% of the BBWAA vote in 2021, his seventh year on the BBWAA ballot.

Manny Ramirez had a reputation for being "flaky" and for being a run-producing machine with 555 HR, 1831 RBI, 1544 R, and a 154 OPS+ in his 19-year career. He was a key contributor to four pennant-winning teams in Cleveland and Boston, including the curse-breaking 2004 Red Sox 2004 World Series champions and another Red Sox championship in 2007. He was also a terrific postseason performer (though not quite as good as Ortiz), hitting .285/.394/.544 with 29 HR, 78 RBI, and 67 R in 493 PA. Although poor defense (-21.7 dWAR) held his unadjusted

CVI to 64.7, that would certainly have been enough to put him in the HOF. Unfortunately, two late-career steroid busts lowered his CVI to 54.3 and ruined his HOF prospects. I really have no idea when Ramirez started using steroids or how much they may have inflated his stats. Since I did not cut his CVI by the maximum amount, he may not even belong in the CVI-Plus category. Ramirez received 28% of the BBWAA vote in 2021, his fifth year on the ballot. If Bonds and Clemens can't get elected, I don't see it happening for Manny.

Hall of the Very Good

Tim Hudson (SP):
57.0 CVI – Oakland AL (*30.9*),
Atlanta NL (*25.7*)

Felix Hernandez (SP):
56.9 CVI – Seattle AL (*50.1*)

John Olerud (1B):
56.8 CVI – Toronto (*22.6*), New York NL
(*17.3*), Seattle (*17.1*)

Mark Buehrle (SP):
56.0 CVI – Chicago AL (48.7)

Kenny Rogers (SP):
55.2 CVI – Texas AL(*31.4*), Oakland (*9.2*)

Roy Oswalt (SP):
55.1 CVI – Houston NL (*46.2*)

Dustin Pedroia (2B):
53.9 CVI – Boston AL (*51.6*)

Nomar Garciaparra (SS):
53.8 CVI – Boston AL (*41.2*)

This grouping contains eight CVI-Plus players, four SP and four hitters. Six (all but Hernandez and Pedroia) are HOF-eligible. Buehrle and Hudson got 11.0% and 5.2% of the votes, respectively, in their 2021 BBWAA ballot debuts; the others were dropped from the BBWAA ballot after failing to garner 5% of the vote in their first year of eligibility. All were very good players, but none is likely ever to be elected to the HOF. A few brief capsule comments on each player will follow.

Hudson, a four-time all-star, accrued 14.6 WAR_p for the 2002-03 Oakland A's "moneyball" teams and another 5.8 WAR_p for the 2010 Braves in the course of his 17-year career. Although he may have been less heralded than A's teammates Mark Mulder and Barry Zito, it was Hudson who had the best career.

Six-time all-star Felix Hernandez burst out of the gate as a 19-year old to amass 49.9 WAR_p in Seattle by the age of 29, including a 7.2-WAR_p season in 2010 at age 24. But "King Felix" hit the wall at age 30 and has accrued only 0.4 WAR_p in the past five injury-plagued seasons. After opting out of his 2020 minor league contract with the Braves due to the Covid-19 pandemic and being cut by the Orioles in Spring 2001, he now finds himself looking for a job. His CVI is stuck at 56.9; a comeback seems unlikely.

John Olerud was a slick 1B with solid on-base skills but modest power (15-25 HR). He had five 5-WAR seasons, topped by 8.0 WAR in 1993 and 7.6 WAR in 1998, but played in only two all-star games and was never viewed as an elite player. He will become eligible for consideration by the VC in 2021.

Five-time all-star Mark Buehrle was a strong mid-rotation SP who was valued for his consistency, rather than star quality, as he won 10-19 games without fail for 15 consecutive years from 2001-15. His 214 career wins included a perfect game against the Rays on May 9, 2010. Other highlights of his career included a 16-win 4.8 WAR_p season in 2005, when he finished fourth in the Cy Young Award voting and the White Sox won their first World Series since 1917. Buehrle was also celebrated for his fielding prowess and led all AL pitchers five times in assists and four times in fielding percentage. Buerle may not be a Hall of Famer, but he certainly is well-qualified for the HOVG.

Four-time all-star Kenny Rogers received only one vote in his 2014 appearance on the BBWAA ballot, but was a steady and versatile performer in starting and bullpen roles for 20 years. He was never viewed as an ace but won 16-19 games five times, including a 16-win, 7.5 WAR_p season with Oakland in 1998. He postseason record was mixed. He pitched brilliantly in the 2006 Tigers World Series run, yielding no runs and 9 hits in 23 IP while winning his three starts in the ALDS, ALCS, and World Series. On the other hand, he was terrible for the 1996 Yankees, who won the World Series Championship despite him. Rogers is not a Hall of Famer, but had a very good career.

For eight years (2001-08), three-time all-star Roy Oswalt was the ace of a very good Astros team that won several division titles and made it all the way to the 2005 World Series. During that period, he never posted less than 3.9 or more than 7.0 WAR_p in any season, averaging 5.1. Oswalt's career faded after age 30, leaving him with 163 wins and a 55.1 CVI, not good enough for the HOF. He received only four votes (0.9%) in his only appearance on the BBWAA ballot.

Four-time all-star Dustin Pedroia was a top-notch 2B who was on a possible HOF trajectory until severe knee problems began to hobble him at age 32 in 2017. However, from 2007-2016 he averaged 5.1 WAR per year, including a 6.9-WAR MVP season in 2008 and an 8.0 WAR season in 2011. He was a key contributor to the Red Sox 2007 and 2013 World Series championship teams, although he hit only .233/.313/.374 in postseason action. He was as strong on defense (15.3 dWAR and four Gold Gloves) as at bat. Indeed Pedroia's dWAR ranks 17th among all 2B, despite playing 100 games or more in only nine seasons. Still, he falls well short of the HOF.

Nomar Garicaparra debuted in 1996 as one of the trio of brilliant young SS (along with A-Rod and Jeter), who would soon take the baton from Cal Ripken and dominate the SS position for the next decade. Unfortunately, injuries would derail Garciaparra's career before he could fully realize that potential. But we should not forget that (except for missing most of the 2001 season, Garciaparra was among MLB's superstars, hitting .325/.372/.557 and averaging 31 HR, 117 RBI, 121 R, 6.6 WAR, and 1.6 dWAR per 162 games from 1997-2003. During this time, he won the 1997 Rookie of the Year award, played in five all-star games, and finished in the top 11 of the MVP voting six times (including a second place finish in 1998). Unfortunately, injuries kept Garciaparra from sustaining this elite performance level into his 30s, and he was finished by age 35. After he received 5.5% of the vote in his 2015 ballot debut, the BBWAA dismissed him from further consideration in 2016.

Still on the Ballot

Since there are not yet any CVI-Minus Hall of Famers from the Steroid Era, I have instead listed the five most notable CVI-Minus players on the 2021 BBWAA ballot (Table 8.4). Some brief comments on their HOF candidacy will follow.

Table 8.4: Notable CVI-Minus Players on the 2021 BBWAA HOF Ballot

A) Players (Position)	MidCareer	2021 Vote (Yr)	AVG/OBP/SLG	OPS+	WAR_{II}	CVI
Kent, Jeff (2B)	2000	32.4% (8)	.290/.356/.500	123	55.4	51.5
Sosa, Sammy (RF)	1999	17.0% (9)	.252/.311/.468	128	58.6	44.2
Hunter, Torii (CF)	2007	9.5% (1)	.277/.331/.461	110	50.7	42.6
Vizquel, Omar (SS)	1998	49.1% (4)	.272/.336/.352	82	45.6	39.1
B) Pitchers	MidCareer	2020 Vote (Yr)	ERA/WHIP	ERA+	WAR_p	CVI
Wagner, Billy (RP)	2003	46.4% (6)	2.53/0.998	187	27.8	46.5

Jeff Kent has drawn modest HOF support because his excellent offensive stats – particularly his 377 HR, 1518 RBI, and 1320 R – are so outstanding *for a 2B*, even in a high-offense era. This argument is predicated on the belief that 2B is such an important defensive position that one should apply a lower HOF standard for offensive stats at this position. So even if no one is clamoring to put 3B Matt Williams in the HOF based on his 378 HR, **Kent**'s 377 HR as a 2B are seen as more special. The problem with this argument is that **Kent** (who began his career at 3B) was never a very good 2B (-0.1 dWAR). His modest 51.5 CVI reflects that fact. Also, his seven 100-RBI seasons in 1997-2004 must be viewed the context that he was hitting behind Barry Bonds, who reached base 255 times per year (or 42% of his PA), *not counting HR*. People who inflate the value of **Kent**'s offensive stats because he played 2B but ignore his defensive weakness at that position are trying to have it both ways. I am willing to give Joe Gordon extra credit for his power numbers at 2B because he was a superlative defensive 2B. But **Kent**? Not so much.

Taken at face value, **Sammy Sosa**'s 609 career HR (9th), including three 60+ HR seasons with an MVP trophy in 1998, would have made him a HOF shoo-in. However, it is abundantly clear that **Sosa** owes his success to steroids, even though he was never actually caught red-handed. MLB did not have drug testing during Sosa's 10-year peak in 1993-2002, when he hit .288/.362/.583 (143 OPS+) and averaged 46 HR, 121 RBI, 104 R, and 5.4 WAR per season. Before 1993, **Sosa** was a skinny free-swinging speedster (like a young Lou Brock) who had almost twice as many SB (67) as HR (37). After 1993, he bulked up and transformed into a lumbering slugger. In 2003, when MLB put its anonymous drug testing protocol in place, the 34 year-old **Sosa**'s WAR dropped to 2.7 (although he still hit 40 HR); he continued to decline rapidly in his few remaining years. Perhaps he decided to stop steroids when testing began, or perhaps he just got old. The steroid adjustment knocks **Sosa**'s CVI down from 63.1 (around the 1.13 percentile) to 44.2 (outside the top 2%).

Torii Hunter, who debuted on the BBWAA ballot in 2021, was a good and popular player, who mixed speed, great defense, and timely hitting for 19 years with the Twins, Angels, and Tigers. Although he is widely respected and may have a managerial or front office career ahead of him, I see him as an unlikely HOF candidate.

Billy Wagner

Although **Omar Vizquel**'s CVI is even lower than **Hunter**'s, there is ample precedent for a great-field-no-hit SS to reach the HOF, going all the way back to Joe Tinker and Rabbit Maranville. Of course, that does not make it right. **Vizquel**'s 29.5 dWAR ranks seventh among all SS, but his 82 OPS+ is well below Ozzie Smith's 88 (74.3 CVI) and would tie Aparicio (46.3 CVI) and Maranville (40.9 CVI) – his two closest comps by similarity score — as the worst OPS+ in the HOF if he were elected. **Vizquel** was never elected to start an All-Star game and only once (1999) received an MVP vote. His support rose rapidly from 37% to 53% in his first three years on the 2020 BBWAA ballot but fell slightly to 49% in 2021, perhaps because of recent domestic abuse allegations.[60] **Vizquel** does have a higher CVI than 22 current Hall of Famers, including recent VC selections Morris and Baines.

Billy Wagner's 422 saves rank sixth on the career leaderboard, and his career 2.31 ERA (187 ERA+) and 0.998 WHIP are unworldly good. He was an extreme 3TO pitcher (45%), and his 11.9 SO9 and 1.99 SO/H would have topped the career lists, but he had far too few BF (3600) to qualify. His 27.8 WAR_p in 3600 BF is good but does not come close to matching Rivera's 56.3 WAR_p in 5103 BF Moreover, **Wagner** was absolutely awful (10.03 ERA) in 11.2 postseason innings – the opposite of Rivera. After lingering around 10% for three years, his BBWAA support rose to 17% in 2019, 32% in 2020, and 46% in 2021. While recognizing the need to relax minimum innings expectations for RP, I cannot support the HOF candidacy of someone who pitched only 900 innings, no matter how good those innings were.

Mike Trout, 2011

CHAPTER 9

THE ANALYTICS GENERATION (2012-PRESENT)

The Game

As MLB's steroid problem has waned, rapid technological advances are revolutionizing all aspects of the game – how hitters are taught to hit (emphasis on launch angle), how pitchers are taught to pitch (emphasis on spin and throwing multiple pitches from the same arm slot), how fielders are positioned (deployment of extreme shifts), how rosters are constructed and managed (13-man pitching staffs, frequent call-ups from AAA), and how players are evaluated and paid. Every team now has a well-staffed analytics department to digest the flood of new information and apply it to personnel decisions, in-game management, and coaching and training. While Billy Beane's "Money Ball" paradigm was *avant garde* in 2002, it is standard operating procedure in 2021.

In the midst of a revolution, it is difficult to sort out true innovations from passing fads. I believe that the new emphasis on breaking down hitting and pitching to their fundamental elements and the development of new metrics to evaluate performance, including defense, are exciting and will gain even more prominence as more and more data become available. However, some aspects of the new order are problematic:

- The accelerating shift in workload from starting pitchers to the bullpen: As recently as 2011, Justin Verlander led MLB with 251 IP. In 2017-19, only two MLB pitchers accrued as many as 220 — Max Scherzer (220.2 in 2018) and Justin Verlander (223.0 in 2019). Moreover, the 30 MLB teams combined for only 42 CG in 2018 and 45 CG in 2010 — down from 173 in 2011, when James Shields led MLB with 11 CG. With managers growing increasingly reluctant to allow pitchers to face any hitter more than twice in a game, only two pitchers (Lucas Giolito and Shane Bieber in 2019) have even thrown even three CG in 2018-20. We now even see "openers," i.e., RP who are used to get the first few outs before the SP (now called a "bulk reliever") enters the game.

- The continuing trend toward three-true outcomes (see Appendix 1, Figures A1.4-6): HR rates have continued to surge, reaching an all-time high of 6776 in 2019, 1083 more HR than at the peak of the steroid era in 2000. Meanwhile, since 1982, strikeout rates have surged 5.04 to 8.81 SO per team per game. in 2018-20, for the first time, MLB pitchers *as a group* had more SO than hits allowed. Thus, the *average* MLB pitcher today misses bats to an extent that legendary hard-throwing Hall of Famers like Rube Waddell, Walter Johnson, Lefty

Grove, and Bob Feller never dreamed of. Similarly, 36.1% of PA in 2019 ended in one of the three true outcomes, which generate little action on the field and are increasingly creating higher pitch counts, slowing the action on the field, and prolonging games. In MLB's first 80 years, no one except Babe Ruth (39.1%) generated a higher percentage of 3TO than the *average* batter in 2019.

- The deployment of extreme defensive shifts: These shifts date back to 1946, when Cleveland manager Lou Boudreau moved all his defenders to the right side of the field against Ted Williams. This strategy never gained wide currency at the time since it was so easy to defeat the shift by bunting or hitting the ball to the opposite field. However, these elementary smallball skills now seem to have been lost. It should not be difficult for modern players to re-learn these skills and keep defenses honest.

- Tanking: The popularization of "tanking" as a strategy to accelerate the re-building process by trading veterans for prospects at the cost of fielding an uncompetitive team, thereby trimming payroll and "earning" high draft choices, has threatened to disrupt competitive balance and to poison MLB's fragile labor peace. While today's tanking has yielded more favorable long-term outcomes – at least for the Cubs and Astros – than it did for the Athletics in 1915 and the early 1930s, when Connie Mack disassembled once dominant teams, fans of the 100-loss Tigers, Orioles Marlins, and Royals had little reason to visit a ballpark in 2019. Meanwhile, the combination of four 100-loss teams and four 100-win teams in 2019, created the worst competitive balance in MLB since 1954, when seven of the 16 teams either won or lost at least 60% of their games.

- High-tech cheating: The use of replay cameras and Apple watches played a central role in recent sign-stealing scandals, which have tainted the 2017 and 2018 World Series champions. Apparently learning from the failure of his predecessors to curb the budding steroid scandal of the 1990s, Commissioner Rob Manfred's has acted quickly and decisively to prevent high-tech cheating from becoming the steroids of the 2020s.

A common thread in these developments has been to make the game less appealing to fans. Baseball has more dead time than ever before due to high pitch counts, frequent mid-inning pitching changes, and tactical discussions on signs and positioning. Moreover, teams shamelessly manipulate the rules for placing pitchers on the injured list and for shuttling pitchers back and forth from AAA, making it difficult for fans to recognize who is on the roster, and resort ever more frequently to deploying position players to pitch in extra innings. Fewer balls than ever are hit into play. While HR provide bursts of excitement, a steady diet of SO and BB (the two more frequent "true outcomes") is boring.

Another closely related offshoot of the analytics revolution is that managers now seem to overthink the game and are sacrificing potentially memorable moments to get a slight or non-existent strategic edge. One need look no further than Blake Snell's removal with a 1-0 lead in the 6th inning of Game 6 of the 2020 World Series after two completely dominant turns through the Dodger lineup, in which he had thrown only 73 pitches and yielded only 2 hits and no walks, while striking out 9. This dubious decision-by-algorithm quickly blew up in Kevin Cash's face when Mookie Betts (who had done nothing against Snell) greeted RP Nick Anderson with a double and came around to score what proved to be the winning run on a wild pitch. However, the point is not that the strategy failed, but that the algorithm that Cash reflexively deployed is ruining the romance of the game.

Consider, for example, what would have happened if an analytics-driven manager like Cash were managing the Twins in the classic Jack Morris-John Smoltz pitching duel in Game 7 of the 1991 World Series.[1] After four scoreless innings in which Morris threw 61 pitches and scattered three hits and a walk, the Braves opened the fifth inning by putting runners on first and third with one out, with switch-hitting MVP Terry Pendleton about to face Morris for the third time. The Twins' actual manager Tom Kelly allowed Morris to remain to retire Pendleton and Ron Gant while stranding both runners and to pitch five more masterful shutout innings to win 1-0 and punch his ticket (arguably) to the HOF. But does anyone doubt that Cash (or any other modern analytics-driven manager) would have gone to his bullpen without even thinking twice? Cash's strategy might have worked and the Twins might have won anyway, but there would have been no classic pitching duel for fans to remember 30 years later.

Cash's quick hook on Snell was not unprecedented. Kyle Hendrick, Rich Hill, and Lance McCullers were each removed before completing five IP in late games of the 2016 and 2017 World Series, despite yielding no more than a single ER. It is quite possible that analytic principles (like not letting starting pitchers face the opposing batting order a third time) may be strategically sound, at least during the regular season, when you can carry 13 pitchers and minor league reinforcements are a phone call away. However, I believe the rote application of so-called analytic principles can easily lead managers astray in a seven-game postseason series, when the opponent has seen all your pitchers and the usual in-season avenues to effectively expand the active roster are closed. While there may be short-term gain from maneuvering a more favorable mid-game match-up, it comes with a long-term cost of limiting your late-inning options and a risk that overexposing your best relief pitchers will limit their effectiveness in subsequent games. That is essentially what happened to Aroldis Chapman and Andrew Miller in the 2016 World Series, when this strategy became popular, and has been happening to other relievers and managers ever since.

However, my larger point is that the current strategy of using more and more pitchers in shorter and shorter stints, whether or not it works, is esthetically detrimental and should be curbed. Frequent time-consuming pitching changes and substitutions interrupt the flow of the game and deprive the fan of the opportunity to experience extraordinary and memorable pitching performances,. They contribute to inexorable rise in SO rates, since RP need only throw as hard as they can for as long as they can when there is an endless supply of fresh arms waiting in AAA. Half-steps like limiting teams to 13-man pitching staffs, requiring that each new pitcher face at least three batters or complete the inning, and restoring the IL to 15 days are not enough. I would like to see limits imposed on the number of mid-inning pitching changes per game, with penalties – like placing a runner on 2B – whenever that limit is exceeded. Similarly, I think MLB should restrict the flow of pitchers between the major and minor league rosters during the season as they do in the postseason.

Despite the recent popularization of tanking, MLB's long-term trend toward competitive parity, which began in the 1960s with expansion, the implementation of the amateur draft, and the collapse of the Yankee dynasty, followed by the end of the reserve clause in 1976, has continued in the Analytics Era.[2] Seven different teams — none of them being the Yankees — have won the World Series in the past seven years, including two first-time champions (the Astros and Nationals) and three others (the Royals, Cubs, and Dodgers) who had not won since 1985, 1908, and 1988, respectively. The addition of a second wild card in each league in 2013 has helped foster an environment where any team at or above .500 entering September can consider themselves contenders. The temporary addition of three more wild card teams in each league in 2020 allowed two sub-.500 teams (the Astros and Brewers) to reach the postseason, something that had never happened before.

However, apart from any impact of tanking on competitive balance, the accompanying deflation in the cost of veteran free agents has poisoned labor relations. Ironically, the MLBPA contributed to this deflation by negotiating away the rights of amateur players entering the annual MLB draft, thereby inflating the value of high draft picks, suppressing the cost of young talent, and rendering older free agents a luxury affordable only by contending teams. While one might take a benign view that MLB front offices have merely become smarter and more efficient in aligning their personnel decisions with the current salary structure, the resulting explosion of dreary 100-loss teams whose fans enjoy no realistic hope of winning and have little reason to go to the ballpark, is anything but benign. Even before the 2020 Covid-19 pandemic played havoc with MLB budgets, a storm has been brewing and may erupt when the current labor agreement expires after the 2021 season.

The Players

Since we are only nine years into the Analytics Era, only 11 players (five hitters and six pitchers) have reached the CVI-Plus range (Table 9.1). Although all were still active in 2020, Trout, Verlander, Kershaw, Greinke, Scherzer, and Votto have already established their HOF *bona fides*, and Betts is really close. As in Chapters 3-8, thematically grouped profiles of these players are presented below.

Table 9.1: CVI-Plus Players

A) Hitters (Position)	Age in 2021	HOF	AVG/OBP/SLG	OPS+	WAR$_H$	CVI
Trout, Mike (CF)	2016	Active	.305/.418/.582	176	74.6	111.4
Votto, Joey (1B)	2013	Active	.304/.419/.517	149	62.1	68.9
Betts, Mookie (RF)	2017	Active	.301/.373/.522	135	45.4	61.8
Longoria, Evan (3B)	2012	Active	.266/.334/.473	120	56.7	58.6
Posey, Buster (C)	2014	Active	.302/.370/.456	128	41.8	55.7

B) Pitchers	MidCareer	HOF	ERA/WHIP	ERA+	WAR$_P$	CVI
Verlander, Justin (SP)	2012	Active	3.33/1.134	129	72.3	91.1
Kershaw, Clayton (SP)	2014	Active	2.43/1.003	158	67.0	87.4
Greinke, Zack (SP)	2013	Active	3.37/1.158	125	67.1	82.4
Scherzer, Max (SP)	2015	Active	3.21/1.110	132	60.6	80.7
Hamels, Cole (SP)	2013	Active	3.43/1.183	123	58.4	59.1
Sale, Chris (SP)	2015	Active	3.03/1.035	140	45.4	53.4

What Greatness Looks Like

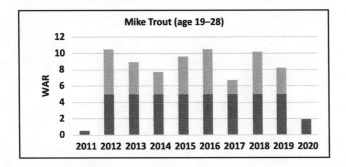

Trout, who is only nearing the midpoint what has already been a historic career, has consistently posted 6.7-10.5 WAR in every full season.

One for the Ages

Mike Trout (CF):
111.4 CVI - Los Angeles AL (*74.6*)

It has taken a worldwide pandemic to slow him down, but Mike Trout is a historic talent, who amassed 72.8 WAR through his age 27 (2019) season. How many position players in the history of baseball do you imagine have exceeded this figure by age 27? Exactly none. Ty Cobb (68.9 WAR) is second and Mickey Mantle (67.9 WAR) is third. In the entire history of MLB, only Walter Johnson (120.7) had a higher CVI than Trout (109.9) through his age 27 season; no other player had CVI $\geq$100 at that age. By contrast, Bryce Harper, with whom Trout is often paired in discussions of MLB's youngest generation of superstars, has only 33.7 WAR through his age 27 (2020) season. In his first eight full seasons, Trout amassed 10.5, 8.9, 7.7, 9.6, 10.5, 6.7, 10.2 and 8.2 WAR. He played in every All-Star game (starting in CF in 2013-19) and finished first or second in the AL MVP voting seven times, winning in 2014, 2016, and 2019 and missing only in 2017, when he was sidelined for two months with a torn ligament in his left thumb and finished fourth.

Due to the pandemic, Trout added only 1.9 WAR in the 60-game 2020 season, and his 74.6 WAR through age 28 now trails Cobb (78.4) and Hornsby (75.9) but still leads Mantle (74.3). Trout already has a 111.2 CVI (0.22 percentile) and has passed DiMaggio and Griffey to rank fifth among all CF. Of the 35 HOF-eligible players currently ahead of him in CVI, only Bonds and Clemens are not in the HOF. His 176 OPS+ ranks fifth on the all-time leaderboard, behind only Ruth, Williams, Bonds, and Gehrig. He would be an elite Hall of Famer if he never played another game. If MLB returns to normal in 2021, Trout's CVI is likely to climb above 120 and pass 10 more elite Hall of Famers. It would not be surprising to see him reach the top 10 before he is finished.

Beyond the Numbers

- Trout was not widely heralded going into the June 2009 amateur draft; the Angels selected him 25th overall with a compensatory draft pick they received from the Yankees when they signed Mark Teixeira.[3]

- Trout arrived in Anaheim to stay in 2012, hitting .326/.399/.564 (168 OPS+) with 30 HR, 83 RBI, 129 R, and a league-leading 49 SB in 639 PA. He led the league with 10.5 WAR and was a unanimous choice for Rookie of the Year but finished second to Miguel Cabrera in the MVP voting, in Cabrera's Triple Crown year.

- The only hole in Trout's resume to date is his lack of postseason exposure. He got only one hit — a home run — in his only postseason, when Kansas City swept the Angels in the 2014 ALDS.

Four Modern Aces

Justin Verlander (SP):
91.1 CVI - Detroit AL (*55.6*),
Houston AL (*16.2*)

Clayton Kershaw (SP):
87.4 CVI - Los Angeles NL (*69.6*)

Zack Greinke (SP):
82.4 CVI - Kansas City AL (*26.3*),
Los Angeles NL (*20.4*), Arizona NL (*17.9*)

Max Scherzer (SP):
80.7 CVI - Washington NL (*38.4*),
Detroit AL (*21.3*)

With 29 ASG appearances, nine Cy Young awards, and an MVP among them, Verlander, Kershaw, Greinke, and Scherzer have already established themselves as future Hall of Famers. Kershaw and Verlander were outstanding from the outset. Verlander underwent a mid-career adjustment when he entered his 30s and physical ailments began to cut into his effectiveness but came back in 2016 as good as ever. Kershaw is making similar adjustments now. Greinke has had an up-and-down career, achieving great heights in 2009 and 2015 and sprinkling a few bad seasons among a half dozen solid ones. Scherzer was a late bloomer, who was only so-so in his 20s but has blossomed into one of MLB's best pitchers in his 30s.

The 2003 Tigers, a historically dreadful 43-119 team, were rewarded with the opportunity to select Justin Verlander in the 2004 amateur draft. From the time Tiger manager Jim Leyland named him as his #5 starter in 2006, the eight-time All-Star has been among the top pitchers in the AL, first for the Tigers and now for the Astros. He led the Tigers (who were only three years removed from their 2003 debacle) to the World Series in his rookie season, winning 2006 Rookie of the Year honors by going 17-9 with a 3.63 ERA (125 ERA+) and 1.328 WHIP with 4.0 WAR_p. Then, from 2009-2013 he averaged 18-9 and 239 SO with a 3.05 ERA (139 ERA+), a 1.120 WHIP, and 6.2 WAR_p in 234 IP per season. He won both the Cy Young and MVP awards with an 8.6-WAR_p season in 2011, when he led the AL in W, ERA, WHIP, SO, and IP and pitched his second no-hitter (on May 7 against Toronto). He was nearly as good in 2012, when he posted 8.0 WAR_p and finished a close second to David Price in the Cy Young award voting and led the Tigers to another World Series.

Justin Verlander, 2018

After a mid-career slump and core surgery in 2014-15, Verlander re-emerged as one of MLB's top pitchers in 2016-19, posting a 2.87 ERA (152 ERA+) and 0.967 WHIP and averaging 17-8 with 266 SO and 7.0 WAR_p and was an ace of the powerful Astros teams of 2017-19. At age 36, his 7.4-WAR_p 2019 season was among his best and brought him his second Cy Young award. He racked up 300 SO for the first time, posted the second lowest WHIP (behind Pedro Martinez) of any pitcher in the last 100 years, and became the 18th pitcher with 3000 SO. He also became only the sixth MLB pitcher to throw three no-hitters. Only Ryan (seven) and Koufax (four) had more.

Verlander has also been an effective postseason pitcher overall, going 14-11 with a 3.40 ERA and 1.066 WHIP in 187.2 IP. His 205 postseason SO total leads all pitchers, and his 14 postseason win total is tied for third with Glavine behind only Pettitte (19) and Smoltz (15). However, Verlander has not fared well in four World Series, going 0-6 with a 5.68 ERA and 1.289 WHIP and yielding 9 HR in 38 IP.

Unfortunately, Verlander had to undergo Tommy John surgery in 2020 and is unlikely to pitch again until 2022, when he will be 38 years old. So 2019 may have been his last hurrah. Still, with 225 wins and 3006 SO through 2019, he has a clear path to the HOF even if he never throws another pitch. Verlander's 91.1 CVI already ranks 22nd among SP and at the 0.39 percentile overall.

At age 31, eight-time All-Star Clayton Kershaw has now pitched in 13 big league seasons and already has compelling HOF credentials. From 2011-15, he won three Cy Young awards (and finished second and third in 2012 and 2015), as well as the 2014 MVP award, and was MLB's best pitcher hands down. During this five-year run, he averaged 18-7 with a 2.11 ERA (172 ERA+), 0.933 WHIP, 250 SO, 6.5 H9, and 7.3 WAR_p over 226 IP per season. Even as he lost time to injuries in 2016-17, he placed fifth and second in the Cy Young award voting, despite posting only 5.8 and 4.9 WAR_p. From 2009-17, his WAR_p always exceeded 4.0, and he always struck out more than a batter per inning. However, Kershaw declined in 2018-19, posting his worst seasons since his rookie year. He seemed to be better in the abbreviated 2020 season with 1.7 WAR_p in 10 starts, but the sample size was too small to be certain. Even if he is no longer the ace he once was, he remains well above average. His 158

ERA+, 6.8 H9, and 1.44 SO/H rank second, second, and third, respectively, on the career leaderboards. His 175 career wins lead all Dodger pitchers, and he has realistic shot at 230-240 wins.

The big blemish in Kershaw's resume has been his relative lack of postseason success, which he partially addressed with a 4-1 record in the expanded 2020 postseason while leading the Dodgers to a World Series championship. Through 2020, he now has a 13-12 W-L with a 4.19 ERA in 189 IP in 20 postseason series. Although his postseason ERA is about 1.8 runs worse than his 2.43 regular season ERA, his 1074 WHIP, 7.3 H9, 9.9 SO9, and 1.36 SO/H fall right in line with his superb regular season stats. His postseason problems are attributable mainly to a few high-profile meltdowns and a general propensity to yield HR—1.33 HR per 9 IP versus 0.70 during the season. The most notorious meltdowns occurred in four games:

> 2009 NLCS Game 1: Phillies scored 5 ER in the fifth inning to erase a 1-0 lead. Phillies won 8-6.

> 2013 NCLS Game 7: Kershaw gave up 3 ER in the third and was knocked out in a 5-run fifth. Cardinals won 9-0.

> 2014 NLDS Game 1: Leading 6-2, Kershaw was chased in an 8-run seventh inning. Cardinals won 10-9.

> 2017 WS Game 5: Kershaw blew a four-run lead in the fourth and a three-run lead in the fifth. Astros won 13-12.

The 24 ER Kershaw gave up in 5.0 IP in these four disastrous outings represent 27% (24/88) of all postseason ER charged to him. In his other 26 postseason starts and seven relief appearances, his ERA was a more Kershaw-like 3.13. So, Kershaw has not been a terrible postseason pitcher. It's more that before 2020, the Dodgers lost nine of 16 postseason series in Kershaw's tenure and that he was too often the man in the spotlight in the pivotal moments. Kershaw's 87.4 CVI currently ranks 26th among SP and at the 0.45 percentile overall. He could attain elite status if he continues pitching effectively into his late 30s.

Who is the only pitcher to post more than 10 WAR_p in the 15 seasons between Randy Johnson's 10.7 in 2002 and Aaron Nola's 10.2 in 2018? It is not Kershaw, Halladay, Verlander, Scherzer, or Kluber, but six-time All-Star Zack Greinke, perhaps the most underrated SP in the game today, with 10.4 WAR_p in 2009. That year, pitching for a 97-loss Royals team, Greinke emerged as the best pitcher in MLB, going 16-8 with a spectacular 2.16 ERA, 1.073 WHIP, 242 SO in 229.1 IP to easily win the AL Cy Young award. His 205 ERA+ in 2009 ranks tied for 39th on the all-time leaderboard. Greinke's 9.1 WAR_p in 2015 was the only other WAR_p >9 from 2003-17, although he finished second to Jake Arrieta (8.3 WAR_p) in the Cy Young voting. Perhaps Greinke has been overlooked because his career has followed a more erratic path

Zack Greinke, 2009

than many pitchers of comparable quality and is pitching for his sixth team. Perhaps a bigger factor is that his social anxiety disorder (which was manifest in high school and nearly ended his career in 2006) makes him painfully shy and uncomfortable with attention from the press and other outsiders.[4] So, Greinke's record—208-126, 3.37 ERA (125 ERA+), 1.158 WHIP, 2689 SO in 2939 IP and 67.1 WAR_p through his age 36 season — must speak for itself. He is on pace to finish with 230-240 wins and close to 3000 SO. However, Greinke has been underwhelming in seven postseasons, going 4-6 with a 4.22 ERA and 1.181 WHIP and 96 SO in 106.7 IP. His 87.4 CVI ranks 30th among SP and at the 0.53 percentile overall. He is entering the twilight of his career, but even if he retired tomorrow, he would be a worthy Hall of Famer.

Late bloomer Max Scherzer debuted at age 23 in 2008 but did not create a big stir until his first Cy Young season at age 28, when he went 21-3 with a 2.90 ERA (144 ERA+), a 0.970 WHIP, 240 SO, and 6.5 WAR_p. In 2013-19, he emerged as one of MLB's elite pitchers, appearing in every ASG and averaging 17-7 with a 2.82 ERA (149 ERA+) and 0.981 WHIP, 266 SO in 212 IP, and 6.7 WAR_p per season, including two more Cy Young awards in 2016-17. He had his first 300-SO season in 2018 and was on his way to another Cy Young caliber year in 2019 until an upper back injury derailed him for several weeks. Scherzer added another 2.2 WAR_p in the abbreviated 2020 pandemic season. His 1.43 SO/H is topped only by Randy Johnson, Ryan, and Kershaw. He has been effective in seven postseasons, going 7-5 with a 3.38 ERA, a 1.134 WHIP, and 137 SO in 112.0 IP. Now entering his age 36 season in 2021, Scherzer's 80.7 CVI ranks 31st among SP and at the 0.55 percentile overall. He has 175 W and 2784 SO through 2020 and will likely reach 220 W and 3200 SO before he is finished. His credentials are already worthy of the HOF, but passing 200 W and 3000 SO would seal the deal.

Beyond the Numbers

- The Tigers actually owed the NL cellar-dwelling Padres a big assist in their good fortune in drafting Verlander. The Padres used the #1 overall pick to select local high school SS Matt Bush, who not only was a colossal bust, but spent more than three years in prison before resurfacing in 2016 as a hard-throwing reliever for the Texas Rangers. A nice redemption story, but hardly what the Padres had in mind.

- In 2004, when negotiations between Verlander the Tigers reached an impasse, his father Richard, who was president of the Communications Workers of America, stepped in and negotiated a $3.1 million signing bonus for his son.[5]

The Man Who Never Pops Up

Joey Votto (1B):
68.9 CVI - Cincinnati NL (*62.1*)

Although Votto has recently been in decline, the six-time All-Star was one of MLB's most consistent stars of the past decade, combining elite on-base skills with 25-HR power. But the oddity that set him apart was his extreme aversion to hitting pop flies. Indeed, if you watched MLB in 2009-18, you were 4-5 times as likely to have witnessed a no-hitter or batting cycle than a Joey Votto pop-up. Votto hit only nine infield fly balls in this period, of which only one came in 2016-18.[8] By contrast, 38 no-hitters (including six perfect games) and 41 cycles occurred in this same 10-year period.[9,10] Indeed, Joey Votto pop-ups were almost as rare as perfect games.

Pop-ups aside, Votto's 0.4194 OBP leads all active players and is the 18th best of all time. His 149 OPS+ is second only to Mike Trout among active players. In 2010-13, Votto hit .317/.434/.544 (164 OPS+) and averaged 26 HR, 86 RBI, 92 R, 38 2B, 108 BB, and 6.5 WAR. He led the NL in OBP in all four seasons, in SLG in 2010, in 2B in 2011-12, and in BB in 2011-13. In 2010, he posted 7.0 WAR and was named NL MVP. After a strained quadriceps ruined his 2014 season, he returned to his previous level of production – 7.8 WAR in 2015 and 8.1 WAR in 2017 – sandwiched around 4.2 WAR in 2016. However, Votto has declined significantly since then to 4.0 WAR in 2018, 1.9 WAR in 2019, and 0.1 WAR in 2020. He even hit four infield fly balls in 2019 – but none in 2020.

Votto did not get a full opportunity with the Reds until he was 24, and his 295 HR, 966 RBI, and 1041 R in 14 years will not excite HOF voters. At age 37 entering the 2021 season, he is running out of time to build on those totals. CVI ranks Votto 15th at 1B and at the 0.99 percentile overall. Votto's 68.9 CVI, which ranks 14th at 1B and at the 0.92 percentile overall, is good enough to make him a viable HOF candidate (comparable to Todd Helton), but not a lock.

Rising Star

Mookie Betts (RF):
61.8 CVI - Boston AL (*41.8*), Los Angeles NL (*3.6*)

Unlike the players discussed earlier in the chapter, Mookie Betts, who just completed his age 27 season still resides in the "very good" category, but he is a good bet to shoot past all the others except Trout before he is finished. Combining speed and surprising power in his 5'9" frame, he has starred from the moment he took the field for the Red Sox as a 21 year-old in late June 2014. Batting mostly in the leadoff spot, he has hit .301/.373/.522 while averaging 30 HR, 98 RBI, 127 R, 26 SB, 7.6 WAR, and 1.9 dWAR per 162 games. A four-time all-star, he has finished in the top 10 in the MVP voting in each of the last five seasons, including a first place finish for the 2018 World Series champion Red Sox in 2018, and second place finishes for the 2016 Red Sox and the 2020 World Series champion Dodgers. He is also a sterling defender in RF with 11.1 dWAR (already 13th best among all OF and 3rd among corner OF) and five consecutive Gold Gloves in 2016-20. He has hit .258/.343/.409 with 3 HR, 12 RBI, 31 R, and 8 SB in 181 AB in four postseasons. His 61.8 CVI currently ranks 19th in RF and at the 1.17 percentile overall, but it could easily double by the time he is 35 if nothing goes wrong. That's a big if, to be sure, but it would put him among MLB's top 30 players of all time.

Still Have a Shot

Cole Hamels (SP):
59.1 CVI - Philadelphia NL (*43.0*), Texas (*10.8*), Chicago NL (*5.6*)

Evan Longoria (3B):
58.6 CVI – Tampa Bay (*51.8*), San Francisco (*4.9*)

Buster Posey (C):
55.7 CVI – San Francisco NL (*41.8*)

Chris Sale (SP):
53.4 CVI – Chicago AL (*30.1*), Boston AL (*15.2*)

Table 9.1 also features four players, all in their 30s and past their primes, who do not yet have compelling HOF credentials but still have time to get there with another strong season or two.

Four-time all-star and 2008 World Series MVP Cole Hamels is closest to the 62.0 CVI threshold that separates the "great" from the "very good," but shoulder problems have sidelined him and he appears to have little left in the tank. After averaging 4.7 WAR_p in 10 full seasons with the Phillies and Rangers in 2007-16 and then 3.2 WAR_p with the Rangers and Cubs in 2017-19, he made only one start with an 8.10 ERA in 2020. As a 37-year old free agent with a dicey shoulder, it is uncertain that he will pitch again. Although his 59.1 CVI (1.23 percentile) is comparable to that of Don Sutton, his 163 career wins and 2560 SO are not even close to Sutton's totals and will not appeal to HOF voters.

One-time Rays uber-prospect and 2008 Rookie of the Year Evan Longoria has fallen short of the early hype but has quietly put together a very fine career with the Rays and Giants. He is one those Grich-like players who is strong in all departments but doesn't bowl you over with any single aspect of his game. He has good but not elite power (304 HR, 1043 RBI, .483 SLG, 120 OPS+) and is an outstanding defender (14.6 dWAR, three Gold Gloves). His three best years (2009-11) came early in his career, when he hit .275/.364/.510 (138 OPS+) and averaged 29 HR, 95 RBI, 91 R, 2.4 dWAR, 7.5 WAR, and had two top 10 MVP finishes. But after making the AL All-Star team in each of his first three seasons, he has not been an All-Star since 2010. Despite this leveling off, he has remained a solid 2-WAR player through his age 34 season, and his CVI could slowly inch up into the low 60s before he is finished. This probably won't be enough to gain entry to the HOF.

Buster Posey also began his career with a Rookie of the Year award (in 2010) and a run of All-Star selections and high MVP finishes but has lost steam after reaching age 30. However, his career track and HOF prospects differ importantly from that of his current teammate Longoria. First, he actually won the MVP award with his 7.6 WAR 2012 season, when the Giants won the second of their three World Series championships of the past decade. Second, he was selected for six NL All-Star teams in seven years (2012-18). Third, he is a catcher, where offensive standards are not as high, and he was regarded as the best at that position from 2010-18, when

Buster Posey, 2013

he averaged 4.5 WAR despite missing most of the 2011 season after a horrific home plate collision with Chase Utley (which led to a major rule change). Posey was on a clear HOF track through 2018, but had a poor year in 2019 (0.9 WAR) and opted out of the 2020 season to protect his at-risk infant from COVID-19. Thus, he will need a comeback season in 2021 to re-establish his HOF trajectory. Although his 55.7 CVI through 2020 is 2.7 below Longoria's, he is a year and a half younger. I think Posey has an excellent chance to reach the HOF.

Chris Sale, who is expected to return from Tommy John surgery at age 32 in mid-2021, is the most difficult of the four players in this group to project. From 2012-18, Sale was a perennial all-star and Cy Young award contender (finishing second in 2017), went 99-59 with a 2.91 ERA (143 ERA+) and 1.024 WHIP, who averaged 240 SO and 5.6 WAR_p per season. The Red Sox paid a king's ransom of prospects (topped by Yoan Moncada and Michael Kopech) to acquire him from the rebuilding White Sox in December 2016, and it paid off in a World Series championship in 2018 (although Sale did not pitch particularly well in the postseason). But Sale was always viewed as a serious arm injury waiting to happen, and it happened in 2020. Sale is young enough to come back strong, but whether he will is anyone's guess. He will need to build on his 109 career wins and 53.4 CVI to have any shot at the HOF.

Other Notable Active Players

Table 9.2: CVI-Minus Players With CVI >40 or Age ≤ 32 and CVI >30

A) Hitter (Position)	Age in 2021	WAR_{II}	CVI
Cano, Robinson (2B)	38	69.1	51.6
Donaldson, Josh (3B)	35	41.4	48.4
Goldschmidt, Paul (1B)	33	45.1	47.6
McCutchen, Andrew (CF)	34	44.6	46.6
Molina, Yadier (C)	38	40.4	43.7
Arenado, Nolan (3B)	30	39.1	41.5
Braun, Ryan (LF)	37	46.9	40.8
Machado, Manny (3B)	28	39.8	40.6
Stanton, Giancarlo (RF)	31	41.0	40.6
Altuve, Jose (2B)	31	36.5	39.0
Heyward, Jason (RF)	31	38.4	37.7
Simmons, Andrelton (SS)	31	36.8	37.2
Freeman, Freddie (1B)	31	38.8	36.6
Harper, Bryce (RF)	28	33.7	34.7
Yelich, Christian (LF)	29	32.3	32.8
Rizzo, Anthony (1B)	31	34.5	32.3
Rendon, Anthony (3B)	31	31.2	31.4
Ramirez, Jose (3B)	28	28.1	30.4

Table 9.2 (cont'd)

B) Pitchers	Age in 2021	WAR$_p$	CVI
deGrom, Jacob (SP)	33	35.9	48.9
Lester, Jon (SP)	37	45.0	46.1
Wainwright, Adam (SP)	39	36.9	45.8
Kluber, Corey (SP)	35	32.3	45.1
Price, David (SP)	35	39.7	41.0
Strasburg, Stephen (SP)	32	32.1	34.3
Bumgarner, Madison (SP)	31	31.9	32.2

Projecting player performance five years into the future is a fool's errand; it is hard enough to forecast what will happen next week. However, I have compiled a list of active CVI-Minus players with CVI ≥ 40 and younger players with CVI ≥30, for whom the HOF is not out of reach.

I believe that the following players (in the order listed) have a realistic chance to reach CVI ≥62, based on their age, current CVI, and performance during the past three seasons:

Jacob deGrom is the surest bet for the HOF. Although 2021 will be his age 33 season, he is coming off Cy Young seasons in 2018-19 (with 17.5 WAR$_p$) and showed no sign of slowing down in 2020 (2.6 WAR$_p$ in a 60-game season). It is not unrealistic to expect him to post at least 6-WAR$_p$ in his age 33-34 seasons, which would raise his CVI to 64.8, comfortably in HOF range. He is likely to remain at least moderately productive through his mid-30s and to finish with CVI >75.

Machado and **Harper**, two 28-year-old stars in their prime years, are also on a realistic HOF trajectory. Of course, history offers many examples of players who perform like superstars in their 20s, only to fall flat in their 30s (Garciaparra, Pinson, and Cedeno, for example), so neither is a sure thing. Still, CVI >70 is a reasonable expectation for both men.

At age 38, **Yadier Molina** is unlikely to attain CVI-Plus status, but HOF voters have traditionally applied different standards to elite defensive performers at C and SS, the two most important positions on the diamond. Molina, a nine-time All-Star and nine-time Gold Glover, certainly fits that description. His 25.4 dWAR ranks fourth among all catchers (behind only Ivan Rodriguez, Gary Carter, and Bob Boone), and his superlative qualities as a receiver and a team leader have helped lead the Cardinals to 11 postseasons, four World Series, and two championships in his 17 MLB seasons. He will likely wind up in the HOF regardless of his CVI.

Arenado, **Freeman**, **Simmons**, **Strasburg**, and **Yelich** will all be 29-32 years old in 2021 and each has had at least one 5-WAR season in 2018-20. Indeed, **Yelich** and **Freeman** were the 2019-20 NL MVPs. **Arenado** (because he has the highest CVI) and **Yelich** (because he is the youngest) are probably the best bets to reach CVI ≥62, but neither is a sure thing. **Simmons**, whose 26.6 dWAR already ranks 11th among all SS (and is running well ahead of Ozzie Smith's 20.8 dWAR at the same age) could benefit from the "Rabbit Maranville effect" that has put so many weak-hitting great defensive SS in the HOF. Simmons's 5.0 dWAR in 2013 (0.2 better than Ozzie's career high of 4.8 in 1989) is the third highest ever recorded. However, **Simmons**, who posted 14.1 WAR and 8.3 dWAR in 2017-18, has declined steeply in 2019-20 (2.4 WAR and 1.8 dWAR) and may have a short shelf life.

Goldschmidt and **Donaldson**, whose CVI are in the high 40s and have remained productive into their early 30s, also have a realistic chance for the HOF. However, while CVI-Plus status is well within reach, each would need four more 5-WAR seasons or three more 6-WAR seasons to raise their CVI past the 62 threshold. **Goldschmidt** posted 6.2 WAR in 2018 but only 4.4 WAR in 2019-20. **Donaldson** posted 6.0 WAR in 2019 but only 0.9 WAR combined in 2018 and 2020. The odds are against them.

Robinson Cano's unadjusted 77.8 CVI would have made him a lock for the HOF, but his two steroid suspensions in 2018 and 2021 have knocked him out of the running. He will not play again until age 39, and is unlikely ever to regain CVI-Plus status.

Most of the others listed in Table 9.2 are either too old or have too much ground to make up to become viable HOF candidates. **Stanton**, **Altuve**, **Rizzo**, **Heyward**, and **Bumgarner** are still under 32, but have not had a 5-WAR season since at least 2017. **Rendon** had 6.4 WAR in 2019, but his CVI is only 31.2 entering his age 31 season. **Jose Ramirez**, who is two years younger than **Rendon** with a 30.4 CVI, may have a better chance. The best years of **McCutchen**, **Lester**, **Wainwright**, **Kluber**, **Price**, and **Braun** (who now has retired) are behind them.

I will not even attempt to project the HOF chances of the many young stars who have not yet attained CVI ≥30. Some will go on to HOF careers and some will disappoint, but it is impossible to predict which is which. As they say, that is why they play the games.

CHAPTER 10

GREATNESS ACROSS THE GENERATIONS

In Chapters 3-9, we have looked at the top players in each generation in the context of the prevailing configuration, rules, and style of play at that stage of MLB's evolution. In this chapter, we integrate this material and compare the best players of all time in various categories across generations. When we do this, it is important to understand that we cannot directly compare players who played 100 years apart. Human beings have grown increasingly bigger, stronger, faster, healthier, and longer-lived between 1871 and 2020. Athletic performance has improved markedly in every sport that can be measured objectively – athletes run faster, jump higher, lift heavier weights than ever before. It is only logical to assume that today's stars are better athletes and ballplayers than those of past generations. So when one looks at rankings across generations, and sees Ruth ahead of Aaron, Walter Johnson ahead of Randy Johnson, Cobb ahead of Henderson, etc. one is not saying that the older players could outperform the more recent players if they somehow were put on the same ballfield in their primes. One can only say that Ruth, W. Johnson, and Cobb stood further above their contemporaries than Aaron, R. Johnson, and Henderson, respectively.

Tables 10.1-4 list the CVI-Plus players in the Elite, Great, Near Great, and Very Good groupings defined in Chapter 2. Table 10.5 lists the best of the CVI-Minus players, i.e., those whose CVI is in the top 2%. Table 10.6 lists the 46 players elected to the HOF despite CVI outside the top 2%. In each of these tables, the men who have been elected to the HOF as players are in boldface type; those who have been elected for accomplishments in management are not bolded. Tables 10.1-5 contain numerical ranks for players who are eligible for the HOF to facilitate counting the top 235. Players who are still active as of 2020 (italics), recently retired, or explicitly banned (gray shading) are listed without a numerical rank. I have indicated in each table the players whose CVI was adjusted for wartime military service, a late start in MLB (segregation, playing in a foreign league), or steroid use by the symbols †, ^, and ~ respectively. Their unadjusted CVI can be found in Appendix 2, Tables A2.1-3 and A2.12). When I discuss each group, I will indicate the players whom I believe deserve to be in the HOF.

With the exception of the three steroid poster boys Bonds, Clemens, and Rodriguez, the "elite" category (Table 10.1) is made up almost entirely of consensus Hall of Famers, most of whom are recognized as among the best of all time. A few of them (notably Blyleven, Carter, and some of the 19th century stars) were not recognized immediately, but most of the recent players listed were elected by the BBWAA on the first ballot. This will undoubtedly be the case for the two active players, Pujols and Trout, when their time comes. I strongly believe that Bonds

Table 10.1: The Elite (CVI ≥ 100, top 0.35 percentile)

	Player	Posn	CVI		Player	Posn	CVI
1	Ruth, Babe (1914-1935)	RF	270.0	29	Robinson, Frank (1956-1976)	RF	118.8
2	Mays, Willie (1951-1973)[†]	CF	232.3	30	Martinez, Pedro (1992-2009)	SP	118.2
3	Johnson, Walter (1907-1927)	SP	211.8	31	Foxx, Jimmie (1925-1945)	1B	117.2
4	Bonds, Barry (1986-2007)~	LF	203.8	32	Mathews, Eddie (1952-1968)	3B	116.7
5	Williams, Ted (1939-1960)[†]	LF	199.5	33	Spahn, Warren (1942-1965)[†]	SP	114.4
6	Cobb, Ty (1905-1928)	CF	198.0	34	Ripken, Cal (1981-2001)	SS	113.3
7	Young, Cy (1890-1911)	SP	194.0	35	Bench, Johnny (1967-1983)	C	111.7
8	Aaron, Henry (1954-1976)	RF	187.5		*Trout, Mike (2011-2020)*	*CF*	*111.4*
9	Hornsby, Rogers (1915-1937)	2B	185.0	36	Clemente, Roberto (1955-1972)	RF	110.9
10	Musial, Stan (1941-1963)[†]	LF	178.1	37	Yastrzemski, Carl (1961-1983)	LF	110.8
11	Speaker, Tris (1907-1928)	CF	174.6	38	Boggs, Wade (1982-1999)	3B	110.8
12	Wagner, Honus (1897-1917)	SS	172.4	39	Anson, Cap (1871-1897)	1B	108.8
13	Clemens, Roger (1984-2007)~	SP	172.3	40	Niekro, Phil (1964-1987)	SP	108.4
14	Gehrig, Lou (1923-1939)	1B	165.4	41	DiMaggio, Joe (1936-1951)[†]	CF	107.4
15	Grove, Lefty (1925-1941)	SP	161.4	42	Feller, Bob (1936-1956)[†]	SP	107.0
16	Collins, Eddie (1906-1930)	2B	154.8	43	Robinson, Jackie (1947-1956)^	2B	106.8
17	Alexander, Grover (1911-1930)[†]	SP	146.6		Rodriguez, Alex (1994-2016)~	SS	106.0
18	Johnson, Randy (1988-2009)	SP	144.1	44	Blyleven, Bert (1970-1992)	SP	104.2
19	Mantle, Mickey (1951-1968)	CF	143.0	45	Gibson, Bob (1959-1975)	SP	103.5
20	Schmidt, Mike (1972-1989)	3B	142.0	46	Carter, Gary (1974-1992)	C	103.1
21	Henderson, Rickey (1979-2003)	LF	134.9	47	Connor, Roger (1880-1897)	1B	102.7
	Pujols, Albert (2001-2020)	*1B*	*132.7*	48	Brouthers, Dan (1879-1904)	1B	102.3
22	Ott, Mel (1926-1947)	RF	131.0	49	Rivera, Mariano (1995-2013)	RP	101.9
23	Lajoie, Nap (1896-1916)	2B	130.6	50	Griffey, Ken (1989-2010)	CF	101.8
24	Mathewson, Christy (1900-1916)	SP	129.2	51	Brett, George (1973-1993)	3B	101.3
25	Maddux, Greg (1986-2008)	SP	128.2	52	Perry, Gaylord (1962-1983)	SP	100.7
26	Morgan, Joe (1963-1984)	2B	120.6	53	Carlton, Steve (1965-1988)	SP	100.6
27	Seaver, Tom (1967-1986)	SP	120.5	54	Roberts, Robin (1948-1966)	SP	100.1
28	Nichols, Kid (1890-1906)	SP	119.9				

and Clemens deserve to be in the HOF because of their body of work before they used steroids. I feel less strongly about Rodriguez, despite his elite CVI after adjusting for steroids, since it is impossible to point with confidence at an authentic season that demonstrates his greatness unambiguously. While my steroid adjustment leads me to believe that A-Rod would have been an elite player without steroids, real empirical data would be more convincing.

Table 10.2: The Great (CVI between 70 and 100, 0.35-0.85 percentile)

	Player	Posn	CVI		Player	Posn	CVI
55	Kaline, Al (1953-1974)	RF	99.0	89	Grich, Bobby (1970-1986)	2B	77.9
	Beltre, Adrian (1998-2018)	3B	98.8	90	Molitor, Paul (1978-1998)	DH	77.8
56	Schilling, Curt (1988-2007)	SP	97.4	91	Heilmann, Harry (1914-1932)†	RF	77.8
57	Mize, Johnny (1936-1953)†	1B	97.2	92	Vance, Dazzy (1915-1935)	SP	77.8
58	Clarkson, John (1882-1894)	SP	96.0	93	Newhouser, Hal (1939-1955)	SP	77.1
59	Gehringer, Charlie (1924-1942)	2B	95.3	94	Snider, Duke (1947-1964)	CF	76.8
60	Vaughan, Arky (1932-1948)	SS	93.8	95	Radbourn, Old Hoss (1880-1891)	SP	76.6
	Verlander, Justin (2005-2020)	*SP*	*91.1*		Utley, Chase (2003-2018)	2B	76.3
61	Mussina, Mike (1991-2008)	SP	91.1	96	Marichal, Juan (1960-1975)	SP	76.1
62	Gossage, Rich (1972-1994)	RP	90.6	97	Eckersley, Dennis (1975-1998)	RP	75.9
63	Martinez, Edgar (1987-2004)	DH	89.7	98	Walker, Larry (1989-2005)	RF	75.7
64	Carew, Rod (1967-1985)	2B	88.7	99	Hubbell, Carl (1928-1943)	SP	75.7
65	Keefe, Tim (1880-1893)	SP	88.5	100	Glasscock, Jack (1879-1895)	SS	74.8
66	Halladay, Roy (1998-2013)	SP	88.4	101	Wood, Wilbur (1961-1978)	SP	74.7
67	Jones, Chipper (1993-2012)	3B	88.3	102	Smith, Ozzie (1978-1996)	SS	74.6
68	Santo, Ron (1960-1974)	3B	88.1	103	Trammell, Alan (1977-1996)	SS	74.5
69	Bagwell, Jeff (1991-2005)	1B	87.8	104	Sandberg, Ryne (1981-1997)	2B	74.3
70	Thomas, Frank (1990-2008)	DH	87.4	105	Wilhelm, Hoyt (1952-1972)	RP	74.3
	Kershaw, Clayton (2008-2020)	*SP*	*87.4*	106	Coveleski, Stan (1912-1928)	SP	74.2
	Jackson, Shoeless Joe (1908-1920)†	RF	87.0	107	Berra, Yogi (1946-1967)	C	74.1
71	Jenkins, Fergie (1965-1983)	SP	86.2	108	Thome, Jim (1991-2012)	1B	73.8
72	Appling, Luke (1930-1950)†	SS	85.9	109	Frisch, Frankie (1919-1937)	2B	73.8
73	Rodriguez, Ivan (1991-2011)	C	85.3	110	Wallace, Bobby (1894-1918)	SS	73.8
74	Yount, Robin (1974-1993)	SS	83.9	111	Boudreau, Lou (1938-1952)	SS	73.7
75	Banks, Ernie (1953-1971)	SS	83.8	112	Bunning, Jim (1955-1971)	SP	73.1
	Rose, Pete (1963-1986)	LF	83.6	113	Simmons, Al (1924-1944)	LF	72.7
76	Walsh, Ed (1904-1917)	SP	83.5	114	McGinnity, Joe (1899-1908)	SP	72.6
77	Davis, George (1890-1909)	SS	83.3		Beltran, Carlos (1998-2017)	CF	72.6
78	Piazza, Mike (1992-2007)	C	83.2		*Cabrera, Miguel (2003-2020)*	*1B*	*72.2*
79	Fisk, Carlton (1969-1993)	C	82.8	115	Smoltz, John (1988-2009)	SP	71.9
80	Galvin, Pud (1875-1892)	SP	82.5	116	Waner, Paul (1926-1945)	RF	71.7
	Greinke, Zack (2004-2020)	*SP*	*82.4*	117	Jeter, Derek (1995-2014)	SS	71.3
81	Greenberg, Hank (1930-1947)†	1B	82.3	118	Dawson, Andre (1976-1996)	RF	71.1
82	Robinson, Brooks (1955-1977)	3B	82.2	119	Dickey, Bill (1928-1946)†	C	71.0
	Suzuki, Ichiro (2001-2019)^	RF	81.9	120	Rolen, Scott (1996-2012)	3B	70.8
83	Jackson, Reggie (1967-1987)	RF	80.7	121	Rusie, Amos (1889-1901)	SP	70.7
	Scherzer, Max (2008-2020)	*SP*	*80.7*	122	Lofton, Kenny (1991-2007)	CF	70.6
84	Delahanty, Ed (1888-1903)	LF	80.5	123	Baker, Home Run (1908-1922)	3B	70.6
85	Plank, Eddie (1901-1917)	SP	80.4	124	Faber, Red (1914-1933)†	SP	70.4
86	Ryan, Nolan (1966-1993)	SP	79.9	125	Larkin, Barry (1986-2004)	SS	70.4
87	Glavine, Tom (1987-2008)	SP	78.7	126	Koufax, Sandy (1955-1966)	SP	70.2
88	Reese, Pee Wee (1940-1958)†	SS	78.3	127	Cone, David (1986-2003)	SP	70.0

The vast majority of players (90%) in the slightly less exclusive "great" category (Table 10.2) have also been elected to the HOF. The most notable exception is Curt Schilling (who has non-baseball-related electability issues), but there are some overlooked gems in the right half of Table 10.2 – Grich, Glasscock, Wood, Rolen, Lofton, and Cone. With the exception of Shoeless Joe Jackson, I would vote to put all of these players, including Pete Rose, in the HOF. The five active players (Verlander, Kershaw, Greinke, Scherzer, and Cabrera) and the four recently retired players (Beltre, Suzuki, Utley, and Beltran) also deserve election to the HOF when their time comes, but I suspect that the underrated Utley and Beltran (due to his involvement in the Astros cheating scandal) may not get there right away.

Table 10.3: The Near-Great (CVI between 62 and 70, 0.85-1.17 percentile)

	Player	Posn	CVI		Player	Posn	CVI
128	Jones, Andruw (1996-2012)	CF	69.8	152	Goslin, Goose (1921-1938)	LF	66.6
129	Helton, Todd (1997-2013)	1B	69.7	153	Saberhagen, Bret (1984-2001)	SP	66.5
	Mauer, Joe (2004-2018)	C	69.7	154	Allen, Dick (1963-1977)	1B	66.5
130	Ferrell, Wes (1927-1941)	SP	69.6	155	Bell, Buddy (1972-1989)	3B	66.2
131	Raines, Tim (1979-2002)	LF	69.5	156	Buffinton, Charlie (1882-1892)	SP	65.8
132	Willis, Vic (1898-1910)	SP	69.4	157	Drysdale, Don (1956-1969)	SP	65.8
133	McCormick, Jim (1878-1887)	SP	69.4		Ortiz, David (1997-2016)	DH	65.4
134	McCovey, Willie (1959-1980)	1B	69.4	158	Winfield, Dave (1973-1995)	RF	65.3
135	Palmer, Jim (1965-1984)	SP	69.3	159	Sisler, George (1915-1930)	1B	65.2
136	Gordon, Joe (1938-1950)[†]	2B	69.2	160	Bando, Sal (1966-1981)	3B	65.1
137	Boyer, Ken (1955-1969)	3B	69.2	161	Simmons, Ted (1968-1988)	C	65.0
138	Waddell, Rube (1897-1910)	SP	69.0	162	Tiant, Luis (1964-1982)	SP	65.0
	Votto, Joey (2007-2020)	*1B*	*68.9*	163	*Torre, Joe (1960-1977)	C	65.0
139	Dahlen, Bill (1891-1911)	SS	68.8	164	Cochrane, Mickey (1925-1937)	C	64.8
140	Biggio, Craig (1988-2007)	2B	68.6	165	Hamilton, Billy (1888-1901)	CF	64.7
141	Gwynn, Tony (1982-2001)	RF	68.3	166	Murray, Eddie (1977-1997)	1B	64.0
142	Bond, Tommy (1874-1884)	SP	68.2	167	Appier, Kevin (1989-2004)	SP	63.7
143	Crawford, Sam (1899-1917)	RF	68.2		Cicotte, Eddie (1905-1920)	SP	63.6
144	Alomar, Roberto (1988-2004)	2B	67.7	168	Stieb, Dave (1979-1998)	SP	63.6
145	Lyons, Ted (1923-1946)[†]	SP	67.6		Sabathia, CC (2001-2019)	SP	63.4
146	Ashburn, Richie (1948-1962)	CF	67.4	169	Campanella, Roy (1948-1957)^	C	63.1
147	Cronin, Joe (1926-1945)	SS	67.2	170	Ruffing, Red (1924-1947)[†]	SP	62.8
148	Reuschel, Rick (1972-1991)	SP	67.0	171	Slaughter, Enos (1938-1959)[†]	RF	62.8
149	Nettles, Graig (1967-1988)	3B	67.0	172	Williams, Billy (1959-1976)	LF	62.7
150	Brown, Kevin (1986-2005)⁻	SP	67.0	173	Mathews, Bobby (1871-1887)	SP	62.7
151	Whitaker, Lou (1977-1995)	2B	66.9	174	Santana, Johan (2000-2012)	SP	62.6

* Joe Torre was elected as a manager in 2014 after failing to be elected as a player.

The "near-great" category (Table 10.3) is where the job of separating the Hall of Fame from the Hall of the Very Good starts to get sticky. This category contains an almost equal mixture of 25 Hall of Famers, (many of whom were not elected immediately), 21 players with similar CVI who have been passed over by HOF electors, and Joe Torre, who was elected as a manager. If one prefers a "Big Hall" with a cutoff at the 1.5-1.6 percentile (230-240 players at present), then all these players belong in the HOF. However, as someone who favors a "Smaller Hall" with a cutoff around the 1.20-1.25 percentile, I would be more selective. I would keep the existing 25 Hall of Famers and definitely add 10 others – Jones, Helton, Boyer, Dahlen, Bond, Nettles, Whitaker, Allen, Bell, and Tiant. I could go either way on Saberhagen (too inconsistent) and Bando (consistent but not spectacular). When added to the 127 eligible players in Tables 10.1-3 plus Pete Rose, this brings my HOF tally up to 163-165. This leaves Ferrell, McCormick (whose CVI would have only been 57.5 without his spectacular half-season stint in the inferior Union Association in 1884), Reuschel, Brown, Buffinton, Appier, Stieb. Mathews, and Santana as near misses. Of the four active or recently retired players, in Table 10.3, I support the HOF candidacies of Mauer, Votto, and Ortiz; Sabathia is another borderline case.

Fewer than one-third (20) of the 61 HOF-eligible "very good" players in Table 10.4 have actually been elected to the HOF, and most of the rest definitely belong in the HOVG, not the HOF. Nevertheless, I would definitely retain 10 current Hall of Famers – Hartnett, Guerrero, Terry, Mordecai Brown, Killebrew, Hoffman, Stargell, Kiner, Doby, and Ward – and would elevate four others to the HOF – Keith Hernandez, Edmonds, Munson, and Minoso. Hartnett and Munson were very close to the 62 CVI threshold and merit special consideration as catchers, especially since each was considered as the best in their league in his prime. Doby and Minoso, whose MLB careers were hurt by the color line, belong because of their historic importance as trailblazers in the desegregation of MLB. Ward belongs because of his major role as an early advocate of players' rights. I believe that dWAR exaggerates the defensive deficiencies of Guerrero, Killebrew, Stargell, and Kiner and skews their CVI downward. (The same is true of Allen, Winfield, Murray, and Williams in Table 10.4.) I also believe that dWAR doesn't give enough credit to strong defensive 1B like Hernandez and Terry or strong defensive OF like Edmonds. In the absence of a truly reliable metric for RP, I would not second-guess the election all-time NL Saves leader Hoffman. Lastly, I would retain Mordecai Brown, the Cubs ace of the early 20th century, who sported a 152 ERA+ in ten years with the Cubs while doubling as an SP/RP. I would could also go either way on seven players from Table 10.4 – Dwight Evans (just misses 62 CVI), Early Wynn and Sutton (no big peaks, but great longevity counts for something), Pettitte, ace closers Smith and Fingers, and Medwick. The addition of these players brings my personal HOF to 177-186 members. One could also make a case for Abreu, Randolph, Sheffield, and Hershiser, but on balance they probably belong in the HOVG.

Table 10.4: The Very Good (CVI between 53.04 and 62, 1.17-1.55 percentile)

	Player	Posn	CVI		Player	Posn	CVI
175	Evans, Dwight (1972-1991)	RF	61.9	205	**Hoffman, Trevor (1993-2010)**	**RP**	56.2
	Betts, Mookie (2014-2020)	*RF*	*61.8*	206	King, Silver (1886-1897)	SP	56.2
176	Hernandez, Keith (1974-1990)	1B	61.2	207	McDaniel, Lindy (1955-1975)	RP	56.1
177	Edmonds, Jim (1993-2010)	CF	61.0	208	Uhle, George (1919-1936)	SP	56.0
178	Hiller, John (1965-1980)	RP	60.7	209	Buehrle, Mark (2000-2015)	SP	56.0
179	**Hartnett, Gabby (1922-1941)**	**C**	**60.7**	210	Welch, Mickey (1880-1892)	SP	55.9
180	**Wynn, Early (1939-1963)**[†]	**SP**	**60.6**	211	Gooden, Dwight (1984-2000)	SP	55.8
181	Munson, Thurman (1969-1979)	C	60.6		*Posey, Buster (2009-2019)*	*C*	*55.7*
182	Minoso, Minnie (1949-1980)[^]	LF	60.5	212	**Stargell, Willie (1962-1982)**	**LF**	**55.5**
183	Pettitte, Andy (1995-2013)[~]	SP	60.1	213	**Smith, Lee (1980-1997)**	**RP**	**55.4**
184	Abreu, Bobby (1996-2014)	RF	59.8	214	Mullane, Tony (1881-1894)	SP	55.3
	*Spalding, Al (1871-1878)	SP	59.8	215	**Kiner, Ralph (1946-1955)**	**LF**	**55.2**
185	Wynn, Jim (1963-1977)	CF	59.4	216	Rogers, Kenny (1989-2008)	SP	55.2
	Hamels, Cole (2006-2020)	*SP*	*59.1*	217	Oswalt, Roy (2001-2013)	SP	55.1
186	**Sutton, Don (1966-1988)**	**SP**	**58.7**	218	**Fingers, Rollie (1968-1985)**	**RP**	**55.0**
187	Evans, Darrell (1969-1989)	3B	58.6	219	Langston, Mark (1984-1999)	SP	54.5
188	**Guerrero, Vladimir (1996-2011)**	**RF**	**58.6**	220	Shocker, Urban (1916-1928)[†]	SP	54.4
	Longoria, Evan (2008-2020)	*3B*	*58.6*	221	Breitenstein, Theodore (1891-1901)	SP	54.3
189	Smith, Reggie (1966-1982)	RF	58.4	222	Ramirez, Manny (1993-2011)[~]	LF	54.3
190	**Terry, Bill (1923-1936)**	**1B**	**57.8**	223	Cedeno, Cesar (1970-1986)	CF	54.2
191	**Clarke, Fred (1894-1915)**	**LF**	**57.8**	224	**Medwick, Joe (1932-1948)**	**LF**	**54.2**
192	**Herman, Billy (1931-1947)**[†]	**2B**	**57.7**	225	Pinson, Vada (1958-1975)	CF	54.1
193	Randolph, Willie (1975-1992)	2B	57.4	226	**Doby, Larry (1947-1959)**[^]	**CF**	**54.0**
194	Sheffield, Gary (1988-2009)[~]	RF	57.2	227	**Ward, Monte (1878-1894)**	**SS**	**54.0**
195	**Brown, Mordecai (1903-1916)**	**SP**	**57.1**	228	Clark, Will (1986-2000)	1B	53.9
196	Davis, Willie (1960-1979)	CF	57.0		*Pedroia, Dustin (2006-2019)*	*2B*	*53.9*
197	Hudson, Tim (1999-2015)	SP	57.0	229	Garciaparra, Nomar (1996-2009)	SS	53.8
	Hernandez, Felix (2005-2019)	*SP*	*56.9*	230	Koosman, Jerry (1967-1985)	SP	53.7
198	Hershiser, Orel (1983-2000)	SP	56.8		*Sale, Chris (2010-2019)*	*SP*	*53.4*
199	Olerud, John (1989-2005)	1B	56.8	231	**Grimes, Burleigh (1916-1934)**	**SP**	**53.4**
200	Tanana, Frank (1973-1993)	SP	56.5	232	Kaat, Jim (1959-1983)	SP	53.3
201	Bonds, Bobby (1968-1981)	RF	56.4	233	Walters, Bucky (1931-1950)	SP	53.2
202	*Griffith, Clark (1891-1914)	SP	56.4	234	Freehan, Bill (1961-1976)	C	53.1
203	**Killebrew, Harmon (1954-1975)**	**1B**	**56.3**	235	Newsom, Bobo (1929-1953)	SP	53.0
204	**Burkett, Jesse (1890-1905)**	**LF**	**56.3**				

* Clark Griffith was elected as a pioneer/executive in 1946 after failing to be elected as a player. Albert Spalding was elected as a pioneer/executive in 1939 without ever being considered as a player.

Table 10.5: The Rest of the Top 2%

	Player	Posn	CVI		Player	Posn	CVI
236	**Sutter, Bruce (1976-1988)**	**RP**	53.0	272	**Puckett, Kirby (1984-1995)**	**CF**	49.9
237	**Ford, Whitey (1950-1967)**[+]	**SP**	52.8	273	**Kelly, King (1878-1893)**	**RF**	49.8
238	**Dean, Dizzy (1930-1947)**	**SP**	52.6	274	**Doerr, Bobby (1937-1951)**[+]	**2B**	49.7
239	Lee, Cliff (2002-2014)	SP	52.6	275	**Klein, Chuck (1928-1944)**	**RF**	49.6
240	Lemon, Chet (1975-1990)	CF	52.6	276	Gonzalez, Luis (1990-2008)	LF	49.5
241	Adams, Babe (1906-1926)	SP	52.6	277	**Sewell, Joe (1920-1933)**	**SS**	49.5
242	Viola, Frank (1982-1996)	SP	52.5	278	McGriff, Fred (1986-2004)	1B	49.3
243	**Flick, Elmer (1898-1910)**	**RF**	52.4	279	Rucker, Nap (1907-1916)	SP	49.3
244	Tenace, Gene (1969-1983)	C	52.4	280	**Gomez, Lefty (1930-1943)**	**SP**	49.2
245	Murphy, Dale (1976-1993)	CF	52.3	281	Johnson, Bob (1933-1945)	LF	49.2
246	Pierce, Billy (1945-1964)	SP	52.3	282	Cash, Norm (1958-1974)	1B	49.1
247	**Wheat, Zack (1909-1927)**	**LF**	52.3	283	**Keeler, Willie (1892-1910)**	**RF**	49.1
248	**Rixey, Eppa (1912-1933)**[+]	**SP**	52.1		*deGrom, Jacob (2014-2020)*	*SP*	*48.9*
249	**Keller, Charlie (1939-1952)**[+]	**LF**	52.0		Zobrist, Ben (2006-2019)	2B	48.9
250	**Ewing, Buck (1880-1897)**	**C**	51.8	284	Cruz, Jose (1970-1988)	LF	48.8
251	John, Tommy (1963-1989)	SP	51.8	285	Martinez, Dennis (1976-1998)	SP	48.7
252	**Jennings, Hughie (1891-1918)**	**SS**	51.8	286	Quinn, Jack (1909-1933)	SP	48.7
	Cano, Robinson (2005-2020)	*2B*	*51.6*	287	**Rizzuto, Phil (1941-1956)**[+]	**SS**	48.7
253	Palmeiro, Rafael (1986-2005)⁻	1B	51.6	288	Giles, Brian (1995-2009)	RF	48.6
	Wright, David (2004-2018)	3B	51.5	289	Vazquez, Javier (1998-2011)	SP	48.6
254	Kent, Jeff (1992-2008)	2B	51.5	290	Cey, Ron (1971-1987)	3B	48.6
255	**Perez, Tony (1964-1986)**	**1B**	51.4	291	Knoblauch, Chuck (1991-2002)	2B	48.6
256	Ventura, Robin (1989-2004)	3B	51.4	292	Wells, David (1987-2007)	SP	48.6
257	**White, Deacon (1871-1890)**	**3B**	51.3	293	**Bancroft, Dave (1915-1930)**	**SS**	48.5
258	**Pennock, Herb (1912-1934)**[+]	**SP**	51.2	294	Harrah, Toby (1969-1986)	3B	48.5
259	Posada, Jorge (1995-2011)	C	51.2		Colon, Bartolo (1997-2018)	SP	48.4
260	Trout, Dizzy (1939-1957)	SP	51.1		*Donaldson, Josh (2010-2020)*	*3B*	*48.4*
261	Harder, Mel (1928-1947)	SP	51.0	295	Campaneris, Bert (1964-1983)	SS	48.3
262	Berkman, Lance (1999-2013)	LF	51.0	296	Lolich, Mickey (1963-1979)	SP	48.2
263	Lynn, Fred (1974-1990)	CF	51.0	297	Moyer, Jamie (1986-2012)	SP	48.2
264	Finley, Chuck (1986-2002)⁻	SP	50.5	298	**Kelley, Joe (1891-1908)**	**LF**	48.2
	Kinsler, Ian (2006-2019)	2B	50.5	299	Blue, Vida (1969-1986)	SP	48.1
265	**Rice, Jim (1974-1989)**	**LF**	50.5	300	**O'Rourke, Jim (1872-1904)**	**LF**	48.0
266	**Averill, Earl (1929-1941)**	**CF**	50.4	301	Jackson, Larry (1955-1968)	SP	47.9
267	Kinder, Ellis (1946-1957)	RP	50.2	302	Schang, Wally (1913-1931)	C	47.9
268	**Beckley, Jake (1888-1907)**	**1B**	50.1	303	Damon, Johnny (1995-2012)	CF	47.8
269	**Collins, Jimmy (1895-1908)**	**3B**	50.1	304	Key, Jimmy (1984-1998)	SP	47.7
	Teixeira, Mark (2003-2016)	1B	50.1	305	Magee, Sherry (1904-1919)	LF	47.7
270	Fregosi, Jim (1961-1978)	SS	50.0	306	Wilson, Willie (1976-1994)	CF	47.7
271	Hack, Stan (1932-1947)	3B	49.9				

Table 10.5 lists 71 HOF-eligible players, of whom 25 (31%) have been elected to the HOF and eight active or recently retired players (of whom only Jacob deGrom is on a likely HOF track). I would choose three players from this table as borderline candidates for my personal HOF – Sutter (higher peak than Smith or Fingers, but shorter duration), Whitey Ford (his post-season dominance is not captured by WAR or CVI), and Buck Ewing (widely regarded as the best catcher of MLB's first half century but his playing time was circumscribed by the nature of the 19th century game). That brings my personal HOF to 177 players (the 1.18 percentile) if I am strict or 190 players (the 1.26 percentile) if I am more lenient.

Table 10.6: Hall of Famers with CVI Outside the Top 2%

	Player	Posn	CVI		Player	Posn	CVI
1	Tinker, Joe (1902-1916)	SS	47.4	24	Wilson, Hack (1923-1934)	CF	39.6
2	Fox, Nellie (1947-1965)	2B	47.1	25	Thompson, Sam (1885-1906)	RF	39.6
3	Aparicio, Luis (1956-1973)	SS	46.4	26	Combs, Earle (1924-1935)	CF	39.0
4	Hoyt, Waite (1918-1938)	SP	46.3	27	Jackson, Travis (1922-1936)	SS	38.9
5	Cepeda, Orlando (1958-1974)	1B	45.7	28	Roush, Edd (1913-1931)	CF	38.2
6	Rice, Sam (1915-1934)[†]	RF	45.7	29	Duffy, Hugh (1888-1906)	CF	38.1
7	Carey, Max (1910-1929)	CF	45.2	30	Morris, Jack (1977-1994)	SP	37.8
8	McPhee, Bid (1882-1899)	2B	44.5	31	Lombardi, Ernie (1931-1947)	C	36.1
9	Bresnahan, Roger (1897-1915)	C	44.5	32	Baines, Harold (1980-2001)	DH	32.8
10	Hooper, Harry (1909-1925)	RF	44.2	33	Schalk, Ray (1912-1929)	C	32.4
11	Lazzeri, Tony (1926-1939)	2B	44.2	34	Marquard, Rube (1908-1925)	SP	31.3
12	Chance, Frank (1898-1914)	1B	44.1	35	Traynor, Pie (1920-1937)	3B	31.0
13	Manush, Heinie (1923-1939)	LF	43.8	36	Bottomley, Jim (1922-1937)	1B	30.6
14	Cuyler, Kiki (1921-1938)	RF	43.2	37	Kell, George (1943-1957)	3B	30.2
15	Chesbro, Jack (1899-1909)	SP	42.6	38	Mazeroski, Bill (1956-1972)	2B	30.1
16	Brock, Lou (1961-1979)	LF	42.3	39	Youngs, Ross (1917-1926)	RF	29.8
17	Joss, Addie (1902-1910)	SP	42.1	40	Haines, Jesse (1918-1937)	SP	29.1
18	Evers, Johnny (1902-1929)	2B	41.2	41	Lindstrom, Freddie (1924-1936)	3B	26.2
19	Bender, Chief (1903-1925)	SP	40.9	42	Ferrell, Rick (1929-1947)	C	26.2
20	Lemon, Bob (1941-1958)[†]	SP	40.9	43	Hafey, Chick (1924-1937)	LF	25.4
21	Maranville, Rabbit (1912-1935)[†]	SS	40.2	44	Waner, Lloyd (1927-1945)	CF	23.4
22	Hunter, Catfish (1965-1979)	SP	40.2	45	Kelly, High Pockets (1915-1932)[†]	1B	22.5
23	Schoendienst, Red (1945-1963)	2B	39.8	46	McCarthy, Tommy (1884-1896)	RF	16.3

The 46 CVI-Minus players in Table 10.6 do not belong in the HOF; most are not even close calls. One might argue that some of the listed middle infielders – Tinker, Fox, Aparicio, Maranville, Mazeroski, Rizzuto and Bancroft from Table 10.5, and current HOF candidate Omar Vizquel – merit recognition for their defensive prowess. But in my view, unless one is talking about a truly exceptional defensive player like Ozzie Smith, plaques in the HOF should be reserved for the best all-around players, not players whose excellence in one circumscribed facet of the game was offset by glaring deficiencies in other important aspects. A few of these players – Brock, who was instrumental in elevating the stolen base to new importance, or Hack Wilson, who holds the all-time RBI record for one season – have historical significance beyond their CVI, but then so do non-Hall of Famers Roger Maris, Don Larsen, and Johnny Vander Meer. The HOF should honor their special achievements, but not by anointing these players as among the best of all time.

Tables 10.7-8 summarize the players who have been retired long enough to qualify for the HOF ballot whom I would add or subtract from the HOF if I had my way. Table 10.7 lists the 24-29 non-Hall of Famers I would add to the HOF and the 13 with CVI ≥60 whom I would leave out. I have not considered adding any players with CVI <60 to the HOF.

I have made room for these additions and trimmed the size of my personal HOF from 235 to 177-190 by "demoting" 74-82 current Hall of Famers (Table 10.8). I have not considered demoting any current Hall of Famers with CVI ≥62 (see Tables 10.1-3) or retaining any of the 57 current Hall of Famers with CVI <50 (see Tables 10.5-6). I have explained the reasoning behind my admittedly subjective selections in Table 10.7-8 earlier in this chapter. Many of these selections are very close calls.

In fairness to the actual HOF selection committees, I must acknowledge that since mine is a virtual Hall of Fame, based only on my assessment of players' performance on the diamond, I need not concern myself about any of my honorees embarrassing me by giving an off-the-wall rant at his induction ceremony or about sending the wrong message about the morality of cheating, gambling, domestic violence, marital infidelity, substance abuse, or the other human failings large and small to which we humans are prone. The directors of the real Hall of Fame, which is a physical entity do not have this luxury. I also understand that they can't actually "demote" players who have already been elected.

Table 10.7: Non-Hall of Famers with CVI ≥ 60: Who Belongs in the HOF?*

	Elevate to HOF	Posn	CVI		Borderline	Posn	CVI
1	Bonds, Barry	LF	203.8	1	Reuschel, Rick	SP	67.0
2	Clemens, Roger	SP	172.3	2	Saberhagen, Bret	SP	66.5
3	Schilling, Curt	SP	97.4	3	Bando, Sal	3B	65.1
4	Rose, Pete	LF	83.6	4	Evans, Dwight	RF	61.9
5	Grich, Bobby	2B	77.9	5	Pettitte, Andy	SP	60.1
6	Glasscock, Jack	SS	74.8				
7	Wood, Wilbur	SP	74.7				
8	Rolen, Scott	3B	70.8				
9	Lofton, Kenny	CF	70.6		**Dismiss**	**Posn**	**CVI**
10	Cone, David	SP	70.0	1	Jackson, Shoeless Joe	RF	87.0
11	Jones, Andruw	CF	69.8	2	Ferrell, Wes	SP	69.6
12	Helton, Todd	1B	69.7	3	McCormick, Jim	SP	69.4
13	Boyer, Ken	3B	69.2	4	Brown, Kevin	SP	67.0
14	Dahlen, Bill	SS	68.8	5	Buffinton, Charlie	SP	65.8
15	Bond, Tommy	SP	68.2	6	Appier, Kevin	SP	63.7
16	Nettles, Graig	3B	67.0	7	Cicotte, Eddie	SP	63.6
17	Whitaker, Lou	2B	66.9	8	Stieb, Dave	SP	63.6
18	Allen, Dick	1B	66.5	9	Mathews, Bobby	SP	62.7
19	Bell, Buddy	3B	66.2	10	Santana, Johan	SP	62.6
20	Tiant, Luis	SP	65.0	11	Hiller, John	RP	60.7
21	Hernandez, Keith	1B	61.2				
22	Edmonds, Jim	CF	61.0				
23	Munson, Thurman	C	60.6				
24	Minoso, Minnie	LF	60.5				

* Retired at least five years.

Table 10.8: Hall of Famers with CVI <62: Who Belongs in the HOF?

	Retain in HOF	Posn	CVI		Demote	Posn	CVI
1	Hartnett, Gabby	C	60.7	1	Clarke, Fred	LF	57.8
2	Guerrero, Vladimir	RF	58.6	2	Herman, Billy	2B	57.7
3	Terry, Bill	1B	57.8	3	Burkett, Jesse	LF	56.3
4	Brown, Mordecai	SP	57.1	4	Welch, Mickey	SP	55.9
5	Killebrew, Harmon	1B	56.3	5	Grimes, Burleigh	SP	53.4
6	Hoffman, Trevor	RP	56.2	6	Dean, Dizzy	SP	52.6
7	Stargell, Willie	LF	55.5	7	Flick, Elmer	RF	52.4
8	Kiner, Ralph	LF	55.2	8	Wheat, Zack	LF	52.3
9	Doby, Larry	CF	54.0	9	Rixey, Eppa	SP	52.1
10	Ward, Monte	SS	54.0	10	Jennings, Hughie	SS	51.8
				11	Perez, Tony	1B	51.4
	Borderline	**Posn**	**CVI**	12	White, Deacon	3B	51.3
1	Wynn, Early	SP	60.6	13	Pennock, Herb	SP	51.2
2	Sutton, Don	SP	58.7	14	Rice, Jim	LF	50.5
3	Smith, Lee	RP	55.4	15	Averill, Earl	CF	50.4
4	Fingers, Rollie	RP	55.0	16	Collins, Jimmy	3B	50.1
5	Medwick, Joe	LF	54.2	17	Beckley, Jake	1B	50.1
6	Sutter, Bruce	RP	53.0		Additionally, 57 Hall of Famers		
7	Ford, Whitey	SP	52.8		have CVI <50.		
8	Ewing, Buck	C	51.8				

TOP PLAYERS AT EACH POSITION

Tables 10.9-11 list the top players at each position. In these tables, I have integrated SP and RP into a single list and have listed DH at their most frequently played defensive position. As in Tables 10.1-8, players who have been elected to the HOF through 2020 are shown in boldface type.

Table 10.9: Top Infielders

	First Basemen	CVI	Second Basemen	CVI	Shortstops	CVI	Third Basemen	CVI
1	Gehrig, Lou	165.4	Hornsby, Rogers	185.0	Wagner, Honus	172.4	Schmidt, Mike	142.0
2	*Pujols, Albert*	*132.7*	Collins, Eddie	154.8	Ripken, Cal	113.3	Mathews, Eddie	116.7
3	Foxx, Jimmie	117.2	Lajoie, Nap	130.6	Rodriguez, Alex	106.0	Boggs, Wade	110.8
4	Anson, Cap	108.8	Morgan, Joe	120.6	Vaughan, Arky	93.8	Brett, George	101.3
5	Connor, Roger	102.7	Robinson, Jackie	106.8	Appling, Luke	85.9	Beltre, Adrian	98.8
6	Brouthers, Dan	102.3	Gehringer, Charlie	95.3	Yount, Robin	83.9	Martinez, Edgar (DH)	89.7
7	Mize, Johnny	97.2	Carew, Rod	88.7	Banks, Ernie	83.8	Jones, Chipper	88.3
8	Bagwell, Jeff	87.8	Grich, Bobby	77.9	Davis, George	83.3	Santo, Ron	88.1
9	Thomas, Frank (DH)	87.4	Utley, Chase	76.3	Reese, Pee Wee	78.3	Robinson, Brooks	82.2
10	Greenberg, Hank	82.3	Sandberg, Ryne	74.3	Glasscock, Jack	74.8	Molitor, Paul (DH)	77.8
11	Thome, Jim	73.8	Frisch, Frankie	73.8	Smith, Ozzie	74.6	Rolen, Scott	70.8
12	*Cabrera, Miguel*	*72.2*	Gordon, Joe	69.2	Trammel, Alan	74.5	Baker, Home Run	70.6
13	Helton, Todd	69.7	Biggio, Craig	68.6	Wallace, Bobby	73.8	Boyer, Ken	69.2
14	McCovey, Willie	69.4	Alomar, Roberto	67.7	Boudreau, Lou	73.7	Nettles, Graig	67.0
15	*Votto, Joey*	*68.9*	Whitaker, Lou	66.9	Jeter, Derek	71.3	Bell, Buddy	66.2
16	Allen, Dick	66.5	Herman, Billy	57.7	Larkin, Barry	70.4	Bando, Sal	65.1
17	Ortiz, David (DH)	65.4	Randolph, Willie	57.4	Dahlen, Bill	68.8	Evans, Darrell	58.6
18	Sisler, George	65.2	Pedroia, Dustin	53.9	Cronin, Joe	67.2	*Longoria, Evan*	*58.6*

Table 10.10: Top Catchers and Outfielders

	Catchers	CVI	Left Fielders	CVI	Center Fielders	CVI	Right Fielders	CVI
1	Bench, Johnny	111.7	Bonds, Barry	203.8	Mays, Willie	232.3	Ruth, Babe	270.0
2	Carter, Gary	103.1	Williams, Ted	199.5	Cobb, Ty	198.0	Aaron, Henry	187.5
3	Rodriguez, Ivan	85.3	Musial, Stan	178.1	Speaker, Tris	174.6	Ott, Mel	131.0
4	Piazza, Mike	83.2	Henderson, Rickey	134.9	Mantle, Mickey	143.0	Robinson, Frank	118.8
5	Fisk, Carlton	82.8	Yastrzemski, Carl	110.8	*Trout, Mike*	*111.4*	Clemente, Roberto	110.9
6	Berra, Yogi	74.1	Rose, Pete	83.6	DiMaggio, Joe	107.4	Kaline, Al	99.0
7	Dickey, Bill	71.0	Delahanty, Ed	80.5	Griffey, Ken	101.8	Jackson, Shoeless Joe	87.0
8	Mauer, Joe	69.7	Simmons, Al	72.7	Snider, Duke	76.8	Suzuki, Ichiro	81.9
9	Simmons, Ted	65.0	Raines, Tim	69.5	Beltran, Carlos	72.6	Jackson, Reggie	80.7
10	Torre, Joe	65.0	Goslin, Goose	66.6	Lofton, Kenny	70.6	Heilmann, Harry	77.8
11	Cochrane, Mickey	64.8	Williams, Billy	62.7	Jones, Andruw	69.8	Walker, Larry	75.7
12	Campanella, Roy	63.1	Minoso, Minnie	60.5	Ashburn, Richie	67.4	Waner, Paul	71.7
13	Hartnett, Gabby	60.7	Clarke, Fred	57.8	Hamilton, Billy	64.7	Dawson, Andre	71.1
14	Munson, Thurman	60.6	Burkett, Jesse	56.3	Edmonds, Jim	61.0	Gwynn, Tony	68.3
15	*Posey, Buster*	*55.7*	Stargell, Willie	55.5	Wynn, Jim	59.4	Crawford, Sam	68.2
16	Freehan, Bill	53.1	Kiner, Ralph	55.2	Davis, Willie	57.0	Winfield, Dave	65.3

Table 10.11: Top Pitchers

	Pitchers	CVI	Pitchers	CVI	Pitchers	CVI	Pitchers	CVI
1	Johnson, Walter	211.8	Carlton, Steve	100.6	Vance, Dazzy	77.8	McCormick, Jim	69.4
2	Young, Cy	194.0	Roberts, Robin	100.1	Newhouser, Hal	77.1	Palmer, Jim	69.3
3	Clemens, Roger	172.3	Schilling, Curt	97.4	Radbourn, Old Hoss	76.6	Waddell, Rube	69.0
4	Grove, Lefty	161.4	Clarkson, John	96.0	Marichal, Juan	76.1	Bond, Tommy	68.2
5	Alexander, Grover	146.6	*Verlander, Justin*	*91.1*	Eckersley, Dennis (RP)	75.9	Lyons, Ted	67.6
6	Johnson, Randy	144.1	Mussina, Mike	91.1	Hubbell, Carl	75.7	Reuschel, Rick	67.0
7	Mathewson, Christy	129.2	Gossage, Rich (RP)	90.6	Wood, Wilbur	74.7	Brown, Kevin	67.0
8	Maddux, Greg	128.2	Keefe, Tim	88.5	Wilhelm, Hoyt (RP)	74.3	Saberhagen, Bret	66.5
9	Seaver, Tom	120.5	Halladay, Roy	88.4	Coveleski, Stan	74.2	Buffinton, Charlie	65.8
10	Nichols, Kid	119.9	*Kershaw, Clayton*	*87.4*	Bunning, Jim	73.1	Drysdale, Don	65.8
11	Martinez, Pedro	118.2	Jenkins, Fergie	86.2	McGinnity, Joe	72.6	Tiant, Luis	65.0
12	Spahn, Warren	114.4	Walsh, Ed	83.5	Smoltz, John	71.9	Appier, Kevin	63.7
13	Niekro, Phil	108.4	Galvin, Pud	82.5	Rusie, Amos	70.7	Cicotte, Eddie	63.6
14	Feller, Bob	107.0	*Greinke, Zack*	*82.4*	Faber, Red	70.4	Stieb, Dave	63.6
15	Blyleven, Bert	104.2	*Scherzer, Max*	*80.7*	Koufax, Sandy	70.2	Sabathia, CC	63.4
16	Gibson, Bob	103.5	Plank, Eddie	80.4	Cone, David	70.0	Ruffing, Red	62.8
17	Rivera, Mariano (RP)	101.9	Ryan, Nolan	79.9	Ferrell, Wes	69.6	Mathews, Bobby	62.7
18	Perry, Gaylord	100.7	Glavine, Tom	78.7	Willis, Vic	69.4	Santana, Johan	62.6

All-Time All-Star Teams

Just for fun, I have used CVI to construct virtual all-star teams of the best single seasons (rather than the best careers) at each position in the 120 years since the modern AL-NL construct was established. Each 32-man all-star roster has 20 position players (two at each position and four "utility" players), 10 starting pitchers, and two relievers. Players are listed at the position they played most often during their peak season. No more than one season from any single player is included. Roger Clemens's 11.9-WAR_P 1997 season is the only steroid enhanced season that made the cut, beating out his natural 10.4-WAR_P 1990 season. Barry Bonds's natural 9.9-WAR_H 1993 season beat out his "enhanced" 11.9-WAR_H 2001 season. The steroid adjustment knocked Alex Rodriguez's enhanced 10.4-WAR_H 2000 season and Sammy Sosa's enhanced 10.3-WAR_H 2001 season off the team.

These All-Star teams include mostly elite players (20 Hall of Famers on the AL team, and 24 on the NL team) but also several "one-year wonders." Several elite players (Henderson, Ott, Frank Robinson, Mathews, Maddux, DiMaggio) who never had a 10-WAR season are absent. Here are the biggest surprises:

American League:

1. Al Rosen (1953) had the all-time best season of any 3B in either league. He had three other 4.5-6 WAR seasons but finished with only 32.6 WAR in 10 years. Mookie Betts (2018) also made the team.

2. Being based on WAR_P, CVI favors old-time 120+ IP relievers over modern 60-IP relievers. So, Hiller (1973) beat out HOF closers Rivera and Eckersley, who had more sustained success.

3. Four White Sox pitchers (Wood, Gossage, Cicotte, Walsh) made the team. A fifth, Red Faber, was tied with Walsh, Ford, Cicotte and Greinke for the final SP slot, but I used his -0.3 WAR_H that season as a tiebreaker.

4. Non-HOF All-Stars:

   a. Eligible but not elected: Ford, Hiller, Petrocelli, Porter, Rosen, Wood

   b. Still on BBWAA Ballot: Clemens

   c. Banned: Cicotte

5. Active or Recently Retired: Beltre, Betts, Greinke, Mauer, Trout.

Table 10.12: All-Time AL and NL All-Stars

C	AL Player (Year)	WAR_{II}	CVI	NL Player (Year)	WAR_{II}	CVI
C	Joe Mauer (2009)	7.8	13.6	Mike Piazza (1997)	8.7	15.8
1B	Lou Gehrig (1927)	11.8	20.3	Albert Pujols (2009)	9.7	15.3
2B	Eddie Collins (1910)	10.5	17.2	Rogers Hornsby (1924)	12.2	21.3
SS	Cal Ripken (1991)	11.5	19.6	Honus Wagner (1908)	11.5	19.6
3B	Al Rosen (1953)	10.2	16.5	Ron Santo (1967)	9.8	15.5
LF	Carl Yastrzemski (1967)	12.5	22.0	Barry Bonds (1993)	9.9	15.8
CF	Mickey Mantle (1957)	11.3	19.1	Willie Mays (1965)	11.2	18.9
RF	Babe Ruth (1923)	14.1	25.8	Stan Musial (1948)	11.3	19.1
Bench						
C	Darrell Porter (1979)	7.6	13.1	Johnny Bench (1972)	8.6	15.5
1B	Jimmy Foxx (1932)	10.4	17.0	Jeff Bagwell (1994)	8.2	13.8
2B	Nap Lajoie (1906)	10.0	16.0	Joe Morgan (1975)	11.0	18.4
SS	Robin Yount (1982)	10.6	17.4	Ernie Banks (1959)	10.2	16.5
3B	Adrian Beltre (2004)	9.6	15.0	Mike Schmidt (1974)	9.7	15.3
OF	Ty Cobb (1917)	11.3	19.1	Lonnie Smith (1989)	8.8	13.1
OF	Ted Williams (1946)	10.6	17.4	Henry Aaron (1961)	9.5	14.8
OF	Mookie Betts (2018)	10.6	17.4	Larry Walker (1997)	9.8	15.5
UT	Mike Trout (2012, 2016)	10.5	17.2	Gary Carter (1982)	8.6	15.5
UT	Lou Boudreau (1948)	10.3	16.7	Bryce Harper (2015)	9.7	15.3
UT	Tris Speaker (1912)	10.1	16.2	Jackie Robinson (1951)	9.7	15.3
UT	Rico Petrocelli (1969)	10.0	16.0	Arky Vaughan (1935)	9.7	15.3
Pitchers	**AL Player (Year)**	WAR_{P}	CVI	**NL Player (Year)**	WAR_{P}	CVI
SP	Walter Johnson (1913)	15.1	26.6	Dwight Gooden (1985)	12.2	21.3
SP	Pedro Martinez (2000)	11.7	20.9	Steve Carlton (1972)	12.1	20.2
SP	Cy Young (1901)	12.6	19.8	Grover Alexander (1920)	11.9	19.0
SP	Wilbur Wood (1971)	11.8	19.5	Randy Johnson (2002)	10.7	18.5
SP	Hal Newhouser (1945)	11.3	19.1	Bob Gibson (1968)	11.2	18.1
SP	Roger Clemens (1997)*	10.7	18.5	Aaron Nola (2018)	10.2	18.1
SP	Ed Walsh (1912)	11.4	17.8	Christy Mathewson (1908)	11.8	17.9
SP	Russ Ford (1910)			Joe McGinnity (1903)	11.7	17.7
SP	Eddie Cicotte (1917)			Sandy Koufax (1963)	10.7	17.7
SP	Zack Greinke (2009)	10.4	17.8	Jacob deGrom (2018)	9.9	17.4
RP	Rich Gossage (1975)	8.2	19.8	Bruce Sutter (1977)	6.5	13.2
RP	John Hiller (1973)	7.9	18.2	Lindy McDaniel (1960)	5.9	12.7

*0.9 steroid adjustment applied to WAR_{P}.

National League:

1. Dwight Gooden (1985) owns the top pitching performance of the modern NL. Only Walter Johnson (1913) was better.

2. McDaniel (1960) beat out Hall of Famers Lee Smith and Hoffman.

3. Ron Santo (1967) edged out Mike Schmidt (1974) as starting 3B.

4. Non-HOF All-Stars:

    a. Eligible but not elected: Gooden, McDaniel, Lonnie Smith

    b. Still on BBWAA Ballot: Bonds

    c. Banned: None

5. Active: deGrom, Harper, Nola, Pujols.

CHAPTER 11

THE HALL OF FAME

Starting in 1936, MLB began a tradition of honoring of honoring its most illustrious players, managers, and executives in a dedicated wing of a museum to be called the Hall of Fame (HOF).[1,2] This museum opened in Cooperstown, NY in 1939 to commemorate the centennial of the apocryphal "invention" of baseball by Abner Doubleday (an event that we can be quite certain never actually occurred). Still, Cooperstown is a beautiful, nostalgic setting and exemplifies the bucolic America in which the more nebulous origins of the sport reside. So what's wrong with a little creation myth?

I suspect that most baseball fans has a love-hate relationship with the HOF. On the one hand, we can't understand when they omit one of our favorites or elect a player we believe unworthy. We quibble that the HOF is too big or too small. We criticize their handling of players tainted by steroids. On the other hand, no true baseball fan can help but be charmed and awed when they visit the HOF and wander among the plaques honoring the icons of the game. I now offer a brief critical history of Baseball's Hall of Fame.

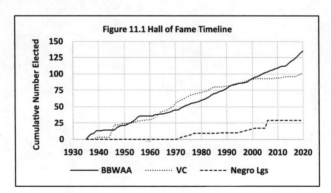

The HOF has used three distinct selection processes. The Baseball Writers Association of America (BBWAA) does the initial screening of recently retired players, the Veterans Committee (VC) deals with managers, executives, umpires, and long-retired players, and a series of special committees were formed to consider the Negro Leagues. The timeline for each of these processes is shown in Figure 11.1.

The first step in selection of players for the HOF was tasked primarily to the Baseball Writers Association of America (BBWAA). The bar was set high, with a 75% majority required for election. Over the years, the BBWAA has sent a steady stream of players to the Hall of Fame (Table 11.1) and have mostly chosen well. Almost 90% (120/134) of the players they selected are CVI-Plus (shown in boldface type).

Table 11.1: MLB Players Elected to the Hall of Fame by BBWAA (1936-2020)

Year	Name	Year	Name	Year	Name	Year	Name
1936	Ty Cobb	1956	Joe Cronin	1985	Lou Brock	2005	Ryne Sandberg
1936	Walter Johnson	1956	Hank Greenberg	1985	Hoyt Wilhelm	2006	Bruce Sutter
1936	Christy Mathewson	1962	Bob Feller	1986	Willie McCovey	2007	Tony Gwynn
1936	Babe Ruth	1962	Jackie Robinson	1987	Catfish Hunter	2007	Cal Ripken
1936	Honus Wagner	1964	Luke Appling	1987	Billy Williams	2008	Rich Gossage
1937	Nap Lajoie	1966	Ted Williams	1988	Willie Stargell	2009	Rickey Henderson
1937	Tris Speaker	1967	Red Ruffing	1989	Johnny Bench	2009	Jim Rice
1937	Cy Young	1968	Joe Medwick	1989	Carl Yastrzemski	2010	Andre Dawson
1938	Grover Alexander	1969	Roy Campanella	1990	Joe Morgan	2011	Roberto Alomar
1939	Eddie Collins	1969	Stan Musial	1990	Jim Palmer	2011	Bert Blyleven
1939	Lou Gehrig	1970	Lou Boudreau	1991	Rod Carew	2012	Barry Larkin
1939	Willie Keeler	1972	Yogi Berra	1991	Fergie Jenkins	2014	Tom Glavine
1939	George Sisler	1972	Sandy Koufax	1991	Gaylord Perry	2014	Greg Maddux
1942	Rogers Hornsby	1972	Early Wynn	1992	Rollie Fingers	2014	Frank Thomas
1947	Mickey Cochrane	1973	Roberto Clemente	1992	Tom Seaver	2015	Craig Biggio
1947	Frankie Frisch	1973	Warren Spahn	1993	Reggie Jackson	2015	Randy Johnson
1947	Lefty Grove	1974	Whitey Ford	1994	Steve Carlton	2015	Pedro Martinez
1947	Carl Hubbell	1974	Mickey Mantle	1995	Mike Schmidt	2015	John Smoltz
1948	Herb Pennock	1975	Ralph Kiner	1997	Phil Niekro	2016	Ken Griffey
1948	Pie Traynor	1976	Bob Lemon	1998	Don Sutton	2016	Mike Piazza
1949	Charlie Gehringer	1976	Robin Roberts	1999	George Brett	2017	Jeff Bagwell
1951	Jimmie Foxx	1977	Ernie Banks	1999	Nolan Ryan	2017	Tim Raines
1951	Mel Ott	1978	Eddie Mathews	1999	Robin Yount	2017	Ivan Rodriguez
1952	Harry Heilmann	1979	Willie Mays	2000	Carlton Fisk	2018	Vladimir Guerrero
1952	Paul Waner	1980	Al Kaline	2000	Tony Perez	2018	Trevor Hoffman
1953	Dizzy Dean	1980	Duke Snider	2001	Kirby Puckett	2018	Chipper Jones
1953	Al Simmons	1981	Bob Gibson	2001	Dave Winfield	2018	Jim Thome
1954	Bill Dickey	1982	Henry Aaron	2002	Ozzie Smith	2019	Roy Halladay
1954	Rabbit Maranville	1982	Frank Robinson	2003	Gary Carter	2019	Edgar Martinez
1954	Bill Terry	1983	Juan Marichal	2003	Eddie Murray	2019	Mike Mussina
1955	Joe DiMaggio	1983	Brooks Robinson	2004	Dennis Eckersley	2019	Mariano Rivera
1955	Gabby Hartnett	1984	Luis Aparicio	2004	Paul Molitor	2020	Derek Jeter
1955	Ted Lyons	1984	Don Drysdale	2005	Wade Boggs	2020	Larry Walker
1955	Dazzy Vance	1984	Harmon Killebrew				

Table 11.2: MLB Players Elected to the Hall of Fame by VC (1939-2020)

Year	Name	Year	Name	Year	Name
1939	Cap Anson	1955	Home Run Baker	1971	Jake Beckley
1939	Buck Ewing	1955	Ray Schalk	1971	Chick Hafey
1939	Old Hoss Radbourn	1957	Sam Crawford	1971	Harry Hooper
1945	Roger Bresnahan	1959	Zack Wheat	1971	Joe Kelley
1945	Dan Brouthers	1961	Max Carey	1971	Rube Marquard
1945	Fred Clarke	1961	Billy Hamilton	1972	Lefty Gomez
1945	Jimmy Collins	1962	Edd Roush	1972	Ross Youngs
1945	Ed Delahanty	1963	John Clarkson	1973	High Pockets Kelly
1945	Hugh Duffy	1963	Elmer Flick	1973	Mickey Welch
1945	Hughie Jennings	1963	Sam Rice	1974	Jim Bottomley
1945	King Kelly	1963	Eppa Rixey	1974	Sam Thompson
1945	Jim O'Rourke	1964	Red Faber	1975	Earl Averill
1946	Jesse Burkett	1964	Burleigh Grimes	1975	Billy Herman
1946	Frank Chance	1964	Tim Keefe	1976	Roger Connor
1946	Jack Chesbro	1964	Heinie Manush	1976	Freddie Lindstrom
1946	Johnny Evers	1964	Monte Ward	1977	Amos Rusie
1946	Tommy McCarthy	1965	Pud Galvin	1977	Joe Sewell
1946	Joe McGinnity	1967	Lloyd Waner	1978	Addie Joss
1946	Eddie Plank	1968	Kiki Cuyler	1979	Hack Wilson
1946	Joe Tinker	1968	Goose Goslin	1980	Chuck Klein
1946	Rube Waddell	1969	Stan Coveleski	1981	Johnny Mize
1946	Ed Walsh	1969	Waite Hoyt	1982	Travis Jackson
1949	Mordecai Brown	1970	Earle Combs	1983	George Kell
1949	Kid Nichols	1970	Jesse Haines	1984	Rick Ferrell
1953	Chief Bender	1971	Dave Bancroft	1984	Pee Wee Reese
1953	Bobby Wallace			1985	Enos Slaughter
				1985	Arky Vaughan
				1986	Bobby Doerr
				1986	Ernie Lombardi
				1989	Red Schoendienst
				1991	Tony Lazzeri
				1992	Hal Newhouser
				1994	Phil Rizzuto
				1995	Richie Ashburn
				1995	Vic Willis
				1996	Jim Bunning
				1997	Nellie Fox
				1998	George Davis
				1998	Larry Doby
				1999	Orlando Cepeda
				2000	Bid McPhee
				2001	Bill Mazeroski
				2009	Joe Gordon
				2012	Ron Santo
				2013	Deacon White
				2018	Jack Morris
				2018	Alan Trammell
				2019	Harold Baines
				2019	Lee Smith
				2020	Ted Simmons

However, recognizing that the BBWAA was ill-suited to evaluate players who retired before 1910, the HOF empaneled two committees with more historical expertise in 1937 — the Centennial Committee, a one-off committee to honor baseball's earliest pioneers, and a broad-based Veterans Committee (VC) to bring historical perspective to players whose careers antedated those of most BBWAA members and to honor worthy executives and managers. Their selections are listed in Table 11.2, again with CVI-Plus players in boldface type, (The Veterans Committee was called the Old-Timers Committee until 1953. Since 2010 there have been four separate committees that each focus on a different era. I use VC as shorthand for the entire process.[3]) On the whole, the VC has selected players more capriciously than the BBWAA; only 43% (43/101) of their selections fall in the CVI-Plus category.

Many years later, a panel was charged to consider players from the Negro Leagues, who were barred from MLB from 1889-1946. Table 11.3 shows the 29 players who were elected by this route between 1971 and 2006, of whom only three (W. Brown, Irvin, Paige) ever received an opportunity to compete in the newly integrated AL and NL. Although MLB now officially recognizes seven Negro Leagues that operated in 1920-48 as major leagues, and their statistics now appear in Baseball-Reference.com, these statistics cannot be taken at face value, since the teams in these leagues played fewer than 100 games per season and statistics from those games are incomplete.[4] Furthermore, many of the greatest black stars (e.g., Grant, Lloyd, Santop, Williams) played mostly before 1920 and/or played several seasons in Cuban, Mexican, or other leagues that are not officially recognized as major leagues (e.g., Dihigo, Mendez, Torriente). Thus, I have included not only their "official" major league WAR from the seven recognized Negro Leagues, but also their unofficial WAR earned in other professional games, as compiled in the Seamheads database.[5] Still, despite the spottiness of the official records, we have enough "official" data for players like Charleston, Foster, Gibson, Paige, Rogan, Stearnes, and Wells, who performed in the heyday of the Negro Leagues, to document unambiguously their lofty place among Baseball's all-time greats.

This division of labor between BBWAA and VC worked well at first. By the time the HOF opened its doors in 1939, 26 men had been elected – 13 by the BBWAA (including Lou Gehrig, who was terminally ill, in a special election), 10 managers-executives, and three 19th century stars (Anson, Ewing, and Radbourn). All but two of the 16 players elected were CVI-Plus (14), and even the CVI-Minus choices (Ewing and Keeler) were defensible. In 1942 and 1944, respectively, Rogers Hornsby (an all-time great) and Commissioner Kenesaw Mountain Landis were added. But then, in 1945-46, the VC election process began to go awry. Fewer than half (8/19) of the new players the VC added were CVI-Plus, and many of the 11 CVI-Minus choices were highly questionable. These inductions markedly lowered the threshold for HOF membership, but at least adhered to the VC's mission of evaluating players whose careers had not been fully considered by the BBWAA.

Table 11.3: Negro League Players Elected to the Hall of Fame (1971-2006)

Player	Posn	WAR Official*	Other**	AL/NL	Year Elected
Paige, Satchel (1927-1965)	P	37.4	13.9	9.0	1971
Gibson, Josh (1930-1946)	C	38.4	18.4		1972
Leonard, Buck (1933-1948)	1B	28.5	3.4		1972
Irvin, Monte (1938-1956)	OF	10.8	5.6	21.3	1973
Bell, Cool Papa (1922-1946)	CF/P	35.4	9.4		1974
Johnson, Judy (1918-1936)	3B	14.0	7.1		1975
Charleston, Oscar (1915-1941)	CF	48.3	30.3		1976
Dihigo, Martin (1922-1945)	P/SS/OF	22.8	37.2		1977
Lloyd, John Henry "Pop" (1906-1932)	2B/SS	14.1	38.4		1977
Dandridge, Ray (1933-1944)	3B	5.1	8.0		1987
Day, Leon (1934-1946)	P/OF	17.8	5.5		1995
Foster, Willie (1923-1937)	P	47.1	-8.4		1996
Wells, Willie (1924-1948)	SS	51.1	10.6		1997
Rogan, Bullet (1916-1938)	P/OF	61.5	0.2		1998
Williams, Smokey Joe (1907-1932)	P	6.6	48.9		1999
Stearnes, Turkey (1923-1940)	CF	49.7	1.3		2000
Smith, Hilton (1932-1948)	P	23.2	4.4		2001
Brown, Ray (1931-1945)	P	39.5	5.3		2006
Brown, Willard (1935-1948)	OF/SS	18.5	10.2	-0.6	2006
Cooper, Andy (1920-1939)	P	26.0	-1.0		2006
Grant, Frank (1887-1907)	2B	0.0	1.6		2006
Hill, Pete (1904-1925)	OF	4.2	42.5		2006
Mackey, Biz (1920-1947)	C	25.6	5.4		2006
Mendez, Jose (1907-1926)	P	7.2	40.9		2006
Santop, Louis (1910-1926)	C	2.5	14.4		2006
Suttles, Mule (1923-1944)	1B	36.8	-0.7		2006
Taylor, Ben (1909-1929)	1B	18.9	16.5		2006
Torriente, Cristobal (1912-1932)	CF	26.0	37.3		2006
Wilson, Jud (1922-1945)	1B/3B	34.5	10.2		2006

* Officially recognized major Negro leagues – Baseball-Reference.com (July 2021).

** Latin American leagues, barnstorming teams, etc. – Seamheads.com (July 2021).

After 14 relatively quiet years (1947-60), in which the VC elected only eight new members — five CVI-Plus and three CVI-Minus, all from the appropriate era — the VC became active again, expanding its mission to become a "court of appeals" for players previously considered and dismissed by the BBWAA. From 1961-80, the VC elected 41 new players to the HOF, almost four times as many as the 11 players they elected before 1945. Only 13 of the new electees (32%) were CVI-Plus. Perhaps even worse, only seven of the 38 newly elected CVI-Minus players – Beckley, Flick, Hooper, Joss, Kelley, Marquard, and Thompson – ended their careers before 1925; the rest all played within the 10 years preceding the first BBWAA election and thus had been (in theory) considered and dismissed by the BBWAA. Worst of all, the newly lowered standards were applied selectively to favor former teammates of ex-players sitting on the VC. Frankie Frisch (1967-73), Bill Terry (1971-76), and Waite Hoyt were the VC's most egregious practitioners of cronyism, but there were others; you can read more in Jay Jaffe's illuminating *Cooperstown Casebook*.[6]

Josh Gibson, with permission from the National Baseball Hall of Fame and Museum

But there was also good news. In 1971, the HOF appointed a subcommittee to study the Negro Leagues and identify players worthy of HOF induction. The subcommittee, relying heavily on eyewitness accounts, selected nine players before disbanding in 1977. The VC continued to elect a trickle of eight Negro League players (plus manager/executive/pioneer Rube Foster) in 1981-2001. Then, fearing that time was running out, the HOF appointed another special panel in 2001 to make one final exhaustive pass to identify and elect all remaining HOF-worthy candidates while some first-hand eyewitnesses were still alive. Twelve additional Negro League stars (as well as five executives) were honored in 2006. While none of this can set right the damage done to the livelihoods of these great ballplayers or the immeasurable loss of their statistical achievements to history, the HOF is only a museum and did what it could.

In 1981-2001, the VC pace slowed again to an average of one electee per year. Only three of the 22 new electees (Davis, McPhee, and Willis) finished their careers before 1925. There was still some cronyism, but overall standards had improved. Ten of the 22 electees were CVI-Plus, including three (Mize, Vaughan, and Davis,) with CVI >80. However, the election of the defensively brilliant but offensively challenged Bill Mazeroski in 2001 elicited considerable criticism and calls for further reform. So, new rules were instituted to make it more difficult for the VC to elect players, specifically limiting each year's ballot to 10 names from a specific era, which would rotate from year to year. The VC has elected eight MLB players since 2001, five of whom were CVI-Plus (Santo, Trammell, Gordon, Simmons, and Smith).

Setting aside the 29 Negro League electees, who (through no fault of their own) never played in the White major leagues or played there only in their declining years, two questions arise about the 235 men elected to the HOF based on their performance as MLB players: (1) Is 235 the right number of such players in the HOF? (2) If this is the right number, did the electors choose the most deserving 235 players? Let's take a look.

The answer to the first question is subjective, but our close examination of players in the "Very Good" group (#175-235 in Table 2.7) in the previous chapters strongly suggests that 235 (which corresponds to 1.55% of all players who debuted before 2004) is too many. I proposed in Chapter 2 that a cutoff of 62.0 CVI, which would admit the top 1.16% of MLB players, is a more discriminating indicator of HOF-worthiness. I cite as empirical evidence the fact that 143 of the 174 HOF-eligible players with CVI ≥62 (81%) have been elected to the HOF, while only 20 of the remaining 61 HOF-eligible CVI-Plus players (33%) are in the HOF.

But even if we accept the number 235, the HOF electors clearly did not choose the best 235 HOF-eligible players. Admittedly, ranking players is not an exact science; there is little meaningful difference between a CVI of, say, 54 versus 52. If one wanted to allow the 235 most worthy eligible players into the HOF, one might realistically have expected a knowledgeable and thoughtful panel of electors to override pure statistics in perhaps 10% of cases and thereby choose 20-25 CVI-Minus players over 20-25 CVI-Plus players. Instead, 72 CVI-Minus players have been chosen over 72 CVI-Plus players, a 31% selection rate of players who are statistically inferior — far inferior in many cases — to those who were left out.

The pre-integration VC selection process is the source of both problems (Figures 11.2-3). The BBWAA has done an excellent job of maintaining high objective standards for election to the HOF (Figure 11.2). Of the 134 elected by the BBWAA, 120 (90%) are CVI-Plus; 109 (81%) have CVI ≥62.0. and another 9 (7%) are CVI-235. Only 13 (10%) are CVI-Minus. By contrast, only 43 of the 101 VC selectees are CVI-Plus, and only 34 have CVI ≥62 (Figure 11.3). The VC process was especially problematic for the Deadball and Classical generations. Of the 58 VC selectees

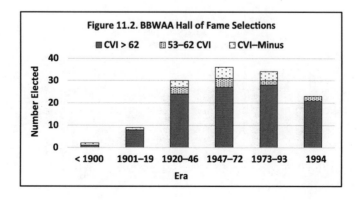

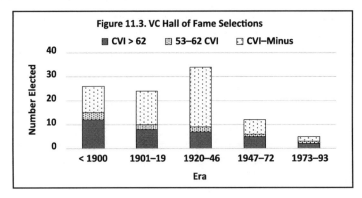

who peaked during 1900-46, only 15 (15%) had CVI $\geq$62.0, and an astonishing 39 (67%) were CVI-Minus. These numbers improved in 1947-1993, when there were 9 CVI-Plus and 8 CVI-Minus VC electees.

Admittedly, the VC process starts with a depleted pool of leftovers from the BBWAA process; the best of the best are elected before the VC gets an opportunity to weigh in. Still, the VC seems to have often been swayed by misguided loyalty to friends and ex-teammates to honor players that the BBWAA could have elected but didn't. Although the volume of VC electees has slowed since 2000, this flawed process, rife with cronyism and subjectivity, continues to put too many CVI-Minus players in the HOF. The unexpected election of Harold Baines (32.1 CVI) in December 2018 (see Chapter 7, Bottom of the Pile) is just the most recent example.

Racial Parity in the Hall of Fame

Apart from selecting so many players with dubious HOF credentials, the VC has also raised some eyebrows for electing very few players of color to the HOF. Until the election of Lee Smith and Harold Baines in December 2018, the VC had elected only one African American and one Latino player (Doby and Cepeda, respectively). Of

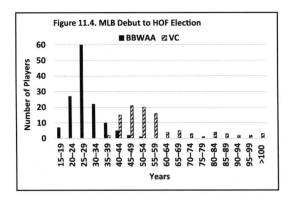

course, the VC has elected only 12 players of any race who debuted after Jackie Robinson blazed the trail for integration in 1947. Since the VC considers MLB players only after they have passed through the BBWAA selection process, players who reached the HOF via the VC have had to wait until 39-142 years (median 52 years) after their MLB debut, versus 15-52 years (median 27 years) for the BBWAA (Figure 11.4). So, the VC did not even get around to the post-integration era until Doby's election in 1998, only three years before the VC process was reformed to make it harder to get elected.

The BBWAA process presents a far different picture. Since 1947, the BBWAA has elected nearly twice as many African American players (30) to the HOF as the number (15.3) that would have been expected from their proportion (14%) in MLB at large.[7-9] This is not because HOF electors have unduly favored African American players, but rather because African Americans also comprise almost twice the expected proportions of HOF-eligible players with CVI $\geq$62 (28 versus 14.9 expected) and with CVI $\geq$53.04 (39 versus 20.9 expected) since 1947. The disproportionate success of a socioeconomically disadvantaged minority with limited opportunities for advancement elsewhere is not unprecedented in baseball or in other sports. One need only look back to the preeminence of Irish Americans in 19th century baseball for a precedent; of the 41 Hall of Famers who began their careers before 1900, 15 (37%) were the sons of Irish immigrants.[10] In any case, the remarkable success of African American players in post-integration baseball certainly put the lie to the old canard that they lacked the capacity to compete with white players on the major league level. Despite Commissioner Landis's absurd insistence that the absence of African American players in MLB for more than 60 years had nothing to do with a deliberate policy of racial discrimination, most MLB executives, like P.K. Wrigley of the Cubs, admitted that their real fear was that integration would adversely affect attendance by white fans; they rationalized that they must wait for the "right time" to integrate – whenever that might be.[11]

Table 11.4 drills down into the electoral process to address the equity of the two-stage HOF voting process by asking whether the best post-integration

Table 11.4: BBWAA and VC Electoral Results for Post-Integration CVI-Plus Players[12-14]

Racial Category	Number of Players	BBWAA			Veterans Committee	
		Elected	On 2021 Ballot	Dismissed	Eligible	Elected
White	95	51 (54%)	7	37	32	7 (22%)
Black^	39	24 (62%)	4	11	10	2 (20%)
Latino	16	9 (56%)	2	5	4	0
Total	150	84 (56%)	13	53	46	9 (20%)

*Includes Joe Torre, who failed to be elected as a player but was later elected by the VC as a manager.

^Derek Jeter (who is biracial) is classified as black in this analysis.

players of the three major racial/ethnic groups (i.e., the 150 CVI-Plus players) are equally likely to win election to the HOF or whether a lingering racial bias exists. The second column contains the number of CVI-Plus HOF-eligible post-integration players in each group. The middle group of columns depicts the BBWAA voting process, in which players who have been retired for five or more years are voted on annually for up to 10 years (formerly 15 years) and are either elected (>75% of the vote), retained on the ballot (5-74% of the vote), or dismissed. The group of columns on the right depicts the VC election process, in which players who were dismissed by the BBWAA may be considered indefinitely in rotating batches of 10 (grouped by era) once they have been retired for 15 years.

The BBWAA has treated all three groups equitably, electing 62% (24/39) of CVI-Plus Black players, 54% (51/95) of CVI-Plus White players, and 56% (9/16) of CVI-Plus Latino players to the HOF. These percentages do not differ significantly. The BBWAA has also elected three Black (Brock, Puckett, and Rice), two Latino (Aparicio and Perez), and four White (Ford, Hunter, Lemon, and Sutter) CVI-Minus post-integration players.

Minnie Minoso

With the election of Smith and Baines to the Class of 2019, the VC now also seems to have treated Blacks and Whites equitably, although the numbers remain very small. They have now elected 20% (2/10) of eligible post-integration Black CVI-Plus candidates versus 22% (7/32) of White CVI-Plus candidates. They have not elected any of the three VC-eligible CVI-Plus Latinos (Minnie Minoso, Cesar Cedeno, and Luis Tiant), but the period they have considered largely predates the 1980s boom in Caribbean players.[15] The results in Table 11.4 differ from those in my prior published analysis, which predated the election of Smith and Baines and used a more restrictive inclusion criterion based on JAWS.[16] The VC also elected one Black (Baines), one Latino (Cepeda), and six white (Fox, Kell, Mazeroski, Morris, Rizzuto, Schoendienst) CVI-Minus post-integration players. The fact that minorities comprise <4% of all MLB players elected by the VC reflects the profligacy of the VC electors of the 1960s and 1970s, who sent too many of their buddies from the pre-integration 1920s and 1930s to the HOF, rather than racial bias *per se*. The VC's fundamental problem is a process that continues to lack rigor and to allow ex-teammates and associates of the players under consideration to vote for their friends at the expense of more deserving players.

Unfinished Business

In summary, the BBWAA has generally done a good job of selecting the best players for the HOF. A few of their choices can be criticized, particularly their handling of the steroid era, but the overall integrity of the process is evident. The 2021 BBWAA ballot includes six players who clearly deserve election based on their CVI: Bonds, Clemens, Schilling, Rolen, Jones, and Helton. Four other CVI-Plus players – Pettitte, Abreu, Sheffield, and Ramirez are close calls. Of course, many BBWAA voters will not vote for several of the aforementioned players because of their involvement with steroids. There is also precedent for electing players like Vizquel and Wagner, but I would not vote for them.

On the other hand, the VC has generally done an unsatisfactory job of selecting the best leftover candidates from the BBWAA process, setting the bar far too low and playing favorites. The December 2019 ballot was an exception, although I would have liked to see Lou Whitaker (66.9 CVI) and Thurman Munson (60.6 CVI) join Ted Simmons in the Class of 2020. Dwight Evans (61.9 CVI) would also have been a solid choice. Murphy (52.3 CVI) and Parker (45.9 CVI) could not sustain their brief reigns among MLB's elite. Indeed, Parker looked like a certain Hall of Famer until he squandered five prime years (1980-84) as a disgruntled, overweight, injury-prone cocaine user; his inspiring late career comeback was not enough to make up for lost time. Tommy John (51.8 CVI) is best remembered as the first pitcher to undergo and successfully return from the ligament replacement surgical procedure that now bears his name, but also won 288 games in his 26-year career. Mattingly (42.6 CVI) and Garvey (32.5 CVI) had their moments but not enough of them to justify a place in the HOF.

Several CVI-Plus players from the Early Baseball (pre-1950) and Golden Days (1950-69) eras – including Jack Glasscock (74.8 CVI), Wes Ferrell (69.6 CVI), Jim McCormick (69.4 CVI), Ken Boyer (69.2 CVI), Bill Dahlen (68.8 CVI), Tommy Bond (68.2 CVI), Dick Allen (66.5 CVI), and Minnie Minoso (60.5 CVI) — might have been under consideration for the December 2020 VC ballot before it was postponed until 2021. Steady Bobby Grich (77.9 CVI), lefty knuckleballer Wilbur Wood (74.7 CVI), speedy CF Kenny Lofton (70.6 CVI, who won't be eligible until December 2023), and underappreciated David Cone (70.0 CVI) top the list of other worthy players who were not on the December 2019 ballot but could be considered in 2021-24, I would also commend colorful postseason ace Luis Tiant (65.0 CVI), and defensive 3B wizards Graig Nettles (67.0 CVI) and Buddy Bell (66.2 CVI).

Before offering suggestions on how to improve the HOF electoral process, let me offer two perspectives. First, the achievements of *all* the players featured in this book are extraordinary. It is an accomplishment just to reach the major leagues, and the vast majority of MLB players come and go without leaving much of a mark. Of the 16,008 men who debuted from 1871-2003, 4672 non-pitchers (55%) and 3340 pitchers (44%) had primary WAR $\leq$0. By contrast, only 737 non-pitchers (8.6%) have at least 20 WAR_H and 518 pitchers (6.8%) have at least 20 WAR_P. Thus, every Hall of Famer except Tommy McCarthy is among the top 9% of players to ever reach the major leagues. When I say that some players don't belong in the HOF, I am applying a standard that would admit only 1.2% of everyone who has played MLB. Everyone in the HOF was at least a good player. The problem is that hundreds of far better players than McCarthy and some others in Table 10.6 were not so honored. It is a matter of fairness and consistency.

Second, the practical application of the concept of "good character" as a criterion for the HOF is problematic. While certain egregious cases (e.g., the Black Sox scandal) may warrant exclusion, human beings are complicated mixtures of good and bad qualities. Not all great players were paragons like Walter Johnson or Mel Ott or Stan Musial or Henry Aaron or Mariano Rivera. Why is Pete Rose (who bet on baseball and lied about it but never actually rigged a game) banned from MLB and the HOF, while Ty Cobb and Tris Speaker, who allegedly conspired to rig a late-season game in 1919 and placed bets on the outcome, were forced to resign from their managerial positions in 1926 but were allowed to continue their careers and to be elected to the HOF?[17,18]

Why are Barry Bonds and Roger Clemens, who were great players before they ever used steroids and trained fanatically to achieve and sustain greatness, being blackballed by HOF voters, while Gaylord Perry, whose performance was enhanced by an illegal pitch, is in? Why has Curt Schilling been passed over for nine years by BBWAA voters for his offensive post-career Twitter posts, while Steve Carlton got a pass for a 1994 magazine interview, given shortly before his HOF induction, in which he embraced antisemitic and other conspiratorial views and accused eight former U.S. presidents of treason?[18] Expecting HOF voters to apply ill-defined criteria consistently and fairly to judge flawed and complicated players is unrealistic.

I would advocate two improvements to the HOF voting process going forward.

1. Clarify the voting guidelines for players who used performance-enhancing drugs and for "character" issues in general. Should any positive drug test be disqualifying, regardless of extenuating circumstances? Is there to be no redemption if a player later gets his act together and compiles HOF-worthy stats while playing clean? It is lazy and unfair to dump this mess in the hands of BBWAA electors. I favor the HOF candidacy of Rose and of guys like Bonds and Clemens, who were all-time greats even without steroids. But if they are to be banned, then set clear criteria for inclusion on the ballot and apply them consistently.

2. VC election committees should not include conflicted ex-teammates and friends (or enemies) of the players being considered as voting members. Long-time teammates, managers, and personal friends of the players on the ballot might be invited as "character witnesses," but should recuse themselves from voting on their candidacy.

The HOF election process will never be perfect, but it can be more fair. Let's take the politics and favoritism out of the Hall of Fame and make it a true homage to Baseball's very best.

APPENDIX 1

CHARTING BASEBALL HISTORY

This appendix provides historical tables covering the entire 150-year sweep of MLB. Relevant sections of some of these charts appear in the state-of-the-game segments of Chapters 3-9.

Table A1.1: Major Historical Milestones in MLB

Year	MLB Milestones
1871	National Association (NA) established
1876	National League (NL) replaces NA
1879	Reserve Clause established
1882	American Association (AA) established
1884	Union Association (UA) opens and closes
≈1884-95	Fielders gloves gradually catch on
1885	Players Brotherhood established
1889	Players of color unofficially banned from MLB
1890	Players League (PL) opens and closes
1894	Infield Fly Rule implemented
1901	American League (AL) established
1901	Implementation of Foul Strike Rule (NL), 56% increase in SO
1903	Implementation of Foul Strike Rule (AL); 52% increase in SO
1903	The first modern World Series
1911-14	The Chalmers Award given to most valuable MLB Player
1914-15	Federal League (FL) opens and closes
1919-20	Black Sox scandal
1920	Babe Ruth becomes a Yankee, hits 54 HR as full-time OF
1920	Ray Chapman killed by a Carl Mays pitch
1921-34	The spitball is phased out
1922	George Sisler wins the first modern BBWAA MVP award
1933	The first All-Star Game is played
1939	Hall of Fame opens
1947	Jackie Robinson debuts in Brooklyn
1951-65	Five franchises move west and south
1956	Don Newcombe wins the first Cy Young award

(continued)

Table A1.1 (cont'd)

Year	MLB Milestones
1961-62	Four AL franchises added
1966	Major League Baseball Players Association (MLPBA) established
1969	Four franchises added; introduction of divisions and LCS
1969	Pitching mound lowered; strike zone tightened
1969-72	Curt Flood rejects trade to Philadelphia and unsuccessfully sues MLB
1973	Introduction of designated hitter (DH) in AL
1975-76	Arbitrator Peter Seitz declares Andy Messersmith and Dave McNally free agents
1977	Two franchises added
1981	Midseason strike in Jun-Aug
1988	Jose Canseco on steroids
1993	Two franchises added
1994	Season-ending strike in Aug; no postseason
1995	Leagues split into three divisions; LDS and wildcards introduced
1996-2002	Peak of Steroid Era (15 50+ and six 60+ HR seasons in seven years)
1997	Interleague play introduced
1998	Two franchises added
2004	Routine drug testing and penalties introduced
2007	Mitchell Report
2012	Two wild cards in each league; one-game wildcard playoffs introduced
2012	Biogenesis scandal

Table A1.2: Key 19th and Early 20th Century Changes in Official Rules[1]

Pitching Distance		
	1871-80	45' (6'x6' box)
	1881-86	50' (6'x6' box)
	1887-92	50' (4x5.5' box)
	1893-	60'6" (hard rubber slab)
Pitching Delivery		
	1879-82	Arm must be below waist
	1883	Arm can be above waist
	1884-1919	No restrictions
	1920-	Spitball outlawed (but 17 practitioners grandfathered)
Strike Zone		
	1871-86	Batter can call for high or low pitch
	1887-	Pitcher can throw anywhere in the strike zone.

(*continued*)

Table A1.2 (cont'd)

Base on Balls Definition		
	1871-78	3 balls (but balls only called on pitches in dirt, behind batter, etc.)
	1879	9 balls (but every pitch must be called a ball, strike, or foul)
	1880-83	8 balls
	1884-86	6 balls
	1887-88	5 balls, batters awarded 1B on hit by pitch
	1889-	4 balls, batters awarded 1B on hit by pitch
Strikeout Definition		
	1871-86	3 strikes
	1887	4 strikes
	1888-1902	3 strikes
Foul Balls		
	1871-82	Not counted as strikes. But batter is retired on foul balls caught on the fly or on one bounce
	1883-93	Not counted as strikes. Batter only retired on foul balls caught before hitting ground
	1894-1900	Foul bunts counted as strikes
	1901-1902	Other foul balls counted as strikes unless the batter already had 2 strikes (NL)
	1903-	Other foul balls counted as strikes unless the batter already had 2 strikes (AL and NL)
The Bat		
	1871-84	Must be round
	1885-92	One side may be flat
	1893-	Must be round
The Ball		
	1871-1910	Hard rubber core, balls replaced infrequently
	1911-1919	Lighter cork core, balls replaced infrequently
	1920-	Lighter cork core, dirty or damaged balls replaced

Table A1.3: Origins and Destinations of 1901 National League Teams

National League 1901	Initial Year	Original League	Original Team Name	Current Team
Boston Beaneaters	1871	NA	Boston Red Stockings	Atlanta Braves
Brooklyn Superbas	1884	AA	Brooklyn Atlantics	Los Angeles Dodgers
Chicago Orphans	1874	NA	Chicago White Stockings	Chicago Cubs
Cincinnati Reds	1882	AA	Cincinnati Red Stockings	Cincinnati Reds
New York Giants	1883	NL	New York Gothams	San Francisco Giants
Philadelphia Phillies	1883	NL	Philadelphia Quakers	Philadelphia Phillies
Pittsburgh Pirates	1882	AA	Pittsburgh Alleghenys	Pittsburgh Pirates
St. Louis Cardinals	1882	AA	St Louis Brown Stockings	St. Louis Cardinals

Statistical Trends:[2,3]

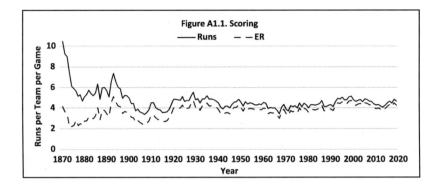

Scoring was highest in the earliest years when pitchers threw underhand and field-ers did not wear gloves. (Figure A1.1). This mostly reflects unearned runs. Earned runs peaked in the 1890s after the pitcher-batter distance increased to 60'6". Scor-ing has been relatively stable at 4.5±1.0 R/T/G since 1900, notwithstanding the Deadball and Steroid Eras.

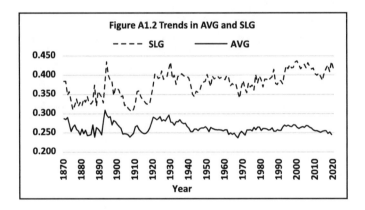

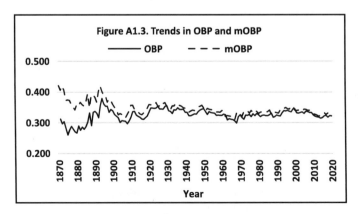

The difference between SLG and AVG (Figure A1.2) is commonly called isolated power (ISO) and has nearly doubled in the past century as longball has driven out smallball. The difference between modified OBP (mOBP) and OBP (Figure A1.3) is the inclusion of ROE in the numerator of the former.[4] As fielding gloves came into use in the 1880s and improved during the Deadball Era, fewer batters reached base on error, and the difference between mOBP and OBP shrank.

Figures A1.4-5 show the steady increase in 3TO and SO per hit over the entire course of MLB history, well beyond the demise of the Deadball Era circa 1920. In Figure A1.5, 3TO includes HBP and excludes inside-the-park HR (IPHR).[5]

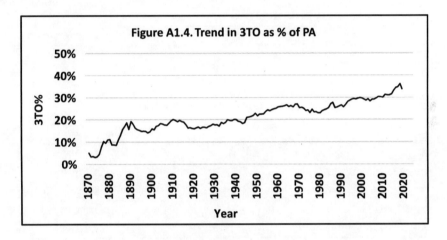

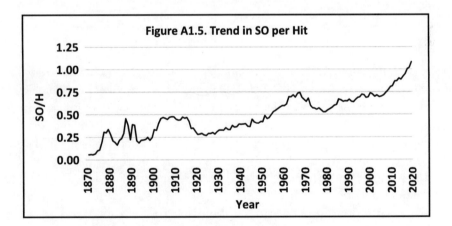

Table A1.4: Progression of All-Time 3TO% Leaders

Years	Hitter	PA	HR	BB+HBP	SO	3TO%
1901-1912	Billy Hamilton	7608	40	1278	362	22.1%
1913-1934	Jimmy Sheckard	9128	56	1227	849	23.4%
1935-1967	Babe Ruth	10623	714	2105	1330	39.1%
1968-1986	Mickey Mantle	9907	536	1746	1710	40.3%
1987-2000	Reggie Jackson	11418	563	1471	2597	40.6%
2001-2011	Mark McGwire	7660	583	1392	1596	46.6%
2012-2013	Jim Thome	10313	612	1816	2548	48.2%
2014-	Adam Dunn	8328	462	1403	2379	51.0%
On Track	Joey Gallo	1785	120	267	672	59.3%

Table A1.5: Progression of All-Time SO/H Leaders

Years	Pitcher	BF	SO	H	SO/H
1893-1909	Tim Keefe	20941	2564	4438	0.578
1910-1965	Rube Waddell	11717	2316	2460	0.941
1966-1992	Sandy Koufax	9497	2396	1754	1.366
1993-2008	Nolan Ryan	22575	5714	3923	1.4565
2008-	Randy Johnson	17067	4875	3346	1.4570
On Track	Yu Darvish	3242	1392	909	1.531
	Chris Sale	6544	2007	1312	1.530

I have set a minimum of 7500 PA to qualify for Table A1.4 (which excludes 3TO poster boy Rob Deer, who had 48.9% 3TO in 4513 PA from 1984-1996) and 9000 BF to qualify for Table A1.5. However, I have included active players who are currently on track to dethrone the current all-time leaders Dunn and Johnson. Joey Gallo whose 3TO% is nearly 60% in his first 1785 PA, is running well ahead of Dunn's pace and is young enough and good enough to accrue the required 7500 PA to pass Dunn. However, Darvish (who is 34 years old and has faced only 3242 batters) and Sale (who will be 32 when he returns from Tommy John surgery) are only slightly ahead of Johnson's pace and are unlikely to dethrone the Big Unit. The top qualifying active hitter, 38 year-old Miguel Cabrera (33.6% 3TO) is no threat to Adam Dunn. The top qualifying active pitchers, 33 year-old Clayton Kershaw (1.44 SO/H) and 36 year-old Max Scherzer (1.43 SO/H), are at an age when their SO/H is likelier to decline than improve.

A few other aspects of Tables A1.4-5 are worth noting. The early 3TO leaders, Hamilton and Sheckard, are there because of their ability to draw walks. They had no power and hit fewer than 100 HR between them. Sheckard eventually passed Hamilton because he struck out more often; the introduction of the foul strike rule in 1902 undoubtedly played a role. After Sheckard, a parade of "usual suspects," big swing-and-miss sluggers (Ruth, Mantle, etc.), follows. Perhaps the most remarkable aspect of either table is the 56-year reign of Rube Waddell as strikeout-to-hit king. His 0.941 SO/H was far ahead of his time and lasted until Koufax came along.

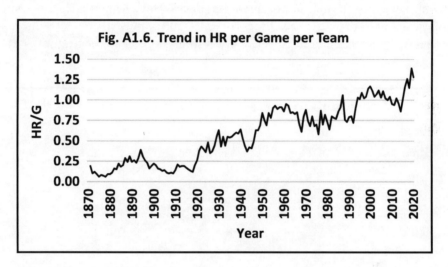

Fig. A1.6. Trend in HR per Game per Team

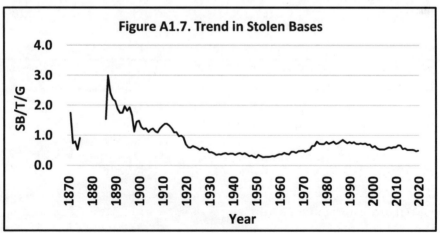

Figure A1.7. Trend in Stolen Bases

The increasing trend in HR (Figure A1.6) also continued will beyond the demise of the Deadball Era. The Steroid Era was just a modest bump in this long-term trend. Stolen Bases (Figure A1.7) enjoyed a renaissance in 1974-99, but despite the efforts of Henderson, Brock, Coleman, Raines, et al, never returned to their 1886-1919 level.

These complementary graphs showing the near disappearance of complete games (Figure A1.8) and the increase in saves (Figure A1.9) reflect the increasing prominence of relief pitching, starting in 1900.

As a result of the distribution of workloads to ever growing numbers of pitchers, pitching wins have become almost useless as a performance metric (Figures A1.10-11). Before 1890, pitching aces at times compiled 600 or more IP and 40 or more W. Currently, 200-220 IP and 18-20 W are often sufficient to lead the league.

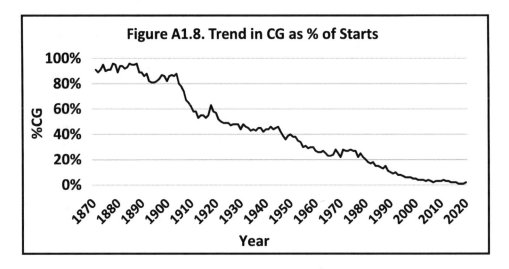

Figure A1.8. Trend in CG as % of Starts

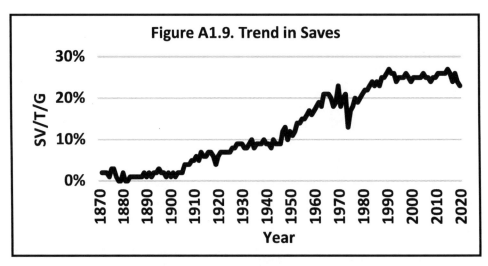

Figure A1.9. Trend in Saves

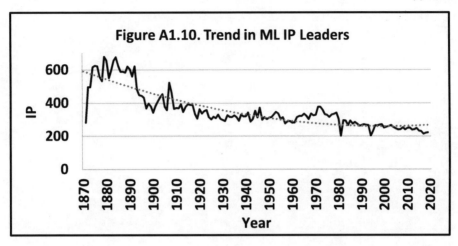

Figure A1.10. Trend in ML IP Leaders

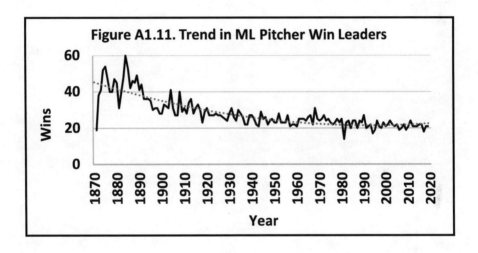

Figure A1.11. Trend in ML Pitcher Win Leaders

APPENDIX 2

MORE ON THE CALCULATION OF CVI

In Chapter 2, I explained how CVI awards extra credit for seasons with primary WAR in excess of a threshold that was appropriate for the length of the season and pitcher workloads in each era, and laid out the rationale for positional adjustments in the threshold for catchers and designated hitters and the use of "leveraged WAR" for relief pitchers. I also alluded to special adjustments for players in three special categories:

- Players with wartime military service

- Players whose MLB career was delayed by external circumstances, while they played in other venues (the Negro Leagues and Japan).

- Players who used steroids and other performance-enhancing drugs (PED)

SPECIAL CATEGORIES

Tables A2.1-3 list the players whose CVI was altered by each of the three special category adjustments.

In Table A2.1, the average of the two complete seasons before and after the gap was imputed to the missed seasons, without using any threshold or multiplier.

The adjusted CVI in Table A2.2 were made by generating a list of all post-1900 position players in the HOF who debuted at a younger age than these players, and was used to generate a range of expectations for the proportional impact of truncating the earlier years of a HOF-level player on that player's career WAR. To be conservative, I used the reciprocal of the 85th percentile of these proportions as the adjustment factor. Taking Jackie Robinson, who debuted in 1946 at age 28, as an illustrative example, the 85th percentile was represented most closely by Tony Perez, who accrued 71.8% of his career WAR at age 28 or later. So, Robinson's unadjusted 77.4 CVI is multiplied by 1/0.718 (1.39) to obtain his adjusted 106.8 CVI.

Table A2.3 lists the adjustments made to steroid users who were considered for inclusion in this book. I did not consider known steroid users Ken Caminiti, Jose Canseco, Juan Gonzalez, Wally Joyner, Chuck Knoblauch, Benito Santiago, Miguel Tejada, and more than 100 other players you have probably barely or never heard of, who were not in the top 2% even when their stats are taken at face value.[1] I have not adjusted the stats of some prominent rumored steroid

Table A2.1: Interpolation of Years Missed for Military Service

Player	Years Missed	Unadjusted CVI	Adjusted CVI
Willie Mays	1952 (partial), 1953	223.9	232.3
Ted Williams	1943-45, 1952-53 (partial)	168.0	199.5
Stan Musial	1945	170.7	178.1
Grover Alexander	1918 (partial)	139.2	146.5
Warren Spahn	1943-45, 1946 (partial)	106.2	114.4
Bob Feller	1942-44, 1945 (partial)	82.2	107.7
Joe DiMaggio	1943-45	92.1	107.4
Johnny Mize	1943-45	82.0	97.2
Shoeless Joe Jackson	1918 (partial)	82.5	87.0
Luke Appling	1944, 1945 (partial)	78.2	85.9
Hank Greenberg	1941 (partial), 1942-44, 1945 (partial)	63.5	82.3
Pee Wee Reese	1943-45	66.2	78.3
Harry Heilmann	1918 (partial)	77.3	77.8
Bill Dickey	1944-45	68.3	71.0
Red Faber	1918 (partial)	69.7	70.4
Joe Gordon	1944-45	60.3	69.2
Ted Lyons	1943-45	63.0	67.6
Enos Slaughter	1943-45	51.6	62.8
Red Ruffing	1943-44	60.6	62.8
Early Wynn	1945	58.9	60.6
Billy Herman	1944-45	53.1	57.7
Urban Shocker	1918 (partial)	53.4	54.4
Whitey Ford	1952-53	48.9	52.8
Eppa Rixey	1918	50.1	52.1
Charlie Keller	1944, 1945 (partial)	45.5	52.0
Herb Pennock	1918	49.8	51.2
Bobby Doerr	1945	45.5	49.7
Phil Rizzuto	1943-45	38.5	48.7
Sam Rice	1918 (partial)	43.2	45.7
Bob Lemon	1943-45	39.6	40.9
Rabbit Maranville	1918 (partial)	37.0	40.2
High Pockets Kelly	1918	22.0	22.5

Table A2.2: Players With Delayed Careers

Player	Rookie Season		Career	Unadjusted	Adjustment	Adjusted
	Year	Age	WAR	CVI	Factor	CVI
Jackie Robinson	1947	28	61.7	76.6	1.39	106.8
Ichiro Suzuki	2001	27	59.7	63.8	1.28	81.9
Roy Campanella	1948	27	35.6	49.2	1.28	63.1
Minnie Minoso	1951	25	50.2	51.2	1.18	60.5
Larry Doby	1948	24	49.3	49.8	1.09	54.0

Table A2.3: Adjustments for PED Use

Player	Unadjusted CVI	Adjusted CVI	Adjustment Made
Barry Bonds	232.3	203.8	20% discount to 1999-2007
Roger Clemens	183.2	172.3	10% discount to 1997-2007
Alex Rodriguez	156.0	106.0	20% discount for 1984-2012
Kevin Brown	78.6	67.0	10% discount to entire career
Andy Pettitte	60.4	60.1	10% discount to 2002
Gary Sheffield	57.9	57.2	20% discount to 2002
Manny Ramirez	64.7	54.3	20% discount to 2009-11; 10% for the rest
Robinson Cano	77.8	51.6	20% discount for entire career
Rafael Palmeiro	65.8	51.6	20% discount to 1993-2005
Chuck Finley	53.4	50.5	10% discount to entire career
Bartolo Colon	48.4	48.1	10% discount to 2010-2012
Chuck Knoblauch	48.6	46.7	20% discount to 1998-2001
Sammy Sosa	63.1	44.2	20% discount to 1993-2004
Mark McGwire	61.0	42.0	20% discount to entire career
Jason Giambi	58.1	41.0	20% discount to 1995-2007
Ryan Braun	48.0	40.8	20% discount to 2007-2011
Nelson Cruz	38.4	37.9	20% discount to 2012-2013

users — Jeff Bagwell, Ivan Rodriguez, Mike Piazza, David Ortiz — because of insufficient evidence of guilt.

The only players in Table A2.3 whose HOF candidacy I support are Bonds, Clemens, and Rodriguez, who clearly were already great players even without PED. I consider Pettitte and Sheffield, who briefly dabbled with PED, to be borderline cases. The unadjusted stats of Cano, Brown, Palmeiro, Ramirez, Sosa, McGwire, and perhaps Giambi would have qualified them for the HOF, were they not inflated by PED use.

Admittedly, Table A2.3 reflects only my best guesses as to who used PED and when they used them. The record is pretty clear for Bonds, Pettitte, and Sheffield, but less so for the others. Brian McNamee testified that he first started injecting Roger Clemens with steroids in 1998, but his performance spiked in 1997.[2] Alex Rodriguez admitted to using steroids in 2001-03 and in connection with the Biogenesis scandal in 2010-12, but he is reputed to have used steroids even in high school.[3] So, I have docked Clemens for 1997-2007 and A-Rod for 1995-2013. Similarly, Kirk Rodomski testified that he sold HGH to Kevin Brown in 2001 (when he was already past his prime), but that Brown was already quite familiar with steroids. Brown and Finley (who are in the Mitchell report) have been silent on this question, so I have docked them for their entire careers. I have also discounted virtually the entire careers of Giambi (an admitted user) and Sosa, who never failed a drug test, but whose sudden transformation from a skinny speedster in 1989 92 into a hulking slugger in 1993-2004 is too striking to ignore.

Palmeiro, Ramirez, and (recently) Cano all failed drug tests late in their careers after not being strongly suspected before then. I have discounted Palmeiro's WAR by 20% starting in 1993, when his annual HR totals suddenly jumped from 22 to 37. Palmeiro had never hit more than 26 HR before then, and never hit <38 HR in any full season afterwards until age 39. I docked Ramirez, who did not exhibit any unusual jumps in performance, by 10% for his career and 20% for the years he tested positive at the end. Cano's positive test for the steroid Stanozolol after the 2020 season removed any reasonable doubt about his 2018 suspension for the masking agent furosemide (a common diuretic, which also has legitimate medical indications).

Sample CVI Calculations

In Chapter 2, I illustrated the calculation of CVI for two players, Fred Clarke and Ernie Banks, in whom the WAR threshold remained at 5.0 throughout their career and the CVI calculation was uncomplicated by any of the aforementioned special adjustments. Here, I will illustrate several more complicated CVI calculations, illustrating the impact of temporal changes in the WAR threshold – including examples from the 19th century (Keefe), the 1994 strike (Maddux), and the 2020 pandemic (Scherzer), how CVI is calculated for catchers (Berra) or RP (Eckersley), and the interpolation of years missed in wartime military service (Greenberg). I have also included an example of how CVI might be projected for a player whose career ended prematurely (Koufax). In each table, negative WAR values are rounded to zero.

The careers of the following six players covered a period of time when the WAR threshold for calculating the "bonus" was not always 5.0. The right column tracks cumulative CVI for the player's career through a particular season. For Maddux and Scherzer, 0.8 times their positive WAR_H (1.8 and 1.7, respectively) are added to CVI in the final line of the table.

Table A2.4: Tim Keefe

Year	WAR$_P$	Threshold	Bonus	CVI Season	CVI Cumulative
1880	4.7	10.0	0.0	3.8	3.8
1881	2.9	10.0	0.0	2.3	6.1
1882	4.5	10.0	0.0	3.6	9.7
1883	19.9	11.0	17.8	30.2	39.8
1884	7.5	11.0	0.0	6.0	45.8
1885	6.9	10.0	0.0	5.5	51.4
1886	10.0	10.0	0.0	8.0	59.4
1887	7.1	9.0	0.0	5.7	65.0
1888	10.3	9.0	2.6	10.3	75.4
1889	4.2	9.0	0.0	3.4	78.7
1890	5.0	9.0	0.0	4.0	82.7
1891	-1.3	9.0	0.0	0.0	82.7
1892	6.0	9.0	0.0	4.8	87.5
1893	1.2	7.5	0.0	1.0	88.5

WAR$_H$ < 0

Table A2.5: Greg Maddux

Year	WAR$_P$	Threshold	Bonus	CVI Season	CVI Cumulative
1986	0.0	5.0	0.0	0.0	0.0
1987	-0.4	5.0	0.0	0.0	0.0
1988	5.2	5.0	0.4	4.5	4.5
1989	5.0	5.0	0.0	4.0	8.5
1990	4.0	5.0	0.0	3.2	11.7
1991	3.5	5.0	0.0	2.8	14.5
1992	9.1	5.0	8.2	13.8	28.3
1993	5.8	5.0	1.6	5.9	34.2
1994	8.5	3.5	10.0	14.8	49.0
1995	9.7	4.0	11.4	16.9	65.9
1996	7.2	4.5	5.4	10.1	76.0
1997	7.8	4.5	6.6	11.5	87.5
1998	6.6	4.5	4.2	8.6	96.2
1999	3.2	4.5	0.0	2.6	98.7
2000	6.5	4.5	4.0	8.4	107.1
2001	5.2	4.5	1.4	5.3	112.4
2002	4.4	4.5	0.0	3.5	115.9
2003	1.3	4.5	0.0	1.0	117.0
2004	3.2	4.5	0.0	2.6	119.5
2005	2.9	4.5	0.0	2.3	121.8
2006	3.1	4.5	0.0	2.5	124.3
2007	2.6	4.5	0.0	2.1	126.4
2008	0.5	4.5	0.0	0.4	126.8

Table A2.6: Max Scherzer

Year	WAR$_P$	Threshold	Bonus	CVI Season	CVI Cumulative
2008	1.2	4.5	0.0	1.0	1.0
2009	1.3	4.5	0.0	1.0	2.0
2010	3.4	4.5	0.0	2.7	4.7
2011	1.4	4.5	0.0	1.1	5.8
2012	4.4	4.0	0.8	4.2	10.0
2013	6.5	4.0	5.0	9.2	19.2
2014	5.8	4.0	3.6	7.5	26.7
2015	6.9	4.0	5.8	10.2	36.9
2016	6.2	4.0	4.4	8.5	45.4
2017	7.2	4.0	6.4	10.9	56.2
2018	8.4	4.0	8.8	13.8	70.0
2019	5.7	4.0	3.4	7.3	77.3
2020	2.2	2.0	0.4	2.1	79.4
WAR$_H$	1.7			1.4	80.7

Table A2.7: Yogi Berra

Year	WAR$_H$	% C	Threshold	Bonus	CVI Season	CVI Cumulative
1946	0.5	86%	3.2	0.0	0.4	0.4
1947	1.0	68%	3.6	0.0	0.8	1.2
1948	2.3	60%	3.6	0.0	1.8	3.0
1949	2.1	93%	3.2	0.0	1.7	4.7
1950	6.1	100%	3.2	5.8	9.5	14.2
1951	5.3	100%	3.2	4.2	7.6	21.8
1952	5.8	100%	3.2	5.2	8.8	30.6
1953	4.9	100%	3.2	3.4	6.6	37.3
1954	5.3	99%	3.2	4.2	7.6	44.9
1955	4.5	100%	3.2	2.6	5.7	50.6
1956	6.2	99%	3.2	6.0	9.8	60.3
1957	3.0	95%	3.2	0.0	2.4	62.7
1958	3.2	79%	3.2	0.0	2.6	65.3
1959	3.9	96%	3.2	1.4	4.2	69.5
1960	2.2	65%	3.6	0.0	1.8	71.3
1961	2.1	15%	5.0	0.0	1.7	73.0
1962	0.1	53%	3.6	0.0	0.1	73.0
1963	1.3	100%	5.0	0.0	1.0	74.1
1964	0.0				0.0	74.1
1965	-0.1	100%	5.0	0.0	0.0	74.1

Berra's threshold is determined by the percentage of games played at catcher in a season – 5.0 for <25%, 4.4 for 25-49%, 3.8 for 50-74%, and 3.2 for >75%. A similar process was used to calculate WAR for DH.

The calculation of CVI for Dennis Eckersley is especially complicated because he was a starter in some seasons and a reliever in other years. In seasons when he did both, his WAR_P is partitioned according to the proportion of games when he appeared in each role. For example, in his rookie year (1975), Eckersley made 24 starts (71%) and 10 relief appearances (29%). So, 3.7 of his 5.3 WAR_P was apportioned to his starts and 1.6 to his relief appearances. When the latter number was multiplied by his gmLI, one gets 3.8 leveraged WAR in the WAR_{RP} column.

Table A2.8: Dennis Eckersley

Year	WAR_P	% RP	gmLI	WAR_{RP}	WAR_{SP}	Threshold	Bonus	CVI Season	CVI Cumulative
1975	5.3	29%	2.45	3.8	3.7	5.5	0.0	6.8	6.8
1976	2.9	17%	1.43	0.7	2.4	5.5	0.0	2.6	9.4
1977	5.1	0%		0.0	5.1	5.5	0.0	4.1	13.5
1978	7.3	0%		0.0	7.3	5.5	3.6	8.7	22.2
1979	7.2	0%		0.0	7.2	5.0	4.4	9.3	31.5
1980	2.1	0%		0.0	2.1	5.0	0.0	1.7	33.2
1981	0.8	0%		0.0	0.8	5.0	0.0	0.6	33.8
1982	4.5	0%		0.0	4.5	5.0	0.0	3.6	37.4
1983	0.0	0%		0.0	0.0	5.0	0.0	0.0	37.4
1984	4.2	0%		0.0	4.2	5.0	0.0	3.4	40.8
1985	4.6	0%		0.0	4.6	5.0	0.0	3.7	44.5
1986	1.9	3%	0.65	0.0	1.8	5.0	0.0	1.5	46.0
1987	3.0	96%	1.67	4.8	0.1	5.0	0.0	4.9	50.9
1988	2.3	100%	1.94	4.5	0.0	5.0	0.0	4.5	55.4
1989	2.6	100%	1.83	4.8	0.0	5.0	0.0	4.8	60.1
1990	3.3	100%	1.68	5.5	0.0	5.0	0.0	5.5	65.7
1991	1.5	100%	1.89	2.8	0.0	5.0	0.0	2.8	68.5
1992	2.9	100%	1.65	4.8	0.0	5.0	0.0	4.8	73.3
1993	0.7	100%	1.86	1.3	0.0	5.0	0.0	1.3	74.6
1994	-0.2	100%	1.71	0.0	0.0	5.0	0.0	0.0	74.6
1995	0.0	100%	1.56	0.0	0.0	5.0	0.0	0.0	74.6
1996	0.4	100%	1.67	0.7	0.0	5.0	0.0	0.7	75.3
1997	0.2	100%	1.83	0.4	0.0	5.0	0.0	0.4	75.6
1998	0.2	100%	1.27	0.3	0.0	5.0	0.0	0.3	75.9

$WAR_H <$ 0

Table A2.9: Hank Greenberg

Year	WAR$_H$	Threshold	Bonus	CVI Season	CVI Cumulative
1930	0.0	5.0	0.0	0.0	0.0
1931	0.0	5.0	0.0	0.0	0.0
1932	0.0	5.0	0.0	0.0	0.0
1933	2.6	5.0	0.0	2.1	2.1
1934	6.3	5.0	2.6	7.1	9.2
1935	7.7	5.0	5.4	10.5	19.7
1936	0.5	5.0	0.0	0.4	20.1
1937	7.5	5.0	5.0	10.0	30.1
1938	6.7	5.0	3.4	8.1	38.2
1939	5.4	5.0	0.8	5.0	43.1
1940	6.8	5.0	3.6	8.3	51.4
1941*	0.2	6.0	0.0	0.2	51.6
1941	5.1			4.1	55.7
1942	5.3			4.3	60.0
1943	5.3			4.3	64.2
1944	5.3			4.3	68.5
1945	2.3			1.9	70.3
1945*	3.0	5.0	0.0	2.4	72.7
1946	6.4	5.0	2.8	7.4	80.1
1947	2.7	5.0	0.0	2.2	82.3

* Played 19 G in 1941 before enlisting and 78 G in 1945 after discharge.

Greenberg missed three full seasons and part of another during World War II (shaded). His CVI calculation involves interpolating the average WAR for the two seasons just before and just after their military service for the missing season. No bonus points were awarded. If one subtracts out the shaded areas, one is left with the unadjusted CVI of 63.5 for Greenberg. Bob Feller's career was impacted by WWII similarly. His exceptional unadjusted CVI of 82.2 bumps up to over 107 when adjusted for time missed in military service.

Table A2.10: Sandy Koufax – What If?

Year	WAR$_P$	Threshold	Bonus	CVI	
				Season	Cumulative
1955	0.9	5.0	0.0	0.7	0.7
1956	-0.3	5.0	0.0	0.0	0.7
1957	1.3	5.0	0.0	1.0	1.8
1958	1.2	5.0	0.0	1.0	2.7
1959	2.2	5.0	0.0	1.8	4.5
1960	1.5	5.0	0.0	1.2	5.7
1961	5.7	5.0	1.4	5.7	11.4
1962	4.4	5.0	0.0	3.5	14.9
1963	10.7	5.0	11.4	17.7	32.6
1964	7.3	5.0	4.6	9.5	42.1
1965	8.1	5.0	6.2	11.4	53.5
1966	10.3	5.0	10.6	16.7	70.2
1967	8.2	5.0	6.4	11.7	81.9
1968	7.4	5.5	3.7	8.9	90.8
1969	6.6	5.5	2.3	7.1	97.9
1970	6.0	5.5	0.9	5.5	103.4
1971	5.4	5.5	0.0	4.3	107.7
1972	4.8	5.5	0.0	3.9	111.6
1973	4.4	5.5	0.0	3.5	115.1
1974	3.9	5.5	0.0	3.1	118.2

WAR$_H$ < 0   1963-66 Avg: 9.10

This table shows the projection of what Sandy Koufax's CVI might have been if he had been able to continue to pitch beyond 1966, while suffering a modest 10% annual attrition from his 1963-66 peak, during which he averaged 9.1 WAR$_P$ per season. In this fantasy scenario, Koufax was on track to attain elite status (CVI >100) by age 34 (1970) and might have finished with a Pedro Martinez-like 118.2 CVI had he been able pitch to age 38. Of course, his arthritic elbow made that impossible, but the projection gives us an idea of how good Koufax was in his short career.

Percentiles

I have calculated CVI for 506 MLB players, including everyone (379 players) with CVI $\geq$45.0. When I say that these 379 players represent the top 2.20% of all CVI, what is the denominator for that estimate? This is not straightforward. Since Deacon White, Bobby Mathews, and 16 others raised the curtain on the National Association on May 4, 1871, 19,902 MLB players have appeared in a major league baseball game.[6] But this denominator is too large, since the book has not closed on the 1292 players who were still active in 2020. (This total includes some who finished their careers in 2020 and does not include some who were sidelined in 2020 but returned in 2021.) Indeed, the book has barely opened on the rising stars who debuted in the past five years.

The remaining 18,610 players who were inactive in 2020 is an unsuitable denominator because it represents a biased sample, in which players with short inconsequential careers are overrepresented, since many of the best players who debuted during the last 10-15 years are still active. To demonstrate this bias, I shift to considering percentiles for WAR, since CVI has been calculated only for a small fraction of players. Using the Baseball-Reference Stathead tool, we find that 9.2% of the 8955 non-pitchers (defined as players who did not appear as a pitcher in $\geq$80% of their games) who debuted in MLB before the start of the 2004 season but only 6.4% of the 1664 who have debuted since then have accrued at least 20 WAR_H in their careers.[5] The contrast is even greater for pitchers; 6.9% of the 7587 pitchers who debuted before 2004 but only 1.6% of the 2406 pitchers who have debuted since then have accrued at least 20 WAR_P in their careers,[6] (Note that Stathead's query tool for pitchers has no filter to remove position players who made pitching appearances. Since these players contribute to the tallies of both non-pitchers and pitchers, these two subtotals add up to more than the total number of players.)

To get an unbiased estimate of percentiles, one must analyze only players who made their major league debut before a fixed date and exclude players (even those who have retired) who debuted after that date. I chose the end of the 2003 season as a suitable cutoff date. Albert Pujols, Miguel Cabrera, and Oliver Perez (none of whose CVI has grown by more than 1.1 since 2016 or is likely to change much going forward) are the only players among the 16,008 who made their MLB debut before 2004 who are active in 2021. I did not include players who debuted in 2004 in the denominators for percentiles, since Zack Greinke (who had 6.8 WAR_P in 2019-20) and Yadier Molina debuted in 2004. Thus, when I cite CVI percentiles in the text players, they are based on a denominator of 16,008; players who debuted in 2004 or later were assigned the average percentile of the players listed immediately above and below them in the CVI ranking.

Table A2.11 provides percentiles of WAR_H for non-pitchers and WAR_P for pitchers who made their MLB debut before the end of the 2003 season.

Table A2.11: Percentiles of WAR$_H$ for Non-Pitchers and WAR$_P$ for Pitchers

Percentile	Non-Pitchers N=8955	Pitchers N=7587	Percentile	Non-Pitchers N=8955	Pitchers N=7587
0.5	77.1	66.4	7.5	24.1	18.8
1.0	66.1	55.0	10.0	18.2	14.2
1.5	57.0	47.2	15.0	10.8	8.5
2.0	50.9	42.3	20.0	6.3	5.4
3.0	43.0	33.0	30.0	1.8	2.0
4.0	37.3	27.9	40.0	0.3	0.6
5.0	32.5	24.6	50.0	0.0	0.1

These percentiles provide useful context for CVI-Minus Hall of Famers. Of the 235 Hall of Famers elected as players, only Tommy McCarthy is outside the top 10% by WAR, and only two others (High Pockets Kelly and Lloyd Waner) fall outside the top 7.5%.

Unadjusted CVI Ranking

The special adjustments to CVI for wartime military service, delayed major league eligibility, and steroid use (Tables A2.1-3) are potentially controversial since they give players credit for hypothetical production in missed seasons or take away credit for actual production in PED-enhanced seasons. Table A2.12 provides un-adjusted rankings based on actual production, regardless of the circumstances. As in Tables 10.1-5, Hall of Famers appear in boldface type and active players are in Italics. Players with wartime military service (†), players with delayed MLB eligibility (^), and PED users (~) are also identified by the indicated symbols next to their names.

Without the three adjustments, the CVI threshold for the top 2% drops slightly from 66.7 to 68.2 and the CVI-Plus threshold (not shown) increases slightly from 53.04 to 53.1. As one would expect, players who used PED (see Table A2.3) fare better here than in Chapter 10, and the players who missed time in military service (Table A2.1) or whose MLB debut was delayed (Table A2.2) fare better in Chapter 10. Although the adjusted values come closer to how I evaluate the achievements of players in these special categories, the reader may prefer to begin with CVI rankings that are based strictly on actual stats accrued and make their own adjustments.

Table A2.12: Unadjusted CVI – Top 1.0 Percentile

	Player	Posn	CVI
1	Ruth, Babe (1914-1935)	RF	270.0
2	Bonds, Barry (1986-2007)~	LF	232.3
3	Mays, Willie (1951-1973)†	CF	223.9
4	Johnson, Walter (1907-1927)	SP	211.8
5	Cobb, Ty (1905-1928)	CF	198.0
6	Young, Cy (1890-1911)	SP	194.0
7	Aaron, Henry (1954-1976)	RF	187.5
8	Hornsby, Rogers (1915-1937)	2B	185.0
9	Clemens, Roger (1984-2007)~	SP	183.2
10	Speaker, Tris (1907-1928)	CF	174.6
11	Wagner, Honus (1897-1917)	SS	172.4
12	Musial, Stan (1941-1963)†	LF	170.7
13	Williams, Ted (1939-1960)†	LF	168.0
14	Gehrig, Lou (1923-1939)	1B	165.4
15	Grove, Lefty (1925-1941)	SP	161.4
	Rodriguez, Alex (1994-2016)~	SS	156.0
16	Collins, Eddie (1906-1930)	2B	154.8
17	Johnson, Randy (1988-2009)	SP	144.1
18	Mantle, Mickey (1951-1968)	CF	143.0
19	Schmidt, Mike (1972-1989)	3B	142.0
20	Alexander, Grover (1911-1930)†	SP	139.2
21	Henderson, Rickey (1979-2003)	LF	134.9
	Pujols, Albert (2001-2020)	*1B*	*132.7*
22	Ott, Mel (1926-1947)	RF	131.0
23	Lajoie, Nap (1896-1916)	2B	130.6
24	Mathewson, Christy (1900-1916)	SP	129.2
25	Maddux, Greg (1986-2008)	SP	128.2
26	Morgan, Joe (1963-1984)	2B	120.6
27	Seaver, Tom (1967-1986)	SP	120.5
28	Nichols, Kid (1890-1906)	SP	119.9
29	Robinson, Frank (1956-1976)	RF	118.8
30	Martinez, Pedro (1992-2009)	SP	118.2
31	Foxx, Jimmie (1925-1945)	1B	117.2
32	Mathews, Eddie (1952-1968)	3B	116.7

(continued)

Table A2.12 (cont'd)

	Player	Posn	CVI
33	Ripken, Cal (1981-2001)	SS	113.3
34	Bench, Johnny (1967-1983)	C	111.7
	Trout, Mike (2011-2020)	*CF*	*111.4*
35	Clemente, Roberto (1955-1972)	RF	110.9
36	Yastrzemski, Carl (1961-1983)	LF	110.8
37	Boggs, Wade (1982-1999)	3B	110.8
38	Anson, Cap (1871-1897)	1B	108.8
39	Niekro, Phil (1964-1987)	SP	108.4
40	Spahn, Warren (1942-1965)†	SP	106.2
41	Blyleven, Bert (1970-1992)	SP	104.2
42	Gibson, Bob (1959-1975)	SP	103.5
43	Carter, Gary (1974-1992)	C	103.1
44	Connor, Roger (1880-1897)	1B	102.7
45	Brouthers, Dan (1879-1904)	1B	102.3
46	Rivera, Mariano (1995-2013)	RP	101.9
47	Griffey, Ken (1989-2010)	CF	101.8
48	Brett, George (1973-1993)	3B	101.3
49	Perry, Gaylord (1962-1983)	SP	100.7
50	Carlton, Steve (1965-1988)	SP	100.6
51	Roberts, Robin (1948-1966)	SP	100.1
52	Kaline, Al (1953-1974)	RF	99.0
	Beltre, Adrian (1998-2018)	3B	98.8
53	Schilling, Curt (1988-2007)	SP	97.4
54	Clarkson, John (1882-1894)	SP	96.0
55	Gehringer, Charlie (1924-1942)	2B	95.3
56	Vaughan, Arky (1932-1948)	SS	93.8
57	DiMaggio, Joe (1936-1951)†	CF	92.1
58	Mussina, Mike (1991-2008)	SP	91.1
	Verlander, Justin (2005-2020)	*SP*	*91.1*
59	Gossage, Rich (1972-1994)	RP	90.6
60	Martinez, Edgar (1987-2004)	DH	89.7
61	Carew, Rod (1967-1985)	2B	88.7
62	Keefe, Tim (1880-1893)	SP	88.5
63	Halladay, Roy (1998-2013)	SP	88.4
64	Jones, Chipper (1993-2012)	3B	88.3

(*continued*)

Table A2.12 (cont'd)

	Player	Posn	CVI
65	Santo, Ron (1960-1974)	3B	88.1
66	Bagwell, Jeff (1991-2005)	1B	87.8
67	Thomas, Frank (1990-2008)	DH	87.4
	Kershaw, Clayton (2008-2020)	*SP*	*87.4*
68	Jenkins, Fergie (1965-1983)	SP	86.2
69	Rodriguez, Ivan (1991-2011)	C	85.3
70	Yount, Robin (1974-1993)	SS	83.9
71	Banks, Ernie (1953-1971)	SS	83.8
	Rose, Pete (1963-1986)	LF	83.6
72	Walsh, Ed (1904-1917)	SP	83.5
73	Davis, George (1890-1909)	SS	83.3
74	Piazza, Mike (1992-2007)	C	83.2
75	Fisk, Carlton (1969-1993)	C	82.8
	Jackson, Shoeless Joe (1908-1920)†	RF	82.5
76	Galvin, Pud (1875-1892)	SP	82.5
	Greinke, Zack (2004-2020)	*SP*	*82.4*
77	Feller, Bob (1936-1956)†	SP	82.2
78	Robinson, Brooks (1955-1977)	3B	82.2
79	Mize, Johnny (1936-1953)†	1B	82.0
80	Jackson, Reggie (1967-1987)	RF	80.7
	Scherzer, Max (2008-2020)	*SP*	*80.7*
81	Delahanty, Ed (1888-1903)	LF	80.5
82	Plank, Eddie (1901-1917)	SP	80.4
83	Ryan, Nolan (1966-1993)	SP	79.9
84	Glavine, Tom (1987-2008)	SP	78.7
85	Brown, Kevin (1986-2005)~	SP	78.6
86	Appling, Luke (1930-1950)†	SS	78.2
87	Grich, Bobby (1970-1986)	2B	77.9
88	Molitor, Paul (1978-1998)	DH	77.8
	Cano, Robinson (2005-2020)~	*2B*	*77.8*
89	Vance, Dazzy (1915-1935)	SP	77.8
90	Heilmann, Harry (1914-1932)†	RF	77.3
91	Newhouser, Hal (1939-1955)	SP	77.1
92	Snider, Duke (1947-1964)	CF	76.8

(*continued*)

Table A2.12 (cont'd)

	Player	Posn	CVI
93	Radbourn, Old Hoss (1880-1891)	SP	76.6
94	Robinson, Jackie (1947-1956)^	2B	76.6
	Utley, Chase (2003-2018)	2B	76.3
95	Marichal, Juan (1960-1975)	SP	76.1
96	Eckersley, Dennis (1975-1998)	RP	75.9
97	Hubbell, Carl (1928-1943)	SP	75.7
98	Walker, Larry (1989-2005)	RF	75.7
99	Glasscock, Jack (1879-1895)	SS	74.8
100	Wood, Wilbur (1961-1978)	SP	74.7
101	Smith, Ozzie (1978-1996)	SS	74.6
102	Trammell, Alan (1977-1996)	SS	74.5
103	Sandberg, Ryne (1981-1997)	2B	74.3
104	Wilhelm, Hoyt (1952-1972)	RP	74.3
105	Coveleski, Stan (1912-1928)	SP	74.2
106	Berra, Yogi (1946-1967)	C	74.1
107	Thome, Jim (1991-2012)	1B	73.8
108	Frisch, Frankie (1919-1937)	2B	73.8
109	Wallace, Bobby (1894-1918)	SS	73.8
110	Boudreau, Lou (1938-1952)	SS	73.7
111	Bunning, Jim (1955-1971)	SP	73.1
112	Simmons, Al (1924-1944)	LF	72.7
113	McGinnity, Joe (1899-1908)	SP	72.6
	Beltran, Carlos (1998-2017)	CF	72.6
	Cabrera, Miguel (2003-2020)	*1B*	*72.2*
114	Smoltz, John (1988-2009)	SP	71.9
115	Waner, Paul (1926-1945)	RF	71.7
116	Jeter, Derek (1995-2014)	SS	71.3
117	Dawson, Andre (1976-1996)	RF	71.1
118	Rolen, Scott (1996-2012)	3B	70.8
119	Rusie, Amos (1889-1901)	SP	70.7
120	Baker, Home Run (1908-1922)	3B	70.6
121	Lofton, Kenny (1991-2007)	CF	70.6
122	Larkin, Barry (1986-2004)	SS	70.4
123	Koufax, Sandy (1955-1966)	SP	70.2

(continued)

Table A2.12 (cont'd)

	Player	Posn	CVI
124	Cone, David (1986-2003)	SP	70.0
125	Jones, Andruw (1996-2012)	CF	69.8
	Mauer, Joe (2004-2018)	C	69.7
126	**Faber, Red (1914-1933)†**	**SP**	69.7
127	Helton, Todd (1997-2013)	1B	69.7
128	Ferrell, Wes (1927-1941)	SP	69.6
129	**Raines, Tim (1979-2002)**	**LF**	69.5
130	**Willis, Vic (1898-1910)**	**SP**	69.4
131	McCormick, Jim (1878-1887)	SP	69.4
132	**McCovey, Willie (1959-1980)**	**1B**	69.4
133	**Palmer, Jim (1965-1984)**	**SP**	69.3
134	Boyer, Ken (1955-1969)	3B	69.2
135	**Waddell, Rube (1897-1910)**	**SP**	69.0
	Votto, Joey (2007-2020)	*1B*	*68.9*
136	Dahlen, Bill (1891-1911)	SS	68.8
137	**Biggio, Craig (1988-2007)**	**2B**	68.6
138	**Dickey, Bill (1928-1946)†**	**C**	68.3
139	**Gwynn, Tony (1982-2001)**	**RF**	68.3
140	Bond, Tommy (1874-1884)	SP	68.2
141	**Crawford, Sam (1899-1917)**	**RF**	68.2
142	**Alomar, Roberto (1988-2004)**	**2B**	67.7
143	**Ashburn, Richie (1948-1962)**	**CF**	67.4
144	**Cronin, Joe (1926-1945)**	**SS**	67.2
145	Nettles, Graig (1967-1988)	3B	67.0
146	Reuschel, Rick (1972-1991)	SP	67.0
147	Whitaker, Lou (1977-1995)	2B	66.9
148	**Goslin, Goose (1921-1938)**	**LF**	66.6
149	Allen, Dick (1963-1977)	1B	66.5
150	Saberhagen, Bret (1984-2001)	SP	66.5
151	Bell, Buddy (1972-1989)	3B	66.2
152	**Reese, Pee Wee (1940-1958)†**	**SS**	66.2

INDEX OF FEATURED PLAYERS

BIBLIOGRAPHY

Baseball-Reference.com is the source of all MLB statistics in this book. References to specific player pages, leaderboards etc. are not listed here. Unless specified otherwise, all internet links were last accessed in December 2020.

1. Chris Cioffi. Raleigh News&Observer. Nov 2016. "Fuquay-Varina man drives 650 miles to listen to Cubs win at his father's gravesite," https://www.newsobserver.com/news/local/counties/wake-county/article112255152.html.
2. Rich Cohen. The Chicago Cubs: Story of a Curse. Farrar Strauss and Giroux, New York, 2017.
3. Terry Cashman, 1981. "Talkin' Baseball (Willie, Mickey and the Duke)" https://en.wikipedia.org/wiki/Talkin%27_Baseball#References.
4. Sean Lahman, 2005, "A Brief History of Baseball: Origins of the Game," www.seanlahman.com/baseball-archive/brief-history-of-baseball/.
5. Ken Burns. *Baseball*. Florentine Films and WETA-TV, 1994.
6. Baseball-Reference.com. The National Association, https://www.baseball-reference.com/leagues/NA/.
7. John Thorn, May 4, 1871: Association Ball: Kekionga vs. Forest City, https://sabr.org/gamesproj/game/may-4-1871-association-ball-kekionga-vs-forest-city.

Chapter 1

1. Baseball-Reference.com, https://www.baseball-reference.com/.
2. Stathead Baseball, https://stathead.com/baseball/.
3. SABR Biography Project, https://sabr.org/bioproject.

Chapter 2

1. Wikipedia. Edwin Starr, https://en.wikipedia.org/wiki/Edwin_Starr.
2. Baseball-Reference.com WAR Explained, https://www.baseball-reference.com/about/war_explained.shtml.
3. Keith Law, *Smart Baseball*. Harper Collins, New York, NY, 2017. Chapter 14, pp 183-203.
4. Marvin Gay. "What's Going On?", http://www.metrolyrics.com/whats-going-on-lyrics-marvin-gaye.html.
5. The Blind Men and the Elephant, https://www.peacecorps.gov/educators/resources/story-blind-men-and-elephant/.
6. Stew Thornley, SABR biography of Jack Morris, https://sabr.org/bioproj/person/7585bcdf, accessed October 2016.

7. John Thorn and Pete Palmer. *The Hidden Game of Baseball*, University of Chicago Press, Chicago, IL 2013. Originally published in 1984.

8. Baseball-Reference, Position player WAR calculations and details, https://www.baseball-reference.com/about/war_explained_position.shtml.

9. FanGraphs, https://www.fangraphs.com/.

10. On-Base Plus Slugging Plus (OPS+), http://m.mlb.com/glossary/advanced-stats/on-base-plus-slugging-plus.

11. Adjusted Earned Run Average Plus (ERA+), http://m.mlb.com/glossary/advanced-stats/earned-run-average-plus.

12. Brian McKenna, SABR biography of Old Hoss Radbourn, https://sabr.org/bioproj/person/83bf739e.

13. Bill James. *Whatever Happened to the Hall of Fame?: Baseball, Cooperstown, and the Politics of Glory.* Fireside, Rockefeller Center, New York, NY, 1994, 1995.

14. Jay Jaffe. *Cooperstown Casebook.* St. Martin's Press, New York, NY, 2017. Chapter 3, pp. 22-27.

15. Tyler Kepner, Jerry Holtzman Obituary, July 21, 2008, https://bats.blogs.nytimes.com/2008/07/21/holtzman-creator-of-the-save-rule-dies-at-82/.

16. Hall of Famers, https://baseballhall.org/hall-of-famers/past-inductions/past-inductions.

17. Based on the fact that Jose Bautista, the first player to debut in 2004, is player #16009 in the Baseball-Reference database. https://www.baseball-reference.com/leagues/MLB/2004-debuts.shtml, https://www.baseball-reference.com/players/b/bautijo02.shtml.

Chapter 3

1. Baseball Almanac. Baseball Rule Change Timeline. http://www.baseball-almanac.com/rulechng.shtml.

2. Evolution of 19th Century Baseball Rules, http://www.19cbaseball.com/rules.html.

3. Baseball-Reference.com. History of Baseball in the United States. https://www.baseball-reference.com/bullpen/History_of_baseball_in_the_United_States#Professionalism_and_the_rise_of_the_major_leagues.

4. Science Non-Fiction, "Hitting a fastball requires more than just quick reactions," https://sciencenonfiction.org/2016/05/23/hitting-a-fastball-requires-more-than-just-quick-reactions/.

5. David J Gordon, "The Rise and Fall of the Deadball Era," *Baseball Research Journal* (SABR), 47 (2):92-102 (Fall 2018).

6. Baseball Glove History and Evolution, http://www.infobarrel.com/Baseball_Glove_History_Evolution.

7. John Thorn, "Why did the baseball glove evolve so slowly?" https://ourgame.mlblogs.com/why-did-the-baseball-glove-evolve-so-slowly-bff30f33737a.

8. Baseball-Reference.com. The National Association, https://www.baseball-reference.com/leagues/NA/.

9. Baseball-Reference.com. The National League, https://www.baseball-reference.com/leagues/NL/.

10. Baseball-Reference.com. The American Association, https://www.baseball-reference.com/leagues/AA/.

11. Sean Lahman, 2005, "A Brief History of Baseball: Origins of the Game," www.seanlahman.com/baseball-archive/brief-history-of-baseball/.

12. Jennifer K. Ashcroft and Charles A. Depken. *The Introduction of the Reserve Clause in Major League Baseball: Evidence of its Impact on Select Player Salaries During the 1880s.* AIESIASE Working Paper Series, Paper No. 07-10. April 2007, http://college.holycross.edu/RePEc/spe/AshcraftDepken_ReserveClause.pdf.

13. Baseball-Reference.com. The American Association, https://www.baseball-reference.com/leagues/AA/.

14. Baseball-Reference.com, The Union Association, https://www.baseball-reference.com/leagues/UA/.

15. Baseball-Reference.com. The Players League, https://www.baseball-reference.com/leagues/PL/.

16. Baseball-Reference.com. The American League, https://www.baseball-reference.com/leagues/AL/.

17. Baseball-Reference.com. The Federal League, https://www.baseball-reference.com/leagues/FL/.

18. Bill Lamb, SABR Biography of John Ward, https://sabr.org/bioproj/person/2de3f6ef.

19. Sherman Anti-Trust Act (1890), https://www.ourdocuments.gov/doc.php?flash=false&doc=51.

20. Ethan M. Lewis, "A Structure to Last Forever. The Players League and the Brotherhood War of 1890." Chapter 1. Introduction, http://www.ethanlewis.org/pl/ch1.html.

21. Ethan M. Lewis, "A Structure to Last Forever. The Players League and the Brotherhood War of 1890." Chapter 2. "If They Could Only Get Over the Idea that They Owned Us," http://www.ethanlewis.org/pl/ch2.html.

22. Ethan M. Lewis, "A Structure to Last Forever. The Players League and the Brotherhood War of 1890." Chapter 3. "It Will Be the Survival of the Fittest," http://www.ethanlewis.org/pl/ch3.html.

23. Ethan M. Lewis, "A Structure to Last Forever. The Players League and the Brotherhood War of 1890." Chapter 4. "Printers Ink and Bluff," http://www.ethanlewis.org/pl/ch4.html.

24. Ethan M. Lewis, "A Structure to Last Forever. The Players League and the Brotherhood War of 1890." Chapter 5. "The Brotherhood is All Right," http://www.ethanlewis.org/pl/ch5.html.

25. Ethan M. Lewis, "A Structure to Last Forever. The Players League and the Brotherhood War of 1890." Chapter 6. "I Have Worked this Season as I Never Did Before," http://www.ethanlewis.org/pl/ch6.html.

26. Ethan M. Lewis, "A Structure to Last Forever. The Players League and the Brotherhood War of 1890." Chapter 7. Conclusion, http://www.ethanlewis.org/pl/ch7.html.

27. David Fleitz, SABR biography of Cap Anson, https://sabr.org/bioproj/person/9b42f875.

28. Brian McKenna. SABR Biography of John Clarkson, https://sabr.org/bioproj/person/47feb015.
29. Charlie Bevis, SABR Biography of Tim Keefe, https://sabr.org/bioproj/person/6f1dd1b1.
30. Brian McKenna, SABR Biography of Old Hoss Radbourn, https://sabr.org/bioproj/person/83bf739e.
31. Charles Hausberg, SABR Biography of Pud Galvin, https://sabr.org/bioproj/person/38c553ff.
32. Ernest Lawrence Thayer, "Casey at the Bat," https://www.poets.org/poetsorg/poem/casey-bat.
33. Charlie Bevis, SABR Biography of Tim Keefe, ibid.
34. The Classical, March 14, 2013, "Pud Galvin's Juiced Balls," http://theclassical.org/articles/pud-galvins-juiced-balls.
35. Bill James, *The New Bill James Historical Baseball Abstract*. 2001. Free Press, New York, NY 2001, p. 978.
36. *Adrian C. Anson, A Ball Player's Career*. Era Publishing, Chicago, IL. 1900.
37. Bill Lamb, SABR Biography of Roger Connor, https://sabr.org/bioproj/person/4ef2cfff.
38. Nicole DiCicco, SABR Biography of George Davis, https://sabr.org/bioproj/person/95403784.
39. David Krell, SABR Biography of Bill Dahlen, https://sabr.org/bioproj/person/571833af.
40. Joe Williams, "SABR 42: Bill Dahlen selected as overlooked 19th century baseball legend for 2012," https://sabr.org/latest/sabr-42-bill-dahlen-selected-overlooked-19th-century-baseball-legend-2012.
41. John Saccoman, SABR Biography of Ed Delahanty, https://sabr.org/bioproj/person/d835353d.
42. MLB.com Glossary. Stolen Base (SB). http://m.mlb.com/glossary/standard-stats/stolen-base.
43. Richard Puff, "Amos Wilson Rusie," in Frederick Ivor-Campbell, Robert L. Tiemann, Mark Rucker, eds., Baseball's First Stars (Cleveland: Society for American Baseball Research, 1996, p 43.
44. Bill Lamb, SABR Biography of John Ward, ibid.
45. John Montgomery Ward, "Is the Base Ball Player a Chattel?" Lippincott's Magazine, August 1887, V40: 310-319. https://books.google.com/books?id=07MRAAAAYAAJ&printsec=frontcover&source=gbs_ge_summary_r&cad=0#v=onepage&q=John%20Montgomery%20Ward&f=false
46. Bill Lamb, SABR Biography of John Ward, ibid.
47. Baseball-Reference. MLB Scores and Standings Thursday, May 04, 1871. https://www.baseball-reference.com/boxes/?date=1871-05-04.
48. Bill McMahon. SABR Biography of Al Spalding. https://sabr.org/bioproj/person/al-spalding/.
49. Michael Grahek. SABR Biography of Clark Griffith. https://sabr.org/bioproj/person/clark-griffith/.
50. David Nemec, SABR Biography of Buck Ewing, https://sabr.org/bioproj/person/d60ea3ca.

51. Joe Williams, SABR Biography of Deacon White, https://sabr.org/bioproj/person/deacon-white/.

52. Stathead, Baseball. Hitters with >16.1 WAR$_H$ and Debut before 2004. https://stathead.com/baseball/season_finder.cgi?request=1&sum=1&order_by_asc=1&order_by=WAR_bat&qualifiersSeason=nomin&minpasValS=502&mingamesValS=100&qualifiersCareer=nomin&minpasValC=3000&mingamesValC=1000&min_year_season=1871&max_year_season=2020&lg_ID=lgAny&lgAL_team=tmAny&lgNL_team=tmAny&lgFL_team=tmAny&lgAA_team=tmAny&lgPL_team=tmAny&lgUA_team=tmAny&lgNA_team=tmAny&exactness=anypos&pos_1=1&pos_2=1&pos_3=1&pos_4=1&pos_5=1&pos_6=1&pos_7=1&pos_8=1&pos_9=1&pos_10=1&pos_11=1&as=result_batter&offset=0&type=b&ccomp%5B1%5D=gt&cval%5B1%5D=16.1&cstat%5B1%5D=WAR_bat&ccomp%5B2%5D=lt&cval%5B2%5D=2003&cstat%5B2%5D=year_min&bats=any&throws=any&min_age=0&max_age=99&min_season=1&max_season=-1&location=pob&locationMatch=is&isHOF=either&isAllstar=either&isActive=either.

Chapter 4

1. Brian Witt and Bob Buege, 2017. "Five Who Did: The founding of the American League by Five-Irish-American Milwaukeeans," https://celticmke.com/CelticMKE-Blog/Founding-American-League-Five-Irish-Americans.htm.

2. Deadball Era, https://www.baseball-reference.com/bullpen/Deadball_Era.

3. David J Gordon, "The Rise and Fall of the Deadball Era," *Baseball Research Journal* (SABR), 47(2):92-102 (Fall 2018).

4. Baseball-Reference.com, Pitcher's Mound, https://www.baseball-reference.com/bullpen/Pitcher%27s_mound.

5. Foul Strike Rule, https://www.baseball-reference.com/bullpen/Foul_strike_rule.

6. Baseball-Reference.com. National League Batting Year-by-Year Averages, https://www.baseball-reference.com/leagues/NL/bat.shtml.

7. Baseball-Reference.com. American League Batting Year-by-Year Averages, https://www.baseball-reference.com/leagues/AL/bat.shtml.

8. Steve Steinberg, The Spitball and the End of the Deadball Era, *The National Pastime*, Number 23 (Cleveland: Society for American Baseball Research, 2003), pages 7-17, http://research.sabr.org/journals/files/SABR-National_Pastime-23.pdf.

9. Baseball-Reference.com, Spitball, https://www.baseball-reference.com/bullpen/Spitball.

10. Wikipedia, Spitball, https://en.wikipedia.org/wiki/Spitball.

11. Zachary D. Rymer, The evolution of the baseball from the Deadball Era through today. http://bleacherreport.com/articles/1676509-the-evolution-of-the-baseball-from-the-Deadball-era-through-today.

12. Don Jensen, SABR Biography of Ray Chapman https://sabr.org/bioproj/person/c2ed02f9.

13. David Fleitz, SABR Biography of Cap Anson, https://sabr.org/bioproj/person/9b42f875.

14. 1906 Chicago White Sox, www.thisgreatgame.com/1906-baseball-history.html.

15. Frank Jackson, Lessons from Lakefront Park, Hardball Times, July 5, 2012, https://tht.fangraphs.com/lessons-from-lakefront-park-1884/.

16. Eliot Asinof, Eight Men Out: The Black Sox and the 1919 World Series. Henry Holt and Company, New York, NY 1987.

17. Wikipedia. Federal Baseball Club v. NL, https://en.wikipedia.org/wiki/Federal_Baseball_Club_v._National_League.

18. Wikipedia. Minor League Baseball, https://en.wikipedia.org/wiki/Minor_League_Baseball.

19. The Society for American Baseball Research, *Deadball Stars of the National League*, Tom Simon (editor), Brassey's Inc, Dulles, VA, 2004.

20. The Society for American Baseball Research, *Deadball Stars of the American League*, David Jones (editor), Brassey's Inc, Dulles, VA, 2004.

21. Daniel Ginsburg, SABR biography of Ty Cobb, https://sabr.org/bioproj/person/7551754a.

22. Ginsburg, ibid.

23. Ty Cobb and Al Stump, *My Life in Baseball, the True Record*. Doubleday & Co., 1961.

24. John Thorn, Cobb and Speaker and Landis: Closing the Books. https://1927-the-diary-of-myles-thomas.espn.com/closing-the-books-cobb-speaker-landis-e7896605fbc1. Fred Lieb, *Baseball as I Have Known It*, Coward, McCann & Geoghegan (1977).

25. Don Jensen, SABR biography of Tris Speaker, https://sabr.org/bioproj/person/6d9f34bd.

26. Jan Finkel, SABR biography of Honus Wagner, https://sabr.org/bioproj/person/30b27632.

27. J. Conrad, "Ty Cobb Talks About the Greatest Pitcher He Ever Faced," https://www.detroitathletic.com/blog/2013/01/02/ty-cobb-talks-about-the-greatest-pitcher-he-ever-faced/ '.

28. Stuart Schimler, SABR biography of Big Ed Walsh, https://sabr.org/bioproj/person/3a0e7935.

29. Charles Carey, SABR biography of Walter Johnson, https://sabr.org/bioproj/person/0e5ca45c.

30. Jan Finkel, SABR biography of Pete Alexander, https://sabr.org/bioproj/person/79e6a2a7.

31. *The Winning Team*, directed by Lewis Seiler, starring Doris Day and Ronald Reagan, 1952, https://www.imdb.com/title/tt0045332/fullcredits/?ref_=tt_ov_st_sm.

32. Eddie Frierson, SABR biography of Christy Mathewson, https://sabr.org/bioproj/person/f13c56ed.

33. David Jones, SABR biography of Home Run Baker, https://sabr.org/bioproj/person/2f26e40e .

34. Paul Mittermeyer, SABR biography of Eddie Collins, https://sabr.org/bioproj/person/c480756d.
35. Mittermeyer, ibid.
36. Jan Finkel, SABR biography of Eddie Plank, https://sabr.org/bioproj/person/339eaa5c.
37. Finkel, ibid.
38. Dan O'Brien, SABR biography of Rube Waddell, https://sabr.org/bioproj/person/rube-waddell/.
39. Jim Sandoval, SABR biography of Eddie Cicotte, https://sabr.org/bioproj/person/1f272b1a.
40. David Fleitz, SABR biography of Shoeless Joe Jackson, https://sabr.org/bioproj/person/7afaa6b2.
41. Scott Schul, SABR biography of Bobby Wallace, https://sabr.org/bioproj/person/59a8cf09.
42. Don Doxsie. SABR biography of Joe McGinnity, https://sabr.org/bioproj/person/joe-mcginnity/.
43. Bill Lamberty, SABR biography of Sam Crawford, https://sabr.org/bioproj/person/11b83a0d.
44. Lawrence S. Ritter, *The Glory of Their Times*. Quill William Morrow, New York, NY, 1984, Chapter 4, pp 47-69.
45. Baseball Almanac. American Indian Baseball Players, http://www.baseball-almanac.com/legendary/american_indian_baseball_players.shtml
46. Wikipedia, Franklin P. Adams, https://en.wikipedia.org/wiki/Franklin_P._Adams.

Chapter 5

1. David J Gordon, "The Rise and Fall of the Deadball Era," *Baseball Research Journal* (SABR), 47(2):92-102 (Fall 2018).
2. Babe Ruth Quotes. http://www.baberuth.com/quotes/.
3. Year-by-Year Top-Tens Leaders and Records for Home Runs, https://www.baseball-reference.com/leaders/HR_top_ten.shtml.
4. Diane Firstman, "The Growth of 'Three True Outcomes': From Usernet Joke to Baseball Flashpoint," Baseball Research Journal 47(1): (Spring 2018), https://sabr.org/journal/article/the-growth-of-three-true-outcomes-from-usenet-joke-to-baseball-flashpoint/
5. Wikipedia. Minor League Baseball, https://en.wikipedia.org/wiki/Minor_League_Baseball.
6. Allan Wood, SABR biography of Babe Ruth, https://sabr.org/bioproj/person/9dcdd01c.
7. James Lincoln Ray, SABR biography of Lou Gehrig, https://sabr.org/bioproj/person/ccdffd4c.
8. *The Pride of the Yankees*, Sam Wood (director), 1942.
9. Fred Stein, SABR biography of Mel Ott, https://sabr.org/bioproj/person/3974a220.
10. Jerry Grillo, SABR biography of Johnny Mize, https://sabr.org/bioproj/person/a7ac6649.

11. Scott Ferkovich, SABR biography of Hank Greenberg, https://sabr.org/bioproj/person/64198864.

12. Jim Hawkins and Don Ewald, *The Detroit Tigers Encyclopedia*, Champaign, Illinois: Sports Publishing LLC, 2003, p 58.

13. Lawrence Baldassero, SABR biography of Joe DiMaggio, https://sabr.org/bioproj/person/a48f1830.

14. Maury Allen, *Where Have You Gone, Joe DiMaggio? The Story of America's Last Hero.* Dutton, New York, NY. 1975.

15. Ruth Sadler, SABR biography of Charlie Gehringer, https://sabr.org/bioproj/person/9fe98bb6.

16. Fred Stein, SABR biography of Frankie Frisch, https://sabr.org/bioproj/person/0bbf3136.

17. JC. Paul Rogers, SABR biography of Rogers Hornsby, https://sabr.org/bioproj/person/b5854fe4.

18. Bill James. *Whatever Happened to the Hall of Fame?: Baseball, Cooperstown, and the Politics of Glory.* Fireside, Rockefeller Center, New York, NY, 1994, 1995.

19. Jim Kaplan, SABR biography of Lefty Grove, https://sabr.org/bioproj/person/8bc0a9e1.

20. John Bennett, SABR biography of Jimmy Foxx, https://sabr.org/bioproj/person/e34a045d.

21. "A League of Their Own," Penny Marshall (director), 1992.

22. Charlie Bevis, SABR biography of Mickey Cochrane, https://sabr.org/bioproj/person/a80307f0.

23. Charles F. Faber, SABR biography of Dazzy Vance, https://sabr.org/bioproj/person/5c1fec75.

24. Mark Stewart, SABR biography of Hal Newhouser, https://sabr.org/bioproj/person/28aff78b.

25. C. Paul Rogers, SABR biography of Bob Feller, https://sabr.org/bioproj/person/de74b9f8.

26. Before Radar Guns Bob Feller. YouTube, https://www.youtube.com/watch?v=IhZ7t_DNi9w.

27. C. Paul Rogers, Bob Feller, ibid.

28. C. Paul Rogers, Bob Feller, ibid.

29. Mark Stewart, Hal Newhouser bio, ibid.

30. Steven Goldman, "You could look it up: The importance of being Paul Waner," Baseball Prospectus, May 12, 2009, https://www.baseballprospectus.com/news/article/8863/you-could-look-it-up-the-importance-of-being-paul-waner/.

31. Joseph Wancho, SABR biography of Paul Waner, https://sabr.org/bioproj/person/9d598ab8.

32. Cort Vitty, SABR biography of Goose Goslin, https://sabr.org/bioproj/person/2e155494.

33. Bill Lamberty, SABR biography of George Sisler, https://sabr.org/bioproj/person/f67a9d5c.

34. Don D'Addona, SABR biography of Harry Heilmann, https://sabr.org/bioproj/person/7257f49c.
35. Bill Lamberty, George Sisler, ibid.
36. Fred Stein, SABR biography of Bill Terry. https://sabr.org/bioproj/person/bill-terry/.
37. Ralph Moses, SABR biography of Arky Vaughan, https://sabr.org/bioproj/person/4e00be9b.
38. Ralph Berger, SABR biography of Luke Appling, https://sabr.org/bioproj/person/4b5272d7.
39. Ralph Berger, SABR biography of Lou Boudreau, https://sabr.org/bioproj/person/3fde9ca7.
40. Joseph Wancho, SABR biography of Joe Gordon, https://sabr.org/bioproj/person/4d6bb7cb.
41. Joseph Wancho, Joe Gordon, ibid.
42. Mark Armour, SABR biography of Joe Cronin, https://sabr.org/bioproj/person/572b61e8.
43. Mark Armour, Joe Cronin, ibid.
44. Larry Gerlach, *The Men in Blue*, Viking Press, New Your, NY, 1980, p. 285.
45. Daniel R. Leavitt, SABR biography of Stan Coveleski, https://sabr.org/bioproj/person/7b589446.
46. Brian Cooper, SABR biography of Red Faber, https://sabr.org/bioproj/person/a6dff769.
47. Fred Stein, SABR biography of Carl Hubbell, https://sabr.org/bioproj/person/fd05403f.
48. Joseph Wancho, SABR biography of Bill Dickey, https://sabr.org/bioproj/person/25ce33d8.
49. Bill Johnson, SABR biography of Gabby Hartnett, https://sabr.org/bioproj/person/ab6d173e.
50. Mark Smith, SABR biography of Wes Ferrell, https://sabr.org/bioproj/person/81a7570e.
51. Warren Corbett, SABR biography of Ted Lyons, https://sabr.org/bioproj/person/b3442150.
52. Warren Corbett, SABR biography of Red Ruffing, https://sabr.org/bioproj/person/7111866b.
53. Warren Corbett, Ted Lyons, ibid.
54. Joseph Wancho, SABR biography of George Uhle, https://sabr.org/bioproj/person/1d015def.
55. Joseph Wancho, SABR biography of Urban Shocker, https://sabr.org/bioproj/person/b63431c6.
56. Jay Jaffe, Cooperstown Casebook. St. Martin's Press, New York, NY, 2017. Chapter 5, pp. 48-61.

Chapter 6

1. Wikipedia, Kenesaw Mountain Landis, https://en.wikipedia.org/wiki/Kenesaw_Mountain_Landis#cite_note-FOOTNOTEPietrusza406-141.

2. Lawrence D. Hogan, Shades of Glory, pp 331-2, National Baseball Hall of Fame, Cooperstown, NY, 2006.

3. David M. Jordan, Larry R. Gerlach, and John P. Rossi. A Baseball Myth Exploded, https://sabr.org/cmsFiles/Files/Bill_Veeck_and_the_1943_sale_of_the_Phillies.pdf.

4. Hogan, ibid, p 334.

5. Andy McCue. SABR Biography of Branch Rickey, https://sabr.org/bioproj/person/6d0ab8f3.

6. Rick Swaine. SABR Biography of Jackie Robinson, https://sabr.org/bioproj/person/bb9e2490.

7. Wikipedia. List of first black Major League Baseball players, https://en.wikipedia.org/wiki/List_of_first_black_Major_League_Baseball_players.

8. Mark Armour and Daniel R. Levitt, Baseball Demographics 1947-2016, http://sabr.org/bioproj/topic/baseball-demographics-1947-2012.

9. George Skornickel. Characters with Character: Pittsburgh's All-Black Lineup. Baseball Research Journal. Fall 2011, https://sabr.org/research/characters-character-pittsburghs-all-black-lineup.

10. Wikipedia. Continental League, https://en.wikipedia.org/wiki/Continental_League.

11. MLBPA, http://www.mlbplayers.com/HomePage.dbml?DB_OEM_ID=34000.

12. Wikipedia, Flood versus Kuhn, https://en.wikipedia.org/wiki/Flood_v._Kuhn.

13. Baseball Work Stoppages, www.stevetheump.com/baseball_stoppages.htm www.stevetheump.com/baseball_stoppages.htm.

14. Bill Dwyre, LA Times, April 9, 2012. Fifty years ago, Maury Wills made crime pay off for the Dodgers, http://articles.latimes.com/2012/apr/09/sports/la-sp-0410-dwyre-maury-wills-20120410.

15. 1968: Year of the Pitcher, http://www.thisgreatgame.com/1968-baseball-history.html.

16. Leo Durocher, with Ed Lynn. *Nice Guys Finish Last.* The University of Chicago Press. Chicago, IL, 1975, p. 385.

17. YouTube, Willie Mays Famous Catch in 1954 World Series New York Giants, https://www.bing.com/videos/search?q=willie+mays+catch+in+1954+world+series&&view=detail&mid=CD19B9DEA982E3F859F3CD19B9DEA982E3F859F3&rvsmid=7B6F05BA3F58B124A5757B6F05BA3F58B124A575&FORM=VDQVAP.

18. Maxwell Kates. SABR biography of Frank Robinson, https://sabr.org/bioproj/person/c3ac5482.

19. John Saccoman. SABR biography of Willie Mays, https://sabr.org/bioproj/person/64f5dfa2.

20. Bill Johnson. SABR biography of Henry Aaron, https://sabr.org/bioproj/person/5a36cc6f.

21. Kates, ibid.

22. Stew Thornley. SABR biography of Roberto Clemente, https://sabr.org/bioproj/person/8b153bc4.
23. Bill Nowlin, SABR biography of Ted Williams, https://sabr.org/bioproj/person/35baa190.
24. Michael McCarthy, "Ted Williams is 'real John Wayne' in fantastic American Masters doc." In The Sporting News, July 23, 2018, http://www.sportingnews.com/us/mlb/news/ted-williams-red-sox-pbs-documentary-greatest-hitter-who-ever-lived-american-masters-bob-costas/xkd8gkmfdxkyl5l4lm4tpj3xj.
25. John Updike, "Hub fans bid Kid adieu," The New Yorker, October 22, 1960
26. Jan Finkel, SABR biography of Stan Musial, https://sabr.org/bioproj/person/2142e2e5.
27. James Lincoln Ray. SABR biography of Mickey Mantle, https://sabr.org/bioproj/person/61e4590a.
28. Ray, ibid.
29. Jane Leavy, *The Last Boy: Mickey Mantle and the Loss of America's Childhood*, Harper Books New York, NY, 2010, p.13.
30. Ray, ibid.
31. Baseball-Reference, The Negro Leagues are Major Leagues, https://www.baseball-reference.com/negro-leagues-are-major-leagues.shtml.
32. Rick Swaine. SABR Biography of Jackie Robinson, https://sabr.org/bioproj/person/bb9e2490.
33. Swaine, ibid.
34. Herb Crehan and Bill Nowlin. SABR biography of Carl Yastrzemski, https://sabr.org/bioproj/person/a71e9d7f.
35. Nick Waddell. SABR biography of Al Kaline, https://sabr.org/bioproj/person/a141b60c.
36. Waddell, ibid.
37. Baseball Almanac, Warren Spahn quotes, http://www.baseball-almanac.com/quotes/quosphn.shtml.
38. Jim Kaplan. SABR biography of Warren Spahn, https://sabr.org/bioproj/person/16b7b87d.
39. Baseball Almanac, Spahn, ibid.
40. C. Paul Rogers III. SABR biography of Robin Roberts, https://sabr.org/bioproj/person/3262b1eb.
41. Rogers, ibid.
42. Baseball Almanac. American Indian Baseball Players, http://www.baseball-almanac.com/legendary/american_indian_baseball_players.shtml
43. Tim McCarver with Ray Robinson. *Oh Baby I Love It*, Dell Publishing, New York, NY, 1987, pp 58-59.
44. Terry Sloope. SABR biography of Bob Gibson, https://sabr.org/bioproj/person/34500d95.
45. Jan Finkel, SABR biography of Juan Marichal, https://sabr.org/bioproj/person/5196f44d.
46. Ralph Berger, SABR biography of Jim Bunning, https://sabr.org/bioproj/person/bcacaa59.

47. Tom Verducci, "The Left Hand of God," Sports Illustrated, July 12, 1999.

48. Luis Tiant and Joe Fitzgerald, *El Tiante – The Luis Tiant Story*, Doubleday, New York, NY, 1976, p.113.

49. Peter Gammons, *Beyond the Sixth Game.* Houghton Mifflin, Boston, MA, 1985, p. 163.

50. Bob Gibson biography, Browse Biography, http://www.browsebiography.com/bio-bob_gibson.html.

51. Sloope, ibid.

52. Finkel, ibid.

53. Berger, ibid.

54. Mark Z. Aaron, SABR biography of Sandy Koufax, https://sabr.org/bioproj/person/e463317c#sdendnote2sym.

55. Aaron, ibid.

56. Lloyd Vries, CBS/AP April 27, 2007, "Koufax Drafted by Israeli Baseball Team," https://www.cbsnews.com/news/koufax-drafted-by-israeli-baseball-team/.

57. Joseph Wancho, SABR biography of Don Drysdale, https://sabr.org/bioproj/person/14c3c5f6.

58. Mark Armour, SABR biography of Luis Tiant, https://sabr.org/bioproj/person/2212deaf.

59. Joe Morgan and David Faulkner, *Joe Morgan: A Life in Baseball.* W,W. Norton, New York, NY, 1993, p. 285.

60. Andy Sturgill. SABR biography of Pete Rose, https://sabr.org/bioproj/person/89979ba5.

61. John M Dowd. Report to the Commissioner in the matter of Peter Edward Rose, Manager, Cincinnati Reds Baseball Club, May 9, 1989, http://www.thedowdreport.com/report.pdf.

62. Mark Armour. SABR biography of Gaylord Perry, https://sabr.org/bioproj/person/f7cb0d3e.

63. Baseball Bullpen, Gaylord Perry. https://www.baseball-reference.com/bullpen/Gaylord_Perry.

64. Gaylord Perry and Bob Sudyk. Me and the Spitter. Dutton, Boston, MA, 1974.

65. Armour, ibid.

66. YouTube. 1970 World Series: Baltimore Orioles vs Cincinnati Reds: The Brooks Robinson Series. https://www.bing.com/videos/search?q=brooks+robinson+1970+world+series+highlights&view=detail&mid=82D3E8B2D022BEDE45C582D3E8B2D022BEDE45C5&FORM=VIRE.

67. David Fleitz. SABR biography of Eddie Mathews, https://sabr.org/bioproj/person/ebd5a210.

68. Maxwell Kates, SABR biography of Brooks Robinson, https://sabr.org/bioproj/person/55363cdb.

69. Gregory H. Wolf., SABR biography of Sal Bando, https://sabr.org/bioproj/person/f33122f8.

70. Peter Patau. December 2, 2006. http://www.peterpatau.com/2006/12/bohr-leads-berra-but-yogi-closing-gap.html.

71. Wikipedia, Yogi Berra: Yogi-isms, https://en.wikipedia.org/wiki/Yogi_Berra.

72. Wikipedia, Yogi Berra, Ibid.
73. Dave Williams, SABR biography of Yogi Berra, https://sabr.org/bioproj/person/a4d43fa1.
74. Williams, ibid.
75. Roger Kahn. *The Boys of Summer*. Harper & Row, New York, NY, 1972.
76. Warren Jacobs, SABR biography of Duke Snider, https://sabr.org/bioproj/person/be697e90.
77. Jacobs, ibid.
78. Rob Edelman, SABR biography of Pee Wee Reese, https://sabr.org/bioproj/person/68671329.
79. Edelman, ibid.
80. David Claerbaut, *Durocher's Cubs: The Greatest Team That Didn't Win*. Taylor Publishing, Dallas, Texas, 2000.
81. Rudyard Kipling, "If," http://www.kiplingsociety.co.uk/poems_if.htm.
82. Mark Armour, SABR biography of Billy Williams, https://sabr.org/bioproj/person/ce0e08ff.
83. Joseph Wancho. SABR biography of Ron Santo, https://sabr.org/bioproj/person/920a36ba.
84. Cindy Thompson, SABR biography of Fergie Jenkins, https://sabr.org/bioproj/person/7b2f6e52.
85. Joseph Wancho, SABR biography of Ernie Banks, https://sabr.org/bioproj/person/b8afee6e.
86. Wancho, Ernie Banks, ibid.
87. Armour, Billy Williams, ibid.
88. Gregory H. Wolf, SABR biography of Wilbur Wood, https://sabr.org/bioproj/person/ac0fe9f8.
89. Wolf, ibid.
90. Mark Armour, SABR biography of Hoyt Wilhelm, https://sabr.org/bioproj/person/635428bb.
91. Armour, Wilhelm bio, ibid.
92. Charles Schultz, Peanuts, Charlie Brown and Willie McCovey. https://www.bing.com/images/search?view=detailV2&ccid=KOVbyDeB&id=B4657E141CC985F75ED96A55C5FA0C9ACDE6B238&thid=OIP.KOVbyDeByDmBg8seTkxkKwHaD4&mediaurl=http%3A%2F%2Fgiantspologrounds.files.wordpress.com%2F2013%2F04%2Fbrowncrop.jpg&exph=346&expw=661&q=peanuts+cartoon+willie+mccovey&simid=608016163091451867&selectedindex=1&qpvt=peanuts+cartoon+willie+mccovey&ajaxhist=0&insmi=m.
93. Mark Armour, SABR biography of Willie McCovey, https://sabr.org/bioproj/person/2a692514.
94. James Forr, SABR biography of Willie Stargell, https://sabr.org/bioproj/person/27e0c01a.
95. Warren Corbett, SABR biography of Ralph Kiner, https://sabr.org/bioproj/person/ralph-kiner/.
96. Rich D'Ambrosio, SABR biography of Dick Allen, https://sabr.org/bioproj/person/92ed657e.

97. Sherry R. Curry, Elizabeth Taylor's Marriage-Divorce Timeline, DivorceSay Lifestyle Magazine, April 11, 2010, https://credovie.wordpress.com/2010/04/11/elizabeth-taylors-marriage-divorce-timeline/.

98. Seamus Kearney, SABR biography of Richie Ashburn, https://sabr.org/bioproj/person/cda44a76.

99. Mark Stewart, SABR biography of Enos Slaughter, https://sabr.org/bioproj/person/fd6550d9,.

100. Jay Jaffe, *Cooperstown Casebook*. St. Martin's Press, New York, NY, 2017. Chapter 5, pp. 48-61.

Chapter 7

1. Wikipedia, Major League Baseball on Television, https://en.wikipedia.org/wiki/Major_League_Baseball_on_television

2. James Quirk, Rodney D Fort (1992), *Pay Dirt: The Business of Professional Team Sports*, Princeton University Press, Princeton, NJ, page 505.

3. Michael Haupert, MLB's annual salary leaders since 1874, SABR Business of Baseball Research Committee newsletter, Fall 2012, update, https://sabr.org/research/article/mlbs-annual-salary-leaders-since-1874/.

4. Roger I. Abrams: "Arbitrator Seitz Sets the Players Free," in *The Baseball Research Journal*, SABR, 38(2) (Fall 2009), pp. 79-85.

5. Doug Pappas, 2002, "A contentious history: Baseball's labor fights," http://static.espn.go.com/mlb/columns/bp/1427632.html.

6. Baseball Work Stoppages, www.stevetheump.com/baseball_stoppages.htm www.stevetheump.com/baseball_stoppages.htm

7. Wikipedia, The 1994-95 Major League Baseball Strike, https://en.wikipedia.org/wiki/1994–95_Major_League_Baseball_strike.

8. Simon Rottenberg (1956), The Baseball Players' Labor Market, Journal of Political Economy, Vol. 64, No. 3, 242–258.

9. Sky Andrechek (January 14, 2010), The Case for the Reserve Clause, in Sports Illustrated, https://www.si.com/more-sports/2010/01/14/andrecheck-freeagency.

10. David J. Gordon, Competitive balance in the free agent era: the dog that didn't bark. *Baseball Research Journal* (SABR). 49(2):48-57 (Fall 2020).

11. Ted Leavengood, SABR Biography of Reggie Jackson, https://sabr.org/bioproj/person/365acf13.

12. Joseph Wancho, SABR Biography of Rickey Henderson, https://sabr.org/bioproj/person/957d4da0.

13. Charles F. Faber, SABR Biography of Joe Morgan, https://sabr.org/bioproj/person/bf4f7a6e.

14. Cosme Vivanco, SABR Biography of Steve Carlton, https://sabr.org/bioproj/person/e438064d#sdendnote7sym.

15. Vivanco, ibid.

16. Maxwell Kates, SABR Biography of Tom Seaver, https://sabr.org/bioproj/person/486af3ad.

17. Gregory H. Wolf, SABR Biography of Bert Blyleven, https://sabr.org/bioproj/person/86826f24.

18. Vivanco, ibid.
19. Talmadge Boston, SABR Biography of Nolan Ryan, https://sabr.org/bioproj/person/4af413ee.
20. Mark Armour, SABR Biography of Jim Palmer, https://sabr.org/bioproj/person/3c239cfa.
21. Steve West, SABR Biography of Wade Boggs, https://sabr.org/bioproj/person/e083ea50.
22. West, ibid.
23. Wikipedia, George Brett, https://en.wikipedia.org/wiki/George_Brett.
24. Joseph Wancho, SABR Biography of Rod Carew, https://sabr.org/bioproj/person/0746c6ee.
25. Wancho (Carew), ibid.
26. Dan D'Addona, SABR Biography of Tony Gwynn, https://sabr.org/bioproj/person/2236deb4.
27. Mark Armour, SABR Biography of Johnny Bench, https://sabr.org/bioproj/person/aab28214.
28. Armour, ibid.
29. Rory Costello, SABR Biography of Gary Carter, https://sabr.org/bioproj/person/1a995e9e.
30. Bryan Stevens, SABR Biography of Carlton Fisk, https://sabr.org/bioproj/person/2160c516.
31. Stevens, ibid.
32. Wikipedia, Ted Simmons, https://en.wikipedia.org/wiki/Ted_Simmons.
33. Bill James, The New Bill James Historical Abstract, Free Press, New York, NY, 2001, p. 435.
34. Jimmy Keenan, SABR Biography of Cal Ripken Jr., https://sabr.org/bioproj/person/8bfeadd2.
35. Wikipedia, Eddie Murray, https://en.wikipedia.org/wiki/Eddie_Murray.
36. Matthew J Prigge, When Robin Yount Almost Quit, Shepherd Express, December 15, 2015, https://shepherdexpress.com/sports/brew-crew-confidential/robin-yount-almost-quit/.
37. Daniel R. Leavitt and Doug Skipper, SABR Biography of Paul Molitor, https://sabr.org/bioproj/person/f9d60ca6.
38. Leavitt and Skipper, ibid.
39. Norm King, SABR Biography of Tim Raines, https://sabr.org/bioproj/person/6fb1015c.
40. Dan D'Addona, SABR Biography of Andre Dawson, https://sabr.org/bioproj/person/8ce7c5bf.
41. Alfonso L. Tusa C, SABR Biography of Rich Gossage, https://sabr.org/bioproj/person/0871f3e2.
42. Larry Hilliard and Rob Hilliard, SABR Biography of John Hiller, https://sabr.org/bioproj/person/bf95ab65.
43. Alfonso and Tusa, ibid.
44. Wikipedia, Dennis Eckersley, https://en.wikipedia.org/wiki/Dennis_Eckersley#Personal.

45. Joseph Wancho, SABR Biography of Dennis Eckersley, https://sabr.org/bioproj/person/98aaf620.
46. City Slickers, 1991, directed by Ron Underwood, https://www.imdb.com/title/tt0101587/.
47. John McMurray, SABR Biography of Bobby Grich, https://sabr.org/bioproj/person/71bf380f.
48. YouTube, "Ozzie Smith makes the greatest infield play of all time!" https://www.youtube.com/watch?v=pCwNNqgrKOM.
49. Ron Fimrite, "No. 1 in His Field," Sports Illustrated, September 28, 1987.
50. Phil Jackman, "O's Have Real Hardnose in Infielder Bobby Grich," *The Sporting News*, February 5, 1972.
51. Charles F. Faber, SABR Biography of Ozzie Smith, https://sabr.org/bioproj/person/a6663664.
52. YouTube, Graig Nettles Highlights from 1978 World Series New York Yankees, https://www.bing.com/videos/search?q=craig+nettles+highlights+from+1978+World+Series&view=detail&mid=58384E86185D50807D0A58384E86185D50807D0A&FORM=VIRE.
53. Doug Skipper, SABR Biography of Dave Winfield, https://sabr.org/bioproj/person/98b82e8f.
54. Wikipedia. Rick Reuschel, https://en.wikipedia.org/wiki/Rick_Reuschel.
55. Wikipedia, Don Sutton, https://en.wikipedia.org/wiki/Don_Sutton.
56. Bill James, ibid, p. 546.
57. Lee Kluck, SABR Biography of Dwight Gooden, https://sabr.org/bioproj/person/d9e52fa4.
58. Baines surprised by Hall of Fame Election _ Many Others Too, USA Today, December 10, 2018, https://www.usatoday.com/story/sports/mlb/2018/12/10/baines-surprised-by-hall-of-fame-election-many-others-too/38708677/.

Chapter 8

1. I use the term steroids as shorthand for anabolic steroids – anabolic because they stimulate the synthesis (anabolism) of protein (the main component of muscle), and steroids because they contain the sterol chemical moiety which reflects their origin as natural physiologic derivatives of cholesterol. Androgens, the male hormones that are responsible for many male secondary sex characteristics (including muscle mass and strength, body hair distribution, libido, and aggressiveness) are the major natural anabolic steroids. Synthetic steroids aim to optimize the anabolic effects while minimizing unwanted side effects.
2. Christopher Klein, 2012. "Baseball's First Fountain of Youth," https://www.history.com/news/baseballs-first-fountain-of-youth.
3. Dave Zirin, 2006, The Nation. "Bonding with the Babe," https://www.thenation.com/article/bonding-babe/.
4. Geoffery Dunn, SABR Biography of Jose Canseco, https://sabr.org/bioproj/person/37e0251c.

5. Jose Canseco images, https://www.bing.com/images/search?q=Jose+Canseco+Muscles&FORM=IRBPRS&=0.

6. Tom Farrey, "The Memos: A Ban Ignored," http://www.espn.com/espn/eticket/story?page=steroidsExc&num=19.

7. Office of the Commissioner, MLB, Memo to all MLB clubs re Baseball's Drug Policy and Prevention Program, http://www.espn.com/espn/eticket/format/memos20051109?memo=1991&num=1. A similar memo was issued by Commissioner Selig in 1997.

8. H.R.4658 - Anabolic Steroids Control Act of 1990. 101st Congress (1989-1990), https://www.congress.gov/bill/101st-congress/house-bill/4658/text.

9. Cliff Corcoran, 2013. "Fifteen years ago today, Steve Wilstein first shed light on the Steroid Era," https://www.si.com/mlb/strike-zone/2013/08/22/steve-wilstein-mark-mcgwire-1998-steroid-era.

10. Mark Fainaru-Wada and Lance Williams, *Game of Shadows*. Gotham Books (Penguin Group), New York, 2006.

11. Jack Curry and Jere Longman, New York Times November 14, 2003, "Results of steroid testing spur baseball to set tougher rules," https://www.nytimes.com/2003/11/14/sports/results-of-steroid-testing-spur-baseball-to-set-tougher-rules.html.

12. Associated Press, March 2014. "A timeline of baseball's drug testing rules," https://www.usatoday.com/story/sports/mlb/2014/03/28/a-timeline-of-mlbs-drug-testing-rules/7024351/.

13. George J. Mitchell, 2007. "Report to the Commissioner of Baseball of an Independent Investigation into the Illegal Use of Steroids and Other Performance Enhancing Substances by Players in Major League Baseball, http://mlb.mlb.com/mlb/news/mitchell/.

14. Mark Armour and Daniel R. Levitt, Baseball Demographics 1947-2016, http://sabr.org/bioproj/topic/baseball-demographics-1947-2012.

15. Bernard Malamud, *The Natural*, Farrar, Strauss, and Giroux, New York, NY, 1952.

16. Damn Yankees, Stanley Donen and George Abbott (directors), 1958.

17. Wikipedia, Alex Rodriguez, https://en.wikipedia.org/wiki/Alex_Rodriguez.

18. Steve West, SABR Biography of Barry Bonds, https://sabr.org/bioproj/person/e79d202f.

19. Frederick C. Bush, SABR Biography of Roger Clemens, https://sabr.org/bioproj/person/b5a2be2f.

20. Wikipedia, Albert Pujols, https://en.wikipedia.org/wiki/Albert_Pujols.

21. BrowseBiography, Adrian Beltre biography, http://www.browsebiography.com/bio-adrian_beltre.html.

22. Emily Hawks, SABR Biography of Edgar Martinez, https://sabr.org/bioproj/person/05b7d71d.

23. YouTube. The Big Unit Randy Johnson strikes FEAR into the heart of John Kruk! https://www.youtube.com/watch?v=DYXTV5lGdUs.

24. Shawn Langlois, "Curt Schilling: Oh, come on, my tweet about lynching journalists was 100% sarcasm," https://www.marketwatch.com/story/

curt-schilling-oh-come-on-that-tweet-about-lynching-journalists-was-100-sarcasm-2016-11-08

25. Bill Nowlin, SABR Biography of Curt Schilling, https://sabr.org/bioproj/person/44885ff3.

26. Stew Thornley, SABR Biography of Greg Maddux, https://sabr.org/bioproj/person/d13d4022.

27. Little League International, Congratulations to our own Mike Mussina in your induction to the Baseball Hall of Fame, https://www.littleleague.org/news/mike-mussina-baseball-hall-of-fame/ January 22, 2019.

28. YouTube. Derek Jeter makes "The Flip" to nab Giambi at the plate in the 2001 ALDS, https://www.bing.com/videos/search?q=derek+Jeter%27s+flip+play+in+2002+ALCS&qpvt=derek+Jeter%27s+flip+play+in+2002+ALCS&view=detail&mid=AB5CC0418A12C4032BEBAB5CC0418A12C4032BEB&&FORM=VRDGAR.

29. Ben Lindbergh, "The Tragedy of Derek Jeter's Defense," http://grantland.com/features/the-tragedy-derek-jeter-defense/.

30. Wikipedia, David Ortiz, https://en.wikipedia.org/wiki/David_Ortiz.

31. Mariano Rivera with Wayne Coffey, *The Closer: My Story*, Back Bay Books/Little, Brown, and Company, New York, NY, 2014.

32. Wikipedia, Mariano Rivera, https://en.wikipedia.org/wiki/Mariano_Rivera.

33. Alan Cohen, SABR Biography of Derek Jeter, https://sabr.org/bioproj/person/c43ad285.

34. Emily Hawks, SABR Biography of Ken Griffey Jr., https://sabr.org/bioproj/person/3e8e7034.

35. Jose Canseco, Juiced: Wild Times, Rampant 'Roids, Smash Hits, and How Baseball Got Big, HarperCollins Publishers, Inc., New York, NY, 2005.

36. Stan Osowiecki, SABR Biography of Mike Piazza, https://sabr.org/bioproj/person/c035234d,.

37. Steve West, SABR Biography of Ivan Rodriguez, https://sabr.org/bioproj/person/2eafa5bc.

38. Osowiecki, ibid.

39. Wikipedia, Joe Mauer, https://en.wikipedia.org/wiki/Joe_Mauer.

40. Jacob Pomrenke, SABR Biography of Chipper Jones, https://sabr.org/bioproj/person/b7c916e5.

41. Wikipedia, Tom Glavine, https://en.wikipedia.org/wiki/Tom_Glavine.

42. Warren Corbett, SABR Biography of John Smoltz, https://sabr.org/bioproj/person/bf321b07.

43. Wikipedia, Andruw Jones, https://en.wikipedia.org/wiki/Andruw_Jones.

44. Greg Erion, SABR Biography of Jeff Bagwell, https://sabr.org/bioproj/person/c8e9ec56.

45. Frederick C. Bush, SABR Biography of Craig Biggio, https://sabr.org/bioproj/person/f4d29cc8.

46. Bush, ibid.

47. Alan Cohen, Todd Helton, in Major League Baseball A Mile High—The First Quarter Century of the Colorado Rockies, 2018, Society for American

Baseball Research, Phoenix, AZ, Bill Nowlin and Paul T. Parker, editors, pp 97-105.

48. Cohen, ibid.
49. Robert Whiting, The Meaning of Ichiro: The New Wave from Japan and the Transformation of Our National Pastime. Hachette Book Group New York. 2004.
50. Whiting, ibid.
51. Whiting, ibid.
52. Wikipedia, Kenny Lofton, https://en.wikipedia.org/wiki/Kenny_Lofton.
53. Wikipedia, Lofton, ibid.
54. Wikipedia, Lofton, ibid.
55. Chris Jones, SABR Biography of Roberto Alomar, https://sabr.org/bioproj/person/24c918e7.
56. Wikipedia, Barry Larkin, https://en.wikipedia.org/wiki/Barry_Larkin.
57. Dan Connelly, Baltimore Sun January 7, 2010, "Alomar falls just short in first bid for Hall of Fame." http://articles.baltimoresun.com/2010-01-07/sports/bal-sp.alomar07jan07_1_roberto-alomar-greatest-second-basemen-ballot/2.
58. Tara Krieger, SABR Biography of David Cone, https://sabr.org/bioproj/person/191828e7.
59. Krieger, Cone bio, ibid.
60. Katy Strong, Ken Rosenthal, "Omar Vizquel accused of domestic abuse: 'He's not the person that you see,'" The Athletic, December 16. 2020. https://theathletic.com/2254716/2020/12/16/omar-vizquel-domestic-abuse/.

Chapter 9

1. 1991 World Series Game 7, Braves at Twins, October 27, https://www.baseball-reference.com/boxes/MIN/MIN199110270.shtml.
2. David J Berri, Martin B Schmidt, Stacy L Brook, The Wages Of Wins : Taking Measure of the Many Myths In Modern Sport, Chapter 4: "Baseball's Competitive Balance Problem," pp 46-68, Stanford Business Books, Stanford, CA.
3. Wikipedia, Mike Trout, https://en.wikipedia.org/wiki/Mike_Trout.
4. Wikipedia, Zack Greinke, https://en.wikipedia.org/wiki/Zack_Greinke.
5. BrowseBiography, Justin Verlander, biography, http://www.browsebiography.com/bio-justin_verlander.html
6. ClinCalc DrugStats Database, The Top 200 Drugs of 2018, http://clincalc.com/DrugStats/.
7. Grant Brisbee, "Robinson Cano is a human infomercial for Performance-enhancing drugs," May 16, 2018, https://www.sbnation.com/mlb/2018/5/16/17358144/robinson-cano-steroids-peds-mariners-hot-take.
8. FanGraphs, Joey Votto, https://www.fangraphs.com/statss.aspx?playerid=4314&position=1B.
9. Baseball Almanac, Official No-Hitters, http://www.baseball-almanac.com/pitching/official-no-hitters.shtml.

10. Baseball Almanac, Hit for the Cycle, http://www.baseball-almanac.com/hitting/Major_League_Baseball_Players_to_hit_for_the_cycle.shtml.

Chapter 10

None.

Chapter 11

1. BaseballHall.org, Hall of Famers by Election Method, https://baseballhall.org/discover-more/stories/hall-of-famer-facts/hall-of-famers-by-election-method.
2. MLB Hall of Fame Inductees, https://www.baseball-reference.com/awards/hof.shtml.
3. Wikipedia, VC, https://en.wikipedia.org/wiki/Veterans_Committee.
4. Baseball-Reference, The Negro Leagues are Major Leagues, https://www.baseball-reference.com/negro-leagues-are-major-leagues.shtml.
5. Seamheads.com, Negro League Data Base, Wins Above Replacement, http://www.seamheads.com/NegroLgs/history.php?tab=metrics_at.
6. Jay Jaffe, Cooperstown Casebook. St. Martin's Press, New York, NY, 2017. Chapter 5, pp. 48-61.
7. Census 2000 Special Reports. Demographic Trends of the 20th Century. Figure 3.3, p77, November 2002, https://www.census.gov/prod/2002pubs/censr-4.pdf.
8. Mark Armour and Daniel R. Levitt, Baseball Demographics 1947-2016, http://sabr.org/bioproj/topic/baseball-demographics-1947-2012.
9. The 30 African American MLB Hall of Famers are Henry Aaron, Ernie Banks, Roy Campanella, Andre Dawson, Larry Doby, Bob Gibson, Ken Griffey Jr., Tony Gwynn, Rickey Henderson, Reggie Jackson, Fergie Jenkins, Derek Jeter, Barry Larkin, Willie Mays, Willie McCovey, Joe Morgan, Eddie Murray, Tim Raines, Frank Robinson, Jackie Robinson, Lee Smith, Ozzie Smith, Willie Stargell, Frank Thomas, Billy Williams, and Dave Winfield (CVI-Plus) and Harold Baines, Lou Brock, Kirby Puckett, and Jim Rice (CVI -Minus).
10. The 15 were: Jim O'Rourke, Pud Galvin, King Kelly, Dan Brouthers, Mickey Welch, Tim Keefe, Tommy McCarthy, Ed Delahanty, Hugh Duffy, George Davis, Joe Kelley, Willie Keeler, Jimmy Collins, Roger Bresnahan, and Joe McGinnity. The SABR Biography Project has biographies of all but Brouthers, searchable at https://sabr.org/bioproj_search. For Brouthers: Roy Kerr, *Big Dan Brouthers: Baseball's First Great Slugger* (Jefferson, NC: McFarland, 2013), 4.
11. Lawrence D. Hogan, Shades of Glory, pp 331-2, National Baseball Hall of Fame, Cooperstown, NY, 2006.
12. The 12 Latino Hall of Famers are Roberto Alomar, Rod Carew, Roberto Clemente, Vladimir Guerrero, Juan Marichal, Edgar Martinez, Pedro Martinez, Mariano Rivera, and Ivan Rodriguez (CVI-Plus) and Luis Aparicio, Orlando Cepeda, and Tony Perez (CVI-Minus).

13. The 13 eligible CVI-Plus African American players who have not yet been elected to the HOF are Dick Allen, Barry Bonds, Bobby Bonds, Willie Davis, Dwight Gooden, Andruw Jones, Kenny Lofton, Vada Pinson, Willie Randolph, Gary Sheffield, Reggie Smith, Lou Whitaker, and Jimmy Wynn.
14. The seven eligible CVI-Plus Latino players who have not yet been elected to the HOF are Bobby Abreu, Cesar Cedeno, Nomar Garciaparra, Minnie Minoso, Manny Ramirez, Johan Santana, and Luis Tiant.
15. Wikipedia, Hispanic and Latino Americans, https://en.wikipedia.org/wiki/Hispanic_and_Latino_Americans.
16. David J. Gordon, "Racial Parity in the Hall of Fame," Baseball Research Journal (SABR), 47(2):49-57 (Fall 2018).
17. Jerome Holtzman, "Cobb and Speaker Got Themselves into a Real Fix," Chicago Tribune, May 21, 1989, https://www.chicagotribune.com/news/ct-xpm-1989-05-21-8902030567-story.html.
18. John Thorn, Cobb and Speaker and Landis: *Closing the Books.* https://1927-the-diary-of-myles-thomas.espn.com/closing-the-books-cobb-speaker-landis-e7896605fbc1.
19. Pat Jordan, "Thin Air: In the Mountains with Steve Carlton, Armed Conspiracist," Deadspin.com, thestacks.deadspin.com/thin-air-in-the-mountains-with-steve-carlton-armed-co-478492324.

Appendix 1:

1. David J Gordon, "The Rise and Fall of the Deadball Era," *Baseball Research Journal* (SABR), 47(2):92-102 (Fall 2018).
2. Major League Baseball Batting Year-by-Year Averages, https://www.baseball-reference.com/leagues/MLB/bat.shtml.
3. Major League Baseball Pitching Year-by-Year Averages, https://www.baseball-reference.com/leagues/MLB/pitch.shtml.
4. Batters who reached base on an error (ROE) are estimated from Baseball Reference Stathead, https://stathead.com/baseball/. Sample ROE query for 2017: https://stathead.com/baseball/event_finder.cgi?request=1&year=2017&year_to=2017&divisory=1&from=button&type=b&event=18, accessed December 2020.
5. I have modified the standard definition of 3TO to incorporate HBP (which is in effect the same as a BB) and to exclude inside-the-park HR (which are really balls in play), as estimated from Baseball Reference Stathead, ibid,. Sample IPHR Query for 2017: https://stathead.com/baseball/event_finder.cgi?request=1&year=2017&year_to=2017&divisory=1&from=button&type=b&event=23&criteria138=hit_location---IPHR-8---to_Location_IPHR%408---locat&criteria139=hit_location---IPHR-7---to_Location_IPHR%407---locat&criteria140=hit_location---IPHR-9---to_Location_IPHR%409---locat, accessed December 2020.

Appendix 2:

1. Wikipedia. List of Major League Baseball players suspended for performance-enhancing drugs," https://en.wikipedia.org/wiki/List_of_Major_League_Baseball_players_suspended_for_performance-enhancing_drugs

2. Mike Lupica, *New York Daily News*, February 13, 2008, "Either Roger Clemens or Brian McNamee will tell lies on the Hill," http://www.nydailynews.com/sports/baseball/yankees/roger-clemens-brian-mcnamee-lies-hill-article-1.311566.

3. Selena Roberts, 2009. A-Rod: The Many Lives of Alex Rodriguez Harper-Collins Publishers, New York, NY.

4. Baseball-Reference.com. 2020 MLB New Debuts. https://www.baseball-reference.com/leagues/MLB/2020-debuts.shtml. (One can navigate from here to other seasons).

5. Stathead.com, Non-Pitchers with >20 WAR_H, https://stathead.com/baseball/season_finder.cgi?request=1&sum=1&order_by_asc=1&order_by=WAR_bat&qualifiersSeason=nomin&minpasValS=502&mingamesValS=100&qualifiersCareer=nomin&minpasValC=3000&mingamesValC=1000&min_year_season=1871&max_year_season=2020&lg_ID=lgAny&lgAL_team=tmAny&lgNL_team=tmAny&lgFL_team=tmAny&lgAA_team=tmAny&lgPL_team=tmAny&lgUA_team=tmAny&lgNA_team=tmAny&exactness=anymarked&pos_2=1&pos_3=1&pos_4=1&pos_5=1&pos_6=1&pos_7=1&pos_8=1&pos_9=1&pos_10=1&pos_11=1&games_min_max=min&games_prop=80&as=result_batter&offset=0&type=b&ccomp%5B1%5D=lt&cval%5B1%5D=2003&cstat%5B1%5D=year_min&ccomp%5B2%5D=gt&cval%5B2%5D=19.9&cstat%5B2%5D=WAR_bat&bats=any&throws=any&min_age=0&max_age=99&min_season=1&max_season=-1&location=pob&locationMatch=is&isHOF=either&isAllstar=either&isActive=either.

6. Stathead.com, Pitchers with >20 WAR_P, https://stathead.com/baseball/season_finder.cgi?request=1&sum=1&order_by_asc=1&order_by=WAR_pitch&qualifiersSeason=nomin&minIpValS=162&minDecValS=14&mingamesValS=40&qualifiersCareer=nomin&minIpValC=1000&minDecValC=100&mingamesValC=200&min_year_season=1871&max_year_season=2020&lg_ID=lgAny&lgAL_team=tmAny&lgNL_team=tmAny&lgFL_team=tmAny&lgAA_team=tmAny&lgPL_team=tmAny&lgUA_team=tmAny&lgNA_team=tmAny&as=result_pitcher&offset=0&type=p&ccomp%5B1%5D=lt&cval%5B1%5D=2003&cstat%5B1%5D=year_min&ccomp%5B2%5D=gt&cval%5B2%5D=19.9&cstat%5B2%5D=WAR_pitch&throws=any&min_age=0&max_age=99&min_season=1&max_season=-1&role=anyrole&games_started=60&games_relieved=80&location=pob&locationMatch=is&isHOF=either&isAllstar=either&isActive=either.

GLOSSARY OF TERMS AND ABBREVIATIONS

Term	Definition
1B	First Base. 2. The defensive player positioned at 1B. 3. A 1-base hit (or single).
2B	Second Base. 2. The defensive player positioned at 2B. 3. A 2-base hit (or double).
3B	Third Base. 2. The defensive player positioned at 3B. 3. A 3-base hit (or triple).
3TO	Three "true" fielding-independent outcomes – SO + (BB+HBP) + OPHR
AA	American Association (1882-91). 2. Class Double-A in modern minor leagues.
AAA	Class Triple-A in modern minor leagues
AB	At-bats
AF	African American - Non-Latino player of at least partly African descent
AL	American League (1901-present)
AOE	Advance on Error - an error that allows one or more BR to advance but does not add a BR
ASG	All-Star game. Held annually starting in 1933 - two per year in 1959-62
AVG	Batting average (H/AB)
BABIP	Batting average on balls in play - similar to 1 - DE, but does not include ROE or IPHR
BB	Bases on balls (or walks)
BBWAA	Baseball Writers Association of America - vote on postseason awards and Hall of Fame
BIP%	Percentage of PA in which the ball is put in play - not OPHR, SO, BB, or HBP
BF	Batters faced (by a pitcher)
BR	Baserunners
C	Catcher
CF	Center field. 2. Defensive player positioned in center field.
CG	Complete games – team uses a single pitcher for entire game
CVI	Career Value Index – Metric used to rank player value (see Chapter 7)

CVI-Plus	Players with CVI in the Top 235 (the number of players currently in the HOF)
CVI-Minus	Players with CVI outside the Top 235 (<53.04)
CYA	Cy Young Award (1956-present) – award recognizing best pitcher in each league
DE	Defensive efficiency – percentage of balls in play converted to outs (see Chapter 6)
DH	Designated hitter (AL, 1973 to present) – batsman designated to hit in the pitcher's place
ER	Earned run – run scored without the help of a fielding error
ERA	Earned run average = 9*ER/IP
ERA+	100 times the ratio of the league ERA to a pitcher's ballpark-adjusted ERA
FL	Federal League (1914-15)
G	Games
gmLI	Game Leverage Index – weighting factor for RP WAR (see Chapter 7)
H	Base hits
H9	Hits allowed per 9 IP
HBP	Hit by pitch – batter awarded 1B
HGH	Human Growth Hormone
HOF	Baseball's National Hall of Fame in Cooperstown, NY
HOVG	Hall of the Very Good, denotes good but not great players who fall short of HOF caliber
HR	Home runs
IP	Innings pitched (numbers 1 and 2 after decimal point refer to thirds of an inning)
IPHR	Inside-the-park HR (considered in play)
ISO	Isolated Power = SLG - AVG
JAWS	Jaffe WAR Score (see Chapter 7)
L	Loss attributed to pitcher
LA	Latino (player of Latin American birth or parentage)
LF	Left field. 2. Defensive player positioned in left field
MLB	Major League Baseball
MLBPA	Major League Baseball Players Association (1966-present)
mOPB	Modified on-base percentage; includes reached on error in numerator
MVP	Most Valuable Player in each league (1922-present)

NA	National Association (1871-75) – first professional baseball league
NABBP	National Association of Baseball *Players* – formed the first professional league in 1871
NBA	National Basketball Association
NL	National League (1876-present)
NFL	National Football League
NHL	National Hockey League
NS Ratio	Noll Scully ratio of actual to "idealized" standard deviation of winning percentages.
OBP	On-base percentage - sum of H + BB + HBP divided by PA - SH
OF	Outfield. 2. Defensive players playing an outfield position
OPHR	Out-of-the-park HR (not considered in play)
OPS	OBP + SLG
OPS+	100 times the ratio of the ballpark-adjusted OPS to the league average OPS
PA	Plate appearances
PED	Performance Enhancing Drugs (includes HGH as well as androgenic steroids)
PL	Players League (1890)
Primary WAR	WAR_H for hitters and WAR_P for pitchers (see below)
R	Runs scored
RBI	Runs batted in
RF	Right field. 2. Defensive player positioned in right field.
ROE	Reach on error - an error that results in a new BR
RP	Relief pitcher
SABR	Society for American Baseball Research
SB	Stolen base
SH	Sacrifice hits (includes bunts and sacrifice flies)
SHO	Shutouts - CG in which the opponent scores no runs
Similarity Score	Quantifies similarity of two players (originated by Bill James, listed in Baseball-Reference.com)
Slash Line	AVG/OBP/SLG
SLG	Slugging percentage – total bases divided by AB
SO	Strikeouts
SO9	Strikeouts per 9 IP
SO/H	Strikeouts per hit allowed

SP	Starting pitcher
SS	Shortstop
SV	Saves – counting stat for RP who close out winning games
T	Team
TB	Total bases (= H + 2B + 3B*2 + HR * 3)
UA	Union Association (1884)
UCL	Ulnar collateral ligament – the ligament repaired in Tommy John surgery
UER	Unearned run – run scored because of an error
VC	Veterans Committee
W	Win attributed to pitcher. 2. White – Non-Latino player of European descent
WAR	Wins above replacement (see Chapter 3)
WARH	WAR as a non-pitcher (includes offense and defense, but is not simply oWAR + dWAR)
WARP	WAR as a pitcher
dWAR	WAR as a defender
oWAR	WAR as a hitter
WHIP	The sum of H + BB given up by a pitcher divided by his IP
W-L	Won-Lost record attributed to a pitcher
WS	World Series

PHOTO CREDITS

The majority of photographs that appear in this book are taken from the public domain. Original sources and credits, when available and/or required, are provided here.

Px. Henry Aaron, with permission from the National Baseball Hall of Fame and Museum.

P10. Fred Clarke, 1903, *Chicago Daily News.*

P19. Willie Keeler, 1909 Tobacco Card. US Library of Congress's Prints and Photographs.

P30. Jack Glasscock, 1888 Cigarette Card. US Library of Congress's Prints and Photographs.

P34. John Montgomery Ward, 1887 baseball card. US Library of Congress.

P42. Honus Wagner, 1910. By Charles M. Conlan.

P47. Ty Cobb, 1924. By National Photo Company.

P50. Walter Johnson, 1910s. By Charles M. Conlan.

P54. Eddie Collins, 1911. From the George Grantham Bain Collection.

P55. Rube Waddell, 1901. US Library of Congress Archives.

P60. Three Finger Brown (hand). Chicago Daily News.

P70. Babe Ruth, 1916. By Charles M. Conlan.

P78. Lefty Grove, 1933. Goudey Baseball Card.

P84. Harry Heilmann, circa 1914. *Chicago Daily News.*

P88. Joe Gordon. 1950 Bowman baseball card.

P93. Gabby Hartnett. 1933 Goudey baseball card.

P100. Chuck Klein, 1936. Created from Klein's Goudey baseball card.

P104. Jackie Robinson, 1945. Kansas City Call (newspaper).

P121. Roy Campanella (with Willie Mays), 1961. By William C. Greene of the *World Telegram & Sun.*

P125. Robin Roberts. 1953 Bowman baseball card.

P128. Juan Marichal, 1962. From *Baseball Digest.*

P166. Mike Schmidt, with permission from the National Baseball Hall of Fame and Museum.

P172. Bert Blyleven, 1987. By Park Press Inc.

P178. Rod Carew, 1975. By Rick Dikeman.

P188. Robin Yount (as coach), 2006. By Scott Ableman.

P220. Barry Bonds, 1993. By Jim Accordino.

P230. Adrian Beltre, 2011. By Keith Allison.

P234. Randy Johnson, 2008. By SD Kirk.

P241. Derek Jeter, 2008. By Keith Allison.

P246. Jim Thome, 2008. By Keith Allison.

P249. Ivan Rodriguez, 2009. By RWHMedia.

P253. Tom Glavine, 1993. By Jim Accordino.

P260. Todd Helton, 2013. By Keith Allison.

P262. Ichiro Suzuki, 2002. By Rick Dikeman.

P276. Billy Wagner, 2007. By Alex Kim.

P278. Mike Trout, 2011. By Keith Allison.

P285. Justin Verlander, 2018. By Keith Allison.

P288. Zack Greinke, 2009. By Keith Allison.

P291. Buster Posey, 2013. By SD Kirk.

P318. Josh Gibson, with permission from the National Baseball Hall of Fame and Museum.